MW00855866

Winner of the Jules and Frances Landry Award for 2013

MILLIKEN'S BEND

A Civil War Battle in History and Memory

LINDA BARNICKEL

LOUISIANA STATE UNIVERSITY PRESS)|(BATON ROUGE

Published by Louisiana State University Press
Copyright © 2013 by Linda Barnickel

DESIGNER: *Mandy McDonald Scallan*
TYPEFACE: *Whitman*
PRINTER: *McNaughton & Gunn, Inc*
BINDER: *Acme Bookbinding*

All maps by Mary Lee Eggart

Library of Congress Cataloging-in-Publication Data
Barnickel, Linda A.
  Milliken's Bend : a Civil War battle in history and memory / Linda Barnickel.
    pages cm
  Includes bibliographical references and index.
  ISBN 978-0-8071-4992-8 (cloth : alk. paper) — ISBN 978-0-8071-4993-5 (pdf) — ISBN 978-0-8071-4994-2
(epub) — ISBN 978-0-8071-4995-9 (mobi) 1. Milliken's Bend, Battle of, La., 1863. 2. United States—History—Civil War, 1861–1865—Participation, African American. 3. United States—History—Civil War,
1861–1865—African Americans. I. Title.
  E475.4.B37 2013
  973.7'415—dc23

                                                                                            2012023811

For Corydon Heath, George Conn, "Big Jack" Jackson, and all the others like them—officers and enlisted men, white or black, who died on the altar of freedom.

It was a much more severe engagement, and more important in results, than was at first anticipated.
—*Chicago Tribune,* June 18, 1863

The war for the Union, whether men so call it or not, is a war for Emancipation.
—Frederick Douglass, "Why Should a Colored Man Enlist?"

CONTENTS

ILLUSTRATIONS, MAPS, AND TABLES

Illustrations follow page 148

MAPS

TABLES

PREFACE

"The only certainty is overwhelming ambiguity," writes Tim O'Brien in his Vietnam War classic, *The Things They Carried*. He could have been writing about Milliken's Bend.

My journey began with misinformation. "Taken prisoner and murdered by the rebels, July, 1862." So read the entry next to "Corodon" [Corydon] Heath's name on the "Shober broadside," a copy of which was sent to me in late 1991 by my friend Paul Rambow. We both shared a deep interest in the history of Corydon Heath's original unit, Battery G, 2nd Illinois Light Artillery, and Paul had already been doing a considerable amount of research and correspondence (back in the days before the ubiquity of the Internet and e-mail revolutionized research). By the time I came along, he and many others affiliated with a reenactment group of the same name as Heath's unit had the basic history of the battery well sketched out. Paul even wrote an extensive and detailed history of the battery, which is now available online.

I left my copy of the broadside filed away for a year or so, referring to it occasionally as I researched other individuals and the battery as a whole. One day, as I looked at it more closely, I was drawn to the entry by Corydon Heath's name. "Murdered." What an odd word to encounter—it was wartime, after all. "Taken prisoner and murdered by the rebels." Murdered after being taken prisoner? Whatever happened to bring about something like that? Was this just a bit of postwar bitterness and exaggeration? What had happened? I wanted to learn more.

Thus began my quest. I soon learned that Heath had died in 1863, not in 1862 as the broadside claimed. The Illinois adjutant general's report said Heath was promoted to captain in the 9th Louisiana Colored Infantry in April of 1863 and mentioned nothing about the circumstances of his death. Why then, did the broadside place his death a year earlier and call it "murder"? The beginnings of my search were representative of what I would find throughout my research. Time and again, one tiny particle of information would lead to another—and create more questions. I spent hours in archives in Washington, DC, and throughout seven states. Research was often painfully slow. An entire day of work might result in only one or two useful bits of information—or none at all. Too often, the records were silent, confusing, or missing altogether. How fitting it was that my fascination with this case began with misinformation.

After obtaining Heath's military service records and the pension file for his children, the basic facts became clearer. Heath had indeed been taken prisoner and reportedly executed for serving as an officer in a regiment composed of recently liberated slaves. This knowledge led me directly to the fight at Milliken's Bend, Louisiana, a nearly unknown action that took place on June 7, 1863 (not July 1862, when Shober placed Heath's death). I was surprised to discover that relatively little had been written about this small but very sharp fight on the west bank of the Mississippi River. Even books that concentrated on African American soldiers during the war gave it scant mention. No doubt overshadowed by the enormous clashes at Gettysburg and Vicksburg, Milliken's Bend seems to have vanished from history almost as soon as it occurred. Furthermore, the site of Milliken's Bend was washed away by the mighty river decades ago. I found the fate of the physical battlefield and the nearby surroundings of the bayous of northeastern Louisiana to be a fitting metaphor for the events themselves, obscured long ago and today all but lost to history. Like trying to navigate through the tangled growth of a bayou, the forward movement and research involved in this project was laborious, painstaking, confusing, and difficult.

Milliken's Bend was part of a trinity of battles in the summer of 1863 in which black troops under the Union banner played a prominent part. The engagements at Port Hudson, Louisiana, in late May, Milliken's Bend in early June, and Fort Wagner, South Carolina, in July—all coming in quick succession—did much to publicize the valor of black troops in battle.

Each battle had its own characteristics, and a brief comparison may be in order. At Port Hudson, the two black regiments of the First and Third Louisiana Native Guards were only a small part of a much larger operation. They had been in the United States Army since late 1862, having originally offered their services briefly to the Confederacy at the start of the war. Composed predominantly of free blacks and Creoles from New Orleans, these regiments initially drew their officers from the same population. By the time of Port Hudson, however, Gen. Nathaniel Banks forced the Third Regiment's black officers to step down and replaced them with white men. The First Regiment had not yet been similarly reorganized. Both regiments served with honor and distinction at Port Hudson, especially in the trying assaults on May 27, earning praise from their peers and the press, despite bloody tactical blundering by their commanders.

On the East Coast, at Fort Wagner, South Carolina, the soon-to-be famous 54th Massachusetts Infantry Regiment, under the command of young Boston abolitionist Robert Gould Shaw, led the assault composed of three Union brigades against the Confederate ramparts. Shaw's regiment was the only African American regiment present and was officered by whites. Most of the enlisted men were free blacks from the North, including two sons of Frederick Douglass. A few former slaves who had fled North were also in the regiment.

The assault on Wagner was doomed from the start. Union commanders optimistically thought that a preliminary barrage had weakened the fort's defenders, but the terrain and the formidable defensive Rebel works made the attack a suicide mission. Despite its bloody losses, the 54th Massachusetts gained fame for its heroism that day. Sgt. William H. Carney received special recognition. When the color sergeant fell, Carney grasped the colors before they touched the ground, and he planted them at the top of the works. When the regiment was forced back, Carney refused to leave the colors behind. He carried them with him, although he was wounded in four places and weak from loss of blood. He became the first African American to be awarded the Medal of Honor. (As for many Civil War–era recipients, the award came years later.) The 54th Massachusetts still lives on in public memory. Today's readers may be acquainted with its story from the 1989 film *Glory*, starring Matthew Broderick and Academy Award–winner Denzel Washington.

Of the three battles, only at Milliken's Bend did black troops compose the majority of the soldiers on the Union side. Black regiments in northeastern Louisiana were still organizing, and none of the regiments were at full strength. The white officers, although veterans of battles like Shiloh, Corinth, and smaller fights in Tennessee and Missouri, were new to their duties. Most were promoted several grades above their previous rank—sergeants became captains, for example—and had a great deal of learning to do. Many of the enlisted men had been slaves just weeks before and had not yet had time to learn even basic skills with their weapons. Some had only had their rifles for two days.

At dawn on June 7, 1863, a brigade of Texans under the command of Brig. Gen. Henry McCulloch attacked the small Union garrison at Milliken's Bend,

Louisiana, in an attempt to do something (if only symbolic) to relieve Vicksburg. If successful, the Rebels could capture much-needed supplies and disrupt Union recruiting efforts. With cries of "no quarter" for the white officers, the Confederates drove the Federals from one levee and, after facing strong resistance at a second levee, forced the Union men to the banks of the Mississippi. Two gunboats, *Lexington* and *Choctaw*, were there to greet the Rebels, and the Southerners retreated from the field around midmorning.

Both sides claimed victory. Confederate superiority overwhelmed the Federal forces almost immediately, and the slaughter would have been even greater if not for the gunboats. The Rebels had the Yankees on the run and wouldn't let the gunboats take away their claims to a crushing victory. Union troops believed themselves the victors because the gunboats had forced back the Confederate troops, leaving the shattered remnants of the African Brigade clinging to the riverbank, bloodied but still holding their ground.

The significance of the small but sharp fight at Milliken's Bend far exceeds its present status as an obscure footnote in Civil War history. It was an early battle in which Federal black troops took part, and along with Port Hudson and Fort Wagner, Milliken's Bend proved to a skeptical Northern public that black troops were indeed fit for combat duty. Soon after the battle, accusations arose stating that some men—both white and black—from the Colored Troops had been executed by the Confederates; these accusations played a significant role in the breakdown and suspension of prisoner exchanges between the North and South.

Exploring and answering the question of "what happened" at Milliken's Bend was my primary motivation in beginning this work. Therefore, I have concentrated on creating a narrative of events and circumstances based upon the compilation and analysis of a range of primary sources heretofore unexamined. In addition, innumerable secondary sources provide the broader context and background necessary for a full understanding of the events surrounding the battle. The presence of these secondary sources permeates this work, though their direct citations may be few.

This book is more than just a recitation of what regiment fought where and a description of casualties. The narrative begins in the earliest days of the war and concludes in the modern era. This structure allows the reader to gain perspective on the beliefs and conditions that added fuel to the volatile situation on the levee that hot June day, as well as the lasting outcomes, many of them unresolved, of the war over emancipation. It also becomes clear that the war over emancipation began well before January 1, 1863, when Lincoln announced his final version of the Emancipation Proclamation and that this war continued long after the guns fell silent at Appomattox.

Perhaps this book will at last rescue Milliken's Bend from obscurity. Those who fought and died there—who labored in the surrounding fields, who fled the terror of the Yankees or escaped with joy and freedom to their lines, all of these individuals who make up the story of Milliken's Bend—must not be forgotten. It is hoped that this volume finds its place within the immense Civil War literature and contributes a greater understanding of the events on the west bank of the Mississippi, in the shadow of Vicksburg, and their importance within the wider war.

ACKNOWLEDGMENTS

At the top of my list, I must thank my dear friend Tina Read. Without her encouragement, this book might never have come to be. Her friendship, faith, courage, and example continue to inspire me.

Playing an equally important role, though much, much earlier in the process—indeed, at the *very* beginning—are the men and women of Battery G, 2nd Illinois Light Artillery reenacting group. It was through my acquaintance with Paul Rambow that I first learned of the "Shober broadside"—the document that contained the tantalizing statement about the "murder" of Captain Heath and that prompted this journey, lasting nearly twenty years.

To both Tina and Paul I owe an enormous debt of gratitude, and their influence is proof positive that even the tiniest of actions—telling a friend to "go for it," to chase her dream and make it real—or simply sharing an interesting research document—can profoundly influence a person's life. Indeed, by so doing, these two individuals have helped to literally "rewrite history"—by prompting me to bring this long-neglected but very important battle to light.

Wayne Henson, Gene Wright, Larry Werline, and the entire Tedrick family, along with many others of Battery G (reactivated) also deserve my thanks for their encouragement and support during the early days of this project. Their dedication to preserving the memory and honoring the men and families of the original Battery G is admirable and important.

My research, of course, has been aided along the way by countless librarians and archivists. The late Phyllis Kelley of the Joiner History Room, Sycamore, Illinois, was a great help early in my research, going out of her way to track down within their collections any reference to Corydon Heath.

Michael Knight, DeAnne Blanton, and Jill Abraham at the National Archives on Pennsylvania Avenue in Washington, D.C., used their intimate knowledge of Federal and Confederate records to guide me in my search. Without their help, this book would have been impossible. It was through their guidance that I found Lieb's report (reproduced in Appendix D), a critical document for discovering what happened to Corydon Heath and George Conn after Milliken's Bend. Of course, they led me to many other important resources, as well.

Larry Foreman and Lora Peppers of the Ouachita Parish Public Library in Monroe were kind enough to assist me when I arrived in the midst of an already busy and hectic day. Their resources and assistance are greatly appreciated.

William Dobak, of the U.S. Army Center of Military History, graciously shared a portion of his research with me. Had he not done so, I may have neglected the story of the 1864 "mutiny" in the 49th United States Colored Infantry (USCI). His assistance was also instrumental in identifying by name some of the black men from the 49th USCI who were taken prisoner at Milliken's Bend and returned to their regiment at the end of the war.

Thomas G. Knoles of the American Antiquarian Society diligently acted on my behalf by obtaining basic information about the unprocessed (and very moldy!) Isaac F. Shepard papers, which are in their holdings and, at the time of this writing, were still closed to research. Although it was not immediately apparent that any information relevant to Milliken's Bend was contained in the collection, Mr. Knoles, as well as the conservator, went to an extraordinary effort to provide me with this preliminary assessment of this collection. I am grateful for their time and assistance.

In addition, staffs at the following institutions greeted me with patience and expertise as I peppered them with questions, picked their brains, and made request after request: Mississippi Department of Archives and History; Vicksburg National Military Park; the Old Court House Museum in Vicksburg; LSU Special Collections, Hill Memorial Library; Louisiana State Archives; Tulane University Special Collections; the Center for American History at the University of Texas—Austin; Texas State Library and Archives Commission; the Austin (Texas) History Center; the Texas Heritage Museum (formerly the Confederate Research Center), Hill College, Hillsboro, Texas; Southwest Arkansas Regional Archives in Washington, Arkansas; Indiana State Library; Indiana State Archives; Indiana Historical Society; State Historical Society of Iowa—Des Moines; Illinois State Archives; and the Abraham Lincoln Presidential Library (formerly Illinois State Historical Library).

I also want to thank those who are so often omitted from acknowledgements—all of those individuals at archives and other institutions who staff the reading rooms, provide security, and pull the materials. I am most deeply indebted to the pages who literally do the heavy lifting on behalf of their patrons every day. All of these individuals are the true "workhorses" of research and play a critical role in the success of any researcher's endeavor. Their work and positions are all too often taken for granted. Thank you.

Much of my earliest research was performed in the collections of the Wisconsin Historical Society in Madison. Were it not for their rich resources, incredible newspaper collection, friendly staff, and ease of access, this book might never have gotten off the ground.

Two interlibrary loan librarians deserve special thanks, as do their staffs: Ellen Burke of the Wisconsin Historical Society in the 1990s, and Meg Sherrill of the Nashville Public Library in Tennessee during the 2000s. Truly, the materials I was able to access through this valuable nationwide lending program supplemented, enhanced, and, at times, proved critical to telling the story I had to tell.

Amy Stewart-Mailhiot of Vanderbilt University provided guidance and expertise when dealing with sometimes troublesome government documents, as did Miriam Barrett of the Nashville Public Library.

Scholars Gregory J. W. Urwin, the late James G. Hollandsworth Jr., M. Scott Legan, and the late Arthur Bergeron generously aided my earliest research years ago by sharing portions of their work with me. I regret that at the time I could not reciprocate Dr. Hollandsworth, as I had not yet made discoveries about white officers from Milliken's Bend and the Mound which may have assisted him in his fine and detailed work on the fate of white officers of Colored Troops.

I had the pleasure to meet Dr. Urwin at a public lecture at Middle Tennessee State University in 2006. Although I was a complete stranger, in a brief conversation afterwards, Dr. Urwin suggested that I look closely at the Confederate response to the Emancipation Proclamation. Doing so led me to the development of Chapter 1 and helped me view Milliken's Bend in its broader context as an event in the overall war for and against emancipation, from 1860 (and earlier) to 1960 (and later).

I am greatly indebted to Terrence J. Winschel of Vicksburg National Military Park for his patience and willingness to answer numerous, perhaps too-detailed questions, especially at the end of my research. He is a man of vast and extraordinary historical knowledge, and a kind and generous scholar. Though there may be certain points of interpretation where we disagree, I deeply respect his wisdom and his kindness.

A number of people in the community of Tallulah, Louisiana, have proven invaluable to my work. Kirk Morley, sadly now deceased, gave generously of his time and knowledge and took me on an enjoyable and informative driving tour of the area around the year 2000. Around the same time, Geneva Williams met me at the Hermione House Museum and helped me learn more about the region and community, as well as Milliken's Bend.

Mrs. Williams, who was instrumental in the establishment of the museum and the Madison Historical Society, and Tina Johnson, Director of the Tallulah-Madison Parish Tourism Commission, kindly gave of their time in 2010 to speak with me about historical memory in the parish and how Milliken's Bend, in particular, has been both forgotten and remembered. Brian Madison Davis, now well into his career, generously allowed me to interview him about his bachelor's degree thesis that he wrote years ago.

Likewise, Tim Kavanaugh and Dr. David Slay of Vicksburg National Military Park, provided very helpful information and insights, and gave generously of their time and expertise. It was a pleasure and a privilege to speak to Robert Walker, former Vicksburg mayor and the driving force behind the Mississippi African American monument that now stands on the grounds at Vicksburg National Military Park. His desire to correct omissions of history, as well as his commitment to honor those men who enlisted to fight for freedom, is impressive and inspiring. I deeply appreciate his willingness to share his story with me.

There are others, too, whom I must thank. Carol Kaplan and Andrea Blackman read and provided feedback on my initial book proposal. Andrea very kindly gave of her spare time to read and comment upon an early draft of the book, in its entirety. She was a sharp eye, a thoughtful critic, and an encouraging friend.

Others have provided less tangible but equally important support. Amy Lyles Wilson and the women of her Writing Circle helped me develop courage and confidence in my writing, and they stretched my creativity, skills, and comfort zone. I learned as much by listening as I did by writing. They are my cheerleaders and, in the words of one Circle member, my "writing-sisters." How lucky I am to have been a part of this group!

My family deserves credit and thanks. My late father planted and nurtured my love of the Civil War; my mother's enduring patience, understanding, and encouragement has nurtured this book. My sister has always been there for me, and I am so very grateful for her encouragement, advice, and support.

My friends Kay, Stacy, Vanessa, Ted, Jacque, Geary, Mark, Andrew, Kourtney, Andrea, Carol, Annie, Tina, Bill, Amy, Cindy, Elaine, Heather, Cece, Sandy, Sallye, Beverly, Donna, and many others have all provided gifts of encouragement, laughter, and support. They have helped me when my spirit has flagged, and seldom lost faith in me (even when I had my doubts). You may not know it, but you have been a part of this, too.

I owe the deepest debt of gratitude to my long-suffering acquisitions editor at LSU Press, Rand Dotson. It speaks to his patience and professionalism that he never discouraged me or this project in the six years it took me to produce a final manuscript. I hope his patience is adequately rewarded by the final product.

I began my research in 1992. Twenty years will have passed by the time this work sees print. Unquestionably, I have forgotten or omitted someone here. Even if your name or institution does not appear, I am deeply grateful to all who have helped along the way.

MILLIKEN'S BEND

"The Dark Pall of Barbarism"
Emancipation as War Crime

WITH US IT IS A question of self-preservation. Our lives, our property, the safety of our homes and our hearthstones, all that men hold dear on earth, is involved in the issue."[1]

Perhaps no voice summed up the Southern psyche better than that of Stephen Hale, secession commissioner from the state of Alabama to Kentucky. In late December 1860, he laid out the stakes for Gov. Beriah Magoffin of Kentucky, and he did not mince words:

> the election of Mr. Lincoln cannot be regarded otherwise than a solemn declaration . . . of hostility to the South . . . nothing less than an open declaration of war . . . this new theory of government destroys the property of the South, lays waste her fields, and inaugurates all the horrors of a San Domingo servile insurrection, consigning her citizens to assassinations and her wives and daughters to pollution and violation to gratify the lust of half-civilized Africans. Especially is this true in the cotton-growing States, where, in many localities, the slave outnumbers the white population ten to one.[2]

Magoffin, unwilling to send his state into secession immediately, nevertheless saw no hyperbole in Hale's grim predictions. "You have not exaggerated the grievous wrongs, injuries, and indignities to which the slave-holding States . . . have long submitted." Perhaps Kentuckians, closer to the North, appreciated "the intolerable wrongs and menacing dangers" even more than citizens of the Deep South. Magoffin agreed that "the importance of arresting the insane crusade" against slavery marked by the election of Abraham Lincoln could not be overstated.[3]

The picture Hale painted was nothing short of apocalyptic: "If we fail, the light of our civilization goes down in blood." Women and children would be driven from their homes in a conflagration. "The dark pall of barbarism" would cast its shadow all across the South, bringing with it "the scenes of West India emancipation, with its attendant horrors and crimes." The Southern cause was not just one of "states rights" and the preservation of the Southern "way of life"—slavery. It was a fight for survival, the defense of home and hearth against abolitionist Yankees who would incite slaves to rise up and kill their masters, burn homes, and rape their mistresses. It was not a political matter but rather a personal one, arousing the deepest feelings of home defense and security. It was indeed, a fight for self-preservation. The very word "emancipation," as Hale's plea indicates, evoked images of torture and bloodbath.[4]

Periodic slave revolts seemed to justify this belief in the latent violence of recalcitrant slaves. Nat Turner's rebellion in Virginia sent shock waves across the South in 1831. And just a little over a year before Hale's attempt to persuade Governor Magoffin to lead Kentucky out of the Union, white abolitionist John Brown led an idealistic crusade into Harpers Ferry in northern Virginia, aspiring to incite a slave revolt across the South. In Mississippi in 1861 near Natchez, a large insurrection plot was discovered, to the horror of local residents. Justice was meted out—not in a moment of passion with a lynch mob but instead with several days of formal testimony in the form of an extralegal "trial."[5]

If all of this paranoia seems far-fetched to the modern reader, who might dismiss Hale's comments as extreme political posturing, one only has to think about the omnipresent fears of terrorism in more recent times to see an analogous situation. A tiny incident could lead to near panic among the population. Anthrax-laced letters sent to senators' offices in Washington, D.C., in late 2001 made people throughout the country afraid to go to their mailboxes for a time. There was a similar atmosphere of fear and panic on the eve of the Civil War, and for Southerners, the fear centered on an equally everyday, intimate, and "harmless" source: their slaves. Whites in every Southern state sensed the threat of an imminent slave insurrection and subsequent bloodbath, even if it remained dormant—or merely more fiction than fact.

Slave rebellion leading to an all-out race war was not the only threat perceived in Lincoln's election. According to Southern politicians and newspapers, the so-called Black Republicans, the party of Lincoln, sought racial equality, including equal suffrage—and worse still—racial "amalgamation" or intermarriage. Hale also expressed these fears: "The slave-holder and non-slave-holder must ultimately share the same fate; all be degraded to a position of equality with free negroes, stand side by side with them at the polls, and fraternize in all the social relations of life . . . Who can look upon such a picture without a shudder? What Southern man, . . . [would] see his own sons and daughters in the not distant future associating with free negroes upon terms of political and social equality . . . ?" The God-given "title to superiority over the black race" would be abolished by the hand of man. Northerners not only sought the destruction of the very fabric of Southern society but desired to impose their will against God's. Black equality was as big a threat to the Southern mind as bloodshed in a race war.[6]

Hale was certainly not the only one making these claims. Secession commissioners from Georgia, South Carolina, Mississippi, and Alabama made similar statements, calling upon the states of Virginia, Maryland, and North Carolina, with equal passion, certainty, and foreboding.[7] Louisiana's secession commissioner, George Williamson, had a similar message in February of 1861 for members of the Texas Secession Convention. Williamson believed the two states had many things in common and should be allied in their efforts. The Texans hardly needed convincing of the danger. They had watched anxiously in the late 1850s as Free-State and proslavery forces battled it out in Kansas Territory. The Free-Staters gained the upper hand when Kansas entered the Union in 1861 without slavery. Like the Free-Staters who poured into Kansas, Texans could expect emigrant aid societies armed with Sharp's rifles to convert the state by force to abolitionism. Williamson forecast that if Texas remained in the Union, "the abolitionists would continue their work of incendiarism and murder."[8]

Williamson's reference to "incendiarism" would have been an obvious reference for his Texas audience. The previous summer, numerous fires of mysterious origin occurred nearly simultaneously in several towns and cities, giving the appearance of a concerted action by unknown parties. Recent scholarship has shown that most, if not all, of the fires were started by spontaneous combustion when newly invented "prairie matches" became unstable at high temperatures. Unaware of this scientific explanation, most of the population believed the "abolition menace" had struck Texas, and the citizens responded in fear and tragic paranoia. Many men, black and white, were hanged or run out of the state.[9]

The delegates to the Texas Secession Convention saw the same threats Williamson did. The states of the North had pronounced their hostility to the "beneficent and patriarchal system of African slavery" and promoted "the debasing doctrine of the equality of all men, irrespective of race or color—a doctrine at war with nature, in opposition to the experience of mankind, and in violation of the plainest revelations of the divine law." Besides being offensive to Southern sensibilities of race and propriety, Northern views were unnatural, even heretical. Fundamentally, for Southerners, the election of Abraham Lincoln and the rise of the Republican Party heralded a thinly veiled declaration of war against the Southern states and opposition to the God-given right and responsibility of white men to enslave and thereby "civilize" members of the African race.[10]

Texas joined the Confederacy on March 2, 1861, and although the firing on Fort Sumter was still a month in the future, to Texans' eyes, the war was already underway. Abolitionists had "invaded Southern soil and murdered unoffending citizens." Worse still, these "actors and assassins" (probably a reference to John Brown's band) had received high praise in the press. Finally, the Texans declared that their state, and the others of the South, were established "exclusively by the white race, for themselves and their posterity; that the African race had no agency in their establishment; that they were rightfully held and regarded as an inferior and dependent race, and in that condition only could their existence in this country be rendered beneficial or tolerable." The Texas Ordinance of Secession made it clear: the Federal government had become a weapon "to strike down the interests and prosperity of the people." There was no choice but for Texas to dissolve the bonds of union, just twenty-five years old, and ally herself with her Southern sisters.[11]

As the fever of secession spread throughout the South, the war of words escalated to a war with weapons. Fort Sumter was fired upon in Charleston Harbor on April 12, 1861, and the conflagration that would eventually engulf the South had begun. As more and more men left for military service, Southern prophecies of slave insurrections were not fulfilled. The fear seemed to subside but still lay dormant. Periodic outbreaks of fierce anti-abolitionism and rumors of insurrections—often accompanied by hangings—would continue to seize individual communities.[12]

When Lincoln issued the preliminary Emancipation Proclamation in September 1862, the cry across the South was predictably hostile. Politicians and editors fanned the flames. The Confederate Congress wasted no time in its response. Sen. Thomas Jenkins Semmes from Louisiana introduced a resolution just seven days after Lincoln's announcement of "the emancipation of slaves and the exciting of servile war." Semmes declared that such a policy was a "gross violation of the usages of civilized warfare, an outrage on the rights of private property, and an invitation to an atrocious servile war," and he urged President Jefferson Davis to take retaliatory measures to dissuade its implementation.[13] Not long after his resolution, Semmes introduced a bill "to repress the atrocities of the enemy." He read off a litany of abuses suffered by the people of the South since the commencement of the war: citizens forced to take treasonable oaths, women and children exiled from their homes or imprisoned, houses burned and plundered, men murdered on a pretext, art stolen and libraries destroyed, and soldiers encouraged to "commit outrages" upon women while commanders looked away. Three actions of the enemy involved undermining slavery: "organizing the abduction of slaves by government officials . . . ; promoting servile insurrection by tampering with slaves; and protecting them in resisting their masters."[14]

According to Semmes, emancipation was an act of "barbarous ferocity." In addition to the catalog of horrors present in any war, the Emancipation Proclamation proved that the North had the "atrocious design of adding servile insurrection and the massacre of families to the calamities of war." The war could no longer be considered a conflict among civilized nations but rather an invasion of the South by a "horde of murderers and plunderers breathing hatred and revenge" for repeated defeats by Confederate armies on the battlefield. The Union had sunk to a new low in its war effort if it was willing to free and enlist slaves.[15] Such a drastic and morally repugnant measure by the North had to be counteracted with equally severe actions to try to discourage its implementation. Semmes proposed that all Federal officers and noncommissioned officers taken prisoner be put to hard labor. For those who served in black units or who recruited, trained, or otherwise aided in the arming of Negro troops, the fate was death. Any officer or noncommissioned officer who incited slave rebellion or "pretended" to give slaves their freedom would also meet the death penalty. Each person accused under the act would be tried by a military court, and the president had the power to commute or pardon. Finally, the Confederate president could "resort to such other retaliatory measures as in his judgment may be best calculated to repress the atrocities of the enemy."[16]

By October 1, 1862, the day Semmes introduced his legislation, the Confederate representatives and senators were competing to see who could condemn Lincoln's preliminary Emancipation Proclamation with the greatest vehemence. Numerous legislators echoed Semmes's sentiments, and many proposed legislation of their own. Their speeches and proposals reveal their conviction that a race war was imminent and that severe measures had to be taken to discourage the North from implementing its horrid plan. Since the proclamation would not take effect until January 1, there was still time for the Federal government to reconsider its actions.

Sen. Benjamin H. Hill of Georgia, usually a moderate, nevertheless saw peril ahead. He introduced a bill entitled, "An Act to punish incitement to servile insurrection and other crimes when committed under pretence of waging War." Hill's proposal had some similarities to others introduced at the same time, but one section was especially noteworthy. *Any* Union soldier captured within the Confederacy after January 1, 1863—not just those directly or indirectly involved in arming former slaves—would be presumed to be inciting insurrection and abetting murder. They were to be assumed guilty unless proof could be provided of their innocence, and their fate would be death. These drastic measures would be rescinded only if the Emancipation Proclamation was revoked.[17]

Senator James Phelan of Mississippi saw the same horror ahead. "Our baffled and brutal foes . . . seek to light in our land the baleful fires of servile war, by emancipating amongst us, four millions of negro slaves, with the design of effecting an indiscriminate slaughter of all ages, sexes and conditions of our people. A scheme so ferocious and infernal is unparalleled in the blackest and bloodiest page of savage strife; . . . and reveals the design of our enemy to be,—regardless of the laws of God or man—the annihilation or subjugation" of the Confederate people. "We are thus confronted with the dire alternative of 'Slavery or Death.'" The choice was simple: "*Extermination* by the *slaughter* of a free people, is preferable to their *extinction* by *subjugation*." The Confederate authorities had to face a "dread necessity," the need to abandon civilized warfare in the face of the new Union policy. It would be a "war of extermination."[18]

Sen. John Bullock Clark of Missouri was a former representative in the U.S. Congress. No doubt he would have known a thing or two about vengeful warfare, given the recent and violent role of Missourians in the settlement of "Bleeding Kansas." He saw the preliminary Emancipation Proclamation as the culmination of "a long series of atrocities utterly subversive of the principles of christian [sic] warfare." The proclamation was a "fiendish" design to invoke "the unspeakable horrors of servile insurrection, and a brutal massacre of the whole people of the Confederate states without regard to age, or sex." In the future conduct of the war, he said, the Confederate States should not ask for quarter for its own troops nor grant it to Federal soldiers until the North was willing to abide by warfare appropriate to "christian and civilized nations."[19]

Many of the resolutions, speeches, and bills introduced in early October went nowhere, but one joint resolution managed to pass both houses of the Confederate Congress. In addition to using parts of Senator Semmes's litany of abuses, the resolution enumerated the heinous crimes of "passing laws to equalize the races" and "preparing armed bands of negroes to fight in the presence of negro slaves for the subjugation of the white race." The North wished to "destroy [the South's] labor system, to subvert the institutions human and divine upon which it is founded, employing slaves and other negroes for these purposes, with an atrocious design of adding servile insurrection and the massacre of families to the calamities of war."[20]

It did not take long for such political rhetoric to meet its first test. On November 7, 1862, Union Lt. Col. Oliver T. Beard of the 48th New York Volunteers commanded a small expedition along the Sapello River in Georgia, near Fairhope. He led Company A of the 1st South Carolina Volunteers, the first Union regiment composed of former slaves recruited in the South. His purpose was to try the men, to see if they would make good soldiers for tasks beyond army labor and garrison duty. The greater significance of his mission may have been his recruiting. If the Confederates had been able to read Beard's account, their worst fears would have been realized. "I started from Saint Simon's with 62 colored fighting men," he reported, "and returned to Beaufort with 156 fighting men (all colored). As soon as we took a slave from his claimant we placed a musket in his hand and he began to fight for the freedom of others."[21]

On November 30, 1862, Confederate secretary of war James A. Seddon addressed Gen. P. G. T. Beauregard about the disposition of armed blacks taken prisoner, as reported by Brig. Gen. Hugh W. Mercer, Confederate commander of the District of Georgia. Although Mercer's original correspondence apparently no longer exists, and Beard reported no enlisted men missing or captured, it seems possible that the "slaves taken in federal uniform with arms in their hands" may have been part of Beard's force.

Seddon conferred with Davis about what to do with the captured blacks, then wrote to General Beauregard. "Slaves in flagrant rebellion are subject to death by the laws of every slave-holding State," he wrote, suggesting that, if circumstances permitted, such slaves should be brought to trial before civil authorities. "They cannot be recognized in any way as soldiers subject to the rules of war" and could not, therefore, be tried by a military court. It was "essential that slaves in armed insurrection should meet condign punishment; summary execution must therefore be inflicted on those taken . . . under circumstances indicative beyond doubt of actual rebellion." Seddon knew he was walking a fine line and warned against the abuse of this kind of justice, concerned that in the heat of battle or a moment of overzealousness a massacre could occur. To prevent such an event, he advised that only the general in command near the location of capture should provide the order of execution. In this particular case, Seddon granted General Mercer this authority and stated that such measures should be taken against any other slaves captured in similar circumstances.[22]

Elsewhere in the South, in late December, apprehension was growing. The *Natchez Daily Courier* carried a story from a Houston paper that warned, "the negroes in various parts of the South are being tampered with by secret abolition emissaries." The plots had been broken up, but "the people of the South cannot be too vigilant, as we know the Lincoln government have now resorted to this means to accomplish our destruction . . . Every planter should be on his guard, and all assemblages of negroes should be prohibited."[23] Just a few days later, the same paper carried news from Florida of Yankee officers who declared that the Union would be restored, even if it meant liberating every slave and exterminating the white race. Although such news was conveyed in an exaggerated tone, it nevertheless reflected the bitterness and apprehension felt in the South, and it created an atmosphere of panic, fear, and dread. Such horrors had to be prevented.[24]

Editors in the South began suggesting solutions. One remedy appeared on January 2 under the headline, "Retaliation." The article posited two options for Southern forces: that "all commissioned officers captured on slave territory, be summarily executed" or that "such officers be turned over by the Confederate Government to the State authorities, to be dealt with as felons." The Yankee "minions of . . . Lincoln" came to the South "for the purpose of inciting slaves to rebellion and insurrection. For such fiends no punishment is too severe, and they should be made to feel and know in advance that the death penalty awaits them if they are captured on Southern soil after the proclamation of Lincoln shall have made its appearance."[25]

Shortly before the new year, when it became clear that the United States would not back down from its policy of emancipation, Davis issued General Orders No. 111, which, among other things, declared Union general Benjamin F. Butler to be a felon, "deserving of capital punishment." If captured, he should be immediately hanged. For justification, Davis enumerated Butler's crimes, including exciting slave insurrection. A servile war was fully supported by the Lincoln government, Davis said, and would exceed "in horrors the most merciless atrocities of the savages." Butler himself was not the only felon, however. Davis also declared that commissioned officers under Butler's command could not be "considered as soldiers engaged in honorable warfare, but as robbers and criminals, deserving death" and, whenever captured, should meet the same fate. Enlisted men and noncommissioned officers, however, would be granted "kindness and humanity" and treated as regular prisoners of war, since they were merely forced to serve the will of their superior officers. Slaves captured in arms should be turned over to state authorities. Finally, Davis declared that such punishments would be meted out to all other commissioned officers, under any command, when accompanied by armed slaves. The Confederate adjutant general, Samuel Cooper, added that if the evidence against a man was uncertain, the case would be referred through his office to the War Department for adjudication.[26]

The Confederate government continued to respond to the Emancipation Proclamation in the weeks that followed, and the rhetoric was much the same as it had been in October. Despite the many resolutions and bills introduced in December and January, it took until April for the two houses of the Confederate Congress to agree on punishment for individuals involved in enlisting former slaves in the Union army. Contrary to Davis's proposition to hand over Federal commissioned officers to state authorities, the final legislation directed that they should be dealt with by the Confederate government. The actions of emancipating slaves, encouraging them to run away or rise up in revolt, or making efforts "to overthrow the institution of African slavery and bring on a servile war in these States" was contrary to all rules of "modern warfare . . . among civilized nations" and could only be met with retaliatory measures. Commissioned officers engaged in enlisting or commanding blacks in uniform would be charged with inciting insurrection and granted a trial before a military court. Guilt would result in the death penalty. African Americans who were taken in arms or aided the U.S. military would be dealt with by state authorities according to state laws. The Senate agreed to the resolution in secret session and passed it along to President Davis for his approval.[27]

Even in the North, some members of the U.S. Congress opposed the policy of liberating and arming slaves. William H. Wadsworth, representative from

Kentucky, had visions of terror and bloodshed like those evoked at the beginning of the conflict by Secession Commissioner Hale. Echoing Hale's words to
Magoffin in 1861, Wadsworth explained to his mostly nonslaveholding audience in early 1863: "We in the South could not live under this policy of arming
the slaves . . . it would be the destruction of our homes, our families, our lives,
our property, and our liberty. We could not live under it . . . we still love the
Constitution, and, if you will let this be a war for the Constitution, will die if
need be in its defense," but Kentuckians would likewise be willing to defend
to the death their "imperiled but imperishable rights" to own slaves.[28]

A few days later, Rep. Henry May of Maryland made similar claims, finding
the proposition of arming black men simply "preposterous." It was a new low
in the Union's war effort and demonstrated how poorly the war was progressing for the North. May declared, "We who recognize the amiable disposition
of the domesticated African, his inert nature, his slovenly habits, his clumsi-
ness, his want of vigilance, and his timidity, know that of all human beings,
he presents the least qualifications for a soldier." Yet despite these inferior
qualities, May nevertheless believed that slave insurrection and violence was
a real threat. He evoked the "horrors of San Domingo" in his speech and made
it clear that Confederate politicians and planters were not the only men who
held such views. Several moves were made in both houses of the U.S. Congress
to prohibit the enlistment of blacks as soldiers, but they were defeated.[29]

According to Southern politicians, emancipation was a radical declaration
that slavery was wrong and a moral evil. Furthermore, it proposed that slaves
would be put in positions of carrying weapons, frightening enough of its own
accord but more terrible and offensive because slaves thus would be made
soldiers—a noble profession, not fit for persons of color. Such a proposition
was ridiculous in its very nature, and it made a mockery of all soldiery, North
and South. Northerners must be truly desperate if they were willing to serve
in the same army with former slaves.

Southerners could not bear the idea of going into battle against former
bondsmen and declared, even before it became a logical possibility, that such
a war would become one of "extermination." They already saw it as such the
moment Lincoln gave his proclamation. According to them, it was Lincoln,
not the Confederacy, who turned the war into one of annihilation. The Emancipation Proclamation could mean nothing less. The document was as repre-
hensible and offensive to the Southern mind as slavery is to the modern reader
today. It transformed the war from a gentleman's fight, where both parties, like

duelists, followed certain rules of warfare (codified in the Articles of War), into an uncivilized war, when the most extreme measures became justified. Emancipation was nothing less than a war crime and an atrocity. Retaliation and retribution were the only responses possible.

Facing former slaves in battle, in the costume of soldiers (for no Southerner took the proposition seriously), Southerners would be fighting not just for their lives and their country but for their way of life, their families, and most of all, perhaps, their virtue as men. The implication that slave-soldiers could be met on the field of battle and treated like ordinary white Yankee soldiers was an impossibility. It was a dishonorable notion, an insult to Southern manhood and honor.

Perhaps even more frightening, emancipation implied that the front lines of battle were no longer around Fredericksburg or Murfreesboro or other far-away places where armies clashed. If slaves were declared free and encouraged to come into Union lines or rage across the plantation, burning homes, ravishing women, and killing children, unleashing the supposedly "savage African" that was safely shackled under slavery—it meant that *everywhere* in the South was threatened. Areas far behind the lines, previously thought quiet and safe, could now become the front in a new form of guerilla war. Slaves across the South could rise up, with little to hinder them, and strike at the very heart of slave owners and white society—their undefended women and children. Such a prospect sent shudders throughout the South, and hysteria was the outcome.

No such universal bloodbath and uprising took place, even though one plot in May 1863 was said to span the entire South. Slaves within a few days' journey of Union lines simply left the plantation. They were interested in freedom, not violence or revenge. Isolated instances of theft, vandalism, "insulting behavior," and some attacks against individual slaveholding families occurred, but these were the exception, not the rule. Most slaves simply walked or ran away, sometimes openly, sometimes in stealth, but rarely exhibiting the unbridled rage and bloodthirstiness that haunted the Southern psyche.[30]

For those slaves far from Union lines, life went on almost as usual. A few individuals might occasionally make a run for freedom, but most knew the futility and risks of such an endeavor and, like the generations before them, tried to make the best of their situation, finding solace in religion, taking strength from friends and family in the quarters, and hoping and praying for the day that freedom would come.

"Eternal Vigilance"
The Insurrectionary Menace and Vigilante Response

T HE BELIEF IN NEARLY omnipresent insurrectionary plots instigated by "outside agitators," coupled with the blazing rhetoric of secessionist fire-eaters, led to predictable and understandable fear in the hearts and minds of white Southern planters. The rhetoric that reached its zenith in 1859, 1860, and 1861 may have been extreme, but it was nothing new. Any detailed examination of events during the summer of 1863 in northeastern Louisiana must take into account an understanding of the depth and breadth of this fear, and its likely and violent outcomes.

Periodic outbreaks of insurrectionary panic shivered the South all during the time of slavery. Civilians and statesmen in Louisiana and Mississippi had their own reasons to fear. Both states had seen their share of uprisings and rebellions and knew such threats were not to be taken lightly. The Haitian Revolution sixty years earlier still had a strong hold on the Southern imagination. Repeatedly in pro-slavery speeches and writings throughout the antebellum period, St. Domingue was invoked to demonstrate the need for strict control over slaves, including brutal punishments, and to justify the continuation of slavery. To abolish it would mean death to those whites who had so "benevolently" provided for the "ignorant African" in a mission of Christian charity, who clothed and fed them, and who oversaw their lives with the heart of a patient and beneficent father. Or so Southerners believed. Historian George M. Frederickson puts it succinctly: "As a slave he was lovable, but as a freedman he would be a monster."[1]

Jefferson Davis, in his last days as a U.S. senator in January of 1861, questioned the growing hostility of the North toward the South and invoked the specter of St. Domingue. There, government intervention from distant France had provoked a revolution. There were no "black heroes," Davis asserted. Only when the slave masters were arrested on charges of treason and removed from the scene did the Negroes rise in insurrection. Indeed, he declared, there never had been a true case of "negro insurrection" anywhere, at any time. Those instances in the United States, as well as Haiti, commonly termed "insurrections" were in fact rebellions led by "bad men" among an "ignorant and credulous people." Negroes did not have the wherewithal to plan, lead, or take such actions of their own accord. Only when they were led and provoked by others, in the absence of their masters, would they rise up, burn, and kill.[2]

The legacy of St. Domingue loomed large over Louisiana in particular. Thousands of refugees, black and white, free and slave, had fled to New Orleans in the period from 1797 to 1809. Sixty years later, nearly three hundred individuals in Louisiana, most still in Orleans Parish, listed their birthplace as Haiti or Santo Domingo. More than one thousand in the state at the time were born in the West Indies, including those born in Haiti.[3] Shortly after the Haitian Revolution, in 1811, five hundred Negroes had plotted rebellion in St. John the Baptist Parish. They marched down the River Road in a martial display with flags and drums, burned homes and storehouses, and killed a few whites. White troops from New Orleans quickly moved to put down the rebellion, militia forces were called out of Baton Rouge, and planters from the west bank of the Mississippi crossed over to assist. Sixty-six blacks were killed; another sixteen were captured, taken to New Orleans, tried, and executed.[4]

Another scare originated near Natchez, Mississippi, in 1835, and fear raced up and down the Mississippi River, reaching as far south as Jefferson Parish in Louisiana. The alleged conspirators were quickly executed. Two years later, several slaves were put to death, without trial, for their supposed role in an insurrectionary plot in Rapides Parish. Later decades were also punctuated by rumors of insurrections. In 1842, planters in the cotton parishes along the west bank of the Mississippi in northern Louisiana feared the uprising of nearly three hundred slaves, with the result that twenty were arrested and a few hanged. In 1856, panic again gripped the entire state, but no evidence was found of an actual plot.[5]

John Brown's attack on Harpers Ferry galvanized the South and prompted the largest insurrectionary scare in the years immediately preceding the Civil War. Shortly after Brown's execution, the *Monroe Register* in Louisiana carried a report of an insurrection plot in Dardanelle, Arkansas. Although excerpted from a Fort Smith newspaper, the final line seemed a direct address to the *Register*'s readers: "These things should arouse the people of the State to prepare for the insidious working of Abolitionists amongst us."[6] In Jackson, Mississippi, readers were alarmed to discover that a man who supposedly was a brother of one of Brown's associates had "traveled through Mississippi, and kept Brown and company posted in regard to the disposition of the slaves." The article, reprinted from the Norfolk, Virginia, *Southern Argus,* went on to detail nine Mississippi counties that had been marked on Brown's map, "visited by abolition emissaries," and where the slaves were "ready for insurrection." Most of the counties—among them Warren and Adams (containing the cities of Vicksburg and Natchez, respectively)—had populations where blacks outnumbered whites by about three to one. By sheer force of numbers, slaves in these counties, with only a little prompting from abolitionists sent from the North, could easily overwhelm their masters in an orgy of destruction, rape, and bloodshed. The article urged officials in Mississippi and other states to beware of "all suspicious strangers," especially "peddlars, mercantile drummers, book agents and teachers in search of situations." Anyone who could "not give a good account of themselves" should be forced to leave immediately. Finally, the paper warned: "Let not the lesson taught by fanatic Brown be forgotten by the South. Let the militia be thoroughly and effectively organized in every Southern State. Eternal vigilance is the price of our peace and happiness."[7]

Whether any of the reports were true or false is today, as it was then, ultimately irrelevant. The statement was made, and people would believe. Numerous scholars have written of the power of the insurrectionary menace, a fateful and tragic cultural bogeyman that cost countless African Americans their lives, and some whites, too.[8] More often than not, the supposed "insurrection"—although earnestly believed in by the white planter elite—was often the product of paranoid imagination. Yet, as Armstead L. Robinson points out, even rumors of insurrections were based on one solid fact: "The slaves wanted to be free and the South knew it."[9]

The panics of the early 1860s show the depth of the planters' fears and the lengths they would go to maintain order on the plantations. It is important to remember that these events took place before the war, long before emancipation became a stated aim of the Lincoln administration. Of course, as the secession commissioners made abundantly clear, many Southern statesmen believed Lincoln was an abolition president, even if he tried to deny it in public. But the point remains—if residents on either side of the Mississippi River felt extreme measures were necessary before the war, what actions might they take or consider when Union forces arrived en masse at their fields, gins, and doorsteps in 1863?

Several specific scares in Louisiana and Mississippi in the early 1860s are especially important to examine, given later events during the summer of 1863. Near Natchez in May 1861, planter Isaac F. Harrison of Tensas Parish, Louisiana, uncovered an insurrectionary plot. It called for the slaves in Adams County, Mississippi, and probably elsewhere, to rise up on the Fourth of July. "Being aware that the negros all knew of the war and what it was for," Harrison eavesdropped on a conversation among his slaves, who expected assistance from Lincoln's army. Once free, it was said, they would kill their masters and take white women as their wives. Harrison acted promptly, and the slave who spoke of the plot was put to death.[10] Two other slaves in Jefferson County, Mississippi, met similar fates. Five white men and one male slave were held in confinement and would soon "pull hemp." Other suspects were still at large. Jefferson County planter Howell Hines wrote Gov. John J. Pettus that fear in the region was so great that some Adams County planters had fled to Europe. Hines had no sympathy for these cowards, recommending that their property be confiscated.[11]

The state of affairs was so unsettled that Hines begged the governor to suspend any further departures of still-organizing military companies from the area. Knowing their obligation to the government, Jefferson County citizens decided to send only a few officers off to training camps to learn the drill; they later would return to instruct the others. Hines advocated similar measures for all of the river counties, where the black population significantly out-numbered the white. In Jefferson County, for instance, John D. L. Davenport gave the population as "650 voters surrounded by 11,000 slaves."[12] To bolster his case for keeping troops at home, Hines stated that across the river in Louisiana, Gov. Thomas O. Moore had already taken similar measures and was even considering billeting troops on a river steamer so that they could be easily rushed to any scenes "where there was an out-break."[13]

News and rumors about the plot must have spread quickly. Kate Stone of Milliken's Bend, Louisiana, nearly one hundred miles to the north, wrote in her diary about her fear of an insurrection occurring over the Fourth of July. Some slaves had "gotten a confused idea" that the war "is all to help them," and she was relieved when the day came and went without incident. Now, she thought with relief, the house servants would return to their work.[14]

Later in the fall of 1861, a second, much larger plot would be discovered in Adams County, Mississippi, prompting a massive orderly but extralegal in-vestigation. At least twenty-seven slaves, possibly more, were put to death. It was said that white men from the North, some of them probably German, had led the plot, though no whites were executed. Historian Winthrop D. Jordan's exhaustive study indicates that in contrast to the Fourth of July plot, probably few individuals outside of Adams County knew of the planned insurrection in the fall. Kate Stone, for one, made no mention in her diary of the larger troubles experienced near Natchez just a few months later.[15]

By the middle of 1862, Alexander K. Farrar, the Confederate provost marshal in Natchez, reported continuing problems with Negroes. Stern measures had been taken in the previous year, with about forty blacks hanged for plotting insurrection and an equivalent number "in irons." Although Farrar felt matters were well in hand, he nevertheless complained that there were still many bondsmen who were being "insubordinate" and who were running away to Federal lines—though at that time Union troops were still quite distant. Farrar blamed inattentive and uncaring slave owners who left their human chattel to fend for themselves by stealing food or clothes to meet their basic needs.[16]

The planters in Louisiana and Mississippi were not alone in their fear of slave uprisings and reliance upon vigilante justice, however. The Texans who would arrive in northern Louisiana in early 1863 came from a state known for its violence, lawlessness, and vigilantism. The men who made up portions of Maj. Gen. John G. Walker's Texas Division, including some of Brig. Gen. Henry E. McCulloch's Brigade, came from this violent culture. Some companies of the 16th and 17th Texas Infantry hailed from Bell County, a portion of central Texas noted for a history of extralegal violence dating back to the Texas Revolution. In the wake of independence, Texans were praised for their valor. Their friends, family, and descendants in the region would cultivate and nurture the memory of their deeds, praising, in the words of one historian, "those early pioneers who did not wait for the arrival of formal legal structures." Justice would wait for no man—not even a judge.[17]

Frequently these vigilante actions had racial motivations—first, against Mexicans, then against Indians. The Texans' struggle against Indian attacks would echo later accusations and fears concerning slaves during the Civil War. The narratives were at times nearly the same. Indians were said to attack and ransack homes, rape women, and kill children. Both Native Americans and African Americans were referred to frequently as "savages," and repressive actions taken against them—such as removal to Indian Territory or enslavement—were the white man's efforts to "civilize" or "Christianize" them. Frontiersmen believed killing Indians to be as much a part of their manly duties to their wives and families as hunting or building a cabin. They grew frustrated and impatient with government efforts to pacify, contain, or remove the Indians and often took matters into their own hands. Bell County alone had several militia-type organizations, just for fighting Indians. According to William D. Carrigan, future vigilante mobs would justify their actions by declaring themselves to be following the precedent set by the great Indian-fighters of the past.[18]

The admixture of the proud revolutionary legacy of the heirs of Texas Independence, coupled with heroic tales of Indian fighters, gave extralegal violence a remarkable and forceful cachet in Texas culture and society, at least in central Texas, if not elsewhere. In 1856, in Colorado County, southeast of Austin, there were rumors of insurrection. Like most plots described in the press, it was said that all white men were to be killed, with the women spared to become wives of the slaves in rebellion. The uprising was supposedly well organized, with a formal structure of "companies," complete with passwords and signs. Nearly two hundred slaves were said to be involved. Two of them would die from the beatings they received, and three men were hanged. Mexicans in the county were also considered to be at fault because they enticed the slaves to flee to Mexico. The Mexicans were exiled from the county, granted five days to leave, and were promised death if they returned. From this county in 1862, would come Company I of the 17th Texas Infantry that would fight on the levee at Milliken's Bend.[19]

William H. Parsons, who would later command a cavalry brigade, wrote a defense of vigilantism in putting down slave rebellions in his newspaper, the *Southwest*, and provided details of a plot and the actions of the "committee of safety" that put it down. His hard riding cavalrymen a few years later would earn a reputation for brutality against former slaves in Union uniform.[20]

One Texan even declared that young men would ride a hundred miles to participate in a lynching and that watching an abolitionist hang had become a great "sport." According to Carrigan, most Texans "worried greatly about the actions of their slaves." And though in the wake of Harpers Ferry insurrections seemed to lurk around every corner in the South, "no state can compete with Texas in the late 1850s and early 1860s for bloody overreaction."[21] Carrigan's investigation into the Bosque County safety committee, established in 1862, demonstrates that some of the leading citizens were at the helm. Like a similar committee organized in 1861 in Monroe, Louisiana, the names of the members would have been well known—and well respected—by the majority of the citizenry. Therefore, because of their prominent position within the community, and the heightened power and esteem conferred on members of the vigilance committee, these men could act confidently on behalf of all respectable citizens.[22]

Of course, as the war dragged on, more and more men left home to serve in the Confederate army. Some evacuated their families and slaves away from areas of active military operations. Courts were often removed to distant counties and parishes or suspended entirely. This meant that even the rudiments of justice might be woefully delayed or altogether inaccessible. Such conditions created an environment ripe for vigilante justice.

Two events in Texas further dramatize the cultural milieu of the men in Walker's Division who tramped through Louisiana in 1863: the fires known as the Texas Troubles, and the Gainesville Hangings. Just nine months after the hysteria following Brown's raid on Harpers Ferry, and as inflammatory rhetoric peaked in the move toward secession, a series of suspicious fires erupted across the state in the summer of 1860. On July 8, the business section of Dallas burned to the ground, and within twenty-four hours, flames would strike more than twelve other towns. Although recent scholarship has laid the blame on the then-new "prairie matches," which became very unstable in the extraordinarily high temperatures that dry summer, it did not take Texans long to decide at the time that such fires were deliberately set by "abolition emissaries."[23]

The entire state was seized by panic, or, as historian Donald E. Reynolds calls it, "abolitionist psychosis." More fires occurred in August. Communities throughout north and central Texas launched manhunts to find the culprits. In one noteworthy case, Rev. Anthony Bewley, a Northern Methodist minister, was tracked down in Missouri by an Arkansas posse. The Arkansans turned him over to members of a vigilance committee from Fort Worth, who traveled all the way to Fayetteville to apprehend him. When the men returned to Fort Worth with their captive, he was lodged in a hotel, where a crowd burst in just before midnight and strung him up on a nearby tree. Hatred was so strong against Bewley that his hastily buried body was exhumed a few weeks later. His flesh was removed from his bones, and his skeleton placed on the roof of a storehouse, where it would become a taunting plaything of young boys. His skeleton remained there until at least sometime after the Civil War.[24]

For every fire that summer in Texas, two more would be rumored, often accompanied by reports of hangings or quick actions by vigilant citizens taken in the nick of time to prevent arson. Rumors of destruction were so rife that the editor of the Mount Pleasant *Union*, for example, had to reassure readers in other communities that the nearby towns of Daingerfield and Mount Vernon remained intact, despite published reports in other papers that they had been burned to the ground. Although there was turmoil elsewhere, the *Union* reported that Titus County remained quiet and peaceful.[25]

True or not, the rumor mill kept everyone on edge and created a siege mentality. As if the fires that summer were not enough to cast suspicions on "abolitionist" outsiders in league with slaves, additional plots surfaced in August. The *True Issue* of La Grange, Texas, reported an extensive poisoning plot in several counties. In Henderson County on August 5, a well was poisoned. "Over 100 bottles of strychnine was found in possession of negroes. On examination the plot was brought to light which was to poison as many people as possible at breakfast and then the knife and pistol, with which they were well supplied, were to do the balance of the work. All the old women and young children were to be murdered and the young women were to be taken as wives by the hell hounds," the paper proclaimed. Two days before, at Science Hill, in the same county, one black man "belonging to Mr. Barron" was hanged after strychnine was found "in his possession and he having confessed to having a hand in the insurrection."[26]

In Rusk, Cherokee County, a plot was uncovered to poison the entire town on election day. "Poison was found in the possession of several negroes, and confessions are elicited of a determination to poison and murder the whole people." Other plots had been found in Anderson County. Vigilance patrols of seventy-five to one hundred men were on duty every night in the affected counties.[27] In an unidentified town, perhaps Rusk, "abolition leaders in our midst" had prompted "incendiary movements" among the black population, according to reprints from a newspaper called the *Enquirer*. "We had thought ourselves comparitively [sic] free from the diabolical plottings which had so alarmed the citizens of northern Texas," ran the article, but suddenly "the negroes on the plantation of Mrs. Timmons . . . became unruly and manifested strong symptoms of insubordination." When two of her slaves were beaten to obtain confessions, one man admitted a plot to poison wells and springs just before election day, "to fire the dwelling[s] in the country and [d]estroy the towns, to get possession of all the arms and ammunition they could and kill the men as they returned from the election. Many negroes were implicated . . . as well as several white men." Numerous enslaved men were said to have confessed throughout the county. Their stories reportedly were consistent—

that universally they expected to be free soon and that "they would be assisted by white men in large numbers." Black preachers were said to be particularly involved, and though the plot was well known among the slaves throughout the county, "comparatively few were willing to participate in it." The plot was disrupted by its discovery just days before it was to be implemented.[28]

Remarkably, the article reported that although the vigilance committee had been busy, "they have not yet concluded that any of the slaves implicated ought to receive the extreme punishment of death." It appeared that much of the blame might fall among white men, most of whom were not residents of the area. "The evidence against them is now the subject of scrutiny and deliberation, by a committee of cool-headed, fearless and correct men," said the article. Two German peddlers were particularly suspect.[29]

The Texas Troubles, as the events of that summer came to be known, resulted in the deaths of at least thirty individuals, though historian Donald E. Reynolds believes there were likely many more. Vigilante action and the harsh penalties exacted that hot summer created an environment where "killings were commonplace occurrences that had become entirely acceptable to a majority of the population."[30] The events (or rumors of events) in Texas had a ripple effect across the South. In Mississippi's Winston County, thirty-five blacks were arrested and a white man named Harrington was hanged. Four other counties had supposedly been victims of abolitionist activity, with at least one editor seeing connections to associates of John Brown. In Louisiana, a fire in Alexandria was attributed to abolitionists and explicitly linked to the incendiarism in Texas. Sarah Wadley, a young Louisiana woman visiting in Vicksburg, wrote in her diary that abolitionists were behind plots by slaves to poison their owners.[31]

By mid-September, however, the panic began to subside in Texas. Some citizens realized that the vigilance committees may have acted hastily and gone too far, even by Texas standards. Others saw vindication for their actions. Only a swift and strong response had averted further insurrections and incendiarism. By October, law and order through the courts had been restored.[32]

Several lessons of the Texas Troubles of 1860 would linger on. First, the events of that summer—real or imagined—solidified in the white mind the notion that black slaves would not willingly rebel on their own initiative. They had to be led, provoked, instigated by "abolitionist emissaries," usually from the North. During the war, local men who stood for the Union or balked at Confederate military service would also become suspect.[33] Second, vigilante action—at times proceeding in quite an orderly way, despite being outside of the law—was collectively judged to be an appropriate and necessary response to restless blacks and the whites who led them. Justice meant violence, and the swifter and more certain, the quicker true law and order would be restored. Third, the Texas Troubles demonstrate the devastating nature of rumors masquerading as fact. Even once the unstable matches began to be suspected as the true source of the fires, some citizens refused to believe it. The damage—physically and emotionally—had already been done. Stores had burned down; people had died, sometimes as a result of forced confessions; and the panic was on. Decades later, some historians still believed there was a genuine abolitionist plot.[34]

In Texas that summer, speaking out against the majority opinion put one's life in peril, particularly if one had Unionist inclinations or preached against slavery, as Bewley did. By 1860, "Texans saw any critic of slavery, no matter how mild, as a potential threat to social order," writes Reynolds.[35] Key to this observation is the emphasis on social order. It wasn't just that abolitionists desired freedom for the enslaved. It was that abolitionism struck at a fundamental part of Southern society, the very basis of its economy and culture. As the presidential election of 1860 drew nearer that fall, even the slightest support of Lincoln and the Republican Party was interpreted as implicit support for "incendiaries" and "abolitionists" who were determined to strike Texas again, just as they had during the Troubles.[36]

Given Texans' history of violence as a mode of self-preservation against Mexicans, Indians, restless slaves, and "abolitionists," it is perhaps not surprising that the momentum from these forces resulted in the largest mass execution in American history at Gainesville in October 1862. Forty-two men were executed, two died while escaping, and others in surrounding counties also were killed, all accused of treason to the Confederacy for supporting the Union. Ironically, Cooke County and other counties in northeast Texas had voted against secession in 1861. But by the second year of the war, support for the Confederacy was crucial. Those who resisted conscription or felt that their primary duty was to protect their families from Indian incursions from the north and west risked being accused of membership in the Union League, a loose, ineffective network of men who came together for common defense. To add to the tension, "incendiaries" had struck once again, igniting cotton gins in north Texas.[37]

The real issue, according to Richard B. McCaslin in his study of the Great

Hanging, was a sense of disorder and instability brought about by menfolk absent at war, fear of Indian attacks, and concern that Northern abolitionists from Kansas and Indian Territory sought to infiltrate northern Texas. McCaslin's theory echoes that of Reynolds. Like the response to the Texas Troubles, the Great Hanging was fundamentally a desire for and an effort to restore order and stability. As McCaslin points out, the irony of such lynchings was that they were an extralegal means to maintain legal order, even going so far as to mimic legal procedures by having trials and testimony before passing judgment. A world threatened with chaos was thought to require extreme measures to maintain stability.[38]

A year before the hangings, in September 1861, Brig. Gen. Paul Octave Hébert arrived to head the Confederate army's Department of Texas. A West Pointer who was something of a dilettante, Hébert had no patience with Texans who desired to remain in the state, protecting the northern border, when their services were needed elsewhere in the Confederacy. He quickly transferred one unit, William C. Young's 1st Texas Regiment, to Confederate service, where it was redesignated the 11th Texas Cavalry. Many of the men were lukewarm to the Confederate cause, more concerned about protecting their homes from Indians than fighting for Southern independence. When the soldiers realized they could be sent anywhere, including outside of the state, many men refused to go and paid substitutes to serve in their place.[39]

Like Young's men, many other Texans resisted conscription. Most simply desired to remain close to home, to directly defend their property and families, but some would later be accused of being Unionists. Some hid out in the brush to avoid military service. By May 1862, the situation in north Texas became complicated when so-called abolitionist arsonists struck again, as they had two years previously. Between the resistance to conscription and the sudden reappearance of fires, the populace was on edge. In response, Hébert declared martial law. Gov. Francis R. Lubbock supported his action.[40]

Several months later, in September, Governor Lubbock and militia general Hugh F. Young pleaded with Hébert to send troops to northeast Texas to put down incursions by "Yankee Guerillas" and to combat resistance to the draft. Hébert refused; he needed every man he had to help defend Galveston against a Federal invasion. About all he could do was to accept into Confederate service a brigade of state troops under William R. Hudson, militia general for the 21st District, a region including Cooke, Jack, Denton, Montague, and Wise Counties. On September 13, 1862, Hudson ordered his troops to muster. When turnout was low, Hudson ordered those with him to round up the slackers.

Their absence was all the evidence he needed to convince him of their infidelity to the Confederate cause and their involvement in a Union plot. Arrests began on October 1.[41]

Hudson's actions heralded the beginning of what would quickly escalate into the hanging of more than forty men for treason against the Confederacy. Some victims naïvely believed they would be acquitted because they were innocent. Only a handful could be considered Unionists; most were simply lukewarm to the Confederate cause. Hébert's lack of interference in the actions of Hudson and the subsequent Cooke County vigilance committee, known as the "Citizens Court," gave his implied sanction to the hangings.[42]

Just before Hudson called a muster of his troops, setting the tragedy in motion, far away in the Confederate capital in Virginia, Adjt. Gen. Samuel Cooper revoked Hébert's declaration of martial law. It was "an unwarrantable assumption of authority" and was not even deemed "a proper administration of martial law." Cooper enclosed a copy of General Orders No. 66, which reiterated a prohibition against the suspension of habeas corpus by martial law—a power reserved for the Confederate president.[43]

Of course, it would take weeks for his message to reach Texas, but when it did, Hébert defended his actions. He responded to Cooper on October 11, after the events in Gainesville had already run their course. Martial law had become "an absolute military necessity" in Texas, due to its vast geography and many threats—Yankee invasion by sea to the south, Indians to the north and west, and Unionists organizing on the northern border. Furthermore, Hébert acted "at the request and petitions of the best citizens of the State and with the full consent and approbation of the Governor." In an attempt to reassure Cooper, Hébert wrote, "There was no interference with the administration of civil law, and no suspension of the writ of habeas corpus, and persons arrested and tried had all facilities of defense as in ordinary trials under the common law." What his statement clearly reveals, however—through the use of the phrase "as in ordinary trials"—is the existence of trials outside of usual civil procedure.[44]

Hébert included a letter from Governor Lubbock in his reply. Dated September 26, just as Hudson's men began their roundup, Lubbock worried about the cessation of martial law. "If such a course is adopted I fear the consequences," he wrote. Disloyal individuals were everywhere, and only martial law could restrain their "vile tongues and bad example." Clearly, Lubbock desired martial law to remain in place, and Hébert simply obliged the governor's wishes.[45]

As Hébert was writing his protest to Cooper, the ink had scarcely dried on

President Davis's October 10 order dismissing Hébert from his command in Texas. Davis cited Hébert's unnecessary declaration of martial law and his over-zealous enforcement of conscription as the reasons. As before, the news would take weeks to reach Hébert in Texas. Within a few months, Hébert found himself relegated to the backwater supply and transportation hub of Monroe. In contrast to the frenzied and overwhelming nature of his responsibilities and threats in Texas, Louisiana must have seemed calm by comparison.[46]

When British Lt. Col. Arthur J. L. Fremantle, of Her Majesty's Coldstream Guards, on a grand tour of the Confederate military, found Hébert in Monroe on May 10, 1863, the Confederate general was in a funk. Fremantle explained, "He used to hold Magruder's position as commander-in-chief in Texas, but he has now been shelved at Munroe [sic], where he expects to be taken prisoner any day; and, from the present gloomy aspect of affairs about here, it seems extremely probable that he will not be disappointed."[47] On the following day, Fremantle set off toward Vicksburg, by way of the Red River. Eventually, he reached the Confederate lines in Jackson, Mississippi, where he was initially mistaken for a Union spy.

While in Mississippi, Fremantle observed that the burning and destruction of cities and property by Yankee forces created "a strong indisposition on the part of the Confederates to take prisoners." He related an anecdote in which one Rebel soldier took a Union soldier prisoner "by accident"—the Union man had surrendered faster than the Confederate could shoot him. Yet Fremantle reported that in all his travels, despite the bitter language used against the Yankees "and all the talk about black flag and no quarter," he had never seen a Union prisoner treated improperly. A few days later, on May 29, he heard of a report from Helena, Arkansas, claiming that an entire regiment of black troops, along with forty of their white officers, had been hanged, but he later found this to be yet another rumor. Nevertheless, his Southern companions greeted the initial news with mixed emotions—wholeheartedly in support of such a fate for the white officers but saddened at such a fate for black enlisted men. When Fremantle met the Confederate president less than a month later, Davis said people would talk about giving the Yankees no quarter, and perhaps even go into battle with that attitude, but that he had yet to hear of a single instance where Confederate soldiers had shot down men who had dropped their guns and raised their hands.[48]

Fremantle gave some indication of his Southern hosts' ideas on the subject of arming slaves when, in his journal, he suggested that doing so might aid the Confederate army. He even went so far as to speculate that "from the affection which undoubtedly exists as a general rule between the slaves and their masters, I think that they would prove more efficient than black troops under any other circumstances."[49] But the Briton admitted that such an experiment was unlikely, partly due to the economic value of slaves, but also because "Southerners consider it improper to introduce such an element on a large scale into civilized warfare." Fremantle raised the specter in a vivid word-picture, about what such a proposal meant to the Southern mind, invoking images of "negro features convulsed with rage," emotions raised to a passion, and the risk of armed blacks roaming at large. He implied that once off the plantation, with guns in their hands, black men might not be able to be controlled by their officers. He did not need to state the fears such a scene invoked. Armed black men meant not only the death of the way of life the Confederates were fighting to preserve but also the destruction of white men's homes, lives, and families—including the horror of "amalgamation" or race-mixing. The South would have to fight against emancipation with all of her blood and treasure.[50]

"All Is Uncertain"
Civilians in Louisiana and Mississippi

ESPITE THE FEARS AND RUMORS, when no large-scale multistate insurrection plot materialized in the wake of John Brown's raid, a sense of normalcy began to return. Planters on both sides of the Mississippi River continued to grow their wealth. Landholdings in the four Louisiana parishes running along the Mississippi River from the Arkansas border to the arch of the "boot" of Louisiana (Carroll, Madison, Tensas, and Concordia) were valued at an astonishing $54.5 million in 1860. This was the heart of cotton country. Tensas, Carroll, and Concordia parishes led the state in the production of cotton, together producing 57,926 tons, or 289,629 (400 lb.) bales. Madison Parish also had strong cotton production, though its primary crop was corn, leading the state with 899,050 bushels. The entire economy of the region relied on three things: cotton, slave labor, and the river route to markets.[1]

Slave labor made the river parishes in Louisiana among the wealthiest in the region. More than 53,000 enslaved persons toiled in the fields, gins, and homes of the planters. These bondsmen and women dramatically outnumbered whites, composing from 77 to 90 percent of the population in the four Louisiana parishes. Approximately 15 to 20 percent of the total white population in the area were slaveholders. Scattered free blacks were also enumerated in the river parishes in 1860, totaling less than seventy individuals in this part of the state.[2]

Before the darkening storm clouds of war rolled in during the spring of 1861, the planters of Madison Parish and the other parishes up and downstream were poised for greatness. The economic growth and expansion in the decade preceding the Civil War was phenomenal—a veritable "boom" had taken place. By 1860, farm values had increased six or seven times from just a decade before. Planters from throughout the South sought their fortunes here, and most prospered—except for momentary setbacks due to flooding or levee breaks.[3]

Abraham Hagaman came to the area in 1856, purchasing four hundred

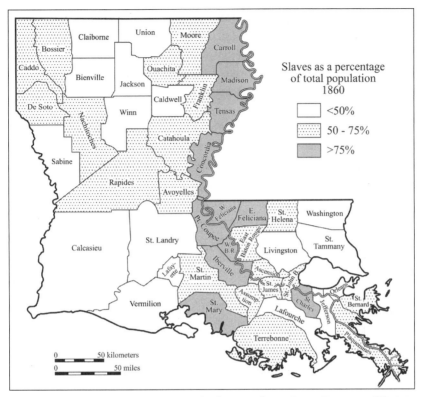

Slaves as a percentage
of total population
1860

☐ <50%

▓ 50 - 75%

▓ >75%

Source: Historical Census Browser, Geospatial and Statistical Data Center, University of Virginia, 2004, accessed Jan. 19, 2012, http://fisher.lib.virginia.edu/collections/stats/histcensus/index .html/.

acres along the Mississippi River, just below Lake Providence in Carroll Parish. His first crop was a success, but in June 1858 the levee broke and flooded his land in three feet of water. Cabins and crops, including cotton and corn, were washed away.[4] Discouraged but determined, he continued his plantation operations but moved his residence to the town proper in 1860, became pastor of a local church, and opened a school for girls. He preached to slaves at Dan Turnbull's place once a month and helped organize a church there as well. Hagaman was happy with his church, the girls' school, and the "refined society" of the area, and he enjoyed owning a nearby plantation, having "faithful servants," a good overseer, and "a mansion for a house." "These were halcyon days for my family," he would recall in 1873.[5]

Hagaman and his community were not the only ones who prospered. In

1858, the *Vicksburg Whig* reported that residents at Milliken's Bend had high aspirations. A steamboat was built in the spring, a new house was "rising like Aladan's palace," and other structures were being refurbished and remodeled. The town boasted Milliken's Bend Academy, an active religious life with a strong Catholic church, at least three shops, and a tavern. One shop, Sartorius's, even offered the latest in "Parisian style." Five years later, almost to the day, the tiny aspiring town would witness some of the most savage fighting of the Civil War. But for now, the storm clouds of war were still far away.[6]

In 1861, when the town of Milliken's Bend was incorporated, the white population was a mere two hundred souls. The town sat on the west bank of the Mississippi River in Louisiana near the border of Carroll and Madison Parishes, about fifteen miles north and west of Vicksburg, as the crow flies. It was part of a string of communities all along the river, though the major commercial centers were in Mississippi—Vicksburg, and farther south, Natchez. The Mississippi River provided the primary north-south route, despite a number of switchbacks. A major east-west route in the area took shape in the form of a rail line about ten miles south of the Bend, leading from the De Soto Peninsula, directly across the river from Vicksburg, running westward and terminating at Monroe, in the central northern part of the state. The railroad line, too, had aspirations, reflected in its name: the Vicksburg, Shreveport, and Texas Railroad. The rest of northeastern Louisiana was served by a loose road network and numerous bayous, with most of the waterways running north and south, more or less parallel to the Great River. A few small lakes dotted the area, but Lake Providence, to the north of Milliken's Bend, was a large body of water formed from an old cut-off channel of the Mississippi River.[7]

Unlike the rugged, carved-up landscape on the high bluffs near Vicksburg, the land to the west in Carroll and Madison Parishes in Louisiana was flat, occasionally interrupted by bayous or swamps. This was cotton country and in many ways was the epitome of what would later be referred to as the "Old South." Plantation agriculture ruled the day, and grand mansions dotted the countryside. More common were humble dogtrot homes. Such small residences were used as the part-time lodging of absentee owners or their overseers. Many planters owned more than one plantation, and often their holdings were on both sides of the river in Louisiana and Mississippi. A significant number of planters owned land in other states as well, including Arkansas, Florida, and Kentucky. Absentee owners managed their affairs through overseers, agents, or extended family.[8]

Slavery in northeastern Louisiana was extremely profitable. Joe Gray Taylor, in his study of the state, said that the prices of slaves in 1859 and 1860 on the eve of war were at "unprecedently high levels." Cotton, too, was selling at a high price, about eleven cents a pound or $44 for a 400-pound bale. On plantations a single bondsman could pick from six to ten bales of cotton each harvest, with the result that his owner could make between $264 and $444 from just one man's labor. Deducting not more than $50 from this amount, as an upper limit on expenditures for feeding, clothing, and otherwise providing for a field hand's everyday needs throughout the year, the planter was left with a significant profit.[9]

Most planters owned between ten and one hundred slaves, though some slaveholders owned more than three hundred. Some slaves had specialized trades and skills, such as blacksmithing or carpentry; others were house servants, carriage drivers, or cooks. Most slaves were field hands who labored in the cotton and cornfields and were forced to rise before dawn, called out by a bell or horn. Abbie Lindsay, a former slave in Morehouse Parish, recalled adults laboring "from can till can't, from the time they could see until the time they couldn't." Litt Young could remember working so late that the cotton was weighed by candlelight. According to latter-day recollections of some former slaves, male slaves were required to produce from 250 to 500 pounds of cotton a day; female slaves about 150. But one scholar believes these figures are inflated when compared to plantation record books, which give an average of about 150 pounds per day for all hands. On some plantations, if a field hand didn't produce the specified amount of cotton, he or she would be punished with the lash.[10]

A few former slaves would, many years later, tell their interviewers that their master didn't allow his slaves to be whipped. But enough former bondsmen and women would speak of beatings, whippings, and other cruelties to make it clear that slaves in Louisiana and Mississippi always lived under the threat of brutal, and often arbitrary, corporal punishment. Rosa Washington had a dinner fork plunged into her head by an overseer who was irate that it was not clean, though washing it was not even her task. Although she herself was spared beatings, she recalled seeing other slaves put in stocks and whipped, with coal oil and turpentine put in their sores. Carlyle Stewart, just a child during the war, would recall, "They had straps and a whip and they'd better not catch you praying to God. When you prayed you had to hide in the woods." "My mother taught me behind the Marse's back," she added. William

Mathews said that his former owner, Buck Adams, "could out-mean de debbil heself," and if a runaway slave was caught, he would be staked to the ground and beaten. Mattie Lee's mother was forced to work in the field the very day she went into labor with Mattie. A male slave threatened the overseer with a hoe in her defense. Not long afterward, the overseer was threatened again with guns, at last forcing him off of the plantation.[11]

Many slaves told chilling tales of cruelty. James Lucas reported his master hanged a slave because he taught other slaves how to spell. Ellen Cragin recalled that a hole in the ground was dug to accommodate the belly of a "stout" woman who was beaten. "I never did get over that," she said, more than seventy years later. Similar measures were taken when pregnant slaves were whipped. Carlyle Stewart explained, "They could whip them without having the child hurt, cause the children were worth money."[12]

Numerous slaves resisted, even at the risk of beatings and bloodshed. Ellen Cragin's father and mother both fought back. Once, her mother fell asleep working at a loom. The plantation mistress asked her young son to beat the exhausted woman awake, which he proceeded to do. "When she woke up, she took a pole out of the loom and beat him nearly to death with it," Ellen recalled in the 1930s. She said her mother shouted out, "I'm goin' to kill you. These black titties sucked you, and then you come out here to beat me." Tom Polk, the young boy, couldn't walk for a time after receiving his thrashing. Ellen's mother ran away, riding to Kansas on the back of a cow named Dolly. "She rode away from the plantation, because she knew they would kill her if she stayed," Ellen said.

Ellen's father, an enslaved Indian known as Waw-hoo'che, also resisted the cruelties of their master. After receiving a beating and having salt rubbed in his wounds, Waw-hoo'che threatened to kill Tom Polk Sr. Each man distrusted the other, and Waw-hoo'che slept in the woods for safety. Ellen herself resisted, though only a child. The other children on the plantation—probably white children from the owner's family—would tease Ellen that her papa got beaten. "I would say to them, 'They better not beat my papa,' . . . and I would beat 'em for tellin' it." Even so, she did not condemn all whites. She remembered an old white man who came and taught her father how to read the Bible. Both men knew they were risking their lives.[13]

With a cotton economy based heavily on slave labor, one might be tempted to think all of northern Louisiana was in favor of secession. Many men were, of course, but a small minority still hoped for a settlement of sectional difficulties that would not involve bloodshed or separation. George Watt, Dr. Andrew Owen and his wife Martha, and two Irishmen, Luke Madden and William Hayden, were among those in Carroll and Madison Parishes who opposed secession and war.[14]

Some of the most loyal Union people in Carroll Parish may have been Col. Hugh Short and his wife, Nancy, of Lake Providence. Colonel Short was a well-respected lawyer and ran as a Union delegate to the Louisiana secession convention. He made many speeches throughout northeastern Louisiana, forcing one of his opponents, despite their vastly differing views, to concede that he was a gifted orator. David Hall had known the Short family since 1848. He described Mr. Short as "a bitter and persistent opponent of secession," who "fearlessly & with great ability used both pen & tongue to prevent the secession of his state." Nicholas D. Ingram called Short "one of the most talented men in the State" when it came to political speeches, and a lawyer "of the first order." But Short's talents were not enough to convince the residents of Carroll Parish to remain in the Union, and his campaign to represent the parish at the convention was defeated. Nevertheless, even after the war began, he continued on his mission, writing several political pamphlets. His dogged persistence in his views prompted threats of violence until consumption took his life in 1862. His widow apparently had similar opinions, though she may have been less outspoken. David Morgan recalled, "During the whole war to its close [she] was in strict accord with the belief and teachings of her late Husband." When Union troops moved into the area, she opened her home to them and was viewed as loyal by such generals as Brig. Gen. Charles Hovey and Brig. Gen. John Hawkins.[15]

Men like Hugh Short were scarce in northeastern Louisiana, especially in the river parishes, which overwhelmingly voted for secession. It was not so to the west. Monroe, in the north-central portion of the state in Ouachita Parish, located on the east bank of the Ouachita River, was a relatively small but bustling commercial town. On the west bank, just upriver, was the town of Trenton, a major cotton port serving northeastern Texas, southern Arkansas, and northwestern Louisiana. A number of Monroe's citizens were born in the North or in foreign countries and included a number of German Jews, many of whom were merchants. Monroe split on the issue of secession, with slightly more than half of the votes cast for delegates to the state convention who were opposed to secession.[16]

Isaiah Garrett was one of the delegates. A well-known local lawyer and a graduate of the U.S. Military Academy at West Point in 1833, he voted as a "Constitutional Unionist"—someone who supported maintaining the Union, regardless of disagreements over slavery. He was in the minority at the state convention, however, and Louisiana seceded on January 26, 1861. Two of his sons served with the Confederate army, including Franklin who became a staff officer for Gen. Paul Octave Hébert. During the war, Isaiah Garrett helped establish a large Confederate hospital in Monroe.[17]

Much like Isaiah Garrett, once secession and war came to pass, Ouachita Parish did its part to support the new nation of the Confederacy. Four companies were raised in short order, and a correspondent writing from their training camp in June 1861 reported with approval that the parish had sent more young men into the army than any other parish outside of New Orleans.[18]

When war did come, communities turned out to celebrate and wish their brave young men off to a speedy and heroic war of glory, defending home and hearth from the Yankee hordes still distant on the coasts and in Virginia. Units bearing such names as the "Jeff Davis Guards," the "Pelican Grays," and the "Ouachita Blues" were some of the first to organize. Among the men enlisting from Milliken's Bend was homeopathic doctor Henry Wirz, who later would gain infamy as the commandant of Camp Sumter, the prison camp near Andersonville, Georgia.[19]

Underneath the patriotism, however, lay a lurking fear that the loss of manpower to the army would leave homes—including women, children, property, and slaves—virtually defenseless. Once war began, the civic leaders of Ouachita Parish took no chances, and the police jury acted promptly. In an extra session meeting on May 8, 1861, a Committee of Police and Vigilance was organized, composed of five men: Robert W. Richardson, Christopher Hunt Dabbs, Charles Henry Morrison, John Ray, and Isaiah Garrett. A quorum consisted of just two men, and members of the committee could appoint three persons in each ward to assist them. Such a committee was deemed necessary because "the public safety under existing circumstances" required an organization that could respond more promptly to threats than the regular police jury. Part of the committee's responsibilities and powers included "authority to make diligent inquiry concerning suspicious characters and persons dangerous to the peace and good order of Society and to make such orders concerning them as in their judgment the Public Safety may demand," seeking assistance from others "to aid them in detecting persons plans or combinations dangerous to society," and to request aid from any military troops in the parish. Perhaps most importantly, the vigilance committee would "have the power and authority to suppress insubordination and put down insurrection among slaves." Although it seems likely that such an organization continued to exist throughout the war, no further mention of it is made in the police jury minutes.[20]

In Monroe, where slaves made up only 60 percent of the population—much less than the Mississippi River parishes to the east—the loss of young white men to the Confederate army nevertheless left some of the civilians feeling vulnerable. The Ouachita Fencibles was a home defense unit composed of boys twelve to sixteen years old, under the command of John B. Ray. Its purpose included the suppression of any insurrections, as well as invasions by the enemy. The Ouachita Rangers was a similar organization, composed of men, for the purpose of maintaining "utmost vigilance" and protecting and defending lives and property in Ouachita Parish. The situation was similar throughout northeastern Louisiana and along the Mississippi River. One Mississippi man even debated how best to serve his new country—by enlisting or remaining at home.[21]

Such precautions seemed a logical necessity now that war had erupted and white men were leaving for the front. These measures seemed even more justified in light of the plot at Isaac F. Harrison's place in Tensas Parish and the much larger but more secretive plot at Natchez. Despite these threats, female diarists like Kate Stone of Milliken's Bend—a young woman who, so the insurrectionary mythos went, had the most to fear from slaves on the rampage—indicated little fear of insurrection, at least until the Yankee presence became more palpable. Even then, her most immediate fear was the Yankee soldiers, not unruly or violent slaves.

On June 25, 1862, Kate, who had two brothers in the Confederate army, had her first encounter with Lincoln's bluecoats. As she sat down to dinner with her family and friends at Mrs. Elizabeth Savage's home near Goodrich's Landing in Carroll Parish, a servant interrupted their meal to announce that Yankee gunboats were coming around the bend. The gathering rushed outside to witness the passage of five boats. "We could have seen every boat and all the men sunk to the bottom of the river without a pang of regret," Kate wrote in her diary. "One transport was crowded with men . . . they had the impudence to wave at us." As one boat turned around and blew its whistle, Kate and her friends feared the Yankees were coming ashore. The men at the house encouraged the women to seek shelter, but before they did, the ladies rushed around the house, picking up valuables. They ran "for the only refuge we could see, the tall, thick cornfield just beyond the fence. Two [Confederate] soldiers who were taking dinner with us were hurried ahead, as we knew they would be captured if recognized." The boat landed at a large island nearby, and later three men came ashore to the house. The next day, Mrs. Savage informed Kate that the Yankee officers had seen the frightened women and came to assure them they had nothing to fear.[22]

At about the same time, Philip Sartorius, a Jewish immigrant from Germany and the merchant in Milliken's Bend who stocked fineries from Paris, temporarily fled his home with his family and sought shelter in the loft of a nearby cotton gin, full of rats, snakes, and rotten cotton seed. A Negro served as lookout. The Sartorius house, just a few years old, was taken over by Federal forces to be used as a smallpox hospital and was later burned. The displaced family settled at nearby Willow Bayou for the following months, and they remained well supplied with food, including eggs, butter, and coffee—sometimes mixed with parched sweet potatoes.[23]

In late June 1862, Union Brig. Gen. Thomas Williams began digging a canal on De Soto Point, just across from Vicksburg. His forces impressed Negro labor from the surrounding plantations for the work. When Joseph Noland had some of his slaves taken from near Omega, just a few miles from the Stone family, Kate felt certain "there would soon be outrages committed on private property." Her mother instructed the male slaves on their plantation that if Yankees came, they were to run and hide. "We think they will," Kate wrote confidently in her diary. Yet the next day, she confessed there was great excitement. The Yankees took from the area more Negroes, who went willingly, "being promised their freedom by the vandals."[24]

Many planters sought safety in central Louisiana or even Texas. Some stayed behind but sent their slaves to the "back country" swamps and bayous. The Stones planned to evacuate their slaves soon, but they feared that the Northerners would burn their house if they found that the slaves had been removed. Just a few days after proclaiming her own slaves' loyalty, Kate wrote that freedom had tempted slaves on other plantations: "Generally when told to run away from the soldiers, they go right to them and I cannot say I blame them."[25]

Yet later in the year, when freedom became an explicit part of the Union's objective in the war, Kate's feelings ran in the opposite direction. On October 1, upon hearing of Lincoln's preliminary Emancipation Proclamation, she wrote: "I wonder what will be the result of this diabolical move." A few days later, she saw headlines in a local newspaper calling for "raising the Black Flag in retaliation" and could not bear to consider the consequences: "Such a war is too horrible to think of."[26] Kate and her family managed to hold on to their dignity and most of their possessions (including their human property) through the winter and into the early spring of 1863, as Union forces seesawed back and forth along the west bank of the Mississippi. The Yankees floundered in the swamps and bayous and dug several canals in an effort to bypass Vicksburg, none of which succeeded.

By February 1863, Confederate mail service had ceased, and Philip Sartorius, local postmaster, could no longer claim exemption from military service. He joined Company B, 15th Louisiana Cavalry Battalion under the command of Maj. Isaac Harrison, the same man from Tensas Parish who had discovered the Fourth of July insurrectionary plot two years previous. In late March in a small skirmish, Sartorius was severely wounded in his upper arm, and his treatment at Yankee hands varied. His first doctor swore at him and reportedly had only a rusty pocket knife with which to operate. A surgeon from a Kentucky regiment arrived with kinder treatment, and Sartorius's condition slowly improved. "Not a day passed where we did not receive oranges, lemons, coffee, tea, and other things," he recalled.[27]

As Federal troops increased their presence at Milliken's Bend and elsewhere in the vicinity, Sartorius's family fared well, while most others suffered from plundering and Yankee quartermasters. One Yankee soldier told Sartorius that it was because of the kind words of his slaves, who pled on his behalf, that his home was spared.[28] Elsewhere in northeast Louisiana, the toll taken on the residents was steep. Not only was their human property running away or being impressed for Federal labor in alarming numbers, but their day-to-day necessities—corn, flour, cattle, horses, carriages, and wood—were being taken wholesale for use by the Union army. Margaret Case, who lived on Roundaway Bayou in Madison Parish, just ten miles from Milliken's Bend, had her plantation so thoroughly foraged by Yankee troops on the move that by the time Union soldiers arrived to more permanently occupy the property, the place had been stripped bare.[29]

After months of unsuccessful attempts to cut canals on the west side of the river, Union general Ulysses S. Grant gave up and decided on a bold move. He would march his army down the Louisiana side of the Mississippi River, bypassing the stronghold of Vicksburg, and cross the river south of the citadel.

Grant established his headquarters at Milliken's Bend in March 1863. Army corps and divisions gathered at Lake Providence, Milliken's Bend, and other landings on the west side of the river, in preparation for the campaign. The Yankee confiscation of foodstuffs, livestock, and black labor began in earnest.

Mark Valentine was the owner of Oasis Plantation and had been a delegate to the Louisiana Secession Convention in 1861, representing Franklin and Carroll Parishes on the side of secession. He noted in his diary on March 21, 1863, that the Yankees had taken all the Negroes from Easlie's place and put them to work on Matt Johnson's place. A few days later, he moaned, "Nothing can [exceed?] the demoralization of this place. The negroes do just as they please." To prove his point, he told how William Davidson and his family were run off of their land. The Yankees took all of their slaves, wrecked the place, and the family "only escaped with the clothes on their backs."[30]

Kate Stone found a similar situation at Benjamin Hardison's house when she visited on March 26. Sensing something was amiss, she was greeted in the garden by George Richards, who informed her that some Yankees with "armed Negroes" had just been there, "carrying [off] with them every Negro on the place," along with clothes and food. Charles, one of the Hardisons' most trusted slaves, had led the group. Inside the house, Kate found Mrs. Mary Hardison and her children distraught, and just as she sat down, word came that the Yankees were coming again. There was no time to run, except to a nearby room. She looked out the window to see "three fiendish-looking, black Negroes standing around George Richards, two with their guns leveled and almost touching his breast . . . We thought he would be killed instantly." No white man was with the armed blacks who burst into the house.

One man came to the room where Kate and her friends were hiding. He cursed and walked around the room with a cocked pistol in his hand, then approached the bed where a baby lay sleeping, saying, "I ought to kill him. He may grow up to be a jarilla. Kill him." Reported Kate, "Mrs. Hardison sprang to his side, snatched the baby up, and shrieked, 'Don't kill my baby. Don't kill him.' The Negro turned away with a laugh and came over where I was sitting with Little Sister crouched close to me holding my hand." The man stood on the hem of Kate's dress. "He looked me slowly over, gesticulating and snapping his pistol. He stood there about a minute, I suppose. It seemed to me an age. I felt like I would die should he touch me. I did not look up or move, and Little Sister was as still as if petrified. In an instant more he turned away with a most diabolical laugh, gathered up his plunder, and went out. I was never so frightened in my life." Although Kate narrated the incident in her diary almost a month later, the terror remained fresh.

The black men, whom Kate never refers to explicitly as soldiers or in uniform, plundered the house for almost two hours. They threatened Mrs. Hardison's mother with a pistol, telling her to keep out of her bedroom, where she tried to protect her belongings, and instructing her to "stop your jaw." The only two white men at home, Mr. McPherson and George Richards, remained outside with guns leveled at them. After spreading a white powder throughout the house, which the residents feared was poison, the blacks lit matches and threw them on the floor on their way out. The flames were quickly extinguished, but the panic remained. The black men threatened to return and burn what was left, so the women gathered up a few belongings and fled to the Stones' house. "Mrs. Hardison was almost crazy," wrote Kate.

When Kate and her family and friends arrived home at Brokenburn, numerous black men from neighboring plantations had gathered in the slave quarters. "They did not say anything, but they looked at us and grinned and that terrified us more and more. It held such a promise of evil." The next day, the Hardisons' place was thoroughly ransacked by slaves fleeing the area. The Stones watched the procession pass by their gate until midnight.[31]

The entire experience resolved Mrs. Stone to leave the area, and the family packed to go sixty miles to the west, to Monroe. Kate sent a note to Mark Valentine, informing him of their intentions. On March 28, he wrote in his diary: "I received a note from Miss Kate Stone written last night they leave in the morning and try to get across Bay[ou] Mason [Maçon]. I hope they may succeed." Although their departure was delayed for a couple of days, the Stones soon left and began to slowly make their way to the west.[32]

Mark Valentine, still at his home along the river, felt helpless. His world was in turmoil. The blacks "think themselves now free except Vernon and perhaps Ned," he wrote. They "are as false and treacherous as they can be I do not interfere with them in anyway—They are destroying everything on the place." By the middle of April, he found out "that the Yankees are conscripting the negroes to form two regiments at [Lake] Providence." Valentine wrote that his own bondsmen did not believe it, but, he admitted, "I have six still absent with the yankees." The next day, on April 14, his diary ends abruptly, with only a note about the weather.[33]

Kate Stone tells the rest of the story. "The Negroes came and stripped the [Valentine] place of everything while he was on it and were exceedingly insolent to him, threatening all the time to kill him. He is quite an elderly man and cannot stand hardships like younger people." Indeed, it was said that "old Mr. Valentine is so overwrought by his losses . . . that it is feared he will lose his mind." He soon fled, "entirely alone in a boat with only a few clothes." He left his diary behind, and one Yankee soldier picked it up and took it with him as a souvenir. It returned to Louisiana more than one hundred years later, where it now resides in the collections of Tulane University.[34]

Not everyone in Carroll Parish anticipated gloom that spring. R. V. Montague had arrived in Carroll Parish in April with grand expectations: "Going down on the boat a man told me that my father had rented six plantations down there & that we would make at least a million and a half of dollars. I was very much elated, but when I got there I was very much chagrined about them, because everything looked very woe begone and destitute to me. I felt when I got there, that if any raids were to be made, we would be the parties that would probably be raided against, because we were Union men and the feeling was bitter against us." He was responsible in part for at least four plantations, formerly belonging to the Morgan-Keene heirs. Among them were Albion, Stamboul, Mound (belonging to one of the Tibbetts), and Wilton, where he made his headquarters. Part of Montague's mission was to "keep the negroes employed" as dictated by the Federal government, and he hired more than two hundred individuals. "There was a large number of them congregated there, and the object of the gov't was to keep them employed, and at the same time to make them self-sustaining," he explained. Yet "a great many negroes were on the plantations that we did not ever employ, and in fact would not employ; it was a very difficult matter to get them to work at all."[35]

Apparently writing of this man's father, Kate Stone contemptuously described a Mr. Montague as a "Southern Yankee." He was hiring blacks at the rate of five to seven dollars a month, not including food and clothes. He had five sons "in the North," two of whom had "gone over to the Yankees," but it is unclear whether Kate meant that they had enlisted in the Union army or that they had simply crossed into Union lines or moved North to live. Kate mused, "It is strange that he could raise five sons in the South to love the North better than their own native land." The irony was unbearable for Kate. She politely began, "Let us hope he is satisfied with them," but then she turned her sharp wit upon him, "no one else is." She had no sympathy: "What a disgrace to belong to that family."[36]

Matt F. Johnson was a tutor to the Morgan-Keene heirs, and his wife was related to them. Members of the 16th Wisconsin Infantry came and took some cattle from Stamboul and Wilton plantations. They returned daily, carrying off more livestock. Johnson said he treated a Lieutenant Thompson with kindness and it was reciprocated, but the raids continued. One day, Johnson, fearful that his family would starve, begged Thompson to stop the raiding, but the officer seemed powerless. Thompson suggested Johnson get an order of protection by taking the loyalty oath, but Johnson felt that was asking the impossible, given the Southern sympathies of his neighbors. Lieutenant Thompson set up a guard for a short time, and Johnson would later recall, "They treated me pretty well in that way." But the hardships would not stop. Troops came and took wagonloads of corn away from Stamboul—fifteen to twenty-five wagons at a time. Johnson was urged to get receipts for the supplies but was thwarted: "I went once, but the lines were closed." Then Johnson's house was rented to Mr. Montague. Trying to save part of his belongings, Johnson moved his furniture out, but he was forced to return it as part of Montague's rental.

Although it is unclear what Johnson's sympathies were before the arrival of Lieutenant Thompson and the rest of the Federal troops that year, he was bitter by the time he was driven off. "I went to an officer and told him I was going to leave the place & join the Confederates," Johnson recounted after the war. "He felt some sympathy for this way in which I had been treated, and did nothing to prevent my going."[37]

Kate had heard of Johnson's troubles, too, and he had lost more than corn and cattle. "Mr. Matt Johnson has lost every Negro off one place and a number from the other places," she reported in March. A couple of months later, the situation had grown worse: "Mr. Matt Johnson, after being beaten by his Negroes, has come out to Floyd with fifteen other men and is trying to raise a company."[38]

Kate Stone and her family suffered their own losses that spring. After the war, Kate's mother, Amanda, filed a claim against the U.S. government for losses totaling over $34,000. She said that twenty thousand bushels of corn had been taken, valued at $30,000 alone. Other claims included seventy hogs, three horses, three mules, a colt, forty tons of corn fodder, a carriage pressed into service as an ambulance, and 16,000 feet of lumber used to build a hospital. Amanda acknowledged that she had four sons in the Confederate army and that, at times, she did "to some extent give aid and comfort to persons who were engaged in the rebellion." Not surprisingly, the postwar Federal government officials remained unconvinced of her loyalty. She would receive no compensation.[39]

By May, the Stones reached Monroe, about sixty miles west of Milliken's Bend. There Kate met Sarah Wadley, whose father worked for the Vicksburg, Shreveport, and Texas Railroad. For a time, the Stones "from the swamp" stayed with the Wadleys, and Kate and Sarah seemed to enjoy each other's company. Sarah also kept a diary. "Miss Kate is a very sweet young lady, so unaffected and agreeable," wrote Sarah. Kate found her surroundings pleasing, with plenty of young people to socialize with, but her heart remained heavy. "I feel out of place with a party of gay young people," she wrote. "Their mirth jars my heart. Life seems too sad a thing to spend in talking nonsense. I feel fifty years old."[40]

In early May, Monroe was thrown into a panic by rumors of approaching Yankees, but Kate remained calm. Her family had nothing left to lose, having been "too thoroughly plucked by the river Feds." In the end, the Federals never materialized. Kate's mother and brother Jimmy went to Delhi in an effort to retrieve some of their slaves still at the plantation. While Mrs. Stone remained at Delhi, Jimmy went with some Confederate soldiers to Brokenburn. Hiding in a canebrake near the house, Jimmy and some of the men approached the slave cabins at night to reconnoiter. He overheard the slave Lucy talking to Maria about "that Woman," Mrs. Stone, and the two women laughed about wearing Mrs. Stone's clothes "and taking her place as mistress and heaping scorn upon her."

At dawn, Jimmy and the other men of the escort surrounded the cabins and told everyone to come out. They all did, except for William, who tried escaping through a window. He was apprehended with the threat of a Bowie knife. Jimmy gathered up the mules and horses, herded the slaves together, and the band set off for the west.

A few elderly slaves were left at Brokenburn, "to protect it as far as possible." The rest of the slaves—except for Webster, who had already joined the Federal army—started with Jimmy for Delhi, still with the Confederate escort. As they neared the Tensas, a band of Yankees approached and began firing. The commander of the escort, a Captain Smith, urged Jimmy to let the slaves go and run for his life, but Jimmy saw to it that the "Negroes and mules" made it safely across the bayou. Mrs. Stone was horrified to learn afterward that the penalty for taking any possessions, including livestock and slaves, outside of Yankee lines was hanging. Not only had Jimmy escaped Yankee bullets—he had also escaped the hangman's noose.

Captain Smith reported that Brokenburn was still in fine shape and had a well-stocked larder of butter, poultry, hams, a fine garden, and coffee, tea and flour bought from the Yankees. The men and women of the slave quarters would be foolish to leave such a place on their own volition, he concluded. It was good that he and Jimmy came when they did. They found William and his family had moved into the big house and were occupying Mrs. Stone's room.[41]

Hope for the beleaguered residents of northern Louisiana, especially those who had fled their homes in the eastern parishes, came in the form of Maj. Gen. John G. Walker's Texas Division, which arrived in Monroe in mid-May. Kate and Sarah's spirits were buoyed by the presence of the troops. Martial displays helped lighten the mood and brought inspiration. The wife of General Walker's adjutant general stayed with the Wadleys, and the staff camped nearby. Kate found General Walker plain but pleasant, and his wife she deemed "stylish." Brig. Gen. Henry E. McCulloch was unimpressive, but Kate dubbed Col. Horace Randal "the finest, most military-looking man of them all." The girls of the house were thoroughly entranced and spent much time visiting with the officers.[42]

Sarah and her friends watched the 16th Texas Infantry on dress parade one evening and were "perfectly delighted." "The division is composed of strong, fine looking men, well clothed and apparently well drilled," she wrote. About a decade later, private soldier Joseph P. Blessington recalled a sharply contrasting scene in his memoir: "But few of the troops had shaved for weeks, and, as a consequence, there was a large and general assortment of unbrushed black, gray, red, and sandy beards, as well as ferocious mustaches and whiskers," giving the men the look of brigands. Their uniforms did not merit the name—every man wore something different, often bordering on the comical. One man might wear the remnants of a straw hat, "fragments" of a pair of pants, and "a part of a shirt." Another might wear pants made out of a blanket and a shirt "as black as the ace of spades."

Blessington and Sarah agreed on one thing. "Our very looks bred good humor," Blessington recalled. While going about their daily duties, "the men looked cheerful and busy," Sarah wrote. She observed them "shaking out their blankets, some cooking, some playing marbles, some watering horses, and engaged in all manner of diverse occupations." Although she found the sights cheerful, Sarah felt an underlying sadness, wistfully remembering those who had died.[43]

While still in Monroe, Kate heard of a fearsome battle, reporting on June 3 that the Yankees had charged Confederate batteries at Vicksburg and met "great slaughter." Undoubtedly, Kate must have been referring to events at Port Hudson instead. She wrote, "Numbers of Negroes, placed by *their friends* in the forefront of the battles, have been slain. Poor things, I am sorry for them." On May 27, Union forces under Gen. Nathaniel Banks had attacked the Confederate stronghold at Port Hudson and were repulsed. Among those attacking the fortifications were the First and Third Louisiana Native Guards—black Union troops from New Orleans.[44]

Uncertainty continued for the Stones, and on June 17 they left the Wadleys' house and headed for Texas, where they would spend the remainder of the war. Kate felt that the Wadleys had become like family, and their parting was a tearful one.[45]

Across the river in Mississippi, Elizabeth Meade Ingraham may have exemplified the experience of all planters in the region. Living near Port Gibson, not far from where Grant's army made its crossing at Bruinsburg, she kept a diary for a little over a month to detail the events for her three daughters, who had fled to Vicksburg. By the time she concluded in mid-June—just as she and her husband received word of their son's death at Chancellorsville—they had watched what seemed like the entire Yankee army march past their front gate.[46]

Ingraham, in her sixties at the time, wrote of the constant coming and going of officers and troops, friends and neighbors, and displaced civilians and refugees. She wrote of rumors and confirmations of slaves leaving their masters—sometimes calmly walking away, sometimes leaving after violent confrontations. She worried constantly about the loyalty of her slaves and strove to hide her family's belongings from Yankee pillaging. After losing many items to Union soldiers, she at last met with limited success by hiding some things in the slave quarters. Weeks later, when she went to retrieve them, she found that some items had been stolen, commandeered by her servants, or were otherwise unaccounted for. One slave, however, was above reproach. Elsie would not cook for the Union soldiers—even generals—until forced, earning praise for her loyalty from the mistress of the house.

After a battle nearly in the front yard, Union soldiers swarmed the home, "as ravenous as wolves." Gen. James B. McPherson tried to offer protection, but by the time he did so, soldiers were back in the house making another raid. "The officers may say what they please, but they wink at and authorize this plundering and thieving," Elizabeth wrote. She resolved to burn some of her things, to prevent them from being taken by the soldiers, and often tried to encourage her husband to burn the entire place, to avoid further losses at the hands of the Yankees. She repeatedly invoked the example of John Perkins, a wealthy Louisianan, who had preferred burning his own home down rather than letting it fall into Yankee hands. Such measures would never be taken on a large scale at the Ingrahams'. Instead, the family endured Union troops passing through again and again. "They tore up and destroyed all the papers in the office, cut a part out of the large map, tore up the sheets, stole every blanket they could find, carried away nearly all the books, even the Dictionary, left the Encyclopedias—nothing came amiss—the house was literally gutted, up stairs and down," she wrote, in one of many entries describing Union depredations.[47]

The next day, another division passed through. Soldiers broke in, discovered some molasses, and helped themselves, carrying it all off. She and her husband sat helplessly looking on as the soldiers feasted on whatever they could find; the couple themselves went without dinner. Some of their bondswomen like Nancy and Elsie ("faithful and true,") brought food for the couple from the slave quarters, and Harriet brought a chicken. Jack and Emma were also "very attentive." One man, Eddens, left with the Union forces, to become a waiter for a colonel, though even he showed some thoughtfulness by setting aside some meat for Elizabeth before he left.[48]

One day, Elizabeth asked the Yankee soldiers if they were fighting to free the slaves. All of them denied it. Yet she attributed the loss of some of her slaves directly to Yankee influence. By May 8, still only a few days after her first encounters with the Union army, at least six of the bondsmen had left the place, including one man named "Jim Crow." Others, mostly women, remained. Like many planters, it was probably inconceivable to Elizabeth that her "loyal servants" would leave of their own volition. She blamed the Yankee soldiers, who would "tamper with them, and hold out inducements for the negro to leave."[49]

The experiences and actions of the slaves on this plantation were as various as the individuals themselves and serve as a microcosm of what was happening throughout the region. Some, like "Jim Crow," left. Others, like Elsie, remained at work on the plantation, only reinforcing her mistress's impression of her loyalty. Regardless of their actions, the experience for all slaves was one of uncertainty and upheaval. Even if they were prone to view the Union soldiers as liberators, the actions of some of the bluecoats made them wonder if the soldiers from the North had their best interests at heart. One African American woman named Kate went in anger and disgust to see Gen. Alvin Hovey and complained to him that Union forces were there "to rob the negroes, not protect them."[50]

A plea from a slave woman would scarcely cause Federal troops to pause. Soldiers soon pillaged the Ingrahams' home again, this time taking linens, tools, china, and molasses. They shot holes in portraits, strewed lard, molasses, sugar, and other items about the house, and busted up a desk "which had stood the St. Domingo insurrection." Some soldiers tried to intervene on behalf of the family and got the reply from their brothers-in-arms, "They are d——d old rebels, ought all to be killed, and the house burnt!"[51]

These were Maj. Gen. William T. Sherman's men, and they came in for especially heartfelt bitterness from Elizabeth, who called them "the quintessence of rascality." Even Elsie called them "Lousy, dirty beasts," and with good reason. The soldiers so terrified the slaves—especially the women—that they were afraid to come to the house. Elsie and Emma were almost captives in their own cabins, sticking together for their mutual protection when Jack was away drawing water. Some Yankee soldiers tried to "abuse" them, but their screams brought Jack back who then called the pickets and the soldiers fled. After the place had been wrecked, Sherman sent guards for the house, which quieted things considerably. But Elizabeth still lived in fear because many of the soldiers declared to her that it was "a war of extermination" and seemed to "glory" in telling it.[52]

Despite the vitriol, she managed to have some conversations with the men. One soldier asked if she was a Union woman, and when she replied that she was not but was indeed "a real old *cantankerous* rebel," he admired her pluck. "Good for you," he said. "I believe in holding up to your own opinions." He might have been surprised to learn that she was the sister of Union Maj. Gen. George Gordon Meade, who would soon gain renown at Gettysburg.[53]

Another soldier told Elizabeth he was opposed to emancipation. He thought that slaves should remain in bondage and "remain where they are." He said that "the army would strike if they thought they were fighting for any thing but the Union."[54] Not all of his comrades held such conservative views about slavery. The next day, Elizabeth reported that Union soldiers were "still tampering with the negroes" and work on the plantation had ceased since all the horses and mules had been taken away. The Yankees were forcing some former slaves to work for them and were paying them in greenbacks, which at times proved a lucrative offer. Two male slaves had been forced to go to the army, and a couple of others left to follow the Yankees but soon returned. "Poor things, I pity them!" Elizabeth wrote in her journal, adding a striking symbol of her own fear: "I sleep in my corset ready for a run."[55]

A couple of days later, Elizabeth noticed changes in the attitudes of some of her slaves. Though Elsie, Kia Jane, and Bowlegs were "attentive," Emma refused to wait on her and Nancy was "not true." Elizabeth seemed to remain calm even though pistols and rifles were now in the hands of some of her bondsmen. "Poor things! I feel sorry for them," she wrote, again, apparently trying to convince herself of her security: "They are not to blame." Her attitude reflected a common conceit, still firmly rooted in the Southern imagination. Slaves were by nature content with their lot and would never rise up or seek freedom on their own. Only when outsiders "tampered with" the slaves could they be coaxed to run away. Even then, it was the slaves' gullible nature that led them astray, not any desire of their own to leave bondage.[56]

By this time, the masses of Yankee troops had advanced to the north and east. Now, instead of Yankee soldiers, the Ingrahams had to face uncertainty with their slaves, and each day their hold on them grew more tenuous. By May 18, Elizabeth didn't think her slaves would stay. "Only a question of time," she wrote, "they are not quite ready." Elsie was still loyal, but Jack (probably Elsie's husband) was "doubtful." That day, Elizabeth went upstairs to find more damage, including mirrors broken or taken. "Our negroes have done the most part of it," she wrote. She continued to speculate about the loyalty of her servants, and she began to realize that circumstances had changed. Perhaps her slaves would be willing to stay and go back to work if she offered to pay them. She made one woman an offer of fifty cents a day to help clean but was refused. In other cases, bribery could produce the desired outcome. Emma had become so disrespectful that she was paid a full dollar, just to stay away.[57]

Elizabeth was frustrated by the new independence shown by her slaves and was uncomfortable not knowing where they were going or what they were doing. "I suppose they would not think they were free if they told us where they went. I do not care; they do not annoy me, and I do not trouble them. I think, in time, we shall lose them all, if we lose Vicksburg." Yet there was uncertainty about living among so many former slaves. On May 27, she reported, "Negro meetings are being held, and the few whites left begin to be very anxious . . . We won't meddle with them, it is certain. [Isaac] Powers was burnt out by his own negroes. I fear the blacks more than I do the Yankees." This last sentiment is particularly important, for it shows the depth of the fear of insurrection that still lingered—and perhaps became even more powerful—as emancipation became reality with the advancing Union troops.[58]

Meanwhile, Jack kept trying to persuade Elsie to leave with him. She would not, until he had found a home for them and a way to earn a living. Elizabeth put out her own offer to Elsie, telling her that if Jack left her, she could live in the washhouse and get paid twelve dollars a month. "I thought it good wages," Elizabeth wrote, and indeed it was. This was more than double what black female laborers on the U.S. government plantations in Louisiana earned. Privates in the Confederate army earned a dollar less, though Confederate currency was so rapidly depreciating that it could not compare to the thirteen a month in greenbacks that white Union soldiers earned. Showing that she had begun to come to terms with the new way of things in the wake of the Yankee army and the Emancipation Proclamation, Elizabeth also told Elsie, "If Jack was free, I should consider her free also, and free to go whenever he found that home for her." Then she sighed, "God knows what she will do."[59]

Perhaps Elizabeth's new attitude was not so much a change of heart as an acceptance of new circumstances. Four weeks went by, "and not a stroke of work" had been done by her former slaves. Elsie called it a "vacation." In bondage a month ago, the servants now "go when they please, and do as they please; no one interferes." Other African Americans came and went, many of them from other plantations. Some sought out spouses and family members. Austin, a slave of "old Dicky H—" drove a buggy on frequent visits to Grace, his wife, one of the slaves on the Ingraham plantation.[60]

The former slaves were well aware of their changed circumstances. Martha, for instance, refused to aid another slave with a sick child unless she was paid for it. Elizabeth was forced to tend to the child. Distressed over this change, she wrote: "Martha . . . is a great rascal" and angrily wondered if "we can ever get our rights again!"[61] As the days passed, Elizabeth's fears grew. "I never feel safe, and am always thankful, when morning comes, that the house has not been fired during the night." The next morning, her thoughts continued along the same lines, fearing the advance of Banks's army, "with his negro regiments to desolate and burn. Surely God has forsaken us."[62]

On May 31, Elizabeth devoted part of her diary to Elsie's situation. No doubt because Elsie was deemed the most loyal of her slaves, Elizabeth wrote more frequently about her than she did most of her other human chattel. She felt some sympathy for her, since "she has a hard time between her duty to her husband and that to her old mistress." A Mr. Hays—probably said in sarcasm and referring to Elsie's husband, Jack—complained "that she waits on me, and none of the others do; that she behaves just as if she was not free, 'coming up here and waiting on me and master' just as usual, which is not quite true . . .

In the morning I do all slops; strip the bed and wash up, while she makes the bed and sweeps up. She is very willing, and does not like to see me work; but he is a rascal, for all the time he tries to make me believe he is true and will never leave me." Elizabeth tried to get Elsie to bring her children up to the house to feed them breakfast, but she did not. Still, Elsie had little respect for the other slaves in the quarter, calling them "common." Perhaps she felt more privileged, as a house servant and an obvious favorite of the mistress. Elsie said she "would be glad to get away from them forever; they are bad people; they are only niggers." Her mistress praised her: "She is strictly honest and true, a rare thing in a black."[63]

But even with these reassurances, trying to maintain their position as slaveholders was becoming precarious. Elizabeth wrote of her husband, "Father beginning to think it is God's will that the Institution should be wiped out, for everything favors [the Yankees]." His health was weakening, and the idea of taking the oath to the Union was more than either he or his wife could bear. "Let us pray to have the strength to resist that despotism, at all events until the whole country succumbs, and there is no Confederate Government," she vowed.[64]

Some Confederate soldiers, or perhaps local militia, called merely "Secesh" by Elizabeth, tried to restore order in the area. They forced slaves to go back to work, whipped a few, and even hanged one man. They had not yet come to the Ingrahams' plantation, but word of their activities apparently had the desired effect. Elizabeth thought most of her slaves were about to flee, but none had left by the next morning, and a few even resumed work. She found the men willing to do what she asked of them, but the situation with the women was the opposite.[65]

On June 11, the Ingrahams received news that their son Frank was killed at Chancellorsville in May. He was the only remaining son, and now there was no male to carry on the family name. Frank had been the only soldier of his company to die in the battle, and this seemed to magnify his mother's grief.[66] Elizabeth longed to bring his body home to be buried in the family plot, but it was impossible. In her grief, she added up the other losses of the family: "No money, negroes, stock; every thing stolen." She closed her diary with a curt entry on June 13: "No news." After the loss of her entire world, except for her husband, her house, and her daughters who were away, it seemed there was simply nothing more to say.[67]

"The Triumph of a Noble Purpose"
Emancipation Comes to Northeast Louisiana

I N THE SPRING OF 1863, as the Union Army of the Tennessee gathered its strength in northeastern Louisiana along the banks of the Mississippi River, commanding general U. S. Grant was confronted with a problem. Hundreds, then thousands, of former slaves flooded into Union lines. Grant seized the opportunity to use the men among them as laborers on one of several canal operations on the west bank of the river as he sought to create a water route to bypass the big guns at the Confederate fortress of Vicksburg.

The use of African Americans' labor for the Union cause was nothing new. In 1861, while in command of troops at Fortress Monroe, Virginia, Brig. Gen. Benjamin Butler refused to return three fugitive slaves to their owner. Although the Fugitive Slave Act was still in effect, Butler declared the slaves "contraband of war." By so doing, he turned the Southerners' notion of slaves as property on its head. Like any other captured "property," Butler reasoned, the slaves could be put to use for the immediate needs of the Union army. A few months later, Congress passed the First Confiscation Act, which essentially put Butler's practice into official policy. White Yankee soldiers everywhere were soon referring to the former slaves as "contrabands," and the term would continue to be used in this fashion throughout the rest of the war.[1]

"Contrabands" soon were turning up in droves everywhere the Union army went. Late in 1862, a formal system was arranged to deal with the influx of black refugees to Union lines in the Mississippi Valley. John Eaton was appointed General Superintendent of Contrabands for the Department of the Tennessee, with his office at Memphis. He proceeded to supervise a number of white subordinates who served as local superintendents at contraband camps on both sides of the Mississippi River in Arkansas, Louisiana, and Mississippi. These camps were essentially gathering places, where the former slaves tried to find family members from whom they had been separated by sale or wartime upheaval and where the Federal government provided basic provisions— or at least, tried to.

In mid-February 1863, Lark S. Livermore, an army chaplain and the super-intendent of contrabands at Lake Providence, Louisiana, wrote to George B. Field, another superintendent, about the general situation in his district and, more particularly, the response among African Americans to the provision in the Emancipation Proclamation calling for the arming of former slaves. More than twelve hundred freedmen and women had come into Union lines in just twelve days, wrote Livermore, and of that number, about seven hundred able-bodied men would be eligible for military service. Livermore believed even more could be obtained from the surrounding countryside if recruiting efforts were actively undertaken. The men were so enthusiastic, they would "gladly take arms & often *beg* the privilege," he wrote. To test their mettle, Livermore often warned them about Confederate president Jefferson Davis's threat of reenslavement or death if they joined the Union army. "The right men *have no fear of it,*" Livermore wrote excitedly. "I see no reason why they wo'd not become the best of soldiers for these times & this region." Livermore believed that the sheer audacity of posting black military units on either side of the Mississippi River would effectively cripple Rebel sentiment and action in the region.[2]

Field, in turn, wrote directly to Secretary of War Edwin M. Stanton about a month later: "Negroes every where are anxious to come within the lines and but for the close vigilance of Masters and overseers, would do so in very large numbers." Even so, about a hundred men a day were coming into the lines at Lake Providence, "notwithstanding *they are generally discouraged* by our *of-ficers,*" who were no doubt overwhelmed with the number of people. Field felt that, with good organization, eight to ten thousand men could be raised among the freedmen with very little effort in a mere forty days. Furthermore, the soldiers could be used to defend the area, and the abandoned plantations and homes could provide work and lodging for soldiers' families. By tilling the soil, these contraband camps could become "self-sustaining, instead of becoming a burthen to the government." Regiments posted along the river could protect the plantations and their workers, help ensure safe navigation, and hinder guerilla operations.[3]

Despite Field's complaint that blacks were discouraged from coming into Union lines, he nevertheless found strong support for their enlistment. Officers he had spoken to were confident in the success of raising black regi-ments. "They firmly believe the negro can fight and are willing to organize and direct his energies against the rebellion . . . with them they can conquer, de-fend & cultivate that region," he said, thus proving that "the Negro can battle successfully for his freedom & country & maintain himself when free."[4]

Field proceeded to provide Stanton with a full report about conditions along a two-hundred-mile stretch of the west bank of the river in northeastern Louisiana and southeastern Arkansas. Based upon conversations with loyal men in the region, Field estimated more than 37,000 African Americans were present, with only 6,000 whites in the area, a ratio of more than six to one. By far, Madison Parish had the widest margin of difference. There, only 700 whites were present compared to 12,000 blacks. Almost all of the white population were women, children, and old men, whom Field found "bitterly hostile to our government." White men of military age were scarce in the region but all together numbered about a thousand, mostly operating as spies or guerillas.[5]

One of the few white families still left in the region, the Stones of Madison Parish, watched and waited. While still at their home near Milliken's Bend, Kate reported that Dr. C. B. Buckner's cook, Jane, had left for the contraband camp on the De Soto Peninsula with her two young children in tow. Along the way, Jane met "one of Mr. Hardison's men," who may have been her husband. Kate and her family were glad to see Jane go, for she was "a constant menace." "We would not have been surprised to have her slip up and stick any of us in the back," Kate wrote, especially since Jane had just wielded a knife on another slave, cutting a gash in the woman's face. Even the blacks thought her fearsome, believing she was a "hoodoo woman." Along with Jane, fifty fleeing slaves sat in the rain that evening, waiting to be ferried across the canal that had been cut into the peninsula. Three escapees from R. W. Graves's plantation drowned in their haste to get across.[6]

A few days later, Kate cataloged the losses from the area. The Watson-Scott place had lost seventy-five people in all; only three little girls remained. Matt Johnson had lost all but one Negro at one plantation and many from other locations. Keene Richards lost 160 from "Transylvania," and about fifty of them died of black measles while working for the Yankees on the canal. Mr. Valentine had been lucky, thus far, but feared all of his slaves would go off en masse, the next time the Yankees came.[7]

While the Stones, Mr. Valentine, and a few other Southern planters still clung to their homes that spring, Field reported that most of the 150 plantations along the river were abandoned and probably all but about ten would be eligible for confiscation by the Union army. None of them, at the time of his writing, were under cultivation. Field went on to propose a system for leasing plantations by which the freedpeople would be hired by white plantation commissioners to work in the fields, with their rate of pay set by the Federal government. Such a proposal was practical on a number of levels. First, it put the men and women coming into Union lines to productive labor, spreading their numbers throughout the countryside instead of living in overcrowded contraband camps where the people were essentially wards of the government, assigned no work, and waiting for handouts of food or clothing. By farming the land on the abandoned plantations, the freedpeople could grow food and cotton for themselves, as well as a surplus for army use.

Field saw benefits beyond the pragmatic however; his vision was greater. "It would be of great importance as establishing the fact that in *Agriculture* free Negro labor under good management can be made a *source* of *profit* to the *employer*," he wrote, advocating the Northern gospel of free labor. "This point once established on the scale proposed, would divest the whole question of emancipation." Field suggested that two counties in Arkansas (Chicot and Desha) and two parishes in Louisiana (Carroll and Madison) could serve as a test project. Once the leasing program proved successful there, the plan could be expanded to the entire Mississippi Valley, from Memphis to New Orleans.[8]

In April, when Adjt. Gen. Lorenzo Thomas spoke to Federal troops up and down the Mississippi River about recruiting black soldiers, he also wrote to Stanton, outlining a plan for bringing abandoned plantations on the west side of the river into cultivation for the provision and profit of the army. Part of Thomas's goal was to prove that blacks could be productive workers under a free labor system. His formal declaration of this policy at Milliken's Bend on April 10 included the goal of organizing contrabands along the river. He appointed Field, Livermore, and Capt. Abraham E. Strickle as commissioners who would oversee the leasing of plantations "to persons of proper character and qualifications." The three men would also ensure that "mutual obligations" between freed people and plantation superintendents were fulfilled. The plantations would grow crops to feed the army and the masses of African American civilians coming into the lines.[9]

Thomas made it very clear that slavery would not be reimposed. "In no case," Thomas declared, "will negroes be subjected to corporeal [sic] punishment by the lash, or other cruel and unusual modes." Families must stay together "when they so desire." Thomas even set out a wage plan: seven dollars a month for able bodied men, five dollars for women, and children between the ages of twelve and fifteen would earn half of what their adult counterpart earned. Children younger than age twelve were prohibited from working in the fields. Although Thomas could not promise protection from Confederate raids when laborers were in the field, he hoped that the new initiative of enlisting blacks in the army would provide all of the military protection needed to safeguard the resumption of plantation operations.[10]

Thomas's plan bears many striking similarities to Field's proposal submitted to Stanton a few weeks earlier. It is not clear if Thomas consulted Field, and he does not credit him for these ideas. If Thomas was not deliberately plagiarizing Field, he must have been aware of Field's plan and perhaps submitted the proposal to Stanton under his own hand, possibly even with Field's blessing. Perhaps Field believed that Thomas's higher rank would give his plan additional clout with Stanton, though the secretary of war had little patience with the adjutant general and had been glad to see Thomas head west.

Just two weeks after Thomas's proposal, a report from Eaton, General Superintendent of Contrabands in the Department of the Tennessee, compiled information from local superintendents in Mississippi, Tennessee, Arkansas, Louisiana, and Cairo, Illinois. Twenty questions covered subjects as diverse as the contrabands' clothing needs to their "notions of liberty." Reverend Livermore at Lake Providence, Louisiana, was one of the respondents. Livermore reported an acute shortage of clothing—some had "not enough to cover their nakedness"—but shipments of clothes from the North helped to alleviate the crisis. Medical supplies and personnel were also scarce; there was one overwhelmed surgeon at Lake Providence who was responsible for providing medical care for more than 2,300 people. The proximity of the Union army to the freedpeople interfered with plantation operations and resulted in "great evils," which Livermore did not detail. Most laborers picked cotton or helped dig the canal by which Grant hoped to bypass Vicksburg. No schools had yet been established, and freedpeople had only occasional religious services, perhaps led by Livermore himself.[11]

Most of the men and women who had come into the lines at Lake Providence were there because they had been abandoned by their masters, wrote Livermore. One can question precisely *who* did the abandoning, but it was certain that many of the planters had fled to the interior, or even farther, like Kate Stone's family soon would do, to Texas.[12] Freedpeople often found their new conditions not much different than slavery, regardless of whether they worked for the army or plantation lessees. David Wray, a private in the 19th Kentucky Infantry (U.S.) reported the harsh nature of some military men who were put over black laborers on the canals: "I tell you the way they did make them work was a sight they was as anxious to run back to there [sic] masters as they was to run away and they would go if they had a chance."[13] Pvt. Samuel H. Glasgow of the 23rd Iowa Infantry wrote in late April from Perkins' Landing, "We have a great many working on Roads and fortifications and that just suits them." "Mack," a reporter for the *Cincinnati Daily Commercial*, witnessed numbers of freedmen running away from government plantations, and he believed they were on their way back to their old masters. The only difference, he thought, was that they received a little pay from the government, but they were often treated worse. "Call it by what name you will," he wrote, "it is nothing but a system of slavery." Brig. Gen. John P. Hawkins would later write to abolitionist Gerrit Smith, begging for something to be done to benefit the Negro. The plantation lessees did not have the best interests for the black man at heart, the general explained, for "cotton closes their eyes to justice just as it did in the case of the former slave masters." To the lessees, like their predecessors the slaveholders, "the Negro is only a nigger."[14]

Among those coming in for criticism from Hawkins was Lewis Dent. Dent was Grant's brother-in-law and became a lessee in the spring of 1863, operating four different plantations near Transylvania Landing in Louisiana. Dent, both as a lessee and, later, as a plantation commissioner, was roundly criticized by army authorities for his apparent greed and lack of proper care for the laborers on his plantation.[15] While Dent may have exemplified some of the worst qualities of the leasing system, the Duncan plantation may have been at the opposite extreme. Land owners before the war, the Duncans pledged their loyalty to the Union cause and were among the first slaveholders in the region to free their slaves and pay them a wage. Despite their professed loyalty, however, the Duncans faced hardship and frustration. Mary Duncan, who owned nine different properties in Louisiana and Mississippi, wrote from New York to the secretary of war, seeking papers "which WILL REALLY 'protect' us in our rights." She proceeded to list her grievances. Chief among them was that all of her male laborers had been impressed into the army. These individuals had been "*freed & hired*," she protested. Even orders of protection from Generals U. S. Grant and James B. McPherson and Acting Rear Adm. David Dixon Porter could not spare her laborers from the recruiter's greedy grasp. She felt she had no other alternative than to appeal directly to Secretary of War Stanton to alleviate her sufferings.[16]

Stanton was unperturbed. "The disturbed state of . . . the Country renders it impossible to prevent or remedy the evils complained of," he wrote, though he directed Grant to look into the matter. Preoccupied with the siege at Vicksburg, Grant finally examined Mrs. Duncan's case in mid-July, more than a month after her letter to Washington. By that time, Grant was aware of the special protection to be provided to the Duncans. Officers involved in the case swore that they had done nothing wrong and placed the blame squarely on the Duncans' shoulders. The freedpeople were hungry and "poorly cared for"—and for those reasons, most were anxious to enlist, so the story went.[17]

General Hawkins knew the real truth of the matter, however. "Like a white man they know when they are justly or unjustly treated," he wrote. Hawkins's own impression was that the freedpeople were willing to work and savvy but that, sadly, the treatment meted out by the plantation lessees was not much of an improvement. In the fall, Hawkins proposed a chilling alternative to the labor situation. If adequate and appropriate employers could not be found for the freedmen, he wrote abolitionist Gerrit Smith, then they ought to "send for their former masters and tell each one to claim his slaves, his treatment of them was parental compared to what we now permit."[18]

Of course, Hawkins was merely making a point, but historian Louis S. Gerteis agrees—the new plantation lessees were sometimes harsher than the old slave masters. He observes, "Nowhere in the South did army commanders or government officials seek to liberate blacks from antebellum conditions of subordination and dependence." Even Adjutant General Thomas advised that the closer plantation conditions approximated slavery—minus the lash—the better it would be for the federal government, the lessees, the army, and the freedmen. It is ironic that the man tasked with the responsibility of seeing to fruition the transformation of African American men from slaves to soldiers— and all that effort entailed, including overcoming opposition, prejudice, and skepticism from white soldiers of all ranks throughout the army—would have such a conservative view of black labor. Gerteis credits the need for immediate social stability, as well as the pressing needs of the sheer numbers of blacks coming in to Union lines, as contributing to Thomas's view.[19]

As the discussions among Hawkins, the plantation commissioners, the secretary of war, and Adjutant General Thomas continued, more Union soldiers poured into northeastern Louisiana in the spring of 1863. Union soldier Charles B. Allaire was blissful after arriving at Lake Providence via steamboat from Memphis, "I think this Country comes as near to my idea of Paradise as is possible for mortals ever to witness." A soldier of the 68th Ohio Volunteer Infantry reported, "For the first time in almost a year, [we] are lying quite still in camp, taking the world easy." The men were receiving good food, clothing, and were in good health. "The camp is one of the most pleasant we have been in," he continued. Col. Manning F. Force, commander of the 20th Ohio Volunteer Infantry, agreed, calling it an "ideal camp." "The bank of the lake was bordered by live-oaks, trailing with gray moss and with glistening magnolias," he wrote. His regiment camped in an old cotton field, and the ground stayed so wet that the men had to create board floors for their tents, which proved to be only a minor inconvenience. Fish and waterfowl were abundant, and in the evenings, "the band would play on a batteau sailing on the water."[20]

Downriver, Kentuckian David M. Wray was gloomier in a letter to his sister. When he arrived at Milliken's Bend, it was in a rainstorm and the mud was a foot deep. It soon dried off, and Wray found plenty to eat. Some men were in good spirits: "The boys seames as lively as if the nation was in peace and all going home." But many of the enlisted men were homesick, and death was still omnipresent.

If you see a man go off and sit to himsefl [sic] then you ma[y] look for a dead man not long since. I saw a white man burried in his blanket onley I did not walk far before I saw a negro burried in a nice dressed coffin with a fine Flag wraped around it. I didnot go far before I saw a negro man sick lying in a swamp dying and a Pup Barkin at him groning thare is a crowd standing by laughing at him as if he was nothing moore than a stump so you can see the difference made her[e].[21]

A few weeks later, on April 8, 1863, Thomas addressed the division under the command of Illinoisan Maj. Gen. John A. Logan, stationed at Lake Providence, Louisiana. Composed of Midwesterners from the states of Illinois, Ohio, Indiana, Michigan, and one regiment of Missourians, Logan's men were part of the 17th Army Corps, under the overall command of Maj. Gen. James B. McPherson. Thomas's purpose was to drum up support among the soldiers for the new policy of President Lincoln, enunciated in the final Emancipation Proclamation issued on January 1. Thomas sought not just to persuade skeptics in his audience but to establish administrative authority and a formal policy for the plan of recruiting and arming regiments composed of former slaves. The white officers in the new black regiments would be veteran soldiers, and even noncommissioned officers and privates could apply for positions. Some had been in the service for more than a year and had fought at the bloody battles at Shiloh, Corinth, and other clashes in Tennessee, Kentucky, and

Mississippi. Thomas also had authority to relieve of command or dismiss from the service any officer or man who was found guilty of mistreating blacks.

Sent on this mission to the Mississippi Valley in the early spring of 1863, Thomas was granted extraordinary power: "I can act precisely as if the President of the United States were himself present. I am directed to refer nothing to Washington, but to act promptly" in regard to promoting and appointing officers to the new African American units.[22] Born in 1804 in the slave state of Delaware, Thomas seemed an unlikely candidate to bring such a message to the troops. In 1861, he was partially responsible for the dismissal of Maj. Gen. John Charles Fremont, who had issued his own emancipation order in Missouri. The Radical Republicans reacted in outrage to this censure, though Thomas had been acting on orders from Lincoln himself. Later, Stanton, who had a strong personal dislike for Thomas, found a convenient solution to their constant clashes by sending the adjutant general to the West in 1863 to promote Lincoln's policy of enlisting black men, especially former slaves, into the army. Thomas would excel in his new duties, putting his heart and soul into the work, and working himself to exhaustion. In just nine months, by the end of the year, over twenty thousand men would be enrolled in the new units. The regiments included men from the states of Arkansas, Louisiana, Tennessee, Iowa, Mississippi, Alabama, Missouri, and one unit of just under one hundred men, designated the "Liberia Guards." By the end of the war, his efforts would result in the enlistment of more than 76,000 African Americans, nearly 41 percent of the total black men in the Union army. Two thirds of the forces guarding posts along the Mississippi River at war's end were Colored Troops, most of them initially organized through Thomas's efforts.[23]

On April 8, 1863, at Lake Providence, his message was received positively—or at least, respectfully—and was endorsed by Generals McPherson and Logan, and brigade commanders Brig. Gen. Mortimer Leggett and Brig. Gen. John D. Stevenson. But Thomas knew many of his listeners might have difficulty swallowing the new policy. He understood. As a native of Delaware, Thomas declared, "I am a Southern man, and, if you will, born with Southern prejudices, but I am free to say that the policy I am now to announce to you I indorse with my whole heart."[24] It was a practical matter. By enlisting former slaves, the North would rob the South of a valuable source of labor. The Confederates would be forced to send white men back to their farms and plantations to ensure adequate food supplies for their armies. Furthermore, such a policy would alleviate many problems faced by the Federal army, which found itself saddled with the responsibility of clothing and feeding escaped slaves who flocked to Union lines. "They are crowding upon us in such numbers that some provision must be made for them," Thomas stated. They could not be resettled in the North, for "some States have passed laws prohibiting them to come within their borders." The members of his audience, mostly from the Midwest, would have been well aware of this. The states of Illinois and Indiana were among those that had such laws.[25]

Despite the difficulty the army already had in providing for the flood of contrabands coming into its lines, Thomas told the soldiers gathered before him that the former bondsmen were to be "to be received with open arms." The plantation leasing system, authorized by Thomas and announced at essentially the same time, would put African American women, children, and old and infirm men to work on the abandoned plantations along the Mississippi River. Men of military age would form black regiments, which would guard these plantations from attacks by cavalry and guerillas, and guard supply lines in the army's rear. "Every regiment of blacks I raise, I release a regiment of whites to face the foe in the field," Thomas declared. Thus, white troops would be relieved of the tedious and often unhealthy tasks of garrison duty and could look forward to the activity and honor of meeting the enemy on the field of battle.[26]

Historian James M. McPherson found, in a limited sample, that nearly twice as many men in the Federal army supported the Emancipation Proclamation as opposed it during the spring of 1863. Some white soldiers, though not abolitionists and generally opposed to emancipation as a war aim, nevertheless saw the pragmatic expediency in what Thomas proposed. One officer in an Indiana regiment reported that his men saw no reason to avoid the employment of blacks as soldiers or in any other capacity that would aid the war effort, since the army had been making use of all sorts of other captured rebel "property." One Michigan man put it bluntly—a black man could stop a bullet as well as a white man. He didn't object to this kind of equality.[27]

Others were indignant. One soldier in the 66th Indiana reported that some of his comrades deserted over the issue, and an officer in a New York regiment stationed near Baton Rouge said twelve officers had submitted their resignations. Even Lt. Col. Arthur Fremantle was getting an earful with the Confederates in Monroe. There, he found some Union deserters who felt betrayed by their government. "We enlisted to fight for the Union," they said, "and not to liberate the G-d d——d niggers."[28]

Thomas was undeterred in his mission. "I am authorized to raise as many regiments of blacks as I can," he declared, and to do so, he needed experienced veterans as officers. Only white men would hold these positions, and Thomas knew that many men would find the opportunity lucrative financially, if not morally. For those among his audience who were considering such a position, Thomas had a firm criteria: "I desire only those whose hearts are in the work." Men of all ranks were encouraged to come forward and apply for commissions. Those individuals who objected to the policy of enlisting black soldiers would have to watch their step. Thomas would firmly punish any man of any rank whom he found mistreating blacks.[29]

David Cornwell, a private who served in the 8th Illinois Infantry at the battle of Shiloh, then transferred to Battery D, 1st Illinois Light Artillery, was among the crowd addressed by Thomas. He found Thomas's speech dull but only because a long-winded introduction by General McPherson had left Thomas with nothing to say. McPherson "talked all around it, on all sides of it, over it and under it and elaborated it until it seemed that nothing more could be said on the subject." Cornwell found Thomas "pitiful." The adjutant general was obliged by the president's orders to address the troops directly, and he repeated McPherson's commentary. McPherson returned to the stage briefly after Thomas's remarks, "smiling sweetly" as if he was a schoolboy who had played a prank, and introduced Gen. John Logan, who "delivered a rattling ten minute speech."[30]

One listener credited Logan with turning hisses of disapproval into all-out cheers for the new policy. "We must hurt the rebels in every way possible," Logan declared. "Shoot them with shot and shell and minnie [sic] balls and . . . shoot them with 'niggers,'" take their laborers from them, and "set them to stopping bullets for us." Logan urged his men to unite behind the policy, "putting the one who is the innocent cause of this war, who has everything to gain or lose in this war, in the front rank." To read this soldier's account, Logan's speech may have appealed to the baser motives of his men. After all of the hardships and battles they had endured, wasn't it about time that the cause of the rebellion, the slave himself, take his place in the ranks, so that he, too, could offer his blood on the altar of the nation? Whatever prejudices Logan's men may have had, the notion of letting the African Americans face Rebel lead and fight for their own freedom opened their minds to ideas they would not otherwise have considered. "From that day, we heard but little against negro troops," wrote the soldier.[31]

"Mack," the correspondent from the *Cincinnati Commercial,* reported a rush for officers' positions in the new regiments. Men of the 7th Missouri were so interested in the prospect that an entire regiment's cadre could be had from their regiment alone. Forty applications came from the regiment, including a captain applying for a colonelcy, and "sergeants too numerous to mention." A few weeks later, a member of the 7th Missouri wrote that eight hundred applications were submitted from an unspecified division—probably Logan's. The idea of Negro troops had his backing: "I have little doubt of the success of the undertaking, if they will place proper officers over negroes."[32]

After ruminating on the issue with a friend, Cornwell approached Maj. Charles Stolbrand, division chief of artillery, to seek a commission as a captain in one of the new black regiments. The higher pay and prestige of an officer appealed to Cornwell, who was always seeking higher rank and was confident of deserving it. He proclaimed to his friend, "I would drill a company of alligators for a hundred and twenty a month." Cornwell's aspirations were partially fulfilled when he received a commission as a first lieutenant in Company B of the 9th Louisiana Infantry, African Descent.[33]

The new regiment's colonel was Swiss immigrant Hermann Lieb, promoted from his rank of major in the 8th Illinois. Despite the positive press given Logan's division from "Mack's" pen, Lieb felt many of his fellow soldiers in the Army of the Tennessee were unenthusiastic about the proposition of enlisting African Americans into the U.S. Army. He felt compelled to stand against such "stupid prejudices" and accepted the position of colonel in the 9th Louisiana Infantry, African Descent.[34]

Sgt. Elisha DeWitt was one of the many men of the 7th Missouri Infantry who put in applications. DeWitt had served with his unit since its organization in June 1861, when he enlisted at the age of eighteen. Thus far, they had marched many miles but had yet to see any real action with the enemy. He would be granted the captaincy of Company I, 9th Louisiana Infantry, African Descent.[35] Another new captain for the 9th Louisiana was Sgt. Corydon Heath of Battery G, 2nd Illinois Light Artillery. A sergeant since the battery's organization, Heath had been interested in obtaining higher rank for some time. In August 1862, he wrote to his friend, Henry Hyde, of his desire to raise a company, thus obtaining the rank and pay of a captain. Another option he was considering was to become a government messenger. With pay about the same as a captain, the position would enable him to "see all parts of the Grand Army of Freedom which would please me much." It is not clear if Heath had abolitionist tendencies, but his referring to the "Grand Army of Freedom"—a month before Lincoln's preliminary Emancipation Proclamation—seems to indicate that something more than just money may have motivated him. A few months after his letter to Hyde, Heath was taken prisoner by Nathan Bedford Forrest's cavalry while ill in the hospital at Trenton, Tennessee. Sent home on parole, he had just returned to his unit on April 10, 1863. Although probably not present with his battery on the day of Thomas's speech, he quickly submitted his application for a position and four days later General Thomas appointed him to the captaincy of Company B.[36]

Organizing at the same time was the 11th Louisiana Infantry, African Descent. Officers for this regiment came predominantly from Brig. Gen. Isaac Quinby's division and hailed from Iowa, Indiana, Illinois, and Missouri, with a sprinkling of Minnesotans. Among them was George L. Conn, a twenty-six-year-old private in the 48th Indiana Infantry. Enlisting in August of 1862, he joined his regiment just after it fought in engagements at Iuka and Corinth. In the spring of 1863, he became a second lieutenant in Company F.[37]

Near the top of the new regiment was Cyrus Sears, who was formerly a first lieutenant in the 11th Ohio Battery. He had served with distinction at Iuka, where his battery sustained one of the highest casualty ratios of any battery during the entire war, losing nearly half its men. The fire was so severe that forty-six out of fifty-four cannoneers were wounded or killed, and only three of their artillery horses—out of eighty on the field—escaped harm. Sears himself was severely wounded but retained his command. (For his heroism and tenacity in the face of battle, he would be awarded the Medal of Honor in 1892.) He left his position in the artillery to become lieutenant colonel of the 11th Louisiana. He would be in charge of the regiment at Milliken's Bend, owing to the cowardice of Col. Edwin W. Chamberlain. Sears's recollection, published in a slim volume in 1909, would be the only substantial Union account written by a survivor of the fight, until Cornwell's memoir was published by a descendent 135 years after the battle.[38]

The newly minted officers had their hands full, most of them bearing significantly more responsibilities than they had in their old outfits. Not long after receiving his appointment as a first lieutenant, David Cornwell was joined by Edward P. Smith as second lieutenant, and Corydon Heath, captain. Together they would form the officer cadre of Company B, 9th Louisiana Infantry, African Descent. Smith and Heath were both artillerymen, as was Cornwell, but because of Cornwell's prior service in the infantry, he was to help the other two learn infantry drill. They soon set up camp, purchased officers' uniforms from the sutler, and began the work of recruiting. Heath obtained a horse from his battery, Cornwell could only get a mule, and Smith had no mount and was left to guard the camp.[39]

Cornwell, Heath, Smith, and all the other new officers in units eventually known as the "Colored Troops," were still considered on "detached service" from their original units and, despite their new uniforms and duties, would still be paid at their old rank until their new units had been recruited to full strength. Forty men had to be enlisted before First Lieutenant Cornwell could officially receive his new rank; only when the company was fully formed, with about one hundred men, could Captain Heath and Second Lieutenant Smith get their rank.[40]

Meanwhile, as the officers of the new Louisiana regiments of African Descent began to organize, Adjutant General Thomas continued his speeches and recruiting efforts. Charles A. Dana, assistant secretary of war, trailed Thomas's path down the Mississippi Valley and reported in April on changes in officers' attitudes. Men who "three months ago, told me they would never serve along with negro regiments, now say that Adjutant-General Thomas makes bad speeches to troops, but that they shall obey orders, nevertheless." Dana's report could hardly be considered a ringing endorsement, but the men's promise of acquiescence was at least an obliging form of support.[41]

"Mack," the correspondent from Ohio, found most soldiers in favor of the new plan, with only a few "growls" coming from those who had sought commissions in the new regiments but were rejected. "Mack" cautioned his readers: "I have no doubt that disloyal men in the North will circulate private advices from the army of disaffection and mutiny among the soldiers on account of the 'nigger equality' scheme now being carried out; but I speak advisedly, when I say that there is no foundation whatever for such a report. Even the regiments raised in Southern Illinois, and which boast of their Democratic proclivities and their eternal hatred of 'abolitionism,' give their sanction to the new policy and wish it God speed."[42]

Although few in the Union army foresaw any direct combat action for the black troops, who were to be used primarily as garrisons in rear areas far from the front, there were hints that they might indeed have to face enemy fire. An editorial in the *Cincinnati Commercial* saw part of their role, as outlined by Thomas, to be guarding posts against guerilla attacks—something that had plagued the Union army periodically throughout its occupation of portions of

the Mississippi Valley. The writer believed that lingering prejudices against
the use of blacks in the military would pass away, but he also recommended
caution to those who supported their recruitment, suggesting that unreason-
able, excessively heroic expectations held by abolitionists needed to be reined
in. The issue at hand was to determine in a balanced and reasonable manner
how the former bondsmen could be most useful to the Union cause and how
the white troops released by the employment of black units could be brought
to bear against the enemy on the front lines.[43]

With the officers now appointed, the hard work of recruiting and organizing the regiments began. "Mack" outlined the procedure for enlisting the
former slaves: "All the able-bodied contrabands now within our lines will be
taken first. All who do not volunteer will be 'conscripted.'" Steamboats would
ply the Mississippi River from Lake Providence to Helena, Arkansas, scouring
plantations along the river for "recruits." An expedition would also be sent to
Bayou Maçon, "where there are large numbers of contrabands, some of whom
are reputed anxious to enlist." "Mack" was confident that ten to twelve regiments could be raised in the area, but he cautioned: "What they will amount
to when raised, is of course, an untried experiment, but there is reason to
hope for good results from it."[44] Despite his optimism, the correspondent had
been skeptical just a week earlier. He thought the task of recruiting among
the freedmen would be difficult. "The negroes here do not favor the idea of
enlisting," he wrote, "but I think, if impressed with the fact that they must
accept one of two alternatives—slavery or soldiery—they will readily choose
the latter."[45] Colonel Lieb of the 9th Louisiana also found recruiting among the
freedmen difficult—in part because so many other regiments were organizing
at the same time.[46]

The rapid organization of so many new regiments brought other difficulties. Brig. Gen. John P. Hawkins reported at the end of April that new black
recruits at Goodrich's Landing had only about one hundred rifles. The ordnance officer would not issue arms to troops who had not been mustered.
This meant that hundreds, probably thousands, of men who were new recruits
could not begin to learn the manual of arms or proper drilling until their units
were recruited to full strength and officially mustered—a task that could take
weeks or months. Hawkins begged Thomas to give a direct order to ordnance
officer Maj. Stephen C. Lyford to make an exception and grant troops weapons
before mustering-in.[47]

A shortage of weapons was not the only problem, however. Hawkins reprimanded Lt. Col. Van E. Young of the 10th Louisiana for allowing his men to visit their families on the nearby government-leased plantations. The soldiers' "influence on the work hands is mischievous," wrote Hawkins. "Allow none of them to recruit on these plantations," he warned, and "allow no families to accompany them" when new recruits came in. The population of dependents was swelling and becoming a hindrance to good military discipline and order. A similar reprimand was dispatched to Col. Hiram Scofield of the 8th Louisiana. Hawkins, like his civilian counterpart, Lark S. Livermore at Lake Providence, found the closeness of the army to civilians to be a liability.[48]

It was not all bad news, however. On the first of May, Hawkins gave Thomas an update on recruiting on the west bank of the Mississippi. Two regiments at Helena, Arkansas, were full strength, armed, and equipped but had not been mustered. Two regiments at Lake Providence were nearly full. Scofield's 8th Louisiana was also nearing completion. Hawkins expected to send out some recruiting expeditions into the "Macon Hills" (along Bayou Maçon) where he expected to find "plenty of recruits." And despite the difficulties in obtaining arms at Goodrich's Landing, Hawkins was encouraged because he deemed it a good recruiting location.[49]

The job of recruiting was not as easy as Hawkins's reports would make it appear. Large numbers of slaves had been driven off of the plantations in northeast Louisiana by their owners and removed to interior parts of the state or taken as far away as Texas. Many white families and plantation owners had fled, as well, abandoning their homes entirely or leaving them in the hands of trusted slaves, from whom they assumed loyalty. Yankee recruiters sometimes expected to find slaves helpless without their owners and believed their work would be made easy by proffering food, shelter, and clothing. However, many slaves were quite capable of taking care of themselves, at the expense of their former masters, as David Cornwell had found out months earlier, while still with the artillery near Lake Providence. One day, he was approached in camp by a slave who was left in charge of a neighboring plantation. The man wanted to sell Cornwell a horse. Cornwell went to the plantation stable, examined the horse though he knew nothing about how to evaluate the animal, and then tried to pass off a counterfeit Confederate fifty dollar bill. The man refused, saying he wouldn't take a "cotton basket full eb such money," and insisted on Lincoln currency. Cornwell held his ground, saying he had no other kind of money, and besides, the man's master was away elsewhere in the Confederacy, where no doubt this form of currency was valid. The bondsman replied (in

Cornwell's words), "ders nobody my master no moah an dat money I gets must be cepterbol to my ownself." Cornwell then came to two conclusions: he did not really want another horse, and "that Darkey did not need a master to take care of him."[50]

This one instance shows the persistent stereotypes carried by Union soldiers as well as their realization of the humanity, independence, and capabilities of those African Americans they encountered throughout their military service. Cornwell was probably typical in many respects, and like more well-known authors of recollections of service with Colored Troops, such as Thomas Wentworth Higginson in South Carolina, Cornwell's reminiscences use language and reflect attitudes of the time that today's readers unequivocally see as racist. What often is lost to the modern reader is just how profoundly changed common soldiers like Cornwell and even adamant abolitionists like Higginson were through their encounters with former bondsmen.

Cornwell uses crude dialect to reflect the Southern accent and the assumed lack of education of former slaves. He uses terms like "darkey," "coon," "buck," and "nigger" but often simultaneously expresses admiration, good-natured amusement, and genuine friendship and affection. It creates an odd tension, particularly given that his memoirs were written years after the war. Probably based on a diary, for they are full of detail, he certainly could have changed his language if he chose. His condescension toward African Americans is clear, but modern objections to his language often render invisible the genuine admiration he at times felt.

Among the first recruits in the 9th Louisiana was a man known to Cornwell as "Big Jack" Jackson. They had known each other for nearly a year because Jackson had served as a cook when Cornwell was a sergeant in the 8th Illinois Infantry. Standing six-and-a-half feet tall, Jackson never wore shoes because of the size of his feet. He had fled Mississippi when he got into an altercation with his overseer, possibly even killing him with a single blow. "Big Jack" joined up with Cornwell's mess somewhere near Jackson, Tennessee. By the time Cornwell was recruiting for a black regiment, "Big Jack" Jackson was driving mules for the army. Jackson joined the new regiment right away and brought a couple of friends with him. Heath appointed him first duty sergeant, but only whites could hold the staff noncommissioned officer positions, since reading and writing was a prerequisite.[51]

As Heath and Cornwell set out on their first recruiting expedition, they found the response among local blacks about like what "Mack" had predicted.

The men were interested in discussing the subject but would not make a decision to enlist. "They had nothing else to do," recalled Cornwell, "and seemed to enjoy the importuning of commissioned officers, as it created a new sensation that was flattering." When the men seemed like they might be persuaded, the women standing nearby would dissuade them, and the men's interest would revert to making conversation but not enlisting. Cornwell found Heath a "candid, honest fellow of unlimited patience, and a persuasive talker." Heath had served on recruiting service several times with his old battery, and Cornwell felt he must have been an excellent recruiting officer among whites. Yet Heath's eloquence found no takers, and the two men returned to camp with no recruits after visiting four plantations. Undaunted, they vowed to return again the next day. "We got plenty of talk, but not a recruit," Cornwell recalled of their second trip out. This time they returned to camp in sorry spirits.[52]

Cornwell lay awake that night, smoking a cigar and reflecting on the situation. The black men on the nearby plantations had it made, he decided. Their masters had left, plenty of provisions were still on hand, and the Union would surely win the war, thus guaranteeing their freedom. Why did they need to join the army, when they were already reaping the benefits of working or relaxing as they pleased, eating from their former masters' larders, coming and going from place to place at their own desire, socializing freely among themselves, and enjoying a life of freedom from the lash? He believed the men had not "the slightest intention of enlisting," though they certainly enjoyed talking about it. Cornwell felt discouraged, and if the whole thing was going to be a failure, he might as well get back to his old unit.

But while Heath and Smith lay sleeping, he hit upon an idea and shared it with "Big Jack." Jack was interested and agreed with Cornwell's plan. The next morning, Cornwell persuaded Heath and Smith to remain in camp. He borrowed Heath's horse, and Jack rode along on Cornwell's mule, his long legs dangling. He was still barefooted, his clothes were too small, and his bare arms and lower legs stuck out from his uniform like a schoolboy, but Jack and Cornwell left the camp that morning confident in their mission.

At the first plantation they visited that morning, the freedmen swarmed Jack. He dismounted his mule and lined up the men "according to rank." Cornwell was amused because Jack thought rank meant the same as height. Undoubtedly, Jack had seen men lining up by height for many months, as he tagged along with the army from Tennessee to Louisiana. Cornwell would have known that forming ranks—two parallel lines of men standing side-by-side—necessitated men arranging themselves from tallest to shortest, according to army drill. Jack was merely lining the men up *in ranks,* as opposed to *by rank.* Jack soon had the men marching down the road, and Cornwell followed on his horse, leading the mule. The women wailed in protest, but Jack marched on with his men. After visiting three other plantations, the two recruiters returned to camp at the end of the day with twenty-one new men, who were promptly sworn in by Heath.[53]

Cornwell feared some would try to run off and warned Jack to keep an eye on them, but he claimed years later that none seemed to want to run away. They didn't complain about how they had entered the service, and none deserted. It is hard to know the truth of these statements, as all of the earliest records for the regiment were lost in the fight at Milliken's Bend. Cornwell recalled that the new recruits were just as happy "as if their enlistment had been voluntary,"—a telling statement that indicates it was anything but.[54] From Cornwell's perspective, it was the black women who had the greatest objection to the men's enlistments, not the men themselves. The women's protests were well founded. Marching their menfolk off to the army left the women defenseless, and events would soon prove they had as much to fear from white Northern soldiers as they had from their former slavemasters.[55]

Even the partnership between Cornwell and Jack could not yield enough recruits for the regiment's needs. After some time of using this technique, the entire regiment still had less than two hundred enlisted men. One day, Colonel Lieb spied Cornwell with "Big Jack," still wearing his too-small uniform and riding a mule. Jack carried his musket at right-shoulder-shift, despite being mounted, and had the bayonet attached as well. Lieb gave Cornwell a sharp dressing-down, calling his parade of troops a "menagery," and fearing ridicule for the entire endeavor of raising Colored Troops. Cornwell defended Jackson and bragged about their success—though not the method—used to bring in new recruits. After listening in stern silence, Lieb scolded Cornwell, insisting that Jackson get a new, properly fitting uniform and shoes, and that he learn the correct way to carry his musket while mounted. Cornwell and Jack continued their recruiting efforts, using the same methods, and added yet more men to the regiment. This time they came from places near Port Gibson, Mississippi, in the very vicinity where the Ingraham family experienced so many difficulties with roving Yankee soldiers.[56]

Cornwell, "Big Jack" Jackson, and the rest of the expedition soon returned up the Mississippi River to Milliken's Bend. Two hundred men came to the regiment from the quartermaster's department and were split up among all the companies. Cornwell's company numbered about forty. While the recruiters had been absent from Milliken's Bend, numbers of women had come into the camp, and army discipline was lax. Cornwell soon took over the daily tasks of the camp for his company, which released Heath and Smith for recruiting. When Lieb returned, the camp was moved closer to the river, the women driven out, and discipline reestablished. Lieb, in charge of the African Brigade at Milliken's Bend on June 2, found that many men had mules, horses, or other livestock in camp and took measures to eliminate this hindrance to good order and discipline.[57]

The 11th Louisiana, like Lieb's regiment, also had too many civilians in camp. On June 4, Col. Edwin W. Chamberlain ordered all "colored women" out of the camp. They were to gather at 10 a.m. and were to be sent downriver under charge of an officer. Even if these women had been employed doing laundry or other tasks, they were to be exiled and not permitted to cross the guard line again.[58] The problem of civilians crossing into military lines would plague the organization of Colored Troops for months, even after the plantation leasing system had been well established. At the same time that Lieb and Chamberlain were driving the women out of their camps, Brig. Gen. Jeremiah C. Sullivan was at his wit's end. He wrote Grant's headquarters that contrabands, mostly women and children, were flooding Young's Point. "Their condition is such that immediate action is needed," Sullivan urged. "No one seems to take charge of them, to feed them, or to attend properly to their sanitary or moral condition. Our soldiers are rapidly becoming demoralized by being thrown in contact with them, and the contrabands are becoming depraved, vicious and unruly." Sullivan understood that plantation commissioners were to see after feeding "negroes who came into our lines" and to provide them with camps and suitable rules and regulations, but it is unclear why this was not happening at Young's Point. The freedpeople kept coming. Sullivan proposed that "a large number of dissolute and idle negroes . . . be 'corralled' near the present encampment of the African regiments." Given the situation, it might be the best alternative. Sullivan explained, "Their Husbands, Brothers and Sons, have enlisted in these regiments, and should be compelled to aid in their support."[59]

Sullivan proposed a detailed plan to solve the problem. First, the contrabands should be gathered together, grouped by families, and an effort should be made to identify and locate their male relatives in the service. Once this was done, the family would be given tickets that would certify that they had a relative in the military. Meanwhile, colonels of the African American units were to obtain information from their recruits about their families, including the number of people "dependent on him for support—and their whereabouts." The two coordinating systems, one civil and one military, would enable the soldiers to support their families by reserving a portion of their pay to cover commissary expenses for them. It is unclear if Sullivan's proposal was ever implemented.[60]

While recruiting in the regiments continued, the plantation commissioners grew worried. Their operations were vulnerable, and they feared an attack almost every day. Abraham Strickle met with Grant in late May, and he focused upon the fragmented method of organization employed with the African American troops as a weakness that could put everyone at risk. The command structure at the time was composed of individual commanders at various posts. Strickle feared that, during an attack, uncertainty about lines of authority and confused orders could lead to catastrophe. For instance, he questioned, where was the dividing line between Reid's authority, based at Lake Providence, and that of General Sullivan, who was based at Young's Point? Who would be in command in the event of an attack between the two posts? (That is precisely where Milliken's Bend lay.) Strickle even went so far as to suggest that the various outposts be united under a single command, and he recommended Col. Isaac F. Shepard for the position.[61]

Strickle also urged that Shepard have authority to draw all necessary supplies. The supply matter had been an ongoing problem and would drive Shepard to near insanity. Because there was no brigade quartermaster or commissary, clothing, food, and other essentials were extraordinarily difficult to obtain—not only for the troops but also for the plantation commissioners. Grant responded promptly to the commissioner's concerns and directed quartermasters and others to cooperate with the organization of black units by providing them the material and other support they required, "without unnecessary delay."[62]

A number of major administrative changes occurred around the same time. On May 22, General Orders No. 143 from the War Department established the Bureau for Colored Troops. Grant created the District of Northeast Louisiana on May 28, placing General Sullivan in charge and thus addressing Strickle's concerns by providing an overall commander for operations on the west bank of the Mississippi River. On June 2, however, Sullivan was relieved of his duties at his own request, citing failing health. He was replaced by Brig. Gen. Elias S. Dennis. Before Sullivan left, he warned Lt. Col. John Rawlins at Grant's headquarters that the men at Young's Point could not "be trusted in an engagement," presumably because they were still untrained. To further complicate matters, Colonel Shepard took over as commander of the African Brigade, while General Hawkins traveled North for an unspecified period of time. On top of that, Shepard was placed under arrest on June 1, and temporary command of the African Brigade at Milliken's Bend devolved upon Colonel Lieb of the 9th Louisiana.[63]

Thus, in the space of two weeks, a new bureau was established at the Federal level, a new district was created in the Army of the Tennessee, and two commanders at the district and brigade level were replaced temporarily. In addition, even the temporary brigade commander, Shepard, had his own temporary replacement, Lieb. All of these transitions came scarcely a month after General Thomas's lackluster speeches to the troops announcing the organization and arming of former slaves in the Union cause. Nearly all of the officers in the regiments of the African Brigade, from colonels to lieutenants, were new to their rank and responsibilities, and of course, all of the enlisted men were the rawest of recruits. The Union forces on the west bank of the Mississippi River were indeed vulnerable. Given the circumstances, this may well have been one of the weakest points in the entire Union army. Nowhere else were so many fresh recruits training and organizing so close to hostile territory, and nowhere else, since the earliest days of the war, were so many officers universally inexperienced in their duties.

In late July, Colonel Lieb summarized some of the problems he had had in the past few months when recruiting for his regiment. Because his new officers were not yet mustered and therefore did not yet have their official rank, they were often thwarted. Officers from other units, especially in the quartermaster department, did not feel compelled to obey requests submitted by Lieb's officers. Members of the Quartermaster and Provost Marshal Departments took Lieb's black recruits to perform duties for their departments and did not send them back to the regiment. "In this way, very many recruits were lost entirely," Lieb wrote in frustration. The regiment could have been organized and mustered nearly two months earlier, he thought, had it not been for these problems.[64]

Lieb's problems were miniscule compared to those of his immediate superior, Colonel Shepard. Shepard found his duties in the wake of Hawkins's departure frustrating and nearly demoralizing. His greatest difficulty was obtaining supplies, clothing, and weapons. Time and again, he had been refused on the grounds that, as a colonel, he had no authority to make requisitions, which required a general's signature. Never mind the fact that Shepard was in command of a brigade, acting in place of General Hawkins. His subordinates fared no better. One quartermaster wryly suggested that Colonel Chamberlain of the 11th Louisiana "get the approval of the *Governor of Louisiana* as he claimed to command *Louisiana troops.*" Capt. Benjamin F. Reno, also of the Quartermaster Department, refused to provide clothing to the troops, finding every officer sent to him deficient in authority or paperwork. He refused one officer who had been acting brigade quartermaster in his old unit and who had authority from General Hawkins. A second officer was turned away on the grounds that he did not have the required bond. To get it, he would have to return North—a trip that would take nearly a month—before he could draw supplies for the brigade. The 10th Louisiana found a way around the stubborn Captain Reno and sent their regimental quartermaster about 250 river miles north to Memphis, where his mission at last met with success. Shepard threatened to follow suit and have all of his regimental quartermasters go to Memphis to obtain supplies. He found Captain Reno's stubbornness frustrating and offensive. "I am bound to suppose that all these obstacles are legal and technically right, but they are *unusual* and I never knew them insisted on before," he wrote, reiterating that though he did not hold the rank of general, he was functioning as one and acting upon General Hawkins's orders. Shepard knew the real cause for the difficulty: "the fact is there is a determined *hostility* to the movement" to recruit black men into the U.S. Army. He vowed, "All this only nerves me *to make success,* . . . I am confident of it, and the more covert hostility the grander the triumph of a noble purpose."[65]

Despite the obstructionist Captain Reno, Shepard remained optimistic and was genuinely pleased with the progress of his brigade. In late May, he summarized the situation for General Thomas. The 9th Louisiana was only partially uniformed and had a few more than three hundred armed men. Despite these handicaps, Shepard was most impressed with their drill. "I witnessed an evening parade which would have been no discredit to many old regiments," he wrote. The officers seemed "faithful and intelligent," and recruiting was progressing swiftly. Likewise, the 11th Louisiana under Colonel Chamberlain was also adding men. Four companies mustered in when Shepard inspected them, and three more would follow in less than a week. Like the 9th Louisiana, the 11th also had not yet obtained uniforms, and only about four hundred rifles were on hand.[66]

Due to Shepard's assumption of duties as brigade commander, his own 1st Mississippi lagged behind the other regiments at Milliken's Bend. Only one company had been mustered, and his recruiting officers had made no report. Still, Shepard was sanguine: "I do not feel impatient as colored men are coming in on the average of at least 75 daily and when the others are fielded, the 1st Miss. will fill even without recruiters." Shepard also pointed out a lurking administrative problem. Another unit designated as the 1st Mississippi was organizing at Grand Gulf, near a refugee camp, and it fielded about four hundred men. Despite the glowing reviews of his infant regiments, Shepard found his circumstances "annoying, trying and difficult." Hawkins had left him no information about his plans, and Shepard did not know what information had been communicated to subordinates. Although he felt he was gaining the upper hand on administrative matters, there were yet "many obstacles."[67]

One continuing difficulty was the matter of recruiting and officer's pay, especially in the 9th Louisiana. Shepard wrote, "This Regiment has *no men mustered in*. Lt. Col. [Charles L.] Paige is in command, and he *distributes* recruits as received to the ten nuclei of companies equally, under the belief that all officers *are under pay from the time of appointment*. In this I think he errs, for my belief is that the *date of muster-in*, with the legal number of men and companies, is the date of payment, and that previously officers are only on *detailed duty*, with their former rank. He is unconvinced." Confident that he was in the right, Shepard asked Thomas to provide a clarifying statement, "because your authority will in no wise be questioned."[68]

Shepard was indeed correct, though the official policy may have been partly responsible for the zeal with which the officers recruited. These men were faced with the formidable tasks of starting a regiment from scratch while simultaneously learning the new responsibilities of their increased rank. Add to this the danger of being in proximity to hostile territory and guerillas, along with the frustrations of trying to bridge the wide cultural gap between Southern African American slaves and white Northern veterans—all while still being paid at their old rank—and the situation must have rankled many of the neophyte officers.[69] Corydon Heath, for example, made seventeen dollars a month as a sergeant in his old artillery outfit. He was still making that amount more than a month later in the 9th Louisiana, though serving in the capacity of a captain, a rank that normally paid sixty dollars a month. Delaying the new officers their rank and pay until they were mustered meant they had extraordinary incentives to fill the ranks as quickly as possible. This often meant adding recruits by forceful persuasion through impressment or enlisting men regardless of their fitness for duty.[70]

The black enlisted men, too, suffered from inequities in pay. They would receive only ten dollars a month, minus a three-dollar clothing allowance, as compared to white volunteers who got thirteen dollars a month, in addition to a clothing allowance of three dollars. The lower pay of black soldiers did not begin as an overtly discriminatory measure. Instead, it originated as a distinction between army laborers and soldiers. Prior to the Emancipation Proclamation, the only blacks working for the army were those men who served as cooks, drivers, or in other capacities, typically in the quartermaster's department. As laborers, these men did not receive the same pay and allowances as soldiers in the army. When African Americans began to be enlisted as soldiers, no other legal provisions were on the books which would enable them to be paid at the rate of soldiers. The *only* provision for paying blacks in uniform was a law of 1862, which assumed them to be laborers. It would take more than a year for the U.S. Congress to rectify this problem, prompting mutinies and discontent in Colored Troops organizations all over the country. In the spring and early summer of 1863 in the Mississippi Valley, however, the opportunity to be paid *anything* for their work, even as soldiers, must have been an appealing prospect to many black men who had labored for so many years without any type of remuneration whatsoever.[71]

As the numbers of African Americans coming into Union lines swelled, Colonel Shepard of the African Brigade, with headquarters at Milliken's Bend, was compelled on May 19 to issue stern orders regarding their treatment. "The entire action and purpose of the Government, both in locating negroes upon plantations and in enrolling them as soldiers," he wrote, announcing just how profound a change in thinking was required, "are intended to recognize in them *the rights of personal liberty,* and to *ensure to them kindness and protection* in the lawful discharge of chosen duties." Apparently, some government lessees were simply reimposing slavery. Shepard expressly prohibited whippings and other severe measures. Wages must be paid, and employment for those on nearby plantations must last under contract until at least February 1864.[72]

In addition, Shepard acknowledged that some recruiting officers had been overzealous in their duties. Lessees could not prevent male laborers from enlisting voluntarily or obstruct the lawful conduct of army business, but neither could recruiters enter the plantation without the lessee's permission. Some recruiters used "threats and force" to get their quotas. Shepard charged them with creating "discontent, distrust, fear and panic among the laborers." Furthermore, he ordered, "No colored man *will be forced*, by threats or by violence into military service" unless the government ordered conscription for black men, an unlikely event. If any men had enlisted under duress, their service obligations were voided, and they were to return to the lessee's plantation from which they were taken.[73]

Shepard established new rules for recruiting on government plantations, and they are revealing for what they say about recruiting methods until that time. Recruiting officers could no longer enter the plantations "to tamper with the hands, at will." Instead, they could only come onto the land with the permission of the lessee, who could demand to be present, if he so desired. A single officer could make no more than three visits to recruit. The lessee would keep a detailed logbook of officers' visits, and any violations or "misunderstandings" were to be promptly reported to Shepard, who promised "all doubts will be promptly remedied." He called upon his officers to exercise "circumspection as well as zeal" in their efforts, for their mission was to lead "a degraded and heretofore enslaved people to the privileges and blessings of freedom."[74]

Despite Shepard's lofty and idealistic goals, the officers in the new African American regiments had tremendous incentives to recruit men as quickly as possible. Once recruited to full strength, the white officers would at last be paid at their new rate and formally assume the rank, title, and responsibilities they had already been undertaking for weeks and months. Given these conditions, it was inevitable that clashes would occur between planters—usually government lessees—and officers on recruiting duty. On May 17, J. E. Walke, the lessee on Dr. Harding's plantation, accused a Mr. Griffith of coming onto his plantation and forcing "eight men against their will to join his Regiment."[75] Even more shocking, Griffith threatened the men that if they did not come with him immediately, he would return with "an armed force" that "would compel them to go regardless of their reluctance." Walke was not the only one offended by this behavior. Walke said his laborers were adamant that he petition the military authorities on their behalf, and he urged that formal protective measures be taken to prevent his laborers from being abducted while at work in the fields, stating, "It not only retards my business but makes great confusion among families when men are forced into the ranks against their will." Shepard had already received complaints about Griffith from some black enlisted men who stated that the officer "'drew his pistol and threatened to shoot them if they did not go with him.'"[76]

A few days later, William Hancock, a chaplain at the infirmary farm, wrote to Commissioner George B. Field about a conversation he had had with Lieutenant Colonel Young of the 10th Louisiana.[77] Young had threatened to take cattle from the farm's corral, and he had eyes for the lumber and furniture there, too. There was more, Hancock said but declined to elaborate. Immensely polite, Hancock wrote his superior: "Would you be so kind as to give me some instructions on what to do and an order to retain such property as you may deem best . . . for our use." Shepard declared Young's actions at the infirmary farm to be "like stealing from a Poor House," and he admitted that he had a poor impression of Young from "other slighter affairs," probably earlier difficulties over recruiting. But the situation was awkward. Shepard was only in temporary command during Hawkins's absence, so he felt compelled to refer the matter to Adjutant General Thomas, though he pledged to impose whatever disciplinary measures might be necessary.[78]

As if the many difficulties of supplies, organization, recruiting, and civilian matters (both with lessees and contrabands) were not enough, Shepard had to contend with nearby white troops disgusted by their proximity to black units. Even his immediate superior, General Sullivan, viewed the black soldiers as nothing more than a labor pool for stevedores and cooks. Shepard's relationship with Sullivan had been rocky from the start. In April, when the regiments were in their infancy, Sullivan had repeatedly addressed Shepard as "Superintendent of Contrabands," requesting male and female laborers, including children, to assist with unloading boats, helping in camps, or "cleaning house." Shepard informed Sullivan more than once that he was not a superintendent of contrabands and therefore could not fulfill his request. General Sullivan countered by threatening Shepard with a charge of disobedience if he refused to comply. Shepard had obliged one of Sullivan's requests, as a courtesy, although he was under no military obligation to do so. His orders instructed him to only obey commands from Maj. Gen. Frederick Steele.[79]

Shepard took temporary command of the African Brigade in late May. When Sullivan made yet another request, again addressed to the "Superintendent of Contrabands," Shepard snapped. The men in his camp were *soldiers*, he explained, "not *negroes* simply, nor '*contrabands*' *at all*, but *free men*, entitled to all the personal and official respect that attaches to the General himself." Concerned that his words might be too harsh, Shepard consulted with Abraham Strickle, who advised against sending the letter. Shepard was well aware that his words might not be persuasive. A few weeks later, he came to the conclusion that Sullivan "utterly abhors the idea of arming negroes" and "wished to see a rebel force come in and wipe us out."

Shepard's trials paled in comparison with those of the enlisted men of the African Brigade, who found themselves and their families under constant personal attack from white soldiers in blue. Plantation commissioner Lark S. Livermore reported, "I have seen a white soldier walk out of his way to see how flat he could knock a Negro down." Maj. Julian E. Bryant (identified as "Bryan") of the 1st Mississippi Infantry, African Descent, reported one black soldier had been cut with a knife (and was expected to lose his eye) after he asked for his hat back from a white soldier who had taken it. In a similar incident, soldiers of the 131st Illinois Infantry attacked an African American soldier who refused to remove his hat when he passed the white men. Unrepentant, a white sergeant involved in the latter case claimed he had every right to "order" the African American soldier to remove his hat. Kicks, cuts, and beatings were a common occurrence, and the white soldiers involved received little, if any, punishment.

All of the plantation commissioners reported hostility and violence toward the African American soldiers in the area, as well as against the men's families on nearby plantations or in contraband camps. Commissioner Field said he had lessees complaining all of the time about "depredations" from the 1st Kansas Mounted Infantry. He even believed that white soldiers were "running off" Negroes from government plantations and then "selling them or getting a bounty for them" in what essentially amounted to a black market operation in human trafficking. Field had complained to the provost marshal and asked that white troops be removed from the area entirely. Commissioner Strickle seconded Field's opinion, believing black troops could never be effective as long as white troops were quartered nearby. Livermore held the same sentiments. Field thought the commanding generals in the area took so little notice of the situation that he felt it was pointless to file complaints any longer—choosing instead to do so only "in very heinous instances."

Although Cornwell belittled the reaction of black women whose menfolk were taken away by the army, they had every right to complain. They feared for their lives. Black women suffered some of the most violent attacks from white Yankee soldiers. Strickle reported, "Black women have come to me and complained of rape on their daughters before their eyes by white soldiers." He failed to apprehend the suspects, despite using "all the means in my power to bring the guilty parties to justice." Capt. Eben F. Cutter of the 3rd Missouri Infantry, serving as a quartermaster with the African Brigade, reported he was "disturbed every night with complaints from black men that their wives were being ravished by white soldiers." Major Bryant of the 1st Mississippi Infantry, African Descent, testified that a dozen or more white soldiers had been arrested for attempting rape.

In just two months, Shepard could report the following offenses: "Forcible violation of female chastity; The rape of women before their husbands' eyes; Negro quarters ransacked, robbed and burned; Their money wrested from them or counterfeit coin forced on them instead." And that was not all. Shepard said the black civilians in his area had met with violence, atrocity, and brutality—even murder. "These outrages have passed with almost utter impunity," he wrote Grant, finding that there was great "sympathy for offenders." The criminals were most often white Union soldiers, sometimes officers. Shepard was deeply grieved. Even God must weep when such a "holy cause" as emancipation was "accompanied by such outrageous atrocities."

One of the units coming in for the severest condemnation was a nearby company from the 10th Illinois Cavalry. Their duty was to serve as scouts for the African American regiments at Milliken's Bend. Capt. Christopher H. Anderson of Company A reported that about half of his men disapproved enlisting blacks and viewed it as "a degradation to come in contact with the Negro soldiers." Anderson also admitted that some of his men might be prone to violence, confessing that some had "abused Negroes," but did not know if the victims had been soldiers or civilians. Hoping to mitigate the situation— either because of his own prejudices or in a genuine effort to avoid further violence—Anderson had asked General Sullivan to send his company elsewhere, but reassignment did not come.

The situation came to a head on May 30, when Pvt. John O'Brien of Company A, 10th Illinois Cavalry got drunk with a friend. Together they wandered into the camp of the 1st Mississippi Infantry, African Descent, looking for trouble. There they found Henry Lee, a black private, tied to a tree as punishment for some infraction. The two white soldiers pulled on the rope and kicked Lee in the genitals so violently that he was still incapacitated days later. From there, the two men proceeded to a nearby cotton shed, where they found Lizzie Briggs and her ten-year-old daughter. They grabbed the young girl by her arm and spread her legs apart, but her mother wrested her away. One of the men threatened the woman with a hatchet. "I'll smash your damned mouth," he shouted and told her she would have been better off staying with the "secesh." Lizzie's mother, who was nearly one hundred years old, tried her best to save her daughter and granddaughter, but she was knocked down near the fireplace and kicked. O'Brien's drunken friend kicked a teenage boy in the face, causing a huge gash, and went to another woman and tore off her clothes. She ran away before he could rape her.

O'Brien's friend, who is never identified, managed to escape, but O'Brien himself was quickly apprehended and brought before Shepard, who ordered him whipped by black soldiers from the 1st Mississippi. Two white soldiers, Sgt. Samuel Shonessy and Captain Cutter, witnessed the whipping and found it inconsequential. The men used small "twigs" that broke after a few strokes. Captain Cutter said they were mere switches that would not even hurt a three-month-old child. The entire whipping did not last more than a few minutes, and Sergeant Shonessy deemed it "very light."

Although the whipping was marginal, Shepard was satisfied that the point had been made and that the African American soldiers had at least had the opportunity to punish their own affronts. It was "time to make an example," and he wanted the "colored men [to] feel I was their protector." Shepard believed he had acted in the best interests of his men, and ultimately, the army. But word quickly came back to Captain Anderson and Lt. Thomas D. Vredenburgh that one of their men from the 10th Illinois was being whipped by Negroes. The two officers flew to the 1st Mississippi's camp, released O'Brien from custody, sent him back to his own camp, and burst into Shepard's headquarters. The two officers were livid. Captain Anderson demanded that Shepard come to his regiment and "acknowledge that he had committed a gross outrage and disgraced the service, his country, cause, and humanity." After doing that, Shepard should be "turned out of the service and decent society."

Anderson stalked back to camp and found his company seething. No doubt Private O'Brien had told them his story. One soldier sought permission to clean "out the damned nigger camp," and a lieutenant called Shepard a "God-damned abolishionist" [sic] who was "not as good as the negroes in his camp." Anderson returned to Shepard's headquarters and warned that his company was "uncontrollable," declaring he could not be held responsible for any actions they might take.

Major Elvis P. Shaw of the 10th Illinois took a calmer, more formal approach. He requested a court of inquiry to examine Shepard's actions. When

General Sullivan heard about the whipping of Private O'Brien, he placed
Shepard under arrest on June 1. Shepard also requested a court of inquiry so
that greater attention could be brought to the violence and intimidation that
he and his men were facing on a daily basis. A court convened at Milliken's
Bend on June 4 and met for ten days, being interrupted twice by attacks from
the Rebels.

In the end, Shepard was exonerated, and the court pointed to the larger
issues at stake. The court agreed that Shepard was justified in having O'Brien
whipped because so many abuses against black soldiers and their families had
gone unpunished and ignored by the military authorities. It was imperative,
therefore, that justice and punishment be swift. Furthermore, the court found
that not a single instance of abuse had been reported in the week since the
whipping had taken place. Therefore, Shepard's disciplinary measures seemed
to have worked. President of the court, Col. Thomas Kilby Smith, praised the
court for looking beyond the immediate circumstances to the larger issues. It
was not just a matter of the whipping of Private O'Brien by a few men of the
1st Mississippi, ordered to mete out punishment by their brigade commander,
Colonel Shepard. No, it was the gross neglect to protect fellow Union soldiers
and their families from abuse by other soldiers.

As the court of inquiry concluded, Shepard provided a supplementary
statement in which he praised the court for its willingness to examine the
broader issue of white soldiers' abuse of African American soldiers and civilians. Shepard blamed Sullivan, who ignored the needs and requests of officers
in the Colored Troops and disregarded complaints. "Gen. Sullivan and no
other is directly responsible for any wrong 'state of affairs' and as Commander
of the District it was obviously his duty to have comprehended and remedied
'faults in the organization of the African Regiments'—which he has never con-
descended to notice," Shepard wrote.[80]

Apparently unrelated to this diatribe, which came in the closing days of
the court, Shepard also scored a victory of a different sort. On June 3, Sullivan
stepped down from command, citing illness. Assistant Secretary of War
Charles Dana, however, claimed Sullivan was relieved on account of his "iner-
tia"—indicating Sullivan's resignation was probably not voluntary.[81]

Despite the positive outcome of the court of inquiry, the situation created
yet more difficulties in the short term. Col. Hermann Lieb took charge of the
African Brigade while Shepard was under arrest. Sullivan's departure resulted
in yet another change in command when Brig. Gen. Elias S. Dennis took over

as commander of the District of Northeast Louisiana. The changes in both positions and the turmoil and hostility between the 10th Illinois and the African Brigade came just days before the attack on the outpost at Milliken's Bend.

Meanwhile, the men of the African Brigade still had work to do. Drills and target practice continued. On May 31, just one day before his arrest, Shepard put Lieb in charge of the pickets at Milliken's Bend, to be composed of men from the 9th and 11th Louisiana. When he requested men for picket duty from the 11th Louisiana, Shepard specified his desire for soldiers "experienced in the manual of arms, and if possible, acquainted with the country." Many of the men could fulfill the second requirement, though few held the first.[82] Most of the new recruits were still learning how to handle their weapons. Earlier in the month, Cornwell, at Lieb's request, began making arrangements for target practice. He made a target measuring twenty-two inches wide and six feet high, about the size of a man, and covered it in canvas with a black bull's-eye in the center. A trench was dug in front of the target, for an observer to remain in safety. The observer would indicate with a small black or white flag whether the shot had been a hit or miss and would indicate its location.

To help the new recruits learn to take careful aim, Cornwell had a simple device built, consisting of a sandbag on top of a tripod. The soldier would place his musket on top of the sandbag, line up the sights with the target, and fire. Few of the men could hit the target at all. Frustrated, Cornwell took the musket, lined it up himself, and showed the next soldier in line how it would look when properly aimed. Once he understood, the soldier would be given an opportunity to try again. Inevitably, it seemed, he would fail. "It would only make a hole through the atmosphere fifty feet above and twenty to the right of the target," Cornwell would recall. The problem was that the recruits failed to use both sights on their guns when aiming. Using only the front sight resulted in fire too high. Using only the rear sight sent the bullet into the ground fifty yards away. Cornwell grew frustrated and threatened to "kill" the man if he didn't get it right. Of course, Cornwell didn't shoot anyone, but his patience wore thin. Meanwhile, other soldiers observed the errors of their predecessors and sometimes learned from them. On the rare occasion when one of the men would score a hit, "he would be as proud as if he had killed his overseer . . . and tell all the other Darkeys just exactly how he did it," Cornwell wrote.[83]

The difficulty of marksmanship may not have been the soldiers' fault. The men were armed with Austrian rifles, which, besides firing a large .69 caliber ball, were notoriously unreliable. In the fall, Brigadier General Hawkins would complain to his superiors: "The Austrian rifle is not fit for a soldier. It is classed a third rate by the Ordnance Department, and I see very little wisdom in requiring voluminous reports and vexatious delays before replacing them with an arm that is known to be first class. Our present arms are constantly breaking and bursting, and their fire is very inaccurate. I could not go into a fight with much confidence in their efficiency. The men fear the effect on themselves of their own fire." Some rifles would burst upon their first firing and were even more prone to do so as the barrel became fouled during battle. "I wish to make good soldiers of what I have got, but they stand a poor chance with the arms now furnished them," he wrote in frustration. He begged for Springfield rifled muskets to be sent to him from eastern armories or St. Louis. "If you could see the *soldier-like appearance* of my troops, you would feel convinced that they deserved the best class of arms and would use them to advantage whenever opportunities occurred," he pleaded. Hawkins had been complaining for months, without results.[84]

Lt. George Sabin, who inspected the regiments that fall, had the same complaint. He found that the men took good care of their arms, inferior though they might be, but this was an indication that they could be entrusted with better weaponry. Sabin found that many of the weapons were castoffs from other regiments, and many were "old, defective, and worthless." The regiments of the African Brigade, he felt, "ought to be better provided with better arms at once. It is absolutely cruel to put men into the field in so defective condition." These were the very same weapons the new recruits of the African Brigade had carried with them into battle at Milliken's Bend the preceding summer.[85]

Meanwhile, "Mack" continued to keep the news coming to his readers in Cincinnati. On the last day of May, near Vicksburg, he reported that a picket post near Lake Providence, manned by members of the 8th Louisiana Infantry, African Descent, had been attacked by guerillas. Two Negroes and a white officer were killed, and one black man was captured and hanged. Nearly 150 guerillas were reported to be in the area, and, it was said, "They aver their determination to hang every negro they catch in arms against them, and to shoot their officers without mercy."[86]

Although such stories made good headlines and propaganda, "Mack" appears to have been in error. On May 27, near Lake Providence, Capt. Frank S. Bishop and sixteen men from Company F of the 8th Louisiana were attacked by guerillas while on picket duty. Bishop was severely wounded in both legs, one enlisted man died, and six others were taken prisoner. No official record has been found indicating any of the men were hanged—though "Mack's" report may have been the first to mention such action by the Rebels—real or imagined. Rumors of similar events elsewhere in northeastern Louisiana would persist throughout that summer and into the fall.[87]

"Mack" was probably just repeating what he had heard, and the rumors of a hanging had apparently drifted southward to Milliken's Bend. "Mack" wrote that Col. Hermann Lieb of the 9th Louisiana Infantry, A. D., swore to shoot "six guerillas for every negro they hang. He will shoot the first six he catches as a measure of retaliation for the act above-related. He is willing to fight against guerillas with his Ethiopian command, under the black flag." Lieb and his men would not have to wait long for the opportunity to seek their revenge. Just a week later, organized Rebel forces would attack Lieb's outpost. Some Federal officers would accuse the Confederates of hoisting the black flag during their attack—a symbol indicating a merciless fight to the death, in which no prisoners would be taken.[88]

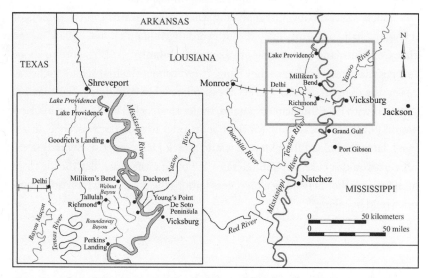

Overview of north Louisiana and detailed view of the area of northeast Louisiana near Vicksburg.

"I Cannot Tell How It Was I Escaped"
The Bloody Battle at Milliken's Bend

THE TEXANS' SPIRITS were high. With over 350 miles behind them in slightly more than a month and after more than a year in the service, most of it spent in fruitless marching and countermarching, they had met the enemy and forced him to flee. In all of their travels across Arkansas and Louisiana, McCulloch's Brigade of Walker's Division had not yet had the opportunity to meet the Yankees. They did so, for the first time, on May 31, 1863, at Perkins' Landing, Louisiana, about twenty-five miles southwest of Vicksburg. Maj. Gen. John G. Walker gave McCulloch the mission of capturing "a camp of instruction and insurrection for negroes" at Perkins' Landing.[1]

The Rebels set out for Perkins' Landing at about 9 p.m. on the evening of May 30. They left Buck's plantation, the head of navigation on the Tensas River, and marched twelve miles out to the landing on the Mississippi River. As the sun rose, McCulloch formed his men in line and advanced.[2] The Federal outpost was held by a single regiment. Far outnumbered by the full brigade under McCulloch, Col. Richard Owen of the all-white 60th Indiana Infantry tried to buy some time with his picket line. While he did so, the remainder of his regiment, with the aid of about three hundred black laborers, built makeshift breastworks out of cotton bales close to the river. The Confederate troops rushed on, into the abandoned camp of the enemy. There they found breakfast still on the fire and began to help themselves. McCulloch quickly reestablished order, and the Southerners continued their advance.[3]

Crossing an open field, the brigade came under fire from a Yankee gunboat. McCulloch ordered most of his infantry to take shelter behind a levee but kept Col. Richard Waterhouse's 19th Texas Infantry in the field to support Capt. William Edgar's artillery. "They did their duty nobly," McCulloch wrote in his report. "Colonel Waterhouse was in front of his regiment, exhibiting coolness and courage worthy of imitation by all officers and men." The men themselves "stood up under the fire like a wall of masonry." Perhaps so, but at least one man in the ranks thought it an unfair fight. E. D. McDaniel later told his wife, "We could not do anything with musketts against the gunnboats I did not like to stand there and be shot at and not get to shoot any not that I am Blood thirsty or want to kill anyone but when I am where they are shooting at me then I want to shoot some myself."[4]

Captain Edgar brought two fieldpieces, known as "6-pounders" for the weight of the solid shot projectile they fired, into action to attack the river transport on which the enemy was trying to make an escape. However, Edgar quickly found himself the underdog in an artillery duel with the Federal iron-clad *Carondelet,* which had come to aid Owen's overwhelmed garrison. Armed with a variety of heavy artillery, the *Carondelet* outgunned Edgar, but, like David meeting Goliath, the Confederate captain was not intimidated. Edgar's guns and the *Carondelet* peppered each other with nearly three hundred shells between them. The ironclad was predictably unaffected, but Edgar's men had nothing to fear either, as almost all of *Carondelet's* shots went far overhead. Despite the noise and bluster of the big guns on the river, McCulloch's Brigade sustained few casualties. Only one man was killed, Capt. Gallatin Smith, a staff officer. More than a year after Walker's Division was organized and left Texas, Smith was the division's first man to die in battle.[5]

While the *Carondelet* blazed away, the transport *Forest Queen* sidled up to the riverbank and evacuated the 60th Indiana. Meanwhile, McCulloch ordered up artillery and infantry reinforcements, and Generals Walker and Taylor had arrived as well. As McCulloch realized his enemy had left, the Rebels began ransacking the Union camp, taking what they could and destroying the rest. Some of the men who had written letters full of foreboding to their loved ones before the battle now glowed with confidence and victory. "If this is all the fear I don't mind a battle," wrote Capt. Elijah Petty. He and others like him would have their braggadocio challenged a week later.[6]

Losses on both sides were light. Only Captain Smith had been killed on the Confederate side, though two other men were wounded, and two more were missing. McCulloch estimated Federal losses at eleven killed and several more wounded.[7] Captain Petty reported that one Yankee soldier had been captured, along with five black men—details that would become more important later. No report from the 60th Indiana has been found.[8]

With the enemy evacuated and the site protected by the gunboat, there was little point for McCulloch to advance farther or occupy the place. In addition, cavalry scouts under Maj. Isaac F. Harrison, who were from the vicinity and would be excellent guides, were nowhere to be found. Late that evening, McCulloch and the rest of Walker's Division would meet up with their wayward cavalry at Bayou Maçon.[9]

The small scrap at Perkins' Landing buoyed the Texans' spirits. If the outcome at Perkins' Landing was any indication of the caliber of the Yankee forces that would oppose them, Walker's Division would soon gain control of the entire western bank of the Mississippi, cutting Grant's supply lines and forcing him to abandon his campaign for Vicksburg. That scenario, however, was a pipe dream. While their men may have been optimistic, both Taylor and Walker were realists. Taylor knew that they could do little to aid Vicksburg. On June 5, his suspicions were confirmed when he discovered that Grant's supplies were arriving in Mississippi up the Yazoo, and most of the Union stockpiles on the west side of the Mississippi River had already been removed to the east.[10] In an undated report, probably written in late June, Walker mentions the futility of the actions on the west bank: "A few weeks previous to our coming, the enemy's operations could have been seriously embarrassed by cutting his line of communication at Richmond, [Louisiana] but the golden opportunity had passed."[11] Nevertheless, Taylor and his superior, Lt. Gen. Edmund Kirby Smith, felt compelled to take some sort of action on behalf of Vicksburg, even if doomed to failure.[12]

Maj. Isaac F. Harrison's 15th Louisiana Cavalry Battalion, whose men hailed from northeastern Louisiana and were serving as scouts for Walker's Division, reported only small Federal detachments guarding the posts along the river. Encouraged by their recent success at Perkins' Landing and anticipating similar easy victories, Walker's men arrived at Richmond, Louisiana, about twenty miles west of Vicksburg, late in the morning on June 6. The men had marched along bayous and through swamps, covering nearly fifty miles in just three days. They battled heat, mosquitoes, rattlesnakes, and water so poor that even the horses refused to drink. Exhausted, they tried to rest despite the growing heat of the day.[13]

Around 2 a.m. on the morning of June 6, 1863, Col. Hermann Lieb, in charge of the Federal outpost at Milliken's Bend while Col. Isaac Shepard was under arrest, conducted a reconnaissance toward Richmond, Louisiana. Two companies of the contentious 10th Illinois Cavalry followed Walnut Bayou, roughly twisting along a route south of Milliken's Bend, while Lieb and his men of the 9th Louisiana progressed generally southwest along the Richmond Road to the railroad depot, three miles out from Richmond, near Tallulah.

When he encountered Confederate pickets at the depot, Lieb calmly retired back toward Milliken's Bend. Meanwhile, members of the 10th Illinois Cavalry engaged portions of Maj. Harrison's Louisiana cavalry near the same location. The two detachments were about the same size, Harrison's force numbering about one hundred, with the Illinoisans mounting about 140 men. Harrison charged first, disrupting the Yankee line, killing eight, and capturing twenty-five men.[14]

A squad of the Illinois cavalrymen came crashing through Lieb's lines during his return to the Bend, the Confederate horsemen hot on their heels. Lieb deployed his regiment and halted the Rebel advance with a single volley. Harrison's troopers fell back to Richmond, and Lieb returned to the Bend. Lieb reported the events to his superior, Brig. Gen. Elias S. Dennis, saying that he thought the Rebels' next move would be to take the bridge over Walnut Bayou. Dennis ordered a detachment of the 23rd Iowa Infantry, which had just returned from escorting Rebel prisoners north, to move upriver from Young's Point to Milliken's Bend in support of Lieb. Dennis also requested assistance from Admiral Porter, who sent the gunboat *Choctaw*.[15]

After the small skirmish between Harrison's cavalry and the probe by Lieb and the 10th Illinois Cavalry, Taylor saw his opportunity and decided to work quickly. He believed Lieb would think Richmond was held only by the cavalry, so splitting up Walker's Division of infantrymen to assault Milliken's Bend and other points on the Mississippi in force would surprise the Yankees.[16]

When Walker's Division arrived in Richmond at 10 a.m. on June 6, they were ordered to fix two days' rations and be ready to march by 6 p.m. that evening, thus avoiding the intense heat of the day. Taylor believed attacking at dawn the next day would lessen the likelihood of defense from gunboats on the river. He instructed Walker to send a brigade each against Young's Point and Milliken's Bend, keeping the third brigade in reserve, six miles out from Richmond. Twenty men from Harrison's cavalry were to serve as scouts for each brigade. After successful strikes against Milliken's Bend and Young's Point, the two columns would advance toward Duckport, midway between the two locations. Walker and his subordinates thought the plan a good one.[17]

Walker assigned McCulloch's brigade the task of capturing the outpost at Milliken's Bend. Brig. Gen. James M. Hawes's brigade would move against Young's Point, and Col. Horace Randal's brigade would remain in reserve. General Walker would remain with Randal's brigade, ready to issue orders as the circumstances required.[18] Although Walker's attack on the river outposts may have been unanticipated by some of the Union forces, Col. George E. Bryant of the 12th Wisconsin, stationed in Mississippi at Grand Gulf, sent an urgent dispatch to Grant's headquarters on June 7: "I am *positively* informed, that *Seven Transports* Crowded with Rebels, under McCullough, Taylor & Walker—a part of whom attacked the force at Pirkins, a week ago—are making their [way] up *'Tansas'* and that they intend to attack Milikins Bend, or failing in that to Capture—a Steam Boat & cross to Miss—The force is 'Six Thousand Strong' estimated at 10'000—*Harrison* was Ordered to join them." Before the ink was even dry on his message, events had already begun to unfold on the Louisiana riverbank.[19]

When Lieb returned to camp around noon after his reconnaissance in the wee morning hours of June 6, he doubled his pickets and sent a squad of mounted infantry out to act as vedettes. The men of the nearby 10th Illinois Cavalry, who normally could be expected to assist by providing vedettes on the outskirts of camp, were nowhere to be found and would take no part in the fight at Milliken's Bend. The African Brigade would be on its own.[20] That day was generally quiet, but Lieb did not expect it to last. The 23rd Iowa Infantry, numbering about 120 men, arrived around dusk but remained on its transport. Lieb ordered the regiments of the African Brigade to be in line of battle by 2 a.m. on June 7.[21]

McCulloch's Brigade left Richmond in the middle of the night on June 6 accompanied by scouts from Harrison's battalion. At about 2:30 a.m. on June 7, Union pickets opened fire on the cavalrymen, driving them back into their own lines. In the darkness and confusion, the Rebel infantry fired upon the retreating horsemen and killed two of their mounts. None of the men were injured.[22] Part of the cavalrymen's good fortune in surviving their own force's fire may have been due to the poor nature of Confederate weaponry. The majority of McCulloch's men carried smoothbore muskets into the fight. These weapons had an effective range of about one hundred yards and shot a .69 caliber ball or a .69 caliber ball with three buckshot—a so-called "buck and ball" cartridge. A few men in Walker's Division, possibly one company in every regiment, carried .577 caliber Enfield rifled-muskets, a far superior weapon, with an effective range of about five hundred yards. Nearly two hundred men in the division carried other inferior weapons, including Colt repeating rifles, Belgian rifles (.70 caliber), and a smattering of Mississippi rifles (.54 caliber). As the Confederates advanced on the Yankee works, they were not much better armed than their opponents.[23]

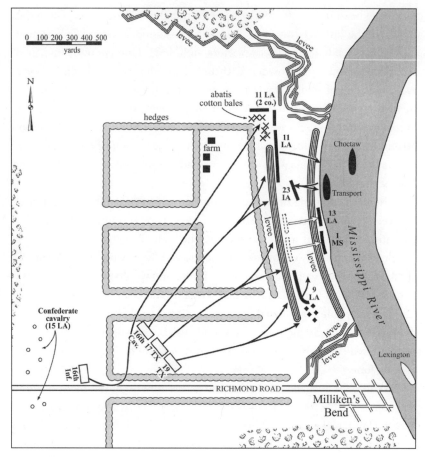

Battle of Milliken's Bend
McCulloch's Brigade, C. S. A. attacks the U. S. African Brigade on June 7, 1863.

After regaining their composure from the cavalry mishap, McCulloch's men moved forward, driving in the Union pickets. The small cavalry detachment from Harrison's battalion guarded the Rebel right. It was still dark, and 2nd Lt. Peter W. Gravis of the 17th Texas Infantry could see only those immediately near him in line. He strained his eyes to make out the Yankees ahead of him but saw nothing.[24] Across the lines in the early morning darkness, Colonel Shepard stared back. Still under arrest and therefore unable to issue orders, he peered across the levee and saw some troops coming from the distant woods. Initially thinking the troops were Federal pickets returning to camp, he soon saw their numbers grow and spread out in a threatening line of battle. The advancing Rebel line under McCulloch anchored its right on the Richmond Road and moved forward.[25]

After the Southerners advanced about a quarter of a mile, Yankee skirmishers opened up with a blaze of fire from behind a thick hedge. McCulloch's force pushed onward, driving back the Union pickets. Six hundred yards on, the Rebels encountered another hedge, with more Union troops behind it, and they again pushed forward. "Thus the fight or skirmishing continued from hedge to hedge and ditch to ditch," wrote McCulloch.[26] The thick hedges caused great disarray in the advancing Confederate lines, forcing them to advance through narrow openings. They had to consolidate their forces into groups, presenting easy and large targets for the enemy. In addition, their route of advance was predictable, confined as it was to the narrow openings in the hedge, and they took heavy fire.[27]

At some point early in the action, more than one astonished Yankee reported that McCulloch's advance was sheltered by a line of "moving breastworks." Mules were being driven ahead of the oncoming Confederates. Although no Southern sources mention deliberately driving mules before them, a few Union soldiers thought it was a calculated and inhumane tactic. What seems more likely, given the circumstances, was that it was a natural outcome of the Rebel advance. Cornwell's memoir makes it clear that mules were routinely used to aid Yankee recruiting expeditions into the countryside. They were also necessary to operate the nearby government-leased plantations. Probably a number of these animals were kept at the post at Milliken's Bend, and as the Rebel line advanced, the frightened animals fled in front of them toward the Union lines.[28]

After passing through the tumult created by the hedges, McCulloch's men struggled back into line. The defenses they now faced were even more formidable—a ten-foot high levee, topped in some places by cotton bales. McCulloch's Brigade stretched out in line of battle with Fitzhugh's 16th Texas Cavalry (Dismounted) on the left, under the command of Lt. Col. Edward P. Gregg, Col. R. T. P. Allen's 17th Texas Infantry in the center, and Col. Richard Waterhouse's 19th Texas Infantry on the right. Col. George Flournoy's 16th Texas Infantry was held in reserve. The Rebel line advanced at an oblique angle upon the far left of the Union defenses and received heavy fire as it assembled for its assault. E. D. McDaniel, a soldier in Waterhouse's regiment, reported that "the musketts was poping worse than any cane brake on fire."[29]

Union forces were arranged behind a levee, and though five regiments would be listed as participants in the battle, none were at full strength. In fact, the 11th Louisiana Infantry, African Descent, had the most men present, counting nearly five hundred among its number, nearly half of a full-strength regiment.[30] It took position on the far right of the Federal line, near an old cross levee topped by felled trees and cotton bales. On the opposite end, anchoring the far left of the Union line, was the 9th Louisiana Infantry, African Descent, numbering slightly less than three hundred men, among them, 1st Lt. David Cornwell, Capt. Corydon Heath, and "Big Jack" Jackson. Filling in the middle of the Union line, from left to right, were about 150 men of the 1st Mississippi, African Descent; roughly one hundred men from the 13th Louisiana Infantry, African Descent;[31] and 125 men of the 23rd Iowa Infantry. The 23rd Iowa, still aboard the transport when the fight began, was the only white regiment present on the Northern side and the only regiment on either side with any substantial combat experience. Lieb would bring roughly the same number of men to the fight as his Southern opponent.[32]

The Union troops behind the levee fired their first volley, causing the Confederate line to waver and sending some men "running in confusion to the rear." Chaplain George G. Edwards of the 11th Louisiana said the Rebel column "trembled" when first fired upon but was rallied by its officers and came on "with yells that would make faint hearts quail." Lieb said the Rebels "came madly on with cries of 'No quarters [sic] for white officers, kill the damned abolitionists, but spare the niggers.'" Second Lt. Matthew Miller, an officer in Lieb's regiment, also said the Rebels came on yelling "No quarters."[33]

The Rebel troops charged the levee, many of them without stopping to reload.[34] One Confederate in Allen's regiment took time to take a bead on a Yankee officer who was yelling to his men, *"give them Hell, give them Hell, give them Hell."* The soldier wrote his father a day later, with satisfaction and precision, "I took deliberate aim at his breast two inches below and to the right of the second button and sent a ball and three buckshot in him. He fell with the word 'Hell' on his lips."[35] Many of the black defenders, due to their unfamiliarity with their weapons, could get off only one or two rounds before the lines of battle closed on each other. The fight erupted into a violent hand-to-hand melee, where both bayonet and musket butt were used—a rare occurrence in Civil War battles.[36]

First Lt. David Cornwell watched the initial attack from his position in reserve with two companies of the 9th Louisiana, just back of the first levee.

Captain Heath and 2nd Lt. Smith were with Company B on the far left of the Union line. Heath took up a musket to aid in the defense, but the Southern forces poured over the levee like a tidal wave. Cornwell saw Heath and a few others nearby cut off, absorbed by the Confederate line as prisoners.[37] Seeing his comrades overwhelmed, Cornwell sprang into action, yelling, "Now bounce them Bullies," as he led his men forward. "Big Jack" Jackson lunged ahead into the melee, smashing his rifle butt into any Rebel within range. Within moments, he held only the barrel of his weapon; the wooden stock had shattered in his hands. Cornwell saw Jack stabbed multiple times by bayonets, but his friend did not slow down. Because of his size and his fury, Jack became a special target for the Confederates. He was soon killed by a bullet to the head. Not long after, a bullet struck Cornwell's right arm, shattering the bone near his shoulder, but he stayed in action. He considered himself lucky—had the bullet gone an inch to either side, it would have entered his chest and killed him.[38]

Meanwhile, the Texans overwhelmed the Yankees on the levee, "carrying it instantly," and inflicted many casualties. Joseph P. Blessington of the 16th Texas Infantry said the Yankees "stampeded pell-mell over the levee, in great terror and confusion. Our troops followed after them, bayoneting them by hundreds." John M. Wright of the 16th Texas Dismounted Cavalry, agreed. "We made it hot for those negroes. There was not one left to tell the tale." Peter Gravis with the 17th Texas Infantry later recalled the scene with an exhilaration borne of battle—and a warrior's memory: "We . . . turned loose our war dogs, and I tell you, my readers, they howled! We clubbed guns, bayoneted, cut with the sword, until the enemy fled helter, skelter."[39]

The plucky soldier who had just sent a Yankee officer to hell recounted, "We charged the Levy and fought Bayonet crossing Bayonet for full one minute. My antagonist was a huge Negro who fired and missed me and then clubbed his gun and tried to strike me. I stapped [stabbed?] my Bayonet through him twice he then struck at me. I thrust up my gun in him to ward off the blow." The black soldier crashed his musket butt onto the Southerner's shoulder, nearly breaking his shoulder blade. The Rebel fought back: "I then sent my Bayonet clear through him and fired into him as Div[ine] service . . . which blew him all to pieces."[40]

McCulloch praised his men in their deadly work: "There were several instances in this charge where the enemy crossed bayonets with us or were shot down at the muzzle of the musket. No charge was ever more gallantly made than this, and the enemy were not only driven from the levee, but were followed into their camp, where many of them were killed."[41] He had mixed reviews for his enemy, including some surprising praise. "This charge was resisted by the negro portion of the enemy's force with considerable obstinacy," he conceded, "while the white or true Yankee portion ran like whipped curs almost as soon as the charge was ordered."[42]

The Iowans were not the cowards McCulloch made them out to be, however. They were simply overwhelmed. As the first shots were being fired, the men of the 23rd Iowa were roused off their transport. "We did not think they were in very heavy force or very near," wrote one soldier, and the regiment methodically disembarked: "We went out to within about twenty steps of the levee, and the front halted till the rear would get off the boat." The colonel rode over to the breastworks, "and to his surprise saw the rebels 200 yards away, four regiments deep." The 23rd Iowa was still struggling into line when the opposing forces clashed on top of the first levee. Col. Samuel L. Glasgow shouted desperately to his men, "Double quick! For God's sake! They are right on us!" but the regiment's left flank was shattered. "We had been in the ditch about three minutes when the negroes gave way on our left and let the rebels in," William M. Littell wrote. "The rebs were on top of them," he recalled. "It was a very hot place . . . They fired a terrible volley right down the ditch and were preparing to give us another when the Col. ordered us to fall back to the next breastworks that run at right angles with the first. We did so when they flanked us again, and we had to fall back to the river bank."[43]

Pvt. Samuel H. Glasgow, not to be confused with his colonel of nearly identical name, was still ill at Young's Point and reported the battle secondhand for his wife. As the black troops were being flanked on the Union left, rolling up the line, the Confederate advance fell hard upon the left of the Iowans. "That left the Old 23 to Fight against 3000 of the Enemy," he wrote, "but they stood there and fought them hand to hand untill [sic] the Colonel ordered them to fall back . . . they said he had to order them the third time before they would retreat." The last man standing from Company B "knocked down 3 rebs with the Butt of his Gun and then run his Bayonet through them," and "some of our men and Rebs lay side by side with their Bayonets through one another." Acting Rear Admiral Porter may have been referring to the same company when he wrote: "A company of the Iowa regiment stood at their post until they were slaughtered to a man, killing an equal number of rebels."[44]

William M. Littell likewise would tell his wife that the entire detachment of the 23rd Iowa—about 120 men strong—faced the entire force of Rebels, reportedly numbering 2,500 men. Littell dismissed the men of the African Brigade entirely, since they "had just drawn their guns the evening before and did not know how to use them." His frustration was palpable. "They did not know how to load their guns, did not know where their caps were. Three of them came to me for caps. I said, 'My God men have you no caps,' one of them answered, 'Massa we dont know where they are' I showed them and each one had his cap pouch full."[45]

All firsthand accounts from men of the 23rd Iowa mention sharp fighting, and their statements are backed up by grim casualty numbers. Lt. Cmdr. Frank M. Ramsay of the *Choctaw* also stated that the Hawkeyes held their ground. But the officers of the African Brigade universally claimed the Iowans had fled the field, allowing the spearhead of the Confederate attack to pierce the Union line and causing enormous casualties among the African American regiments. Even Confederate accounts state that the white troops fled, and it is difficult to reconcile the two versions of events. However, it seems likely that Littell's account is reasonably accurate. The Iowans were probably just forming their line of battle when the close-quarter fighting surged their way, and they were forced to fall back toward the riverbank, after a momentary attempt to hold at one of the cross levees. These men were experienced veterans. Finding their position immediately untenable, they withdrew to find a stronger position; at this point, the only option left would have been the riverbank, which formed a natural breastwork. A regiment that ran away would not have sustained such high casualties. The two regiments to the 23rd's immediate left—the 1st Mississippi and the 13th Louisiana—had shockingly low casualties. It seems much more likely that these two very small units of the African Brigade may have been the ones who fled, leaving the 23rd Iowa in an immediately un-sustainable position. This theory gains further credence when one compares Lieb's statement of the deployment of his forces—in which the 13th Louisiana would have been on the 23rd Iowa's immediate left—and the statement of 2nd Lt. Matthew Miller of Company I, 9th Louisiana, who remarked that the right of his company was adjacent to the 23rd Iowa. Miller, too, says the Iowans fled, but one wonders what became of the two other regiments deployed be-tween the two units at the outset of the fight.[46]

The memories of the action lasted a lifetime, whether one wore blue or gray. Thomas F. Mays of the 17th Texas would recall in 1913 the events of fifty years earlier. Though in 1863 he was "a beardless boy," he remembered the thick hedgerows and "that scene of carnage and gore . . . as if it had happened only yesterday." He recalled that Colonel Allen was "shot through the arm and shoulder, and had to retire," which led some Yankees to think he had been killed. Mays mentioned some of his friends who died that day but stated that once the regiment reached the Yankee breastworks, "we never lost another man." "In less than thirty minutes the victory was ours," he boasted, probably referring to the initial breach of the Union line. Most of the white Union officers "as the boys used to say 'Sidaddled' [sic] . . . and left their poor negro comrades to their own fate. We killed 750 negroes in the trenches and the blood ran in some places several inches deep. A few of them would jump up and run, but they fell with a bullet before they went very far. I think that very few, if any, escaped alive." Richard H. "Dick" Tutt of the 19th Texas Infantry boasted years later that his regiment was credited with killing "1000 negroes in eight or ten minutes."[47]

E. D. McDaniel's company of the 19th Texas Infantry was detailed as pickets for the advancing graycoats early in the fight and after the initial contact, pulled back to serve as rear guards. Still, "it was the most oneasy time I ever beheld," he would write his wife, more than a month later. Though not involved in the vicious hand-to-hand fighting at the Yankee breastworks, McDaniel's company was still exposed to fire: "There [sic] balls whistled all around us but thank the good lord none of us got hurt."[48]

On the Union side, Chaplain George G. Edwards of the 11th Louisiana estimated three hundred men killed in just ten minutes during the Rebel onslaught. Second Lt. Miller of the 9th Louisiana witnessed the annihilation of his entire company. Out of thirty-three men present in Company I, nearly half were killed and almost all of the survivors were seriously wounded. One man had six wounds, and most had at least two. Miller himself was wounded twice by bayonets, though only slightly. He grew heartsick over the scene: "I never more wish to hear the expression, 'The niggers wont fight.'" The bodies of sixteen of his slain men, not to mention those who still lived, provided the proof to discredit such a statement. In an attempt to provide some grim perspective, Miller wrote that it was "the worse I was ever engaged in, not even excepting Shiloh."[49]

Colonel Shepard, under arrest and prohibited from issuing orders, "stood for the encouragement of the blacks, side by side with them in the trenches, as long as to stand was possible," and reported "muskets were clubbed, and bayonets used freely." Colonel Lieb, who commanded the African Brigade that day, described the hand-to-hand fighting as "desperate," but his black soldiers displayed "unprecedented bravery," resisting the charge until Rebel numbers overwhelmed them.[50]

The Union line gave way on the far left, and the Rebels brought down a devastating enfilading fire all along the Yankee line. Lieb said the oncoming Southerners took special aim at the Yankee officers, and his casualty report bore this out. The black line crumbled, and some of the men took shelter in the camps behind wagons, boxes, and other camp equipage. Others "doggedly contested every inch of the ground" as they were pushed back to the river.[51]

The Confederates followed in pursuit, assaulting a second levee along the riverbank which sheltered the remainder of the Union force. Taylor had given Walker "strict orders . . . to drive the enemy into the river, so as to permit no time for escape or re-enforcements," and McCulloch's men had every intention of obeying. But as the Rebels topped the second levee, the blue defenders would not budge—in part because they had nowhere else to go. The far right of the Federal line, tenaciously held by a portion of the 11th Louisiana Infantry, African Descent, still held firm on the first levee, and some of these men were able to train their guns on the rest of the advancing Rebel forces, firing into the side and rear of the Confederate line. Straight ahead of the Texans, the guns of the Choctaw were brought to bear, prompting the Confederates to beat a hasty retreat to the landward side of the first levee. Using this as a breastwork, they continued their fire. It was about 4 a.m.[52]

The Choctaw, under Lt. Cmdr. Frank M. Ramsay, arrived near Milliken's Bend at 3:15 a.m., when it was flagged down by an officer on shore, who shouted that his pickets were under attack. Twenty minutes later, Ramsay opened fire with his one-hundred-pounder rifled and nine-inch guns. Ramsay reported that the Union troops then broke immediately, except for the 23rd Iowa, and sought shelter at the riverbank. Ramsay could not see the Confederate forces, due to the high banks of the river, and had to rely on instructions from the shore to direct his firing. The Choctaw continued firing throughout the morning.[53]

As the Union forces tumbled back to the second levee and the riverbank, Colonel Flournoy's 16th Texas Infantry tried to gain the right of the Federal line, where the 11th Louisiana was making its stubborn stand. At some point during Flournoy's movement, the regiment began receiving occasional fire from some farm buildings on the regiment's left. Fearing the Federals might be attempting to turn the entire Rebel brigade's left, Capt. George T. Marold was sent with his company to investigate. Marold's men soon captured nineteen black men. Although certainly armed, it is not known if the African Americans were in Federal uniform, since at least some recruits had not yet been properly clothed. It is possible that some of these men were still wearing the clothes they wore as field hands. If so, these circumstances could, at least in theory, legitimize claims by Confederates that they fought "armed slaves in insurrection."[54]

One member of Flournoy's regiment, Pvt. Anton Shultz, got out of a tight spot by using his wits and was hailed a hero. Shultz was a musician detailed to assist Dr. William Cocke, the regimental surgeon. Shultz took Dr. Cocke's horse to look for some water at a nearby house, when he suddenly found himself surrounded "by a company of armed negroes in full United States uniform, commanded by a Yankee captain, who took him prisoner."[55] Shultz kept his wits about him, though. When the captain asked him where the main Confederate force was, he pointed to the southwest—a completely different direction from where the fight was going on. The captain thought to try to make it to the transport on the river. Shultz, the helpful and compliant captive, informed him that it would be easy to do so—and he would even show the way! "The Yankee suffered himself to be humbugged by our German youth, or young man, and he led him and his entire company of 49 negroes through small gaps in thick hedges until they found themselves within 60 yards of Colonel Allen's regiment, who took them all prisoners without the fire of a gun," McCulloch proudly reported.[56]

McCulloch later suggested that both Marold and Shultz be compensated for their heroics by having their pick from the captured slaves. "These negroes had doubtless been in the possession of the enemy, and would have been a clear loss to their owners but for Captain Marold," McCulloch wrote. "Should they be forfeited to the Confederate States or returned to their owners, I would regard it nothing but fair to give to Captain Marold one or two of the best of them." McCulloch recommended Shultz have the same privilege. "If such things are admissible, I think he should have a choice boy from among these fellows to cook and wash for him and his mess during the war, and to work for him as long as the negro lives." Furthermore, because "the horse of Dr. Cocke was lost in the praiseworthy effort to procure water for our wounded, another of these fellows might be well and properly turned over to him to compensate him for his loss."[57]

McCulloch's statements are particularly revealing for what they say about the fate of captured black Union soldiers. His report expresses no hint of bitter

animosity or insurrectionary paranoia. He does not shout for blood and vengeance. Instead, very matter-of-factly, he suggests that the slaves be returned
to servitude, given as rewards to Marold, Shultz, and Dr. Cocke, and the remainder returned to their former owners or put to work for the Confederacy.
Not once does he ever advocate or hint that they should be executed—a fate
that many Northern newspapers, officers, and politicians fully expected and
reported—possibly without any substantiation whatsoever.

If McCulloch's sentiments are any indication of the overall Confederate
feeling toward captured blacks in uniform, then it is clear that instead of being
executed as "insurrectionists," these former bondsmen were to be returned to
a lifetime of servitude. Decades later, Beverly G. Goodrich would write to the
Confederate Veteran magazine of a resentment that still smoldered: "With their
usual disregard of the truth, the Yankees accused us of shouting 'No quarter,'
but the Sixteenth [Texas] Infantry captured an entire company of negroes."[58]

While these captures were taking place somewhere on the Confederate
left, the bulk of Flournoy's regiment and a portion of the 11th Louisiana continued battling it out near the same vicinity.[59] Pvt. Joseph P. Blessington believed
his commander to be "entirely ignorant of the plan of attack." Blessington
reported that during the opening phase of the battle, the 16th took a position
on the far Confederate right. When the rest of the brigade advanced across the
first levee, Colonel Flournoy felt compelled to follow, despite a thick hedge
that blocked the way forward. After struggling through the hedge, the regiment dressed ranks, fixed bayonets, and prepared to charge. Flournoy ordered
an advance at the double-quick. In the midst of this movement and despite his
protests, he suddenly received orders from McCulloch to move his regiment—
still on the double-quick—to the far left of the Confederate line. Apparently
McCulloch was fearful of being outflanked on his left, and Flournoy obeyed.
McCulloch personally observed the regiment's new position and ordered a
number of men detailed from each company to serve as sharpshooters across
the top of the levee. It was at this time, wrote Blessington, that the regiment
began receiving scattered fire from the rear, and Flournoy sent Marold's company to investigate.[60]

Although Private Blessington claimed his commander was ignorant of
the battle plan, it was probably his uninformed position as a private in the
ranks that led him to that conclusion. McCulloch indicated in his report that
Flournoy's regiment was deliberately held back from the initial charge. When
the 16th Texas Infantry finally came into action on the Confederate left, it

found its advance stubbornly blocked by two companies of the 11th Louisiana, posted behind cotton bales and part of an old levee. The precise location of this levee is unclear. Colonel Lieb, in his report, makes it sound like it was part of or near the second levee, since he tells about the shattering of the first line of the Union defense before he tells about the Confederate advance on the Union right. Private Blessington's narrative makes it sound like it is an extension of the first levee. General Walker's map places a cross levee at either end of the Union line, roughly perpendicular to the two levees that ran parallel to the river. The cross levee on the right of the Union line is probably where the 11th Louisiana was posted. Walker's map also indicates some buildings not far from this location. As the Confederate forces advanced against this cross levee, these buildings were on either the regiment's left or rear, depending on the precise maneuvers used to attack the 11th Louisiana's position. These buildings are almost certainly the buildings referred to in McCulloch's report, where the captures by Captain Marold's company and the crafty Private Shultz took place.[61]

McCulloch reported that Flournoy's men took and held the position on the levee under intense fire from the Yankee gunboat, but low casualties in the 16th Infantry cast doubt on this report. Blessington also does not indicate that the position was taken. In fact, gunboats may have prevented an advance of the Rebel regiment. Lt. Col. Cyrus Sears of the 11th Louisiana reported heavy casualties in his regiment caused by Federal shells from the river falling short. Despite being pummeled by their own gunboat's heavy artillery and facing an entire regiment on their front, all Union accounts state that the tiny force of two companies from the 11th Louisiana tenaciously held their position. Indeed, theirs was the only part of the Union line which stood firm throughout the entire fight. Posted behind an old levee reinforced with cotton bales, the bluecoats held off the Confederate advances until midmorning, when the Rebels at last withdrew.[62]

The *Choctaw* continued firing its heavy guns throughout the engagement, though Ramsay reported dissatisfaction with some of his ammunition for his one-hundred-pounder gun. "Every one of our 5-second shells commenced turning over as soon as it left the gun," he complained. This might be one reason some of the shells fell short, hitting men of Sears's regiment and others. By contrast, Ramsay reported, shells captured from the enemy at Haynes' Bluff were "superior to all the shells that have been furnished this vessel for the 100-pounder . . . Not one of them turned over, and only one or two failed to explode." No problems were reported with the shells for the nine-inch gun.[63]

Around 8:30 a.m., Ramsay reported the Confederates in retreat. He be-lieved the *Choctaw*'s presence was instrumental in saving the day: "Had not a gunboat been present the enemy would have captured everything." Late to the fight, the timberclad *Lexington* arrived around 9 a.m. and joined in, throwing twenty-four rounds after the Rebels, though it ceased firing an hour later.[64] Most Confederate accounts agree with Ramsay that the fighting broke off around 10 a.m. Despite the navy's heavy artillery and Ramsay's claims to the contrary, Lieb reported that the battle did not peter out until much later in the morning, about noon. Chaplain Edwards of the 11th Louisiana reported the action subsiding around 11:30 a.m., and a Rebel soldier likewise said that his regiment did not leave the field until noon. The discrepancies between Ramsay's account and others may have been because the Confederate troops withdrew from the immediate vicinity of the riverbank and the main assault had ceased. The comparative quiet after the early morning's fury probably led Ramsay to think that Confederate forces had left entirely. Instead, scattered remnants of the Yankee infantry harassed the Rebel withdrawal, although by this time, both sides were spent. It also seems likely that Southern forces may have withdrawn but not yet left the field entirely, as they rested and waited for reinforcements.[65]

By the time the fighting ceased, the thermometer measured "95 degrees in the shade." It had been about seven hours since the first shots were fired, and McCulloch's men had been on the move since before midnight. The men of the African Brigade had been on high alert for just as long. Exhaustion was setting in for both sides.[66] Sometime, probably late in the morning but before disengaging, McCulloch called on Walker for reinforcements, but by the time a courier galloped to Walker's headquarters and Randal's Brigade marched out to Milliken's Bend, it was too late. Walker found McCulloch's men in-capable of further action due to exhaustion, the heat, and a lack of water. Randal's Brigade would have been forced to renew the attack by itself, and Walker believed the enemy had been reinforced by several troop transports and gunboats by this time. "Success would be an inadequate compensation" for the number of additional lives that would have been lost, he felt, so he called off any further attacks. Walker sent the wounded to the rear, rested the men for the afternoon, and then started back to Richmond "in the cool of the evening."[67]

Meanwhile, Walker informed Taylor that an advance to Duckport was now impossible. Taylor disagreed and was sorely disappointed in Walker's execution of his mission. Taylor sniped, "Had common vigor and judgment been displayed, the work would all have been completed by 8 a.m." He complained, "I discovered too late that the officers and men of this division were possessed of a dread of gunboats such as pervaded our people at the commencement of the war."[68]

To be fair, McCulloch had no supporting artillery at Milliken's Bend; only two artillery pieces were with Walker in reserve, and these were certainly no match for the heavy guns of an ironclad, though the Confederate artillery had already demonstrated their pluck at Perkins' Landing the week before. Taylor probably thought that the gunboats posed no real threat, particularly in close-quarter fighting like at Milliken's Bend, since they would be prevented from firing due to fear of hitting their own troops. It also seems likely that fire from the gunboats would fall far inland, as it did at Perkins' Landing, and overshoot the troops battling it out on the riverbank. The high bank due to the low river at Milliken's Bend also meant the naval gunners would be firing blind, presenting even less of a hazard to the assaulting troops.

What Taylor overlooked, however, and Walker failed to emphasize was that McCulloch's men had received a steady pounding from the huge guns of the *Choctaw* for seven hours. Continuing to fight under this kind of barrage—even if most of the shells fell short into Federal lines or overshot their mark and fell harmlessly in the Confederate rear—nevertheless took courage and commitment on the part of officers and men. This commitment to the task at hand is made more apparent when one considers the Texans had passed through the horrors of bloody hand-to-hand combat early in the fight and certainly had not faced anything like this kind of a defense from their opponents before. Perkins' Landing a week earlier had been a frolic compared to the bloodbath at Milliken's Bend. The brigade and the stubborn blue-clad defenders continued fighting throughout the morning, until it was simply impossible to continue any longer. In truth, it was exhaustion, as much as the gunboats, that forced McCulloch's hand.[69]

D. E. Young of the 17th Texas would have disagreed with Taylor's assessment, too. Gunboats held no fear for him. He put the matter in context: "i had ruther fite A [dozen?] gunboats than to charge one breast work." The gunboats "throde shell and shot at us too but tha dun no damege to us tha kill too men." In contrast, the assault on the Union line came at a terrible cost. "Hour compiney went in withe 41 Men and lost 19 i dont see how we kept from all being kill," he told his wife.[70] Like him, others who survived the fight were genuinely stunned. On the Union side, Maj. William Cotton of the 11th Louisiana "was in the thickest of the fight" but escaped with only "a few bullet-holes in his clothes." Lt. Matthew Miller of the 9th Louisiana felt especially lucky despite two relatively minor bayonet wounds. Many of his comrades had died from bayonets and clubbed muskets during the vicious close-quarter fighting. He marveled, "I cannot tell how it was that I escaped."[71]

Others were not so lucky. Lt. Jonathan W. Ayers of Company K, 9th Louisiana, though wounded, was fished out of the river by the crew of the *Choctaw*. Probably after the navy guns ceased firing around 10 a.m., Ensign Ezra Beaman took the boat's cutters and brought about twenty of the wounded aboard, including Capt. Thomas Blondin of the 11th Louisiana, other officers and privates, and two "civilian prisoners." Aboard ship, Acting Assistant Surgeon Eugene P. Robbins tended to their wounds and injuries. At 10:45, Captain Blondin died, and shortly after noon, his body was sent ashore for burial. Later that afternoon, the prisoners and all of the wounded except two lieutenants were transferred to the steamer *J. S. Pringle*. Lt. Charles Clark, quartermaster of the 9th Louisiana, died of his wounds at 7 p.m., and carpenters aboard the *Choctaw* promptly went to work to build him a coffin.[72]

White soldiers, both Federals and Confederates who fell within Union lines, were sent to Van Buren General Hospital at Milliken's Bend, where Surgeon Joseph B. Whiting of the 33rd Wisconsin Infantry was in charge. Among the many men admitted on June 7 were some members of the 23rd Iowa. The number and severity of their casualties would seem to refute accusations that their regiment ran away, leaving the black troops to fend for themselves. Among the wounded was Henry Buson, who had his right arm amputated and died three days later. Henry Bittman of Company K had a head fracture, John S. Walker of Company B was shot in the face, and William W. Shoemaker was shot in the thigh. Lambert B. Gardner, shot in the hip and arm, died of his wounds a week later.[73]

Nearby, Contraband General Hospital treated most of the wounded African American soldiers. Established to aid sick laborers on government plantations, including men, women and children, the hospital usually cared for about twenty-five persons in late May. On June 6, it held thirty-two patients, but the following day its census swelled to 146 with the influx of wounded soldiers. Many of the men died from their wounds in the weeks and months that followed, some lingering into the deep heat of August before succumbing. Charles Evans of Company D, 9th Louisiana, must have been one of the men wounded by so-called friendly fire from the gunboats, since the boats were the only artillery present at the fight. A shell struck him in the spine, paralyzing him from the waist down. He died a few weeks later. William Jeffreys of the 11th Louisiana had both arms amputated. Numerous men were admitted with "contusions" and "compound fractures," though the surgeon did not make explicit mention of any bayonet wounds.[74]

The body of John Jackson, a black enlisted man of Company G, 9th Louisiana, who survived the ordeal of battle, testified to the nature of the fighting. Early records state he was wounded in the right arm, twice in the head, and in the thigh, which was fractured by a clubbed musket. A surgeon who examined him for his medical discharge said he had a severe scalp wound from a bullet, had been bayonetted in the right breast, and had his right arm broken by a blow from a musket. Though descriptions varied, it is clear that this man was in the thick of the fight and suffered a number of serious wounds. Jackson returned to his regiment about six months after the battle, serving as assistant company cook, but his wounds never fully healed, and he was discharged in late 1864.[75] Among the officers of the 9th Louisiana, Colonel Lieb was severely wounded in the thigh, and the surgeon was unable to remove the bullet. David Cornwell was severely wounded in the arm, where a bullet fractured a bone and lodged deep in his triceps. The doctor expected him to be back in active service at the end of two months.[76]

At first left for dead "in the ditch at the rifle pits," 1st Lt. William A. Skillen of the 9th Louisiana nevertheless survived. Decades later, Cornwell would cite a source that credited Skillen with taking on five Rebel soldiers at once: "He killed or wounded three of them before he was himself struck down. He was bayoneted in several places, his skull fractured with a musket butt, and several shots were fired into his body. But in spite of all of this he lived, being one of the worst wounded men who survived during the war." Lieb would testify later, "I considered it at the time all but a miracle that Lieut. W. A. Skillen could survive his many injuries."[77]

Later that day, Union acting rear admiral David Dixon Porter of the U.S. Navy arrived on the flagship *Black Hawk* and surveyed the battlefield. He estimated the number of Confederate dead at eighty and gave a vivid description of the scene: "I . . . saw quite an ugly sight. The dead negroes lined the ditch inside of the parapet, or levee, and were mostly shot on the top of the head. In front of them, close to the levee, lay an equal number of rebels, stinking in the sun . . . They were miserable looking wretches." Later historians would read Porter's description of the dead Negroes and conclude that they had been "cowering," but the dead Rebels in front of them cast doubt on such a claim. The gruesome scene convinced Porter that the black troops had "stood at their post like men." Indeed, the nature of their wounds would indicate this was so. Standing behind a breastwork, firing their rifles, only their heads and the uppermost parts of their torsos would have been exposed. Had they been cowering, they would have been stooping and cringing behind the levee, fully protected. Their heavy losses, and that of their opponent, testified that both sides had fought with courage and fury.[78]

Despite being the defenders, protected by levees as breastworks, Federal losses were startling. The inexperience of the men of the African Brigade, coupled with the flanking of the Union line, was devastating. The most accurate reports would tally 492 men killed, wounded, or missing. The entire defending force counted 1,148 men present for duty that morning, resulting in a total loss for the brigade of 43 percent. Even if one excludes the large number of missing, the losses in killed and wounded still come in at 360, or 31 percent, a heavy loss, even by Civil War standards.[79]

Among the African Brigade, the 9th Louisiana Infantry was the hardest hit. Its officer corps, including experienced white first sergeants, was decimated, with fifteen men either killed or wounded. Captain Heath of Company B, 9th Louisiana, was taken prisoner and, as of June 8, the day of Lieb's report, was said to be "in the negro prison at Richmond." Another white officer, Elisha DeWitt, captain of Company I, was also missing. Of the African American enlisted men, there were sixty killed, ninety-eight wounded, and twenty-one missing. Total losses for the 9th Louisiana, according to Lieb's figures, were 195. This was a loss of 68 percent, giving the 9th Louisiana the highest-ranking percentage losses of any African American unit during the entire war. Furthermore, its percentage killed comes in at 23 percent—exceeding the 19 percent sustained by the famous 1st Minnesota at Gettysburg. The total number of officers and men killed in action for the 9th Louisiana was sixty-six, the highest number for any regiment in a single action during the entire Vicksburg campaign.[80]

In the 11th Louisiana Infantry, the losses were less severe but still striking. Four officers were killed, eight wounded, and among the African American enlisted men, twenty-four were killed and fifty-eight wounded. Over one hundred men were missing, with probably most of these accounted for in the two major captures that took place on the Union right. Bringing 482 into battle, this regiment sustained a loss of 42 percent from all causes. Capt. James P. Hall's Company F is a good example of the devastation. On the morning of June 7, fifty-eight privates reported for duty. The day after the battle, there were only twenty-eight.[81]

The other units of the African Brigade suffered minimal losses. Between the 13th Louisiana Infantry and the 1st Mississippi Infantry, there were only two killed, twenty-six wounded, and three missing. Their small losses probably indicate that they fled to the riverbank and took shelter there, while both the regiments on the brigade's flanks—the 9th and 11th Louisiana (left and right, respectively) suffered horribly. In addition, the small losses among the 13th Louisiana and the 1st Mississippi, even though they were initially posted next to the Iowa regiment, which sustained heavy losses, seems to provide further proof that these two regiments must have fallen back quickly, leaving the Iowans to fend for themselves.[82]

The all-white veterans of the 23rd Iowa arrived in line toward the center of the Yankee defenses just as the crushing weight of the Confederate attack crumbled the Union left. Rumors would circulate that they put up no resistance and ran for their lives, but their casualty figures show they were in the thick of the fight. The 23rd Iowa entered the fight with about 120 men. Twenty-three men were killed, and about forty-two were wounded. In terms of raw numbers, its losses at the Bend nearly equaled the casualties it had sustained just a few weeks earlier at the Big Black River in Mississippi, where it began the fight with nearly twice as many men. At Milliken's Bend, the regiment lost an incredible 54 percent from all causes, with *no* missing men. The percentage of men killed in action at Milliken's Bend is 19 percent—equal to the percentage killed in battle of the 1st Minnesota at Gettysburg. Surely, such grim accounting demonstrates that the 23rd Iowa must have fought stubbornly at Milliken's Bend, despite rumors to the contrary.[83]

A few weeks after the fight, Colonel Shepard submitted his own figures for the brigade. His numbers vary somewhat from those of Lieb's account, though it is difficult to make precise comparisons since Shepard broke his numbers down by race and rank. Still, it is noteworthy that by mid-June, many of the missing men had undoubtedly returned or were accounted for. Shepard states only ninety-seven enlisted men were still missing, compared to more than twice that amount reported shortly after the battle. Of that number, sixty men were "known" to be prisoners, most of them from the two large captures that took place on the Union right. This leaves about thirty men unaccounted for.

It seems likely that at least some of the remainder who were still missing may have simply deserted. Nelson Gibbs, Isom Lee, and Thomas Watkins of the 11th Louisiana did, and there were probably others.[84]

Among the officers, Shepard reported that out of forty-nine men, seven died on the battlefield, fourteen were wounded, and three were taken prisoner—a loss of fifty percent. Shepard also tallied the losses among the five white first sergeants, one for each regiment present that day—three of them were killed, and one was wounded, leaving only one man unscathed.[85]

Confederate losses, though substantial, were not nearly as severe. For his entire brigade, McCulloch reported "44 killed, 130 wounded, and 10 missing." Many of the wounded were not expected to recover. A sampling of men from the 16th Texas Cavalry (Dismounted) shows the variety and severity of wounds. For instance, William R. Brinley had his leg amputated, Jonathan Huff had a bayonet wound in his arm, William McWhorter was shot through the shoulder, David Ramby lost his leg, Frank Parsley had his leg broken, and P. Finus Tweedle was wounded in the lungs and was dying. Several of the missing men from the 19th Texas were wounded and being treated at Van Buren Hospital, within Yankee lines. Capt. Samuel J. P. McDowell of Company K, 17th Texas Infantry, reported his company of just thirty-nine men lost half its number in killed and wounded. His regiment suffered the highest losses of the brigade, accounting for nearly half of the entire Confederate losses.[86]

The Confederates evacuated most of their wounded, and established a field hospital in some slave cabins on the road back to Richmond. Regimental and division surgeons went to work, and the medical corps of Randal's Brigade was drafted to assist.[87] Second Lt. Peter W. Gravis of the 17th Texas was shaken by what he saw: "It was a horrible sight after the battle to see the arms and legs amputated at the field hospital, and the suffering wounded pleading for help; the dying praying for mercy." George T. Boardman of the 16th Texas Infantry straggled behind the main forces due to his sore feet and missed the fighting, but he got a grim look at its outcome. Boardman aided in unloading ambulances and lifting men from the operating table, where he saw "wounds in every conceivable form and character." The situation was made even worse by the intense heat.[88]

Joseph P. Blessington recalled the scene with horror a decade after the fact: "So fearful, so horrible are the scenes, that, long after you leave the place, perhaps haunting you to the verge of life, the screams of the wounded, the groans of the dying will ring in your ears." He shook them off by remembering those who gave him inspiration. One youth in an ambulance hailed his fellow, shouting faintly with what strength he had, "They have broken my thigh, but it is in a glorious cause." Another man, shot in the face but undaunted, called out with determination: "I will be at them again."[89]

Like his men, McCulloch was stunned. "In proportion to the number [wounded,] more are severe and fewer slight than I have ever witnessed among the same number in my former military experience." Although McCulloch had served as a Texas Ranger, fought Indians, and was a Mexican War veteran, his combat experience in protracted military engagements was relatively minimal. For him, as for many of his men, the scene at Milliken's Bend must have come as a gory awakening. Reviewing his losses, the general mourned, "My loss is truly deplorable, and my very heart sickens at its contemplation."[90]

McCulloch tallied 185 killed, wounded, and missing. Two regiments, Allen's 17th Texas Infantry and Fitzhugh's 16th Texas Cavalry (Dismounted) under Lt. Col. Edward P. Gregg, were especially hard hit, suffering more than three-fourths of the casualties for the entire brigade. Walker also estimated Confederate losses at nearly two hundred killed and wounded. However, by the time Taylor made his report, only twenty men were listed killed and just eighty wounded. Taylor either minimized McCulloch's losses, or some of those initially thought killed or wounded made their way back to Confederate lines. It seems likely that McCulloch's figures are the more accurate, given the sheer violence of the fighting.[91]

Although commanders on the same side gave varied casualty reports about their own losses, estimates of enemy casualties were even more inaccurate. McCulloch came in with the wildest estimate. He cautioned, "It is true that no certain or satisfactory estimate could be made of the loss of the enemy," but he continued with certainty, "I know, from the dead and wounded that I saw scattered over the field in the rear of the levee, and those upon and immediately behind it, it must have been over a thousand." General Walker's report put estimated Federal losses at about eight hundred killed and wounded, still a gross exaggeration, more than double the actual losses incurred by the Yankees.[92]

Lieb, in turn, magnified Confederate losses, reporting that McCulloch lost over one hundred killed and "a large number wounded," most of whom were evacuated from the field by the Southerners. Chaplain Edwards of the 11th Louisiana thought Confederate losses in killed and wounded must have been more than seven hundred. He theorized that Rebel losses must have been higher than Union losses because the bluecoats were protected behind breastworks during the initial moments of the battle, while the Confederates were organizing their assault on open ground. Including the pummeling of the Southern troops by Yankee gunboats, Edwards was confident that more than two hundred Rebels had died, and four or five hundred men had been wounded.[93]

Lieb also erroneously reported that "Colonel Allen of the tenth Texas" was among the killed, an error that Dennis would repeat in his report, though he attributed Allen to the 16th Texas. Colonel Allen, of the 17th Texas Infantry, was indeed seriously wounded but remained with his regiment. In a similar manner, Charles A. Dana wrote Secretary of War Stanton on June 10 that among the 130 Rebel dead buried on the field was General McCulloch, who died of his wounds. McCulloch survived the fight, unharmed.[94]

While both sides magnified the losses inflicted on the enemy, they also exaggerated the number of troops they faced. Lieb reported that McCulloch had a brigade of infantry and about two hundred cavalry, "nearly treble our number with two brigades in reserve." It is unclear what led Lieb to think two brigades were in reserve, unless scouts spotted the Rebels leaving Richmond that morning before Walker split his forces. Similarly, an early report observing Harrison's cavalry, before they were split up among the brigades, might also have led Lieb to think more Rebel cavalrymen were present.[95] Admiral Porter, who was not even present at the time of the fight, estimated Rebel forces at about three or four thousand. Likewise, Chaplain Edwards of the 11th Louisiana, who was on the scene, claimed the enemy "were at least three thousand strong."[96]

McCulloch was just as inaccurate in his assessment of the numbers his brigade faced. He reported that he brought about 1,500 men into battle and was opposed by two or three times that number. The Union forces were also reinforced by "three gunboats that were kept constantly playing shot and shell upon us during the whole engagement." Although only the *Choctaw* and the *Lexington* were engaged, McCulloch may have mistaken two different sized guns firing from the *Choctaw* as two separate boats, or he may have thought the transport *Ft. Wayne*, which had brought up the 23rd Iowa from Young's Point, was a gunboat.[97] It is noteworthy that both sides consistently thought they were heavily outnumbered. The viciousness of the fighting probably led each commander, as well as many of their enlisted men, to believe the opponent had more forces engaged. Surely such severe casualties had to be inflicted by a numerically superior foe.

Two days after the battle, the news finally reached Monroe. Sarah Wadley heard that the Yankees had fled, resulting in a Confederate victory, "but the negroes fought desperately." The black soldiers "would not give up until our men clubbed muskets upon them, we lost three hundred killed and wounded and it is said there were three thousand of the negroes killed." She could scarcely believe it was true. "It is terrible to think of such a battle as this, white men and freemen fighting with their slaves, and to be killed by such a hand, the very soul revolts from it. Oh may this be the last."[98]

The next day, June 10, Kate Stone had a different view, thinking the battle had been a Confederate disaster. "It is hard to believe that Southern soldiers— and Texans at that—have been whipped by a mongrel crew of white and black Yankees," she wrote, desperately hoping that the report was in error. She busied herself by making mattresses for the wounded expected to arrive soon. "It is said the Negro regiments fought there like mad demons, but we cannot believe that. We know from long experience they are cowards."[99]

Later that same day, the first casualties arrived. The hospitals in Monroe were given just one hour's notice to prepare. Eighty-two men arrived that day, and more than 250 arrived about a week later. Two hospitals in town were already caring for more than two hundred men before receiving the wounded from Milliken's Bend, which filled them beyond capacity. The additional casualties forced the Nebraska House hotel, Union Church, the Male Academy, and even a carriage shop to be pressed into service as makeshift hospitals. The women of the town, like Kate and Sarah, knitted socks, made bandages, cooked, and aided as they could. Some of them even organized entertainments to lift the men's spirits and to raise funds for medical supplies.[100]

As the hospitals tended to their wounded, the commanders took stock of their performance in battle. McCulloch, like many other commanders at Milliken's Bend, expressed a sentiment that could only be called mournful pride: "The scathing ordeal through which my little brigade was compelled to pass has increased my confidence in and love for them." He felt the gunboats made the fight unfair and knew that any claims to victory were tarnished by having to yield the field. He wished for "at least one fair chance" for his men to "gain a complete victory to compensate them for the gallant fighting they have done and always will do."[101]

McCulloch blamed his lack of success on poor intelligence work. Although Taylor's orders were "to engage the enemy before day and carry his works at the point of the bayonet," McCulloch believed the instructions must have been based on erroneous information. Taylor must have been expecting only one battalion of cavalry and one battalion of Negro infantry at the post, with no artillery or gunboats. McCulloch declared that the Yankees knew of his approach and had been reinforced the night before with three transports full of additional troops, though in actuality, only 120 men of the 23rd Iowa supplemented Lieb's garrison. McCulloch further complained: "I was entirely misinformed by our guide with regard to the ground over which we had to advance. Instead of finding it a smooth, open field without obstructions, I found the ground exceedingly rough, covered with small running briars and tie-vines, through which infantry could scarcely march, and so much cut up with ditches and obstructed with hedges that it was impracticable to make any well-regulated military movement upon it." McCulloch continued, "I would not have been the least surprised if we had made an entire failure; and nothing but the best and bravest fighting, under the providence of God, could have crowned our efforts with even partial success."[102]

McCulloch's superior, General Walker, praised the efforts to take Milliken's Bend. "Nothing could have been more admirable than the gallantry displayed by officers and men," he wrote Taylor, as if gallantry alone could carry the day. Walker, like McCulloch, blamed the guides from Harrison's cavalry and insufficient knowledge of the terrain for McCulloch's failure. Walker reported in a sketch map that the position of the defender was strong and that the front of their position was cut up by numerous hedges and two levees. The enemy's flanks were protected by cross levees, a short line of breastworks composed of abatis and brush, and stands of timber. Combined, the natural ground and man-made defenses left little room for maneuvering. In hindsight, Walker assessed the task of taking the Union position by a frontal assault as one of "extreme difficulty." If Taylor was still skeptical about the outcome of the battle, Walker added that the fire from Union gunboats rendered McCulloch's efforts to take the post impractical. "It would have been folly to have persisted in the attack."[103]

But Taylor was not satisfied. Although he acknowledged the bravery of McCulloch's men in the ranks, he had bitter words for those in command. McCulloch demonstrated "great personal bravery, but no capacity for handling masses." Disappointed in nearly all of his subordinates, Taylor complained, "Nothing was wanted but vigorous action in the execution of the plans which had been carefully laid out." Years later, Taylor acknowledged the futility of the entire mission: "I was informed that all the Confederate authorities in the east were urgent for some effort on our part in behalf of Vicksburg, and that public opinion would condemn us if we did not *try to do something*."[104]

In contrast to their commanding officers, many Confederate soldiers saw Milliken's Bend as a smashing victory. The enthusiastic accounts sent home to their families and recorded in their diaries and memoirs reveal confidence, pride, and a bit of verbal swagger. "We ran them to their gunboats and held our ground till all our wounded were taken off," recalled James H. Pillow, who was downright offended that the Yankees declared it their victory. The Rebels had taken the Yankee works and sent the bluecoats scrambling amid great slaughter. What else could a victory look like? Individual Rebel soldiers like Pillow would have been surprised to learn that McCulloch, Walker, and Taylor saw their mission as a failure.[105]

On the Union side, one could almost hear the black men's cheers echoing all the way to Washington. Assistant Secretary of War Charles Dana made sure of it. In his report to Secretary of War Stanton, Dana rightly praised the actions of the green troops of the African Brigade, but he gave an exaggerated sense of their gallantry when he failed to mention the role—or even the presence—of the gunboats in stemming the Rebel tide. In his initial report on June 8, Dana stated that the black troops "at first gave way, but hearing that those of their number who were captured were killed, they rallied with great fury and routed the enemy." Two days later, he filed a second report, painting a vivid picture of the nature of the fighting: "Many men were found dead with bayonet stabs, and others with their skulls broken open by butts of muskets." His figures of killed and wounded approximated those reported by Dennis and Lieb. Dana made a slight retraction when he acknowledged that Dennis did "not know whether it is true that the rebels murdered their negro prisoners." But the gunboats and their important role in the fight still went unmentioned.[106]

Dana's was the only report given close to the time of the battle which accused the Confederates of deliberately killing African American prisoners. In mentioning the battle cry of the Rebels, Colonel Lieb reported that the white officers were the special targets of Southern hatred—not the African American enlisted men, recently freed from slavery. Targeting the white officers—virtually all of them experienced soldiers from Grant's Army of the Tennessee—also would have made tactical sense, given the inexperience of the soldiers they commanded. Creating heavy casualties among the leaders of companies and regiments was certain to shake the morale, not to mention the efficiency, of a green unit in battle that suddenly found itself leaderless. The fate of Union prisoners captured at Milliken's Bend is the focus of the next chapter, but here, suffice it to note that Dana claimed African American prisoners were murdered during the battle itself—a statement not made by commanders who were actually on the scene at the time.

However, more than one Yankee officer reported the Rebels made their assault bearing the "black flag" of no quarter—designating their intent to take no prisoners. Dana stated that Col. Thomas Kilby Smith, who had been present at the battle due to Shepard's court of inquiry, "certified in an official statement that the rebels carried a black flag bearing a death's head and cross-bones." Lt. Col. Cyrus Sears of the 11th Louisiana recalled more than forty years later that "the enemy fought us under the skull, coffin and cross bones (black) flag." Shepard mentioned in his report shortly after the battle, "I *think* they displayed the white flag, with a black crossbones and coffin. I was on the breastworks *in line* with it and so saw indistinctly. Others assert it without question." Whether such a flag ever existed remains a point of controversy.[107]

It seems unlikely that the Confederates—who had been constantly on the move for more than a month, covering more than three hundred miles— would have taken the time to create or have made a flag of this nature. Supplies in the Trans-Mississippi by this time were scarce and getting scarcer. The men in Joseph P. Blessington's unit were wearing pants made out of blankets and jackets of penitentiary cloth, and one soldier wore a pyramid-shaped hat festooned with buttons and a tassel. If fabric was in such short supply that the men of Walker's Division were having to resort to these measures, it seems highly improbable that they would have designed a "no-quarter" flag, when their battle cry—and most of all, their bullets—could serve the same purpose.[108]

Perhaps the black flag accusations were more metaphorical than literal. At least two Union officers reported the Rebels came on with cries of "no quarters," thus fighting under the sentiment of a black flag, even if not literally carrying one into battle. The controversy over a Confederate "no quarter" policy toward black Union soldiers and their white officers at Milliken's Bend would persist for months and would drag on well into 1864. Indeed, 150 years later, the fate of Union prisoners taken there remains a point of controversy.[109]

"A Disagreeable Dilemma"
The Fate of Union Prisoners, Black and White

RUMORS ABOUT THE execution of Union prisoners taken at Milliken's Bend began almost immediately and would persist for the rest of the year. The Louisiana swamps and bayous became a fitting metaphor as the rumors became a tangle of fact, fiction, and half-truths. Even the generals had difficulty sorting out the facts, and report after report would appear to be about one incident but would turn out to be about another. Not surprisingly, the veracity of some of these stories has been debated to the present day, though only a few historians have examined them in any detail.[1]

Trying to discern the truth of what happened is difficult because whatever the fate of the white officers and black enlisted men, both sides had reasons for making the statements they did, regardless of their veracity. By accusing the Confederates of ruthless brutality and a flagrant violation of the rules of war, the Federals stood to gain by offering revenge as a motive to spur enlistments among blacks. They could renew the vigor with which the war was prosecuted, and they quite naturally could place themselves in the morally superior role of being "civilized" against the "barbarism" of the Rebels. Finally, and perhaps most importantly, they could use the opportunity to place an embargo on prisoner exchanges, thus locking up a significant number of Confederate soldiers, who otherwise would probably find their way back into the Rebel ranks after they returned South.

The Confederates, on the other hand, stood to gain either way. If they executed the men, they were, after all, simply following Confederate law on the matter. On April 30, 1863, the Confederate Congress authorized the execution of white officers in command of black troops, on the charge of "inciting servile insurrection," and blacks taken in arms against the Confederacy were to be handed over to state authorities, to be dealt with according to state law. Confederate president Jefferson Davis and the Trans-Mississippi department commander, Lt. Gen. Edmund Kirby Smith, expressed their dismay that black prisoners had been taken at Milliken's Bend. When Smith heard that some armed Negroes were taken prisoner, he admonished Taylor: "I hope . . . that your subordinates . . . recognized the propriety of giving no quarter to armed negroes and their officers." If the soldiers were executed or faced threats of no quarter on the battlefield, the hope would be that slaves would be too frightened and intimidated to run away or enlist and that any white Union soldier would think twice about volunteering to serve with the Colored Troops. Ultimately, perhaps the North would reconsider its policy of enlisting blacks.[2]

Yet rumor sometimes gains its own force. When Richard Taylor denied any knowledge of hangings or executions, he might in fact have been stating *the truth*—but the accusations were so strong, and so heinous, that any denial began to sound like a fabrication, regardless of actual events. However, strong evidence persists that executions took place in the aftermath of Milliken's Bend, with or without Taylor's authority or knowledge.

To get at the truth, four incidents are particularly critical to examine: the capture of Thomas Cormal, a Confederate deserter; accusations against two of Gen. Paul Octave Hébert's staff officers; Col. William H. Parsons's cavalry raid along the Mississippi River near Goodrich's Landing in late June; and Union Brig. Gen. John D. Stevenson's expedition to Monroe, Louisiana, in late August. Each of these events prompted reports of the execution of prisoners taken at Milliken's Bend or elsewhere in northeast Louisiana, and such reports were complicated by charges and countercharges. The result was a confusing mish-mash of rumor, innuendo, accusation, and denial that propagated itself in various forms. Although details changed and the players shifted, the core of the story universally suggested that white and black prisoners from African American units had been killed. Initially, almost every significant accusation appeared to be without merit. But the rumors persisted, and eventually, a few firm facts began to take shape.

Assistant Secretary of War Charles Dana, a day after the battle, was the first to report that black prisoners had been murdered on the battlefield. He believed that this occurrence rallied the African American troops, who until that point had supposedly fled in fear. As they saw their captured comrades dispatched on the spot, the black soldiers came back with a vengeance, said Dana. Two days later, he had gathered more details from Brig. Gen. Elias Dennis. Dana then backpedaled from his previous statements, reporting that the African American soldiers had fought with great gallantry and that it was unclear if black prisoners had been murdered.[3]

Both of Dana's reports to Secretary of War Edwin M. Stanton seem suspect. Dana was not present at the fight; neither, for that matter, was Dennis. It is likely that by this time Dennis had been to Milliken's Bend to survey the scene, count casualties, and consult with regimental and brigade officers. Still, at least one glaring error appeared in Dana's second dispatch. Dana declared Confederate general Henry McCulloch dead on the field of battle. If Dana (and perhaps Dennis) could make an error this significant, he certainly could have been wrong about any number of other details, including the killing of black prisoners by Confederates.

No Union officer present—not even Lieb or Shepard—nor even Sears or Cornwell in their later memoirs—said that black prisoners were murdered on the battlefield. To be sure, many men died, but no one who was actually present reported that these men were killed in anything but the heat of battle. True, some may have been shot when they could have been made prisoners, and a few Confederate letters recount the bloodbath with something approaching glee. Given the furious nature of the fighting, it was likely the forward momentum of men in battle that brought about their deaths, not cold-blooded murder.

Still, just a week after the fight, there was more disturbing news. On June 14 and 15 the USS *Louisville* took aboard several Confederate prisoners, among them Thomas Cormal, a deserter who served in Maj. Isaac F. Harrison's "battery of light artillery," and Cormal's wife. Lt. Cmdr. Elias K. Owen of the *Louisville* reported that Cormal "witnessed the hanging at Richmond, La., of the white captain and negroes captured at Milliken's Bend. General Taylor and command were drawn up to witness the execution." Cormal further reported that a sergeant in command of a company of contrabands who had been captured by Harrison's cavalry a few weeks before "was also hung at Perkins' Landing." It will be recalled that Confederate captain Elijah P. Petty of the 17th Texas Infantry noted the capture of "1 fed prisoner & 5 negroes" at Perkins' Landing in late May. Perhaps Cormal was describing the fate of these men.[4] A close examination of similar events by historian James G. Hollandsworth Jr. does not mention any executions taking place at or near Perkins' Landing or Richmond, Louisiana. Whether Union officers and enlisted men were put to death at these places remains unclear.[5]

Likewise, the identity of Cormal remains a mystery. No record has been found of a Thomas Cormal in the compiled Confederate service records at the National Archives, *The Roster of Confederate Soldiers, 1861–1865,* or *Records*

of Louisiana Confederate Soldiers and Louisiana Confederate Commands. Major
Isaac F. Harrison, of Tensas Parish, commanded a cavalry unit, the 15th
Louisiana Cavalry Battalion, which later in 1863 became the 3rd Louisiana
Cavalry Regiment. Cormal may have belonged to a battery that was temporarily attached to Harrison's cavalry or perhaps to Company F, which became a
battery in late May, but even so, no records for any Confederate soldier, of
any command, have been found under this name. A more likely explanation
is that the abbreviation for "Battery" and "Battalion" could easily have been
confused by an inattentive Yankee officer or clerk. A closer examination of the
logbook for the *Louisville* on June 14 indicates that "Thos. Conall, a deserter
from Major Harrisons La. Battallion" came aboard at 8:50 a.m. Still, no record
of a Thomas Conall (or Connell) from Harrison's Cavalry has been found.
Allowing for nineteenth-century penmanship, the individual in question may
be Thomas B. Carroll, who served in Company K, 3rd Louisiana Cavalry, the
later designation for Harrison's command.[6]

At about the same time, on June 13, Lt. Gen. Edmund Kirby Smith reprimanded his subordinate, Maj. Gen. Richard Taylor. "I have been unofficially
informed that some of your troops have captured negroes in arms," he wrote,
referring to Milliken's Bend. "I hope this may not be so, and that your subordinates who may have been in command of capturing parties may have recognized the propriety of giving no quarter to armed negroes and their officers. In
this way we may be relieved from a disagreeable dilemma." Smith here clearly
approves a no-quarter policy on the battlefield. His comments indicate that
he considered living black prisoners to be a far more serious problem than if
they were simply shot down without mercy on the battlefield.[7]

Smith's language is also revealing. Not once does he refer to these black
men as soldiers. Instead, they are "negroes . . . in arms," "armed negroes," or
"negroes . . . in . . . insurrection." By avoiding even the linguistic implication
that these men were soldiers, Smith reflects the Confederate point of view that
saw the Union recruitment of black men as a heinous crime, a terrible prelude
to countless slave uprisings that might break out at any minute. Indeed, by
arming slaves and giving them uniforms, the apocalypse of slavery and the
entire South had begun.[8]

If black soldiers had in fact been taken prisoner by the Confederates, Smith
instructed Taylor, they were to be turned over to the authorities of the State
of Louisiana for trial. "I am told that negroes found in a state of insurrection
may be tried by a court of the parish in which the crime is committed," Smith

continued, adding, "Governor Moore has called on me and stated that if the report is true that any armed negroes have been captured he will send the attorney-general to conduct the prosecution as soon as you notify him of the capture." It is unclear if a trial took place, though Confederate correspondence on this and similar matters indicates a clear concern for legality and a desire to follow proper procedures in the midst of a distasteful situation. No record has been found showing that Smith ever requested or used the attorney general's services, though extant records are, of course, quite scarce.[9]

Many parish courts had suspended operations long ago, and Taylor had left Richmond, the seat of Madison Parish, several days before. On June 15, after strong resistance and an artillery duel, Union troops rode into Richmond and burned it to the ground. It thus became an impossibility for the Confederates to bring the black enlisted men to trial in Madison Parish.[10] Chaplain George G. Edwards of the Union 11th Louisiana Infantry, A. D., reported that Rebel Louisiana troops—probably Harrison's cavalry—advocated killing prisoners at Richmond but that the Texans (presumably McCulloch's Brigade or portions of Walker's Texas Division) "drew up in line of battle and declared it could not be done." It is not clear where Edwards got his information, but if it is correct, then it could explain Confederate prisoner Thomas Cormal's story. Cormal, especially if he was associated with Harrison's troops, may have witnessed or heard about this event and provided this information to his captors on the *Louisville*. He may have been unaware that the proposed executions did not take place.[11]

On the same day that Smith encouraged Taylor to turn over prisoners to state authorities, Smith's assistant adjutant general, Samuel S. Anderson, responded to a similar inquiry from Brig. Gen. Paul Octave Hébert of June 6. Hébert wanted to know what should be done with captured former slaves who were bearing arms against the Confederacy. Anderson directed his response through General Taylor and informed him that "no quarter" should be shown to "negro slaves taken in arms" on the battlefield. However, he warned Taylor against executing black soldiers already in his custody as prisoners, stating that such an act committed by Confederate military forces "would certainly provoke retaliation. By turning them over to the civil authorities to be tried by the laws of the State no exception can be taken." Anderson's response, straight from Smith's headquarters, makes the Confederate policy in the Trans-Mississippi quite clear. On the battlefield, black soldiers would be shown no mercy and would be cut down where they stood. It was imperative that they *not* be taken prisoner. It was too late to implement this policy at Milliken's Bend, and because there was still great confusion among subordinates about proper procedures, those African American soldiers already in Confederate custody should not be executed by the military. Such an action, taking place away from the battlefield, would prompt the United States to call for a retaliatory policy, resulting in the deaths of Confederate prisoners of war in Union hands. Instead, the black soldiers would be brought to trial in a civilian court of law and punished by the state. Undoubtedly, though Anderson did not say so, these "slaves in arms" would be condemned to death, if found guilty.[12]

Smith himself was uncertain about the official Confederate policy for dealing with prisoners from black units. He wrote to the Confederate capital in Richmond, Virginia, on June 16 for clarification. Knowing the tenuous and slow nature of communications with the capital, he excused himself: "I saw no other proper and legal course for me to pursue except the one which I adopted."[13] More than a month later, Smith received his reply from the Confederate capital, dated July 13, informing him that the secretary of war recommended a different policy. The former slaves were to be considered "deluded victims" who "should be received and treated with mercy and returned to their owners," although "a few examples might perhaps be made." However, the general practice of "no quarter" was discouraged, since "to refuse them quarter would only make them, against their tendencies, fight desperately." Perhaps Confederate authorities back in the capital saw this as the reason the fighting at Milliken's Bend had been so unexpectedly fierce.[14]

Meanwhile, as Smith and his generals corresponded about what to do with prisoners from black units, Federal Lt. Cmdr. Elias K. Owen's report about Cormal worked its way through the Union military bureaucracy. Acting Rear Admiral Porter forwarded the report to Maj. Gen. Ulysses S. Grant, recommending that Taylor "should be hung himself on the spot if ever taken—or any of his gang."[15] When Grant received the report, he quickly dispatched a letter of inquiry across the lines to General Taylor on June 22. Grant repeated the information obtained from Cormal and informed Taylor that U.S. forces were treating Confederates captured at Milliken's Bend as prisoners of war, "notwithstanding they were caught fighting under the 'black flag of no quarter.'" Grant said he felt "no inclination to retaliate," but if no quarter was shown or prisoners had been killed, he would "accept the issue." Grant knew that the Confederates might treat solders from black units differently than white troops. Anticipating such an objection, he reiterated that all soldiers wearing the Federal uniform had the right to be treated as prisoners of war, regardless of race or regiment. Grant told Taylor he hoped that there had been some mistake in the information he had received or that, if true, "the act of hanging had no official sanction, and that the parties guilty of it will be duly punished."[16]

When the couriers returned from delivering the dispatch to Taylor, they reported that all Confederate officers they encountered vehemently denied that any "soldiers or officers, black or white, have been hanged or are likely to be hanged." However, the couriers learned that the white officers were being "held as hostage in some way, and the negroes have been handed over to the State authorities, by whom they will probably be sold." These statements were not an official reply from Taylor—that was still a few days away—but they do provide a glimpse into the situation about two weeks after the battle, indicating that the prisoners taken at Milliken's Bend were probably still alive. Still, the situation was extremely tense. Local civilians, as well as Confederate soldiers, expressed "great dismay at the idea of our arming negroes, which they suppose must be followed by insurrection with all its horrors," wrote one of the couriers.[17]

Taylor was appalled at Grant's charges. On June 27, he responded, calling such accusations "disgraceful." Taylor confirmed that he had remained at or near Richmond for several days after the fight at Milliken's Bend, "and had any officer or negro been hung the fact must have come to my knowledge." He believed the accusation against Colonel Harrison's cavalry regarding prisoners taken at Perkins' Landing to likewise be without merit, but he assured Grant that he would begin a full investigation, promising swift and certain punishment if it turned out to be true. "My orders at all times have been to treat all prisoners with every consideration," he replied. But as to "negroes captured in arms, the officers of the Confederate States Army are required, by an order emanating from the General Government, to turn over all such to the civil authorities, to be dealt with according to the laws of the State wherein they were captured."[18] What Taylor did not say, but Grant surely knew, was that state laws already on the books mandated the death penalty for slaves in insurrection. Significantly, just two weeks after Milliken's Bend, two bills relating to the enlistment of slaves into the Union forces and slave rebellions were passed into law by the Confederate Louisiana Legislature, meeting in exile in Shreveport. One law, concerning slaves enlisting in the Union army, carried the death penalty.[19]

Grant responded to Taylor's statement on July 4, 1863, the same day he accepted the surrender of Confederate forces at Vicksburg from Lt. Gen. John C. Pemberton. Grant expressed his relief: "I could not credit the story, though told so straight, and I am now truly glad to hear your denial." He reassured Taylor that no harsh actions had been taken against Confederate prisoners in response to the accusations.[20] The matter seemed settled. Grant had his hands full with 29,000 prisoners from Vicksburg, a starving civilian populace, and his own weary army. He needed to make immediate arrangements for occupying and garrisoning the river fortress, and paroling the prisoners. His polite acceptance of Taylor's denial seemed to put the matter to rest.

Yet the rumors persisted. Several months later, on September 24, Lt. Col. Loren Kent, Provost Marshal General, reported to Grant's headquarters disturbing news from Monroe, Louisiana. Two officers on Hébert's staff were charged with the murder of two Federal officers captured near Lake Providence in June. M. W. Sims, one of the accused, was also said to be involved in the murder of four local ministers and the hanging of a Negro soldier near Delhi around the same time.[21]

Oddly enough, a month before Kent's report, on August 11, Grant had issued orders for the exchange of a Major "Semmes," after Hébert informed him that Sims was a civilian, not a soldier. Sims had been in Federal custody since July and had been sent to Johnson's Island prison in Ohio. Hébert desired that Sims be exchanged for an unnamed civilian who had been working on leased plantations for the Union army. Grant was almost apologetic, "Many whose interests and inclinations incline them to remain at home enroll themselves as volunteer aides on the staff of some general, and this I understand to be the case with Major Semmes. I would respectfully ask that Major Semmes be released and returned to his home, in exchange for Judge L. Dent, who has been released by General Hebert and allowed to return to his plantation." The judge was Lewis Dent, Grant's brother-in-law, who leased government plantations along the Mississippi River. It is not clear when he was captured, but by July 19 he was reported in Confederate hands, where he was being "treated with kindness and courtesy." By July 27, Dent was released by Gen. Edmund Kirby Smith, who petitioned Sims's case as a civilian to Grant.[22]

Sims had been captured near Natchez on July 13 while delivering dispatches from General Smith to Gen. Joseph E. Johnston. After his capture, Sims was sent up the Mississippi River to St. Louis, where he was imprisoned at Gratiot Street Prison and subsequently transferred to Johnson's Island, Ohio. On September 5, he was ordered to report to General Grant in Vicksburg, prior to his being exchanged. But when Kent's report accused Sims of murdering two U.S. Army officers from the Colored Troops, Grant responded promptly. Sims was thrown into the Vicksburg jail.[23]

On October 5, "O. H.," who had been on the same steamboat with Sims headed downriver to Vicksburg, sought help from Reuben Davis, a Confederate congressman and prominent lawyer from Aberdeen, Mississippi. "O. H." reported that Major Sims had expected to be exchanged for a member of Grant's staff but "was placed in close confinement in the VBurg jail on the charge of having shot or caused to be shot two Federal prisoners after the Milliken's Bend fight." Sims's friend pleaded for assistance and asked Davis to forward information to Maj. Gen. Stephen D. Lee or General Johnston.[24]

On October 16, Davis wrote to Johnston that he had been acquainted with Sims since childhood. He described Sims as a gentleman and a scholar of strong intellect and prudence. Sims had even studied law under Davis. "I am certain he would not have had any man shot without sufficient reason," Davis wrote. "I hope you will have justice done him and save his life if possible. I suppose Genl Hebert will be able to afford you some information."

Benjamin Sims, fearing for his brother's life, was panicking and desperate. He wrote directly to the Confederate president on October 19, explaining that his brother "thought he was being exchanged and knew not to the contrary until he landed on the wharf & was ordered to prison. He is now in goal [sic], charged with having ordered the execution of two Federal prisoners in the engagement at Milliken's Bend." He pled, "If the case will not admit of a threat of retaliation, may he not have, by a flag of truce, at least all the evidence that can be obtained from our side in his favor. In giving this matter your prompt attention you may perhaps save from an untimely & shameful death a soldier & a gentleman, and confer a favor upon his distressed brother, that will never be forgotten."

On October 26, Capt. Samuel W. Mosby of the 5th Mississippi Infantry wrote to Col. Benjamin S. Ewell from the Officers' Hospital in Lauderdale Springs that Sims was "at present lodged in a common jail at Vicksburg *as a felon*, on the charge of having ordered the execution of two federal prisoners, at Milliken's Bend. This order must have been issued upon the authority of a command from a Superior and Maj. Sims is not responsible for his order. He, as an officer, has served with much gallantry and deserves such treatment, which our foe seems unwilling to bestow upon brave men. I beg that some thing be done in this case as it requires prompt and immediate attention."

Curiously, Mosby's correspondence does not deny—and even seems to implicate, with the alibi of "following orders"—Sim's involvement in killing the two Yankee officers.

Meanwhile, across the river and far to the west in Vienna, Louisiana, Hébert grew increasingly concerned. Unaware of the drama in Vicksburg, he sent a dispatch on November 4 to Judge Dent, who had been released three months earlier and was now safe at his plantation near Lake Providence. Hébert wanted to know if Dent knew anything about the whereabouts of Sims, since Dent had given his word that Sims would be released. Hébert had released Dent in good faith, but Sims had not been heard from. Had Sims been released by U.S. authorities? Had he been returned to Confederate lines? Where was he now? Hébert believed that Dent's "relations social and political" and his relationship to General Grant put him in a position to find out what had happened.[25]

Back in Mississippi, Benjamin Sims remained in distress. He wrote to General Johnston on November 15, 1863, reporting that "on the 8th of this month, Brother and I sent in our petition by flag of truce as you directed, to *his Majesty* Jas. B. McPherson Comdg. at Vicksburg, requesting permission to have an interview with him . . . This he peremptorily refused." McPherson informed Benjamin that his brother had been sent to Memphis. Despondent, and recognizing that any further pleas in Vicksburg were pointless, Benjamin returned home.[26]

Benjamin's despair turned to joy when he found a letter waiting for him from his brother, who had escaped! While on a steamer headed north on the Mississippi River toward Memphis, M. W. Sims overheard a conversation in which he learned of his impending execution. A woman on board helped him escape, and he left his watch with her, and the address of his parents, in case his attempt was unsuccessful. After jumping into the river and swimming to shore, Sims hid in the swamplands, "wandering for weeks, with no food but roots and berries." Wending his way westward through northern Louisiana, Sims at last arrived at Hébert's camp. "He was a man considerably over six feet tall and finely proportioned," Hébert recalled, "but on his return, he was so gaunt haggard and emaciated that no one recognised him." Despite his hardships, there was also good-natured laughter at his expense. Sims entered the camp wearing a suit made out of "Calico window curtains . . . of a very gaudy and striking pattern" provided to him by a kindly woman he met somewhere along the way. Sims's escape prevented a resolution of the Federal charges against him.[27]

Before the war, Sims had been a wealthy lawyer and farmer from Austin,

Texas, owning $55,000 worth of real estate and $97,000 in personal property, much of it in human chattel. In his home county of Travis and at a place
in Burleson County, he owned a combined total of more than 120 slaves.
Regardless of his guilt or innocence in the events associated with Milliken's
Bend, it is easy to imagine how he might have felt about the Union policy of
making soldiers of former slaves.[28]

First Lt. Jesse W. Sparks was aide-de-camp to General Hébert during June
1863 and also was named as a suspect by Union Provost Marshal Kent in his
September dispatch. Sparks's service records indicate he was paroled in 1863
but provide no details about his capture or release. On August 1, 1863, he was
serving on Hébert's staff and accompanied Judge Dent under a flag of truce into
the Union lines at Goodrich's Landing. This was presumably the day of Dent's
formal exchange for Sims. In November, Sparks was still on Hébert's staff, so
his capture must have taken place in July, at the same time as Sims's, or in the
early fall, and he apparently spent very little time in Union custody.[29] Mention
of Sparks's involvement never reappears after Kent's initial report. In contrast,
the evidence against Sims is strong but inconclusive. It seems that neither man
was ever brought before a court—civil or military—so their role in the deaths
of any officers or enlisted men from the Colored Troops remains unclear.

Although Southern correspondence about Sims nearly always refers
to Milliken's Bend, Union Provost Marshal Kent's initial report linked him
to Lake Providence. This discrepancy demonstrates that events across the
Mississippi River from Vicksburg often became one indistinguishable blur,
particularly to Union authorities. Once again, a report about one thing—
Sims's association with events at Lake Providence—would turn out to be about
something different—his actions supposedly taken against prisoners from the
Milliken's Bend fight who were held in Monroe.

Despite Kent's inaccuracy, the events near Lake Providence in late June
merit closer examination. His initial report about the execution of two officers did not indicate if the victims were from Colored Troops regiments, but
his reference to a clash near Lake Providence is undoubtedly to the events
of June 29 and 30. Two Confederate cavalry regiments and a battery of artillery under the overall command of Col. William H. Parsons encountered
two companies of the First Arkansas Infantry, African Descent, fortified atop
an old Indian mound, at a place known as Mound Plantation, not far from
Goodrich's Landing. Although the Yankee soldiers briefly held their own,
Parsons's troops were soon reinforced by a brigade of infantry under Brig. Gen.

James C. Tappan. Now hopelessly outnumbered despite their strong position, the Union commander chose to surrender. He asked that the white Federal officers be treated as prisoners of war but surrendered unconditionally the black enlisted men, placing them in an extremely vulnerable position. One Confederate soldier claimed that during the advance Colonel Parsons told his troopers to take no black men prisoner.[30]

Though it may be difficult to see the Union commander's decision to surrender his African American soldiers as anything but cowardly, it ironically may have saved many of their lives. When the guns went silent, Confederate troops were suddenly faced with an overwhelming number of black enlisted men. Any attempt to slaughter them wholesale after the firing ceased would be a violation even of the convoluted and still-evolving Southern policies. Had the Union commander continued the fight, the black soldiers almost certainly would have become victims of the no-quarter battlefield policy implemented by Smith—if for no other reason than they were outnumbered at the time of their surrender by about ten to one. Suddenly placing more than one hundred African American enlisted men literally at the mercy of their captors created a situation where it would have been extraordinarily difficult for Southern forces to justify their execution. Furthermore, the black soldiers, former slaves, represented more than $100,000 worth of "property"—human capital that could be sold or put to work for the Confederacy. The Confederates would be fools if they destroyed this valuable labor pool.[31] Although the Federal commander essentially deserted his men by leaving them to the uncertain mercy of their captors, it may have been a calculated risk.

It did not save everyone, however. Pvt. John Simmons of the 22nd Texas Infantry wrote that about a dozen black soldiers died shortly after the fight. It is possible that some may have died of exhaustion or wounds. However, firsthand accounts from black soldiers on the retreat reveal that some were beaten and a few were killed. It is not clear if they were executed outright for wearing the uniform of a Northern soldier or if they were killed because they were straggling and slowing down the Confederate withdrawal.[32]

Most of the black soldiers of the two companies of the 1st Arkansas Infantry, African Descent, were spared and sent westward, enduring a hard forced march from Goodrich's Landing to the railhead at Delhi. Anticipating objections from his superior, Maj. Gen. John G. Walker complained, "I consider it an unfortunate circumstance that any armed negroes were captured." Still, Walker absolved Colonel Parsons for accepting these terms and blamed the Yankee commander. The Union officer's actions essentially forced the Confederates' hand into accepting these men as prisoners.[33]

In the end, the Confederates reported a total of 113 black enlisted men captured. However, company-level numbers from the Union side indicate that as many as 128 men may have been taken prisoner. The difference between the two figures neatly correlates with the approximate number of enlisted men who may have died shortly after their capture.[34] Discrepancies also persist about the number of white officers captured at the Mound. Most recent examinations, most notably the detailed work of Anne J. Bailey and James G. Hollandsworth Jr., indicate only three officers were taken prisoner. However, it now appears that four officers may be the correct number. Hollandsworth establishes that Lt. John East was one of the men captured. William B. Wallace, captain of Company E, was another. His pension record provides the names of two other men—Capt. Hugh Maxwell of Company G and 2nd Lt. James M. Marshall of Company E—who were taken prisoner at the same time. It seems that all three of these men were confined together, or at least in close proximity, for they returned to their regiment around the same time later that year. This may be why Walker reports only three officers captured. Curiously, East is not mentioned with these other men, possibly because he spent the rest of the war in a prison camp in Texas. It is not clear why he was treated differently than the other three, but all four Federal officers taken at the Mound are accounted for—and even more importantly, *none* were executed.[35]

After the encounter at Mound Plantation, Parsons's troopers rode on toward Lake Providence, setting fire to houses, cotton, and other property and scooping up about two thousand contrabands working on Federal leased plantations along the river. The former slaves were to be returned to their owners, offered for sale, or set to work for the Confederacy. Parsons endeavored to take them away from Yankee threats along the river, evacuating them toward the interior of the state. Some Rebel soldiers found it tempting to claim a slave for themselves, a practice Parsons soon prohibited.[36]

Before dawn on June 30, the Mississippi Marine Brigade disembarked at Goodrich's Landing to meet Parsons's threat. Composed of infantry, artillery, and cavalry forces, the brigade was a Union army unit, not navy or marines. It was designed to be a flexible and highly mobile force, relying upon riverboats for swift movement to get to the scene of action. As the men left their transport that morning, the still-dark sky was lit up in all directions from burning plantations and cotton gins.

Later that day, as the brigade moved inland, Brig. Gen. Alfred W. Ellet found charred human remains in some of the slave cabins set afire by the raiding Texans. "We were shocked by the sight," he reported to Acting Rear Adm. David Dixon Porter, "No doubt they were the sick negroes whom the unscrupulous enemy were too indifferent to remove."[37] Ellet's reliability on this and other matters has been questioned, with some historians seeing him as prone to exaggeration and outright lying. However, Ellet also wrote to his wife about the gruesome discoveries. "We found . . . in the ashes of the negro quarters frequent evidence of human remains, the charred bones, and grinning skull, and baked carcass, of some poor sick negro who was unable to remove himself from the burning pile." The Rebels were "too indifferent to use any effort to save a 'sick niggar.'" Ellet told his wife he had passed three plantations where he had seen five burned bodies without even leaving the road or searching them out. He thought that twenty other plantations probably held similar horrors that could be solidly documented if a formal investigation were launched.[38]

Even if Ellet had exaggerated such a tale for Porter, it seems unlikely that he would have burdened his wife with such sickening details if there were not some truth in it. Indeed, Ellet provided more description to her than he included in his report to Porter. Although he mentioned in passing to his wife the need for a formal investigation, Ellet's brigade would not have the wherewithal to sustain a longer operation. The Mississippi Marine Brigade was designed to be a quick "strike force" based on the river, not a unit of protracted operations inland. In fact, one account claimed that the brigade's actions that day were expected to be a "'before-breakfast' job" and that the men had nothing to eat for twenty-four hours except a fortunate find of blackberries on the march. If there were to be an investigation, the Mississippi Marine Brigade would not perform it.[39]

Other soldiers told tales like Ellet's. Lt. Col. Samuel J. Nasmith of the 25th Wisconsin Infantry described in his official report similar scenes, which he had heard about from Maj. James Farnan, who was in charge of a detachment from the 5th Illinois Cavalry. The Rebels "spared neither age, sex, nor condition. In some instances the negroes were shut up in their quarters, and literally roasted alive. The charred remains found in numerous instances testified to a degree of fiendish atrocity such as has no parallel either in civilized or savage warfare. Young children, only five or six years of age, were found skulking in the canebreak pierced with wounds, while helpless women were found shot down in the most inhuman manner. The whole country was destroyed, and every sign of civilization was given to the flames."[40]

Josiah Goodwin of the Mississippi Marine Brigade wrote in his diary that Rebel forces

> even went so far as to kill some of the negro soldier & throw them into the negro quarters where there was black women & children that was at that time sick & helpless & then set fire to the houses & burn all within they captured the day before 2 companies of negros with 4 white officers & it is generaly supposed that they off cours burnt them officers but however we are not certain of that being a fact yet we saw the remains of some human beings but we could not find enough of them to asertain wheather they were black or white.[41]

These scenes of destruction were likely what prompted a sensational news article in the *Missouri Democrat,* which Union general in chief Henry W. Halleck brought to Grant's attention a few weeks later. "Rebel Barbarism" screamed the headline, and the article went on to detail a scene of torture and conflagration.

> The day after the battle of Milliken's Bend, in June last, the Marine Brigade landed some 10 miles below the Bend, and attacked and routed the guerillas which had been repulsed by our troops and the gunboats the day previous. Major Hubbard's cavalry battalion, of the Marine Brigade followed the retreating rebels to Tensas Bayou, and were horrified in the finding of skeletons of white officers commanding negro regiments, who had been captured by the rebels at Milliken's Bend. In many cases these officers had been nailed to the trees and crucified; in this situation a fire was built around the tree and they suffered a slow death from broiling. The charred and partially burned limbs were still fastened to the stakes. Other instances were noticed of charred skeletons of officers, which had been nailed to slabs, and the slabs placed against a house which was set on fire by the inhuman demons, the poor sufferers having been roasted alive until nothing was left but charred bones.[42]

Blacks who had been recaptured from Confederates confirmed the story, and a Lieutenant Cole of the Mississippi Marine Brigade swore to the truth of the statement, said the *Democrat*. The two officers named in the article must be Maj. James M. Hubbard and 1st Lt. Stephen S. Cole, both correctly identified as belonging to the Mississippi Marine Brigade.

The veracity of such reports remains controversial today. Terrence Winschel, historian at Vicksburg National Military Park, finds the *Democrat* account to be nothing but outrageous propaganda, stating: "I am satisfied (as too was Grant) that these accounts were sensationalism of the grandest scale." Winschel insists that "had such atrocities been committed there would be irrefutable evidence and an array of scholarly works detailing the crimes." Another source is less certain, finding the doubt so great on both sides of the issue that no verdict can be made either way. Other scholars apparently have found the *Democrat* so exaggerated as to be beneath notice.[43]

However, closer examination of the undated *Democrat* report reveals that it must be referring to events near Goodrich's Landing and Lake Providence, not Milliken's Bend. Although the newspaperman got some of his geography wrong and exaggerated to the extreme, the kernel of the story still might be true. It was the day after the battle at Mound Plantation, not Milliken's Bend, that the brigade pursued Confederate cavalry to Tensas Bayou.[44] The location of Goodrich's Landing in relation to other significant points along the river adds to the confusion. Moving from north to south, each about ten or fifteen miles apart, are Lake Providence, Goodrich's Landing, Milliken's Bend, and Young's Point. Near Lake Providence is where Parsons's raid took place. Ten miles below, at Goodrich's Landing, is where the Mississippi Marine Brigade disembarked to pursue Parsons. Milliken's Bend has no significance in this account other than being erroneously mentioned in the *Democrat* report, but ten miles below it was Young's Point, where the Marine Brigade had been stationed since mid-June. Having confused the Mound (Lake Providence) with Milliken's Bend, the *Democrat*'s reference to a location "ten miles below" likewise becomes erroneous. But when one substitutes Lake Providence for Milliken's Bend in the report, the other geographic references fall into place.

The "repulse" of "guerilla" troops by "gunboats" mentioned in the article must refer not just to the Mound, where the mounted Confederates withdrew after capturing the outpost, but also to shells from the *John Raine* and the *Romeo*, which fell among Parsons's cavalry along the river. Confederate cavalry was only peripherally involved in the fight at Milliken's Bend, and infantry troops were unlikely to be confused with guerillas. Parsons's cavalry was the primary force responsible for the raid near Goodrich's Landing and Lake Providence in late June, and the hard-riding Texas troopers could easily have been mistaken for a guerilla band. Yet, this information is misleading. At no time did any of the Union forces engaged ever doubt that their enemy was part of organized Confederate forces.[45]

Of course, the claims in the *Democrat* about crucifixion are extreme, and one wonders how the race of an individual—and his rank—would have been discernable from a charred corpse or skeleton. Colonel Wood of the 1st Arkansas Infantry, African Descent, whose troops were attacked at the Mound, was also on the Tensas expedition and certainly would have reported the matter if the remains of any of his officers had been found. Four white officers were captured at the Mound, and all can be accounted for, alive. All three officers captured at Milliken's Bend are also accounted for, as will be elaborated later. Several official Union reports remark on the presence of charred corpses, though all of them were believed to be bodies of slaves because they were discovered inside the ruins of slave cabins. Ellet believed their deaths were deliberate torture, but that seems unlikely given the speed and wide swath of Parsons's destruction and the emphasis upon gathering up slaves to move them to the west. More likely, they were incidental casualties, caught in the conflagration along the river. These were not atrocities, per se, but horrifying accidents, what today would be called "collateral damage." There may indeed have been corpses, but the notion that soldiers had been crucified and burned at the stake was surely a fabrication.[46]

Halleck, at the time, obviously thought the matter of enough concern to send a dispatch from Washington to Grant in Mississippi, enclosing the article. There must have been something in the story that concerned him, despite its sensationalism. For his part, Grant remained unconvinced. In response to the claims that white officers from Colored Troops had been crucified and burned, Grant told Halleck on August 29, "I have no evidence of ill-treatment to any prisoners captured from us further than the determination to turn over to Governors of States all colored soldiers captured." Grant considered the tale in the *Democrat* "entirely sensational." No mention was made in Grant's exchange with Halleck about the events a month earlier, involving the Mississippi Marine Brigade and Parsons's raid of destruction near Goodrich's Landing. It is possible Grant did not connect the two because the Marine Brigade reports referred to burned bodies of slaves, not soldiers. Furthermore, because the *Democrat* article referred to Milliken's Bend, Grant likewise could dismiss it, since no reports of such torture or fires had come in after that battle. Grant took the newspaper article strictly at face value, reading it as a completely fabricated narrative of events that supposedly transpired after Milliken's Bend. But viewed in context of discoveries by the Mississippi Marine Brigade as they moved inland in the aftermath of Parsons's raid, it seems likely that the news article, exaggerated though it might be, was at least partially based upon actual events.[47]

In the same letter that enclosed the *Democrat* article, Halleck also requested an update on Grant's inquiry to Taylor about prisoners taken at Milliken's Bend. Grant obliged by providing him with copies of their correspondence. Even Grant was having some difficulty keeping the details straight; he erroneously refers to Milliken's Bend as occurring in July. Grant told Halleck that he remained satisfied with Taylor's denial, and, again, it seemed the matter was closed.[48]

Although rumors about the events of the summer of 1863 in Louisiana would swirl around Grant's headquarters at Vicksburg and Halleck's office in Washington for months, the truth about Milliken's Bend remained elusive. What had happened to the prisoners, white and black? Late in 1863, the testimony of E. J. Conner, whose identity is otherwise unknown, shed some light. As a prisoner of the Confederates in Monroe, Louisiana, in late June, and later rescued, Conner testified in November that a captain and a lieutenant from the black troops captured at Milliken's Bend had been killed at Monroe after a brief imprisonment. The rank he gives for the two prisoners precisely matches that of Capt. Corydon Heath and 2nd Lt. George L. Conn, two officers who went missing during the fight at the Bend. Conner's source for this information was Confederate soldiers, "Union ladies," and, later, "common talk" in Shreveport, though he himself had not personally encountered the men.[49] His testimony was forwarded with an inquiry across the lines to Taylor in late December. Taylor denied Conner's statements, saying that "the rumors upon which Conner's affidavit is based are utterly without foundation."[50]

Also that December, Col. Hermann Lieb declared, concerning his own investigation, "I have now ample proof to convince me" that Heath and a lieutenant from the 11th Louisiana (undoubtedly referring to Conn), had been "executed at Monroe, La. by a military mob." Union Brig. Gen. John D. Stevenson's expedition to Monroe in late August, although brief, enabled Lieb to find out the details. "The black crime of murder on a prisoner of war has been committed," he wrote Assistant Adjutant General, Col. Edward

Townsend in Washington, enclosing testimony from Maj. John G. Davis and Brig. Gen. Mortimer Leggett.[51]

Davis was a subordinate of Colonel Lieb in the 9th Louisiana and had been on the expedition under Stevenson. He made it a part of his duty to inquire about the fate of Heath, who had not been heard from since his capture at Milliken's Bend nearly three months ago. The citizens of Monroe told him that Heath had been "held in close confinement." Not long before the arrival of the Yankee expedition, "he was taken out of Prison at night and put to Death," but the civilians could not tell Davis how he had been killed. Davis then went to the Confederate hospital and inquired of the soldiers there. "I found several men who had seen Captain Heath while a Prisoner, and their statements all agreed concerning his Death," he wrote. He also spoke to Confederate prisoners captured near Monroe who made similar statements, adding that Heath was "taken out of prison by the Rebel authorities at night and hung until dead."[52]

Leggett had been briefly in charge of the post at Monroe before Union troops withdrew less than twenty-four hours after taking the town. While there, he had heard a rumor "that two of our officers who had been taken prisoner were killed in Monroe some weeks before." After questioning "some responsible citizens," Leggett learned that the two officers

> were hand-cuffed together and confined in the jail at Monroe. The irons with which they were fastened, being too small, caused them great distress, their limbs became badly inflamed and swollen. The citizens complained to the military authorities of the barbarity, and were answered that "they would soon end their misery." The next night they were taken from the jail just after dark, put under charge of a squad of soldiers who took them across the river, that soon after guns were heard, and the squad returned without the prisoners & reported that they had shot them. One citizen said he went to the place where the firing was heard and found where they were buried.

Leggett planned to take sworn statements from citizens and to disinter the bodies, but he and his force were recalled to the Mississippi River at daybreak.[53]

Although Lieb did not address the discrepancy between Davis and Leggett's reports as to the manner of the two officer's deaths, he nevertheless found the evidence convincing enough to write Townsend directly at the U.S. adjutant general's office. Based upon these statements, the adjutant general agreed that Heath and Conn had been murdered after being taken prisoner. Not all of the white officers captured at Milliken's Bend met the same fate, however. Capt. Elisha DeWitt of Company I, 9th Louisiana Infantry, was also taken prisoner but by mid-July was "absent on parole of honor" at Benton Barracks, Missouri. Like most of the other officers in his Colored Troops regiment, he would have still held his old rank as a sergeant of Company K, 7th Missouri Infantry. He could not be mustered in as captain in his new regiment until a sufficient number of men had enlisted in his company.[54]

One of his fellow officers in the 9th Louisiana, the chatty David Cornwell, recalled in his memoir:

The only one [of the officers captured at Milliken's Bend] who ever returned was the Captain of Co. I. whose name I cannot recall. I remember him as of medium height, square and solid built with a strong fine face. He had been a sergeant in the 6th [sic] Missouri Infantry and still wore his old uniform with the chevrons on the jacket. Fortunately for him there was nothing about his person to indicate his rank, or his connection with a colored regiment, and he was able to convince them that he had incidently [sic] happened to be there when the attact [sic] was made, and felt bound to take a hand in it. So they let him off. He returned to the Bend, picked up his traps and went back to his old regiment. He did not propose to take such chances.[55]

Although Heath, Conn, and DeWitt were the only officers captured at Milliken's Bend, a few other white officers were taken elsewhere in northeastern Louisiana that summer. It does not appear that any other officers taken during this time met the same fate as Heath and Conn.[56] While in Tyler, Texas, Kate Stone wrote in her diary that some white officers from black units were imprisoned at nearby Camp Ford. When her diary was published in the 1950s, editor John Q. Anderson believed these men were captured during Parsons's raid near Goodrich's Landing and Lake Providence in late June. Hollandsworth, in his investigation of the fate of white officers serving with black troops, confirmed that Lt. John East of the 1st Arkansas Infantry, A. D., who was captured at Mound Plantation, spent the rest of the war at Camp Ford and was apparently the only officer from the Colored Troops imprisoned there.[57]

In addition to Lieutenant East, three other white officers were taken at the Mound. One of them was Capt. William B. Wallace, of Company E. He spent two months "in close confinement" in the hands of the Rebels but was freed when Union forces took Monroe in late August. Two of his colleagues, 2nd Lt. James M. Marshall of Company E and Capt. Hugh Maxwell of Company G, returned to duty with their regiment in December. Although it is not clear what happened to Marshall and Maxwell in the interim, it is certain that none of the Yankee officers taken at the Mound were executed.[58] All three of these men from the 1st Arkansas appear to have been confined in Monroe at about the same time as Heath and Conn. Why those two were executed and the rest spared is unclear. Captain Wallace undoubtedly provided further details about his own captivity in his testimony as part of Lieb's investigation, but the record of what he said has been lost.[59]

The fighting at Milliken's Bend was extraordinarily violent, even by the horrific standards of the Civil War. Nearly all of the black regiments at Milliken's Bend were raised from northeastern Louisiana. Both of these factors may have prompted the executions of Heath and Conn. By contrast, the small force at the Mound quickly capitulated when it was outnumbered, and most of the African Americans composing this force came from southeastern Arkansas. Because the officers at the Mound surrendered their black enlisted men unconditionally, the officers' lives may have been been spared. Furthermore, Confederate general Walker's report states that the white officers surrendered on the condition of being treated as prisoners of war. Southern honor and the word of gentlemen, such as Colonel Parsons and Gen. James C. Tappan, may have ensured these officers' safety.[60]

Although tracing the fate of the white officers captured at Milliken's Bend and Mound Plantation is difficult, precise information about the fate of black enlisted men who were taken prisoner is almost nonexistent. Early regimental records for the 9th Louisiana Infantry, African Descent, were lost in the fight, and details about individuals from this unit, even those killed or wounded in the battle, are difficult to come by. Many compiled service records for men in this unit are simply a name on a card, and nothing more.

Some of the records of Conn's regiment, the 11th Louisiana Infantry, African Descent, do survive. Numerous men are simply listed as "missing," with no further information provided. Some may have wandered off, fled, deserted, joined up with other Federal units, or gone to contraband camps or Federal leased plantations to find their families. If in Confederate custody, they may have been returned as slaves to their former owners, retained as slaves in direct service to the Confederacy (such as through the quartermaster department), taken to Texas and possibly confined in the state prison, or sent to a prison camp where they may have died before release at the end of the war. The possibility remains that a few may have been executed as "an example," as Confederate assistant adjutant general Henry L. Clay recommended to Gen. Kirby Smith.[61]

Among those African American soldiers taken prisoner were Andrew Shields, Pious Berry, Jerry Gaines, Morris Wall, Josiah Howard, Andrew Jackson, and Henry Turner. It is not clear what happened to them, as no further information is provided in the regimental records. Others, such as Nelson Washington, George Washington, Pleasant Boner (also known as Pleasant Barnett), and Jadon[?] Turner, were taken prisoner, held in Texas (specific location not stated), and later returned to their regiment on various dates, most in late 1865.[62]

Like the 9th and 11th Louisiana regiments, the fate of the African American soldiers from the two companies of the 1st Arkansas captured at Mound Plantation is unclear. Company records were burned or captured, and twelve enlisted men from Company E remain completely unaccounted for, without so much as their names recorded. Soldiers like Lewis Bogan, Charles Bogan, William Harris, and Charles Fremont were taken up, along with many of the captured contrabands taken on the larger raid, and force-marched toward the west. A few who straggled, like Jim Albert, were shot down. Some of these men were treated as prisoners of war; others were returned to slavery or set to laboring on Confederate fortifications.[63] Other African Americans taken by the Confederates were removed to the west. George T. Boardman of the 16th Texas Infantry took the train from Delhi to go to the hospital in Monroe, and "300 captive Negroes taken at Lake Providence" were on board with him. It is not known where their final destination was, nor if they were soldiers or civilians, but their presence proves they were not executed on the battlefield nor consumed in a conflagration.[64]

More specific information about the fate of at least a few African American men is found in the records of Confederate captain Nathan A. Birge, who served as quartermaster at Monroe and elsewhere in the Trans-Mississippi. His records for the summer of 1863 show numerous African Americans hired for a variety of positions, including laborers, teamsters, blacksmiths, and hostlers. Most of the men were hired out for thirty dollars a month from

persons who still held them in bondage. However, a few men—identified by
first name only—are noted as being "captured from the Yankees." They were
put to work for the Confederate government without compensation for themselves or anyone else. These men captured from Northern hands may have
been laborers on federally leased plantations or persons staying in contraband
camps or otherwise within Yankee lines, though it seems most likely that they
were Federal soldiers. It seems odd that the designation "captured from the
Yankees" would be used for anything other than soldiers, though a number
of contraband camps had been established near the Mississippi River within
Yankee lines, and their residents could have been referred to in this manner.
David Cornwell's account of Yankee recruiting tactics, other Union soldiers'
comments, plantation commissioners' complaints, and the later reports from
black soldiers about the circumstances of their enlistments reveal that virtually all able-bodied African American males were taken from the area and put
into the Union army unless there were compelling reasons why they could not
serve, such as medical conditions. It is not certain, based on Birge's records,
that these men were soldiers, but it does seem likely. However, even this information is sparse, and it is not known what happened to these men after
August 1863.[65]

This sliver of information from Confederate quartermaster Birge and the
return of black enlisted men from Texas to the 49th U.S. Colored Infantry
(the later designation of the 11th Louisiana) at the end of the war provides
proof that many black enlisted men captured in Louisiana that summer were
not executed by the Confederates for wearing the uniform of a Union soldier.
The exact details of their fate remain obscure. Even their service and pension records are remarkably unrevealing. For instance, Nelson Washington's
service record merely states, "captured by the enemy and held as prisoner"
until November of 1865, when he returned to his regiment. He apparently did
not file for a pension, which might have yielded more information. Pleasant
Boner's service record states that he was taken prisoner while on picket duty at
Milliken's Bend but returned to his regiment on September 1, 1863. Although
it is not stated in his record, it is possible that he may have been freed from
Confederate hands during Stevenson's raid on Monroe in late August. By the
1890s, he was living at the National Military Home in Leavenworth, Kansas,
under the name Pleasant Barnett. Although his pension record provides similar information about his being taken prisoner, mostly abstracted from his
service record, no further details were provided in his personal testimony.[66]

Like Nelson Washington and Pleasant Boner/Barnett, precise details are lacking about exactly what happened to those black enlisted men who were taken prisoner that summer. It is not clear if they were transferred to a prisoner of war camp, put at hard labor, or sold into slavery. Because many men returned to their regiment—at least those from the 49th USCI—in late 1865, it seems likely that the majority may have been held and treated as legitimate prisoners of war.[67] Yet it is equally apparent that at least some men were probably killed after their capture, though this was the exception, not the rule. A dozen or so men were killed after the Mound, and Thomas Cormal's earlier admission to his Yankee captors indicated that about eight or twelve black men may have been killed near Perkins' Landing.

Cormal's statement is supported by Gen. Richard Taylor's admission that Captain E. S. McCall's forces killed one captain and "twelve negroes" at nearby Lake St. Joseph. However, this action was entirely separate from the attack on Perkins' Landing by McCulloch's Brigade at the end of May. McCall's company of sixty men, part of Harrison's cavalry battalion, attacked a "negro camp" on June 4. It is not clear if this was a recruiting depot, a contraband camp, or something between the two. Nor is it readily apparent whether the black men were soldiers or laborers, although they were apparently under the command of a captain. Taylor's account makes it sound like they were offering resistance, as if they were soldiers. He also does not explicitly state whether the thirteen men were killed during the course of fighting or if they were captured and then killed. His report implies that these were routine battle casualties. Taylor also mentions that "the remainder" of the Union force was captured, along with about sixty women and children. It seems unusual that no casualties were reported for McCall's force, even though he was outnumbered. If Thomas Cormal, the prisoner taken up by the USS *Louisville*, was part of Harrison's command, his account might be referring to these events, since Lake St. Joseph was only a few miles from Perkins' Landing.[68]

Another explanation for some of the executions may have been a general lack of discipline among the Confederate cavalry. Although the situation grew worse after the fall of Vicksburg, discipline problems may have already been developing among the horsemen earlier that summer. The situation came to a head in October, when troopers from Col. Isaac F. Harrison's and Col. William H. Parsons's commands committed "thefts and depredations" throughout north central and northeastern Louisiana. Lt. Gen. Edmund Kirby Smith took the matter so seriously that he ordered Brig. Gen. Paul Octave Hébert to have the guilty parties shot. The troopers' lack of discipline and the wartime record of Parsons's unit, in particular, raises questions about their possible involvement in the execution of Yankee prisoners captured that preceding summer.[69]

Hébert recounted some of the difficulties he had had with men from both units, admitting that there had been problems for some time. "Col. Parsons Command [sic], both officers and men, like many of the same arm in our service, are not models of discipline or of soldier-like behavior," he confessed. "The regiment of old . . . gave me much trouble in Texas, particularly in regard to their warfare on pigs and bullocks." Hébert complained that the orders he issued had been constantly ignored and that neither subordinate officers nor enlisted men had been punished for their actions. "When brought up there is always a wo[e]ful want of evidence," he moaned. But, he admitted, Parsons's men "have one redeeming quality, *they have fought when called upon.*"[70]

Hébert went on to elaborate that not all of the "depredations" had been committed by Parsons's troopers. "His men, no doubt, suffer the penalty of a bad reputation," he explained. Thieves and bandits, loyal to no one except themselves, infested the region. Hébert had been at war with these ruffians since he assumed command in Monroe. At Smith's urging, he vowed to rid the area of these disreputable characters. "All such, where taken will be shot or hanged on the spot," he wrote, assuming his own undisciplined cavalrymen would follow his orders at least in this regard.[71]

Given the unsettled nature of the situation and the continuing discipline problems among the cavalrymen of Parsons's and Harrison's commands, it is plausible that some of the reported hangings and executions of white Union officers and black enlisted men may have come at the hands of these troopers. Anne J. Bailey's studies of Parsons's Brigade convincingly demonstrate that these men were capable of such acts. In both 1862 and 1863, Parsons's men were accused of killing black soldier-prisoners or civilians, and strong evidence points to their guilt.[72]

Harrison and his men did not have quite such a record, although his men were implicated more than once. Undoubtedly, the Yankee presence near their homes in northeastern Louisiana gave these men extra commitment to their cause, as well as a sense of urgency and desperation. Their worries would have only increased after the fall of Vicksburg, when most Confederate troops were pushed toward the central part of the state. Such conditions may have prompted some individuals to take extraordinary measures, with or without formal orders. Harrison himself probably would have had no compunction about the matter. He had had his own slave executed before the war for plot-ting a rebellion.[73]

Men from Parson's and Harrison's commands were likely suspects for these reasons. Their lack of discipline made them more prone to acting outside of legal or authoritarian boundaries, and it is conceivable that a few rogue sol-diers, such as a small group of men guarding Yankee prisoners, might have decided to take matters into their own hands. Of course, their lack of disci-pline and a fondness for pigs and bullocks does not make them guilty of killing Union prisoners in cold blood. As Hébert claimed, these units "suffered from a bad reputation," and there were numerous bands of guerillas roaming about the countryside who may have shared in the guilt of executing black soldiers in uniform, or their white officers. However, all of the reports concerning such executions, whether they originate from Confederate or Federal sources, unanimously indicate that the guards, captors, and accused executioners were members of the Confederate military. Even Richard Taylor, in his denials, never evaded the issue by claiming that guerillas were the guilty party. Instead, he directly denied any involvement by soldiers under his command. This de-nial may be the crux of the issue. The men who did the killing may have been under another general's authority. Taylor could rightfully deny the accusations and be legitimately absolved of any guilt. The fact that the execution of Heath and Conn took place in Monroe—where Hébert had his headquarters—makes this general look like a leading suspect, in authority if not in deed. Just as in Texas during the Great Hanging, Hébert's inaction may have been his way of passively supporting his subordinates' actions.

The discipline problems with the cavalrymen escalated so much that fall that Hébert was relieved of his command in early December. This was the second time during the Civil War that Hébert, a former Louisiana governor and Mexican War hero, had been relieved of command because of troubles with his subordinates and his own lack of oversight and poor leadership. Given Hébert's experiences in 1862 and 1863, and the command difficulties he had in Texas and Louisiana, it is possible that some executions were committed by soldiers under his command, even if it was done without his authority. Or, he may have chosen to turn a blind eye and avoid sullying his hands. Either way, Hébert was held responsible for events that took place within his jurisdiction and actions performed by soldiers under his command.[74]

Meanwhile that fall, within the Federal lines, rumors persisted about ex-ecutions of men from the Colored Troops. On October 5, two Confederate deserters, Henry S. Warrick of the Bell Battery and Charles A. Gitchell [?] of the 13th Louisiana [Cavalry?] Battalion passed through Union brigadier general John P. Hawkins's headquarters at Goodrich's Landing. One man gave statements about the hanging of "negro soldiers" and Hawkins forwarded an affidavit to the provost marshal in Vicksburg. Hawkins urged the matter be brought to the attention of General Grant and pledged, "If the Gen. will authorize retaliation I will exercise it." By this time, four months after the fight at Milliken's Bend and slightly over a month since the deaths of Heath and Conn had been confirmed during Stevenson's expedition to Monroe, Hawkins was ready to take the most forceful steps to ensure that black and white soldiers received equal treatment by Confederate forces.[75] He would not be the only man who called for "retaliation." The events at Milliken's Bend and the murky fate of many captured Union soldiers that summer would eventually lead to debate at the highest levels of the opposing governments.

"This Battle Has Significance"
Milliken's Bend and the Wider War

MILLIKEN'S BEND, although one of the smaller actions of the war, nevertheless is important for three main reasons. First, along with Port Hudson and Fort Wagner, Milliken's Bend helped change attitudes and answered in the affirmative the question of whether black troops would fight. Secondly, it was sometimes invoked to aid recruiting, particularly among literate, free blacks in the North, showing them that if former slaves were willing to fight, then they, too, should be ready to enlist to help their Southern brothers. Finally, and most importantly, the capture of a number of officers and enlisted men at Milliken's Bend and elsewhere in Louisiana that summer brought the Confederate treatment of soldiers from the Colored Troops into the forefront, ultimately resulting in the cessation of prisoner exchanges.

Immediately after Milliken's Bend, abolitionists reaffirmed and even skeptics were persuaded that African Americans—even those who had been former slaves—could make good soldiers. Even Confederate brigadier general Henry McCulloch praised the black soldiers' tenacity at Milliken's Bend. In the North, as word spread about the repulse of the Southerners by the raw brigade of former slaves, Milliken's Bend was trumpeted as proof that black men would fight, and fight well. Union colonel Isaac F. Shepard's report, for example, glowed with pride. "I think there will be a future that will make this *first regular battle against the blacks alone* honorably historic. The best of all is our troops are not demoralized by the sad result to them. Not at all disheartened. Indeed they have risen with the event, and proudly walk with a loftier tread then [*sic*] before."[1]

White soldiers who had been skeptical were now converted. With an attitude typical of many whites at the time, a convalescing Union soldier wrote just prior to the battle, with apparent sarcasm, "Did I ever tell you there is a Negro brigade a couple of miles up the bend, *valiant soldiers?* It would amuse you to see them drill." Two days after the battle, he was more enthusiastic:

"All are astonished at their fighting qualities . . . They have proved themselves worthy of the name of soldiers."[2]

About a month after Milliken's Bend, and immediately after the surrender of Vicksburg, Benjamin Stevens left the 15th Iowa Infantry to become an officer in the 10th Louisiana Infantry, African Descent. He wrote his mother in late July that "the thing is demonstrated, the nigger *will fight*." Among paroled Confederates at Vicksburg, he found the Rebels more willing to fight two regiments of white soldiers over one regiment of blacks. "Rebel Citizens fear them more than they would fear Indians," he wrote. Although Stevens had become an officer in the Colored Troops, he nevertheless expressed his preference for the war to remain one for the restoration of the Union, rather than for the abolition of slavery. But he supported the use of former slaves as soldiers against the Confederacy, seeing it as a practical matter: "We are using their own strength against them."[3]

Chaplain George G. Edwards, of the 11th Louisiana Infantry, African Descent, thought the evidence incontrovertible. "This battle has significance. It demonstrates the fact that the freed slaves will fight." Pointing to the casualties, Edwards continued, "Our figures are our arguments that colored men will fight, and they need no comment. We leave them as the battle-field gave them, mournfully brave."[4]

But it was not just the soldiers nearby who praised the black troops at Milliken's Bend. Word soon got to the newspapers. The *Chicago Tribune* lauded operations at Port Hudson but called Milliken's Bend the "crowning glory" of Negro soldiers, erroneously crediting them with saving Grant's supply lines, which, by this time, were safely east in Mississippi. The article also, like many accounts, failed to mention the gunboats, which were the true saviors of the day. Despite the factual inaccuracies, the praise was sincere.[5] "Mack" of the *Cincinnati Daily Commercial* reported that the former slaves met the enemy "with remarkable coolness and courage," even though some of the men had not had their muskets for more than a few days.[6]

Word spread far. A Fourth of July speech to the "colored citizens" of San Francisco mentioned the battle and said that Rebel prisoners taken at Richmond, Louisiana, were relieved to have been captured by white troops, "as they expected no quarter from the blacks" since the fight at Milliken's Bend. Whether these prisoners were part of McCulloch's Brigade is unclear, and the precise reason for their expectation that black Union soldiers would grant no quarter is likewise unknown. Prior to the fight at the Bend, Colonel Lieb was reported to have made such a threat in retaliation when it was rumored that guerillas had put to death some black soldiers elsewhere in the region. Direct charges were never leveled at black troops in the way that persistent rumors—and eventual investigations—followed Confederates in northern Louisiana that summer.[7]

While many in the Northern press gave positive reports about the fight at the Bend, not all of the press was favorable. Robert Hamilton of the *Weekly Anglo-African* waited in vain for a formal report from the U.S. Army. In an editorial, he summarized the basic facts of the fight and mentioned that many of the Federal wounded had been "killed under the 'no quarter' cry." White officers were rumored to have fled, and Hamilton, suspecting a coverup, thought this might be the cause of delay in the official report. White troops did not have "the same incentives to fight" as the black man, wrote Hamilton. "Our life, our liberty, our country, our religious privileges, our family, OUR ALL is at stake . . . These things are well understood by every black man in the army; and this knowledge and the determination to be free will carry him over entrenchments and into the very jaws of death itself." Hamilton felt it was even more important that "officers for colored regiments may be from the bravest of the brave, or many such scenes will be witnessed as took place at Milliken's Bend."[8]

Other Northern newspapers leveled the charge of cowardice against the officers. These accusations probably originated with Colonel Chamberlain's hasty escape to a gunboat during the fight. Shepard promised to investigate but felt the casualties spoke for themselves: "54 white officers in all, *and 28 of them* among the list of casualties! What fight shows so grand a record?"[9] Ultimately, few officers came in for official reprimand, and most evidence indicates the black men fought with great valor and tenacity, despite minimal training, poor equipment, and a precarious tactical position, with their backs to the river. Although it was the Yankee gunboats that forced Confederate troops to withdraw, newspaper reports often omitted the gunboats, crediting the Colored Troops with single-handedly sending the Rebels on the run.

The valor of the African American soldiers provided incentive for recruiting. A July 6 broadside from a mass rally evoked Milliken's Bend and Port Hudson to encourage free blacks to enlist. Of the three major battles involving black troops that summer, only at Milliken's Bend was the Union force composed almost entirely of black troops, nearly all of whom had been held in bondage just a few short months or weeks before. "Though they are just from the galling, poisoning grasp of slavery, they have startled the world by the most exalted heroism. If they have proved themselves heroes, can not we prove ourselves men?" urged the broadside, endorsed by a number of individuals, including Frederick Douglass. Other versions of the same broadside featured the words "Valor and Heroism" in large print, just above "Milliken's Bend and Port Hudson," and prodded its readers with the taunt: "ARE FREEMEN LESS BRAVE THAN SLAVES"?[10] In Xenia, Ohio, a convention of African Americans adopted resolutions supportive of the soldiers at Milliken's Bend and Morris Island (Fort Wagner) and encouraged volunteers for a black regiment then forming at Camp Delaware.[11] And when the 6th U.S. Colored Troops received their regimental colors at Camp William Penn in September 1863, Milliken's Bend was the first battle to be invoked to inspire confidence and courage in the men. Fort Wagner and Port Hudson followed.[12]

Passionate abolitionists or journalists prone to exaggeration fanned the flames of hysteria and outrage in the North, hoping to stiffen Northern resolve. In the month prior to the Union victories at Gettysburg and Vicksburg, the heroism of the black troops gave new hope for the Union war effort. Abolitionists felt such reports could encourage hesitant individuals to have compassion for black soldiers and their officers. Some men, like the Iowan who opposed emancipation but found himself an officer in the Colored Troops, might be converted to the abolitionist cause, motivated by practical expediency rather than moral sentiment. It was hoped that actions like Milliken's Bend and Port Hudson would increase recruiting for the army in general and the Colored Troops in particular, including their officer corps.

Playing up the hysteria over reported executions and atrocities by the Confederates—whether or not they were true—nevertheless served a purpose. Both slave and free African Americans could be motivated to join the army to fight in the cause of freedom against a ruthless enemy, conscious that their own self-interest and personal liberty were intimately tied to the Union cause. If that was not enough, some enlistees might be inspired to join the Federal army simply to seek revenge for their fallen brethren. Reports of the execution of white officers gave greater incentive to all Union soldiers to fight more stubbornly and with greater vengeance. Such news articles also had the effect of discouraging lukewarm applicants for commissions in the Colored Troops. No longer could such positions be seen as low risk. Although the vast majority of Colored Troops would continue to serve as garrison troops, the prospect of battle and possible execution—whether true or not—meant that just as Adjt.

Gen. Lorenzo Thomas had originally desired, only men "whose hearts are in the work" would apply for commissions.[13]

Certainly, the most important consequence of the fight at Milliken's Bend—and other clashes involving African American troops that summer throughout the Confederacy—was the breakdown of prisoner exchanges. Throughout the summer, sensational news articles reiterating rumors of executions of white officers and black enlisted men circulated in Washington, sparking correspondence between U.S. and Confederate authorities.

Confederate president Jefferson Davis thought that Lincoln's Emancipation Proclamation was nothing short of a call for a massive, bloody, and horrific slave uprising, backed by the military power of the United States. In Confederate eyes, the North had thrown down the gauntlet: "the African slaves have not only been excited to insurrection . . . but numbers of them have actually been armed for a servile war—a war in its nature far exceeding in horrors the most merciless atrocities of the savages." The acts of emancipation and enlisting former slaves as soldiers were nothing short of an atrocity and a violation of the rules of war. Davis said that only "just retribution" could deter the United States from such "crimes."[14]

No wonder, then, that a furious war of words broke out. Both sides accused each other of violating the laws and usages of war in their public policy, long before the issues came to a head on the battlefields the following summer. While the Confederate government railed against the crime of the Emancipation Proclamation, U.S. authorities vehemently protested the official Confederate policy concerning prisoners taken from black units, even though it had yet to be tested on the battlefield. Charges and countercharges flew between Washington and Richmond, each side firmly claiming its right to pursue the policies outlined by the respective governments.

On May 1, 1863, the Confederate Congress in a joint resolution took Davis's earlier proclamation one step further and dictated that captured officers of Colored Troops should be put to death. Black enlisted men—or, in Southern parlance, "negroes in arms"—were to be handed over to state authorities for punishment. The Confederate Congress also made it clear that they were compelled, regretfully, to take these steps in retaliation for the Emancipation Proclamation, a document "inconsistent with the spirit of . . . modern warfare . . . among civilized nations."[15]

To Confederates, the enlistment and arming of slaves was indeed a violation of the laws of war and, as such, should be met with the penalty of death.

Confederate secretary of war James Seddon sent an extended response to Robert Ould, Confederate agent of exchange, on June 24, 1863, just two weeks after Milliken's Bend, in which he deplored the Union strategy of insurrection. "The employment of a servile insurrection as an instrument of war is contrary to the usages of civilized nations," he wrote. "The enlistment of negro slaves as a part of the Army of the United States cannot be regarded as having any object but one. It is a part of the system of the United States Government to subvert by violence the social system and domestic relations of the negro slaves in the Confederacy and to add to the calamities of war a servile insurrection. The savage passions and brutal appetites of a barbarous race are to be stimulated into fierce activity. Such a war involves necessarily the abandonment of all rules, conventions, mitigating influences, and humanizing usages"; it becomes a war of "mutual extermination." Seddon and the Confederate government embraced this policy, which they believed they were driven to by the actions and policies of the United States. If the United States objected to such a policy, there was no sympathy from the Southerners; the Yankees had brought it upon themselves.[16]

As reports about the mistreatment and possible murder of black Union soldiers at Milliken's Bend and elsewhere that summer continued to come in, Frederick Douglass lost all patience with Lincoln. It had been more than six months since Jefferson Davis told the world that "he meant to treat blacks not as soldiers but as felons." To Douglass, Lincoln now became just as guilty: "Until Mr. Lincoln shall interpose his power to prevent these atrocious assassinations of Negro soldiers, the civilized world will hold him equally with Jefferson Davis responsible for them." When Douglass met with Lincoln in August, the president explained his position: "'Remember that Milliken's Bend, Port Hudson and Fort Wagner are recent events . . . these were necessary to prepare the way." Always a shrewd politician, Lincoln knew that if he had acted prematurely, before blacks had met the test of bravery on the battlefield or before Confederates had put their words and threats into action, all of the prejudice against "the Negro race would be visited on his administration." It took these battles, and the casualties on and off the battlefield, for Lincoln to issue his policy of retaliation.[17]

On July 30, not long before Douglass's visit, Lincoln had declared that U.S. soldiers would be granted equal protection, regardless of race. Likewise, they should receive equitable treatment from Confederate authorities. He insisted, "The law of nations and the usages and customs of war, as carried on by civilized powers, permit no distinction as to color in the treatment of prisoners of war as public enemies. To sell or enslave any captured person on account of his color and for no offense against the laws of war is a relapse into barbarism and a crime against the civilization of the age." Lincoln outlined a policy of retaliation. For any Union soldier "killed in violation of the laws of war," a Confederate soldier would be put to death. For any Union soldier enslaved, a Confederate soldier would be placed at hard labor.[18]

Even before the battles that summer, the two sides had long ago reached an impasse on the Negro prisoner problem. Prompted by the Confederate Congress's edict of May 1, which called for the execution of white officers and the punishment of "negroes in arms," formal exchanges between North and South were suspended by order of General Halleck on May 25, 1863. This was just two days before Banks launched his assault against Port Hudson and less than two weeks prior to Milliken's Bend. Occasional "special" exchanges would continue, however, and both sides tried to work out agreements for an overall cartel plan, but by late November the exchange of prisoners between the two belligerents had ceased, hung up on the intractable problem of Negro soldiers.[19]

Ethan Allen Hitchcock, Federal commissioner for exchange of prisoners, felt compelled to address the concerns of an anxious public about the cessation of prisoner exchanges. In a letter published on November 28, 1863, in the *New York Times*, he laid the blame squarely on the Confederacy. He referred to Davis's address at the start of the year, which declared that officers in command of Colored Troops would be considered "criminals engaged in inciting servile insurrection." Hitchcock reviewed the Confederacy's howls of protest against the Emancipation Proclamation and the enlistment of blacks, including former slaves, into the U.S. Army. Given Southerners' cries for vengeance and no quarter, Hitchcock also stated, perhaps unknowingly exaggerating, that "in no single instance has the smallest evidence come to light tending to show that any officer connected with colored troops has been captured alive and held in the South as a prisoner of war; nor has any colored man employed as a soldier of the United States been captured in the South and accounted for as a prisoner of war." Hitchcock leveled a serious charge against the Southerners: "we do not know of a single instance in which they have respected those laws [of war] in their treatment of colored troops . . . They are not recognized in the South as soldiers."[20]

In a postscript to that letter, Hitchcock quoted an editorial from the

Richmond Enquirer paraphrasing the May 1 action of the Confederate Congress. The resolution declared "the commanding, organizing, or aiding negroes in arms against the Confederate States to be inciting servile insurrection, and those so offending, when captured, are punished with death or in the discretion of the court. The law further punishes with death the inciting a servile insurrection or rebellion; and that all negroes and mulattoes taken in arms" were to be delivered to state authorities. No distinction was made between free and slave persons of color, Hitchcock pointed out. "It is inconceivable how any one can favor the proposition of a general exchange of prisoners while the law in the South is what their own papers represent and approve, and while the practice . . . according to a good deal of evidence, goes beyond the law itself in barbarity."[21]

Matters concerning prisoners taken at Milliken's Bend and elsewhere continued unresolved until December, when the U.S. House Committee on Military Affairs sought information from the secretary of war about "the alleged acts of inhumanity" by the Rebels against dead and wounded Union soldiers and those taken prisoner. Although the investigation was not specific to Milliken's Bend, one of the reports sent by the secretary of war was that of Col. Hermann Lieb, of the 9th Louisiana (by this time now temporarily known as the 1st Mississippi Heavy Artillery). Lieb's report of the fate of Heath and Conn reached the secretary of war sometime in December and was promptly passed along to the House Committee. Details of the committee's actions are unclear, due to a paucity of records, but by January 22, 1864, a "mass of evidence" had been gathered in response to the initial resolution. How much of this evidence related to Milliken's Bend is not known. The secretary of war's response, and further action by the House Committee, likewise remains unknown.[22]

A year after the Emancipation Proclamation, the charges and countercharges continued. On February 3, 1864, a motion was introduced in the Confederate Congress resolving, in part, that "the emancipation of the negro slaves within the Confederate States by the enemy is not among the acts of legitimate warfare, but is properly classed by writers on public law, including the most eminent publicists of the United States, among such acts as 'putting to death all prisoners in cold blood.'" It is no surprise then, that executing officers and enlisted men with the Colored Troops was adjudged to be the proper course of action. Although the Federal government imposed a policy of retaliation in response to Confederate executions or reenslavement of black soldiers, the Confederates, in law and rhetoric, were already following a policy of retaliation in response to the enlistment of slaves by the United States. Enlisting slaves as soldiers into the U.S. Army and killing prisoners in cold blood were seen as equally heinous acts to Confederate eyes. If the United States was determined to pursue the former policy, the Confederacy was compelled to respond with the latter.[23]

In a joint resolution a few days later, the Confederate Congress conceded that free blacks and slaves should be treated differently. The use of Colored Troops meant that Southern slaves would be "seized, abducted and impressed into the military service of the United States and armed for warfare against their masters." It was preposterous to think that, if recaptured, this human chattel would not be returned to their proper "owners." Such measures would not apply to free blacks, though, nor their officers.[24]

The Union response remained unchanged. No prisoner exchanges would take place until *all* U.S. soldiers received equal treatment. The result of this policy was that prison populations on both sides swelled, bringing about horrors that would not be seen again until the Nazi concentration camps of the twentieth century. Camp Sumter, Georgia, more commonly known as Andersonville, was built in 1864 in response to prison overcrowding elsewhere in the South. Originally designed to house about eight or ten thousand Union prisoners, its population grew to over thirty thousand. Quarters were so tight that more than one thousand men crowded into each acre. Twelve thousand prisoners died. Those that survived were so emaciated that they were living skeletons.[25] The situation was only slightly better in the North. Elmira prison in New York was designed to house about four thousand inmates; more than twice that amount were confined there within two months of the prison's opening in the summer of 1864. During the following winter, Confederate soldiers had to contend with bitter cold and months of snow and ice, with little protection against the elements.[26]

The cessation of prisoner exchanges by Federal authorities, prompted by the Confederate policy against white and black soldiers of the Colored Troops, did not have all Yankees' support, not even those who were serving in the Colored Troops. David Cornwell, now promoted to the rank of captain to fill Corydon Heath's old position, thought a retaliatory policy of executing one Confederate prisoner for each Union soldier killed would be more appropriate than suspending all POW exchanges. In his memoir, Cornwell deplored the end of exchanges and blamed Grant for being indifferent to prisoners' fates.

Always finding fault with Grant about something, Cornwell blamed him—not Lincoln, Congress, the secretary of war, nor even the Confederates—for the suffering of Union POWs. "The boys in the ranks would to a man have voted for an immediate prisoner exchange even if they had known it would pro- long the war five years," Cornwell wrote. "The cruelties practiced upon our prisoners can never be forgotten," but it was "through the cruel and heartless reasoning of General Grant" that they had suffered so.[27] Although the men of Cornwell's regiment would never again meet the enemy on the field of battle, the war was far from over. While Federal authorities advocated equal treat- ment of black soldiers as POWs in Confederate hands, not everything was equal within the Federal lines.

REVENGE TAKEN BY THE BLACK ARMY FOR THE CRUEL-
TIES PRACTISED ON THEM BY THE FRENCH

This image, taken from a sympathetic account of the Haitian revolution written in 1805, exemplifies the horrors white Southerners imagined would occur if slaves were emancipated or took up arms in insurrection. (Marcus Rainsford, *An Historical Account of the Black Empire of Hayti*, courtesy Library of Congress)

ADJT. GEN. LORENZO THOMAS, USA

In spite of his lackluster speeches, Thomas was tasked with initiating the entire Colored Troops endeavor in the Mississippi Valley. By the end of 1863, just nine months after he began the effort, more than 20,000 black men—most of them former slaves—had enlisted in the U.S. Army. (Courtesy Library of Congress)

BRIG. GEN. JOHN P. HAWKINS, USA

Hawkins found officers in the Union army as well as government lessees to be almost a greater problem than threats from the Rebel military. Though not present at Milliken's Bend, Hawkins did battle with the Federal bureaucracy and complained about obstructionist tactics taken against him by individuals who opposed the use of Colored Troops. He even declared to abolitionist Gerrit Smith that some ex-slaves might be better off with their former owners, due to the poor treatment they received at Federal hands. (Mass.-MOLLUS, USAMHI)

KATE STONE

Twenty-two years old, observant, and articulate,
Kate Stone fled with her family from their home
near Milliken's Bend in April 1863. For a while, they
stayed with Sarah Wadley and her family in Monroe. Both women's diaries present vivid portraits of
the war in northern Louisiana. (John Q. Anderson
Papers, Mss. 2156, 2162, Louisiana and Lower Mississippi Valley Collections, LSU Libraries, Baton
Rouge, LA)

JOHN GORDON, USA

John Gordon was just fifteen years old when he joined the 11th Louisiana Infantry, African Descent, in early May 1863. He likely fought at Milliken's Bend. (John Gordon pension file, 49th USCI, NARA-DC)

FIGHT AT MILLIKEN'S BEND

As it appeared in *Harper's Weekly*, July 4, 1863. (Courtesy Library of Congress)

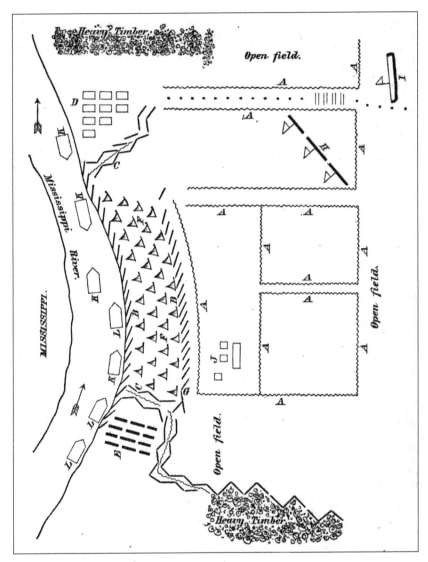

GEN. JOHN G. WALKER'S MAP

The only known map of the action at Milliken's Bend created near the time of the battle, Walker included it with his report to Taylor. (*ORA*, series 1, vol. 24, part 2, p. 463, Nashville Public Library, Special Collections)

USS *CHOCTAW* OFF VICKSBURG

Choctaw was commissioned just three months prior to Milliken's Bend. Undoubtedly its big guns saved the Union garrison from annihilation. (NH 55218, Naval History and Heritage Command)

COL. ISAAC F. SHEPARD, USA

Shepard was in the midst of turmoil when Confederates attacked the outpost at Milliken's Bend. Commanding the African Brigade during the absence of Gen. Hawkins and under arrest at the time of the battle, he nevertheless proved his commitment to the cause of freedom by standing with his men. He beamed afterward, "This *first regular battle against the blacks alone* [is] honorably historic." (Mass.-MOLLUS, USAMHI)

COL. HERMANN LIEB, USA

Colonel Lieb led the 9th Louisiana Infantry, African Descent, and was in temporary command of the African Brigade while Shepard was under arrest. At Milliken's Bend, Lieb's regiment lost more men killed than any other Union unit in a single engagement during the entire Vicksburg campaign. (L. B. Paul Collection, USAMHI)

BRIG. GEN. HENRY MCCULLOCH, CSA

In command of the Confederate brigade that attacked Milliken's Bend, McCulloch conceded that the Union black troops he faced fought well, though the "white or true Yankee portion ran like whipped curs." He proposed that black Union prisoners be returned to slavery or given as rewards to some of his men. (Courtesy of Texas State Library & Archives Commission)

MAJ. GEN. JOHN G. WALKER, CSA

Walker considered the capture of black troops by Confederate forces "unfortunate" and felt compelled to apologize to his superiors. (Ag2008.0005, DeGolyer Library, Southern Methodist University, Dallas, TX)

MAJ. GEN. RICHARD TAYLOR, CSA

Taylor repeatedly denied any knowledge of the rumored executions of black and white Union soldiers from the Colored Troops. Grant was satisfied with Taylor's denial, and for a time the matter was dropped. (Courtesy Library of Congress)

LT. GEN. EDMUND KIRBY SMITH, CSA

Smith was distressed to hear that black troops had been taken prisoner by his subordinates at Milliken's Bend and elsewhere. Instead, he advocated a "no quarter" policy on the battlefield. (Courtesy Library of Congress)

BRIG. GEN. PAUL OCTAVE HÉBERT, CSA

Hébert was a former Louisiana governor and planter. He was in charge of the Confederate post at Monroe, Louisiana, when two white Union officers captured at Milliken's Bend were taken to the woods and killed in cold blood. It is unclear if he had any direct involvement. However, his staff officer, Maj. M. W. Sims, was implicated, imprisoned by the Yankees, and threatened with execution before he made his escape. (Courtesy Library of Congress)

"We Intended to Fight for the Country"
The Limits of Freedom, 1863–1865

A S THE AUTHORITIES in Washington and Richmond bickered, the shattered soldiers in the African Brigade were busy regrouping. Col. Hermann Lieb returned from his recuperation a month after Milliken's Bend in mid-July to find his regiment in shambles. Both his major and lieutenant colonel were absent, and Lieb reported to Adjt. Gen. Lorenzo Thomas that "the order, discipline, and spirit of the regiment" were in "deplorable condition." Numerous line officers were also absent, some due to illness or wounds, others for unspecified reasons. Lt. Adam H. Hill, Lieb wrote, was "entirely unfit for military duty" and worthless to the regiment. Lt. Edwin Cheney and Lt. John Fareweather had similar accusations leveled against them. Second Lt. Edwin C. St. Clair deserted twenty days after Milliken's Bend. Capt. Corydon Heath was still listed as missing, and it would be another month before Lieb learned of his fate. Capt. Elisha DeWitt was absent on parole, and Capt. William Skillen was still recovering from his many wounds. Lieb made his point graphically—of thirty-five officers, seventeen were killed, missing, sick, or otherwise absent or unfit for duty. Virtually half of his officer corps was incapacitated. Despite this situation, Lieb wrote to General Thomas and reiterated Thomas's own proviso that only (white) men whose hearts were in the work should become officers in the Colored Troops. To prove his point, Lieb recommended that five men's appointments to his regiment be revoked.[1]

Lieb had mixed reviews of the enlisted men and echoed the popular view of many white men that former slaves were compliant and "easy to drill" but required constant attention by their white officers to "do justice to the uniform they wear." He had to continue recruiting to fill up his regiment, which was understrength from summer sickness and the casualties at Milliken's Bend. His task was nearly as large as it had been in May, but he was doing what he could to recruit up to full strength. In less than a month, he had added 800 enlisted men to the rolls, even though he had few officers to command them.

His regiment would soon be redesignated as a heavy artillery unit—requiring even more men to fill the rolls.[2]

As summer passed into fall, Thomas ordered Hawkins—now back with the brigade from sick leave—to scour the area for black men who were serving as laborers to private individuals and firms not associated with the government, instructing him that all "able bodied negroes as may be found suitable will at once be enrolled into organizations of African Descent."[3] It wasn't until two months after the fight at Milliken's Bend that the 9th Louisiana Infantry, African Descent, was finally and formally mustered into the U.S. service. Less than six months before, these men had been slaves, and on August 8, 1863, they stood clothed in the uniform of the U.S. Army—not yet full citizens (that would take the Fourteenth Amendment to the Constitution in 1868) but certainly free men—or at least as free as any enlisted man in either army could be.

Colonel Lieb soon let them know that freedom in a uniform had its limits. He issued a stern order in which he outlined his expectations of the men, and their duties and responsibilities. Lieb emphasized in every paragraph the importance and necessity of obedience to orders and respect for officers. He put special emphasis on the crime and penalty of desertion; soldiers could be shot if caught. Perhaps Lieb was telling his soldiers this for their own good. Some units, including perhaps the 9th Louisiana, had had difficulty with soldiers straying off to nearby plantations, hospitals, or contraband camps to visit their families. Former slaves who had run away to Union lines might be tempted to run again if they found their conditions unsatisfactory. Lieb also reminded the men that their freedom had been purchased at a terrible price, by "the blood of thousands of white soldiers." Incredibly, he made no mention of the regiment's harrowing fight at Milliken's Bend, where so much of their own blood had been spilled.[4]

As the hot summer dragged on, more men in the 9th Louisiana died, this time from disease. Lieb petitioned for more medical aid, but none came. One surgeon assigned to duty with the regiment was "old, slow, and impractical," and Lieb considered him worthless. A second surgeon Lieb thought was overwhelmed, although he was doing his best. By November 1863, the situation had not improved. Men were suffering from typhoid and dying at the rate of three or four a day, reported Surgeon Henry Penneman. The steward had succumbed to the same illness. The contract surgeon, the one Lieb complained about, had only inspected the men's tents once, "and then upon the run," because either the smell or the sights were "offensive." Few men under his cursory care ever returned to the regiment. The hospital was in a good, healthy location and had good water. The source of the mortality, Penneman thought, was the ignorance and incompetence of the contract surgeon.

In contrast to the belief that African Americans were better suited to the heat and humidity of the South and had a stronger resistance to tropical diseases, Penneman found them to be more susceptible. They were prone to homesickness, which in turn made their constitutions weaker and vulnerable to disease. Penneman wrote that they were "greater sufferers both in frequency of cases and mortality from Home sickness than the Whites often becoming from this cause so debilitated in mind and body as to fall easy victims to any disease." Many men were dying of "nostalgia"—an affliction that could range from depression and homesickness to what today is called posttraumatic stress disorder.[5]

Penneman also complained that the initial medical inspections of recruits were found wanting. Men as old as seventy and boys as young as fourteen were admitted to the service. There were recruits with hernias who, although unable to perform the duties of a soldier, were essentially trapped in the army, due to an administrative unwillingness to grant discharges once the men had been enlisted. Discharging these men was even more difficult because they had been given a clean bill of health by a medical officer upon their entrance into the service. These were just some of the problems Penneman pointed out, and he felt they fully explained the large number of dead and sick during the month of November 1863.[6]

Also in November, Lt. George Sabin came to inspect the troops. His impressions varied. Lieb's regiment was commended for its appearance, its neat and orderly camp, and the knowledge of its officers. Other regiments were not as fortunate, and some came in for severe censure. Apparently ignorant of the fact that some of the men had fought at Milliken's Bend, the inspector concluded his remarks: "If these troops shall give as good an account of themselves in the field as they have in camp, the most sanguine Hopes of the Friends of Colored troops will be fully realized."[7]

Meanwhile, Hawkins was still complaining about the inadequacies of the brigade's Austrian rifles. These were the same weapons used in the fight at Milliken's Bend, months earlier. Hawkins expressed his frustration at the "Ordnance circumlocution" to Adjt. Gen. Lorenzo Thomas. The situation might be compared to the quartermaster department furnishing regiments with "wheel barrows for transportation" and putting wagons in storage "to count often and look at, and denying any Regt. the use of one of them unless it could prove that . . . a wagon was better than a wheel barrow." Hawkins continued, "The Ordnance Dept. *knows* that an Austrian Rifle is almost worthless, but before it will act it wants other proof than its own knowledge." Hawkins ended his scathing diatribe with a small and bitter consolation: "Should I ever lead my Brigade into battle and get whipped I will at least have the satisfaction of knowing that it was permitted according to rule."[8]

Hawkins's concerns were no small matter. Even though Confederate troops were far to the west, reports were still coming in to Milliken's Bend of raids and guerillas in the area. Five men under a "Captain Elliott," who operated as an independent band, had been raiding and carrying off "negroes and mules." Sometimes they came within a few miles of the Federal post but always eluded capture. Col. Richard H. Ballinger, in charge at Milliken's Bend, thought one man might even be present in his camp. Ballinger vowed "to hang them according to the laws of war" if caught.[9] Difficulties beset troops elsewhere in the region. The 8th Louisiana Infantry's morale sank extremely low in the waning months of 1863. Stationed at Vicksburg, the men were at work on the fortifications of the city, armed with shovels, spades, and picks. One officer complained that the excessive fatigue duty would "prevent us from ever acquitting ourselves creditably as soldiers."[10] Still, Hawkins's enthusiasm would not be dampened. He wrote Ohio abolitionist Caleb Mills and declared, "I will show you a new world and a new people, and perhaps the best Colored Troops in the United States. Everybody that comes here speaks well of them."[11]

The following spring, a new officer arrived in the camp of the 11th Louisiana. Marshall Mills, Caleb Mills's son, took George Conn's place as a lieutenant in Company F under Capt. James P. Hall. Lieutenant Mills was encouraged by the educational and religious efforts underway in his regiment. After studying their tactics in the morning, the white officers gave over their schoolhouse to black children, who, along with the soldiers, were taught the alphabet and the rudiments of an education by two young white women from the North. So devoted were the African American soldiers to their lessons, Mills wrote, that they could be seen in their off-duty hours studying their books and learning to write. He believed they learned twice as fast as any white man.[12]

Some lessons were hard to learn, however. Many of the African American soldiers found that their ideas of freedom did not mix with army regulations. Even without the fatigue duty, at times, there were disturbing echoes of slavery. Take, for example, the military pass, a routine bit of army paperwork that granted an enlisted man permission to be absent from camp for a designated but brief period of time. Men who left camp without their commander's permission faced charges of being absent without leave, which was punishable by court-martial. Worse, a prolonged absence could result in charges of desertion, punishable by death.[13]

The pass was a universal and normal army procedure, not unique to the Colored Troops. But the system—having to request permission from a white man in power, obtain a piece of paper that granted the soldier permission to be absent, and show that piece of paper upon request or face firm punishment if found abroad without it, or if he overstayed his absence—was essentially no different than the slave pass system, which the black soldier no doubt thought he had left behind forever. The situation must have been especially difficult when the soldier desired to see his family. He was a free man now, or so he had been told. Did he not have a right to go about as he pleased, when and where he chose, without reference to any white man's pleasure? The army, quite predictably, responded with a forceful "No." This may have been one reason for Colonel Lieb's emphasis upon discipline and obedience to orders.[14]

The army's strict hierarchical discipline permeated every aspect of the soldiers' new lives. Many standard army camp punishments for infractions were designed to humiliate the offender, like standing on a log for hours on end. More serious offenses involved corporal punishment, such as hanging by the thumbs, being put in stocks, or wearing a ball and chain. One punishment, known as "bucking and gagging," seated the offender on the ground, legs drawn and bent at the knees, with a pole or rod run under the knees. The man's arms would be outstretched, elbows underneath the rod, with his hands bound and grasping his knees. A gag would be placed in his mouth. Such punishments, which were relatively standard practice all throughout the army, must have galled many a black soldier, who took his freedom as his right. As a new recruit, in particular, he may not have understood the fate that awaited him if he told his captain he was going to see his family, pass or no pass.[15]

As Louis Gerteis points out, African Americans' definition of freedom was based upon how free they were from the white man's control—*any* white man's, including Union officers, Northern missionaries and abolitionists, and planter lessees, not just their former masters or overseers. Rebellions both on the government plantations and in the army typically had their origin in one of two things. One was a protest against a specific injustice, such as laborers not being paid wages or, infamously, the lower monthly wage paid black soldiers during the first year of emancipation. The second type of rebellion was against white authority. Tired of taking orders for their entire lives as slaves, and believing it their right as free men to decide for themselves when to come and go, and to do what they pleased without interference, some blacks clashed with their officers. Usually, in the end, the officers had the upper hand, and a young man who was merely asserting his newfound freedom was put in irons and his wages stopped.[16]

This situation turned tragic for some men in Company F of the 49th U.S. Colored Infantry—the new name of the former 11th Louisiana Infantry, African Descent. Pvt. Washington Fontaine and fifteen other soldiers found themselves before a general court-martial on a charge of mutiny in the summer of 1864, almost exactly a year after the fight at Milliken's Bend. While the men were absent from their quarters one day, Capt. James P. Hall, upon the urging of his regimental surgeon, went into the men's tent, found spoiled food and candles, and threw out the mess. The next day after the noon roll call, the soldiers took up their arms, marched in an orderly fashion to Hall's tent, stacked their arms, and refused to do further duty unless Hall would treat them better. Private Fontaine, despite his act of insubordination, remained respectful, saluting Hall prior to informing him of the reason for their actions.[17]

The men were immediately arrested, marched to the guardhouse, and charged with mutiny. Six other men were arrested later in the evening on the charges that they had failed to act to prevent the mutiny, and Sgt. Giles Simms was charged with encouraging the entire company to join in on the protest. Testimony would reveal that Simms had given the initial order to "fall in" for the march to the captain's tent, but he and several men fell out as the others marched on. Robert Randall, a Milliken's Bend veteran, was scurrying for his bayonet and was left behind—luckily for him. He received the lightest punishment meted out by the court-martial. He forfeited his pay and was sentenced to hard labor, wearing a ball and chain, for the remainder of his term of service. He would be released from his sentence early, in March 1865.[18]

The majority of the men involved—seventeen in all—were sentenced to hard labor for life. Among these were Milliken's Bend veterans Albert Rodgers and Price War(e)field.[19] All of these men would be imprisoned at the military prison in Alton, Illinois. Sergeant Simms and Pvt. Washington Fontaine, as the supposed "ringleaders" of the event, were sentenced to execution by firing squad, which was carried out on September 25, 1864.[20]

The man they rebelled against, Captain Hall, was one of the first officers of the regiment, promoted to that position from his humble beginnings in the 93rd Illinois Infantry as a private. He, too, was a veteran of the fight at Milliken's Bend. Marshall Mills, the new lieutenant who took George Conn's position in Hall's company, found Hall an admirable, dedicated, and strict officer.[21] Although it was not directly mentioned in the court-martial proceedings, the rebellion in Company F had apparently been simmering for a while. "The cruelty of those in command of us compelled us to do something," the soldiers recounted in a joint letter addressed to the secretary of war in early 1865. Having already complained to the colonel more than once about their treatment, the men felt they "had no other recourse but to do as we done." Their actions were not directed against the United States, they said, but against their immediate superiors. "There is no set of Men More willing to serve the United States Than ourselves & we intended to fight for The country expecting to be treated as human beings," they wrote. More than once, the men mention their intention to "do our duty as soldiers."[22]

After the violent clash at Milliken's Bend, the 49th USCI had spent the rest of the war on the bluffs at Vicksburg. One wonders if their long stint at garrison duty may have added to their frustrations. Garrison life and the tedious labor associated with it probably resembled too much the life of slavery the men had just left behind.[23]

The men continued pleading their case: "We were not aware what the consequences of Mutiny would be . . . we did not understand what would be the result . . . we think our ignorance [of the laws and regulations of the United States] should gain our pardon." The men were even willing to serve an additional three years in the military after their original term, if clemency was granted. They reassured the secretary that they would perform their duties as soldiers and "obey all orders coming from our superior officers promptly." Numerous officers wrote in support of them, and on May 4, 1865, a month after the end of the war, they were returned to duty. The reprieve came too late for Hector Mearbly and Price Warfield, however. They both died in the military prison at Alton, Illinois, just weeks after the end of the war.[24]

At about the same time, some of the black enlisted men who were captured at Milliken's Bend began to drift back to their regiments, which were still in service. Company records indicate most of them had been held as prisoners of war in Texas. Some men did not return to their regiments until nearly a year after the war ended. Among them were Thomas Banns, Eli Gibson, Robert Jones, William Huttoon, Haz. Young, George Washington, Nelson Washington, and William Hunter, all of the 49th USCI.[25]

By 1866, many of the veterans of Milliken's Bend were nearing the completion of their terms of service. Discharged from the army, it was now time to rebuild their lives and their families. It would not be easy. Disgruntled ex-Confederates and equally assertive blacks would see to it that there would be no truce in the war over emancipation.

"A Terrible Aftermath of Injustice"
Violence in the Postwar Era

EACE DID NOT COME to northern Louisiana after the war. Within months of the cessation of hostilities, the city officials in Monroe enacted repressive measures against the freedmen. Among their first acts was implementing a registration policy for persons of color who lived in the town or operated a business there. The resolution was adopted on June 19, 1865, and African Americans were granted less than a week to comply. Individuals who failed to register would be arrested and if convicted, would perform ten hours of labor for the city. People who hired unregistered blacks were subject to a ten-dollar fine. In June and July, the city council passed six additional ordinances specifically directed at persons of color. Some concerned drunkenness and vagrancy. One measure even reinstituted the pass system, ostensibly in an effort to comply with an order issued by the U.S. Army commander of the area.

Some of the ordinances affected the day-to-day business of the city. If a resident dismissed a black employee, the employer had to provide a written notice of discharge to the employee. A mere scrap of a note would not do. Instead, it must provide the reason for discharge, the length of time the person had been employed, and a statement about the employee's "character." A black person without a paper discharge, upon conviction, would be fined $2.50 or, if unable to pay, sentenced to work ten hours on the public works. It is unclear if the employer—almost certainly a white person—suffered any penalty for not providing the necessary paperwork to their former employee. It is easy to see how local whites could manipulate this process to create trouble between city officials and black residents. Through no fault of their own, black residents could be forced to pay the penalty for their employer's negligence.

The African American residents of Monroe must have strongly protested these regressive efforts, for ordinances were soon passed concerning persons of color who resisted arrest "in word or deed," refused to show passes, or made false entries in the town registry. A little relief came in September, when some of these ordinances were struck down by a General Order emanating from the U.S. War Department.[1]

Between the end of the war and 1868, circumstances grew far worse for Ouachita Parish's black residents. Early in 1868, white men gathered in a mass meeting in Monroe to defend their "supremacy as the ruling race on this continent" and to protest the new Louisiana constitution, then being drawn up in New Orleans. Fear was rampant that the new constitution would place the former slaves in a superior position—"an abhorrent and unnatural proposition." The meeting at Monroe passed a series of resolutions that held the Radical Republicans responsible for an impending race war throughout the state. Furthermore, it was imperative that blacks recognize that the Radical position was "utterly subversive of their future prosperity as a separate race, and wholly destructive of the cordial feelings which have hitherto subsisted between the two races." To the relief of Monroe's white residents, there was no "desire on the part of the blacks to infringe upon the recognized social rights of the white race," and the situation remained calm. The white men there "supported" local African Americans, declaring that laws should protect white and black alike— with the caveat that black men should not have the right to vote.[2]

The language and expressions used in the resolutions echo similar dichotomies expressed by Southerners during slavery, particularly during times of fearfulness over incipient slave insurrections. Negroes were a threat, yet local blacks were content. Blacks might try to be politically active elsewhere, but African Americans within the parish knew their "place." The contradictions and mental machinations that are apparent to us today upon a reading of the resolutions make it clear that the white citizens were merely trying to reassure themselves and the black residents, hoping that each race would contain any violent impulses toward the other over politics, civil rights, and social customs.

Words were not enough to alleviate any vengeful tendencies, however. By the summer of 1868, violence was becoming so commonplace that the assistant commissioner for the Freedmen's Bureau in Louisiana devoted an entire ledger to the subject, entitling it, "Murders and Outrages." It covers only eight months from May to December 1868. Both whites and blacks were victims and perpetrators. Many actions crossed racial lines, although some threats and killings were white-on-white or black-on-black, and race or politics were not always factors. Any attempt to summarize the details found in these records falls short. To say there were three murders in Ouachita Parish, for example, does not begin to convey the hardship and terrorism faced by blacks in Louisiana in the years immediately following the war. What the records do show is violence that, though occurring in isolation and taking only a few victims at a time, nevertheless was equal to and perhaps even exceeded the violence endured during the war. The terrorism of the Ku Klux Klan and unreconstructed white Southern Democrats against the freedmen and their efforts to build schools, vote, own property, and become men, rather than chattel, appears to have gone essentially unchecked. African Americans feared for their lives and for their families.

It is unclear if the violence in 1868 was part of an ongoing pattern, already established, or if much of the violence was related to broader issues unique to that year. In June, Louisiana was readmitted to the Union. In July, the Fourteenth Amendment was ratified, granting citizenship to thousands of African Americans who had legally been considered property only a few years before. And on November 3, former Union general Ulysses S. Grant was elected president of the United States. Each of these events brought tremendous changes; to have them fall so swiftly together was a harbinger of further Republican rule—an unbearable outcome for most former Confederates.

The catalog of "murders and outrages" demonstrates unequivocally the lengths to which Southerners—black and white, Republican and Democrat—felt they must go to aggressively defend their own particular vision of political freedom. For instance, freedmen from Franklin Parish were driven out of their homes "by disguised white men." One day, twenty-five men rode up, killed four freedmen, and wounded a man, woman, and six-year-old child. A few of the band were recognized, but apparently no action was taken. In another incident, Calvin Ross, a freedman who worked on John H. Moore's place, fled after he saw the bodies of two men and a woman lying on the road. Moore told Ross that a bureau agent and two other men had been killed as well.[3]

In Carroll Parish, where Lake Providence was located, the situation was no better. The local authorities received reports that both blacks and whites had been murdered in the back country. Just ten days later, it was noted: "Reports of a horrible nature continue to come in from the interior of the parish. Freedmen from near Delhi report that several of their race have been murdered within the past few days." Near Oak Grove—the fork in the road where Walker's brigades had split up to move on Milliken's Bend and Young's Point in June of 1863—Thomas Hawkins was found hanged. "Freedpeople are very uneasy and are flying in all directions for protection," wrote the Freedmen's Bureau official, but it seemed impossible to escape the violence.[4]

It indeed appeared that the race war predicted by the mass meeting in Monroe was coming to pass. From Delhi to Franklin, freedmen took up arms to defend themselves. Whites were "killing and driving off all colored people that voted the radical ticket." Some people had already been killed, the Freedmen's Bureau agent had been threatened with a knife, and a band of angry whites were believed to be on their way to Madison Parish to continue the work.[5]

Even government officials participated in the terror. In August, several men were arrested for an unidentified reason and sent to the Bastrop jail. When the troops sent for protection left, Justice of the Peace Thomas Reno held a "pretended" trial, a jury sentenced the men to death, and the men were taken to a thicket and shot. One of the accused, Henry Dade, was left for dead but survived his wounds for two days. The bodies were left where they fell, and Reno refused to hold an inquest.[6] Off to the west in Shreveport, the former Confederate state capital-in-exile, more men died. "Freedmen are found shot and hung but short distances from their homes. No clue to perpetrators. Freedmen joining Democratic clubs through fear of their lives," wrote the bureau agent. The civil authorities had no interest in investigating or prosecuting any of these cases.[7]

At the same time, the Ku Klux Klan was growing in power, confidence, and boldness, establishing "Guards of Honor" to force freedpeople to leave. The Klan's actions were so disruptive and effective that even the planters began to complain. They were losing their labor force right at the time of year that they needed workers the most for cotton picking.[8]

Even a few whites were threatened. Luke Madden, an Irishman of Madison Parish who had been captured and taken to Texas late in the war, was run out when he received a polite but chilling request to "please leave the parish . . . within 48 hours, and return no more." The note was embellished with a primitive drawing of a hand pointing to a man dangling from a gibbet.[9]

With the exception of Luke Madden's warning, almost all of the events mentioned in the preceding pages occurred in a two-month period, July and August 1868. The violence would not subside with time, although the precision with which it was recorded might lapse. Decades later, northern Louisiana would still be racked with outbreaks of violence and vigilantism. A full and detailed examination of lynchings and racial violence after the war is outside of the scope of this book, but even a cursory glance at lynching statistics, like those compiled by Michael J. Pfeifer, reveals a horrifying pattern.[10] A number

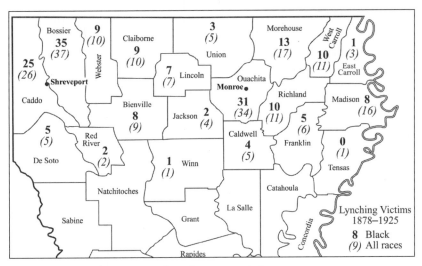

Lynchings Victims by Race, Northern Louisiana, 1878–1925
Source: Map based upon data compiled by Michael J. Pfeifer (see chap. 9, note 10)

of towns and parishes that figure prominently in the story of Milliken's Bend also show up in later accounts of postwar lynchings. In Ouachita Parish and the seat at Monroe, Caddo Parish and Shreveport, and neighboring Bossier Parish combined, there were nearly one hundred lynchings between 1878 and 1925. An almost equal number of victims were spread among seventeen other northern Louisiana parishes.[11]

Predictably, the majority of the victims were African Americans, although Ouachita, Morehouse, and Madison Parishes witnessed the killing of several men who were white, Latino, or Italian. A few cautious generalizations from Pfeifer's study can be made. Murder was the primary charge leveled at lynching victims, and many times, the victim met his death at the hands of a small number of people, rather than a large mob.

Events in Ouachita Parish are of special interest, since Monroe, the parish seat, was where Captain Heath and Second Lieutenant Conn are said to have met their deaths. The citizens of Ouachita Parish clearly had no qualms about resorting to extralegal violence in the decades after the war. In 1878, eleven African Americans were killed in three separate incidents over a five-month period. The reasons for their deaths are not known. From 1878 to 1897, twenty African Americans were killed outside of the law in the parish, most of them accused of murder. Even the turn of the century did not bring peace. Eleven more men would die in extralegal killings between 1906 and 1919. Only a few of the deaths from 1878 to 1919 are clearly identifiable as killings for what Stewart E. Tolnay and E. M. Beck call breaches of "racial codes of etiquette." Most victims were informally charged with a criminal offense, though few lived long enough to be given a trial or offer a defense.[12]

In spite of the dangers, African Americans were not helpless. To the contrary, as Pfeifer's study of Louisiana lynchings points out, the prevalence of lynching may reflect greater resistance by blacks toward white authority. Scholar W. Fitzhugh Brundage persuasively demonstrates that it is naïve and ignorant to read the catalogs of lynchings as victimization and disempowerment of African Americans. If oppression was omnipresent, so was resistance. Brundage advises us all to rethink our assumptions and to look deeper into the historical record for new interpretations, new evidence, and new voices.[13]

Nell Irvin Painter brought a number of new voices to light when she told the story of the Kansas "Exodusters." In 1870, black men banded together in Caddo Parish, forming a committee to examine the state of African Americans in the parish and to determine whether they should remain in the area or migrate elsewhere. By 1878, this committee had grown into the Colonization Council of Caddo Parish, and its president, Henry Adams, called for the Federal government to set aside lands in the West for former slaves, much like the government had created an Indian Territory for those tribes removed from areas east of the Mississippi River in the 1830s. Adams described an environment of intimidation, violence, and cruelty in the parish, with elections being especially risky. One man died a mere thirty minutes after he dared to cast the *only* Republican vote in the entire parish. In one ward, nearly two hundred men were run off, and some were killed or wounded. Three women were killed because of actions taken by their husbands. Adams claimed more than two thousand blacks had been killed, and he believed that as long as blacks remained in the South, they would fear for their lives. The only answer to the problem was to move to lands elsewhere, in a place specifically designated for the former slaves.[14]

With indifference to this proposal at the Federal level, Adams began to advocate emigration to Liberia. Interest was high, and some blacks did manage to raise the funds necessary to make the ocean crossing, but by and large it was out of reach for most. A desire to maintain ties with their families and a strong sense that they were Americans of African descent, not Africans, made many individuals seek to leave the South but remain in the United States. Kansas seemed a better prospect. Eventually, Adams encouraged many residents from Louisiana and other Southern states to move to Kansas in a mass migration known as the "Exoduster" movement.[15]

In the South, the horrific number of lynchings, the swift disenfranchisement of black men, the rise of the Ku Klux Klan, and Jim Crow laws made a sad and disturbing mockery of the Union victory of the Civil War. Indeed, as some historians have observed, though the South lost the war, they won the peace. Many Southerners remained thoroughly unreconstructed. As late as 1896, a former Confederate general would declare, "The great crime of the century was the emancipation of the Negro." F. T. Roche of Georgetown, Texas, would no doubt agree. In 1910, he wrote to the *Confederate Veteran* magazine, declaring, "I regard the enlistment of negros in the army of the United States as one of the most infamous things done in the war between the states." Flatly denying that blacks had played any part in any earlier conflicts of the United States, Roche continued: "I am truly glad to know that it had no precedent in our earlier history. Let the facts be made known."[16] Such sentiments are not surprising coming from men who fought against the Union cause. But the greatest injustice may have been the inability and unwillingness of the Federal government to secure the rights granted to African Americans under the Thirteenth, Fourteenth, and Fifteenth Constitutional Amendments and the additional civil rights legislation enacted in the 1860s and 1870s.

Cyrus Sears, the former lieutenant colonel of the 11th Louisiana, grieved at what his country had become by the early twentieth century. After narrating his story of the battle at Milliken's Bend for his audience of fellow Union veterans in the Loyal Legion, Sears launched into an extended diatribe against lynching. After proclaiming, more than once, that the United States averaged over one hundred lynchings a year, Sears mocked the nation's claim to be a beacon of liberty and justice in the world. He declared, "The people of the United States are the most lawless people of any on earth." Referring to the epidemic of lynchings, Sears believed Union veterans were acutely responsible, having abdicated their obligation to ensure justice for black Americans. "What a terrible aftermath of our injustice, indifference and complaisance is this *saturnalia* of crime," he said, urging his hearers to take action. To Sears, the lynchings, race riots, political and economic oppression, and the blatant disregard for African American rights throughout the country at the turn of the century imperiled the Union once again. Having fought against "anarchy" (secession) once before, it was time to rally to the colors again, to ensure "an impartial square deal to every citizen without reference to color of hair, eyes or skin."[17]

Undoubtedly, the outspoken Sears did not fulfill his audience's expectations of propriety and patriotism. It was probably because of this indictment against his fellow veterans and his criticism of the U.S. government that Sears's paper was not published by the Loyal Legion, as was customary. The Legion told Sears that his unfavorable comments about the 23rd Iowa, earlier in his speech, were the reason they chose not to publish his talk. But Sears believed the reason went deeper—a refusal to give "the negro a 'square deal.'" He resigned from the Legion in disgust.[18]

Forgetting and Remembering Milliken's Bend

ILLIKEN'S BEND WAS never a prominent battle, not even during the war. A few newspapers, North and South, carried short reports, often only a paragraph or two. Even the abolitionist press gave it less attention than Fort Wagner and Port Hudson. To two nations consumed with news of Lee's advance into Pennsylvania and the siege at Vicksburg, Milliken's Bend was born in obscurity.

Perhaps, then, it is not surprising that it has remained obscure and nearly forgotten to the present day. The site of the battlefield and nearby village literally vanished from the face of the earth in the early twentieth century when the Mississippi River changed its course. There is nothing there to mark, to walk, to see.

If Milliken's Bend was born in obscurity, little wonder that it was quickly forgotten in the larger narrative of the war. After four bloody years of struggle, it was time for the nation to reunite and move on. Historian David Blight sees the urge toward reconciliation in North and South as a key point in ensuring that the memory of African Americans and their role in the war would be omitted from the historical record. The issue of slavery and its consequences, the need for emancipation, and the role of black soldiers in the fight for freedom had to be left out of this narrative in order to have Southern support for reconciliation with the North. Furthermore, many Northern veterans had negative opinions about their black counterparts, as did their former Southern enemies. The white veterans on both sides had to remember their fight as noble, brave, and for a just cause. For most white Union veterans, this cause was the restoration of the Union. Emancipation, although conceded as an important outcome of the war, was given secondary status. White supremacy and sectional reconciliation overruled any attempt at racial reconciliation and justice, with the result that black veterans' contributions to the war effort were minimized.[1]

Andre Fleche takes issue with Blight's thesis, making a convincing case based upon veterans' own recollections as published in the organ of the Grand Army of the Republic (GAR), the *National Tribune*. Fleche sees substantial evidence that the GAR was keenly aware of the role of emancipation in the war, took pride in the downfall of slavery, and, more often than one might expect, praised black troops and the men who led them.[2] Donald R. Shaffer, too, sees the GAR as generally supportive of black veterans, although not without controversy. In 1891, some white members in the Mississippi and Louisiana Department proposed the creation of an entirely separate department for blacks. Though it was not unusual to find GAR posts in individual communities segregated by race in the South, in part to keep the peace among their Southern-born neighbors, the proposal to create two entirely separate departments based on color met with resistance and even condemnation from most veterans who lived outside of the South. Many Northern black veterans were especially critical, believing that shared sacrifice on the battlefield with their white comrades demanded equal treatment within the organization. The effort to create twin departments in Mississippi and Louisiana failed, but it pointed out a fracture within the GAR. Despite being a more racially tolerant organization than most others of the late nineteenth century, racism persisted.[3]

Frederick Douglass saw that the memory of the black man's role in his own liberation, and the greater cause of full citizenship for the American Negro, in practice as well as in theory, was disappearing from the nation's consciousness. After the war, he urged Northern Republicans to make justice for the black man a central tenet of lawmaking, politics, and commemoration, especially as Southern Democrats began to regain power through violence, exploitation, and intimidation. He fought to ensure that the black man's contribution to freedom and the war effort was not forgotten.[4]

As Milliken's Bend quickly vanished from the larger historical narrative, some men worked to keep its memory alive. Three black authors—two of them Civil War veterans—mentioned Milliken's Bend in their works. In 1867, William Wells Brown was the first to write a history of blacks' actions during the war. He quoted extensively from other sources about Milliken's Bend, most notably Lt. Matthew Miller's letter. Brown wanted to make sure his readers recognized the importance of the battle, even if they could not quite grasp it from the gore and thrill of Miller's account. Not only did the battle prove that slavery was obsolete, it also served as an indictment against the Southern soldier. Brown made no distinction between the Southern soldier and the slave owner; to him, they were synonymous and came in for quick condemnation. Brown proclaimed their guilt: "No negro was ever found alive that was taken a prisoner by the rebels in this fight." While this statement, probably unbeknownst to Brown, was untrue, it was clear he viewed the fight as a massacre, plain and simple.[5]

Two other black historians, George Washington Williams and Joseph T. Wilson, both writing in the 1880s, wanted to make sure that the heroic exploits of the soldiers at Milliken's Bend were not forgotten. Williams got a number of the basic facts wrong, stating that Milliken's Bend was in Arkansas and that McCulloch had six regiments instead of four. Like Brown before him, he accuses the Rebel troops of a massacre: "Of the three officers and one hundred thirteen men missing, no word was ever had, and it is fair to presume they were murdered." But also like Brown, he praises the black troops' valor, wanting to make sure that this small but extraordinarily violent fight was not forgotten.[6]

Wilson, writing a few years later, also invoked Milliken's Bend. Lt. Matthew Miller's account was a favorite with all three authors, in part, perhaps, because it was one of so very few sources publicly available at the time. Miller's letter had been reproduced in a number of newspapers, and Williams and Wilson must have consulted Brown's volume, where Miller's letter figures prominently. Miller's account is written with verve and declares the fighting worse than Shiloh. Even if most of Williams and Wilson's readers had never heard of Milliken's Bend, everyone would have known about the horrific fighting at Shiloh. To say that Milliken's Bend was even worse was one way to declare the valor and fighting capabilities of the black troops at the Bend as equal to—or even surpassing—that of white soldiers in one of the bloodiest engagements of the entire war.

The first and only substantial published account by a Union veteran of the battle came from Cyrus Sears. His experience before the Loyal Legion prompted him to publish his paper at his own expense in 1909. He worried that blacks' contributions to the Union war effort were being forgotten, and he wanted to ensure that the men who fought at Milliken's Bend would at last receive their due. His paper, "The Battle of Milliken's Bend and Some Reflections Concerning the 'Colored Troops,' the Debt We Owe Them, and How We Paid It," would remain the most detailed and lengthiest published personal account on the Union side until the close of the twentieth century.

Brown, Williams, and Wilson's works were well received, but because they focused on the black experience of the war, they were unlikely to be read by mainstream white America. Sears's account, due to the circumstances of its publication, found only a small audience. A brief biographical sketch of Sears appeared in the *National Tribune* in 1907. It mentioned in a few sentences his actions at Milliken's Bend, including his assumption of command of the 11th Louisiana, when the errant Col. Edwin W. Chamberlain fled to the safety of the gunboats.[7]

David Cornwell read the piece, and he objected to the statement that Sears "became the ranking officer." Most likely the reference was to Sears's assumption of regimental—not brigade—command, but Cornwell thought the statement an affront to Hermann Lieb, who commanded the African Brigade that day. Cornwell felt compelled to compose a rejoinder. His article spanned more than two columns and included a simple sketch map of the battle. He did not attack Sears as strongly as he does in his memoir, but Cornwell's bickering rebuttal put Milliken's Bend before a national readership of a white audience, something that likely had not occurred since the battle itself.[8]

On the Confederate side, the earliest and fullest published personal account of the battle came from Joseph P. Blessington. His memoir, *The Campaigns of Walker's Texas Division*, published in 1875, recounted the events of the summer of 1863, including Milliken's Bend, in considerable detail and with sharp wit. It remains the richest resource from the point of view of a Rebel in the ranks. Former general Richard Taylor wrote his memoir a few years later in 1879 and belittled the actions at Milliken's Bend and Young's Point. It had been a desperate move, doomed to futility, but political necessity forced Taylor and Smith's hands. "Public opinion would condemn us if we did not *try to do something*" to relieve Vicksburg, Taylor wrote.[9]

As the veterans began to pass away, so did the memory of many of the smaller battles fought during the war. Now and then, Milliken's Bend appeared in a collection of letters or a memoir published years after a veteran's death. At midcentury, scholars of African American history like Dudley Taylor Cornish and Benjamin Quarles included it in their works on blacks during the Civil War. Periodically, the battle would be recounted in the pages of the *Crisis* or the *Journal of Negro History*, and other historical journals published brief articles or edited letters mentioning the fight. By and large, however, the battle remained a forgotten footnote.[10]

Beginning in the 1980s, Milliken's Bend began to get growing attention, with numerous articles and books examining events on the levee in more detail. Most accounts fell into three categories: (1) battle narrative; (2) examination of the murder of Union prisoners at Confederate hands; or (3) Milliken's Bend as a small part in a larger narrative of events in the Trans-Mississippi or of black troops during the war. At last, what took place on the riverbank that June day was no longer forgotten. This important story was beginning to be told.

In the past decade, the growth of studies of historical memory has shed a little more light on Milliken's Bend, but even there, one finds the battle more forgotten than remembered. Christopher Waldrep traces the convoluted route of historical memory and collective amnesia at Vicksburg and discusses the efforts of black Union veterans to commemorate their service. Many of these men likely came from the 5th U.S. Colored Heavy Artillery, which garrisoned Vicksburg after its surrender. This regiment was the reorganized 9th Louisiana Infantry, African Descent, that fought under Colonel Lieb at Milliken's Bend. The 49th U.S. Colored Infantry (formerly the 11th Louisiana Infantry, African Descent), Cyrus Sears's regiment, also served most of the war and mustered out at Vicksburg. Many of the black veterans that Waldrep mentions likely came from these regiments. A few had probably fought at Milliken's Bend.

When the Grand Army of the Republic began organizing a post in Vicksburg, white Union veterans excluded their black comrades. Black veterans chose to organize their own post. As Union veterans, blacks had the right to be buried in the new national cemetery at Vicksburg, although they remained segregated in separate sections, just as they had been during their service. Still, the cemetery became a great gathering place for black veterans—a sacred plot of ground where they and their community could come together to remember what had been sacrificed in the war for freedom. Memorial Day became almost as sacred as Emancipation Day celebrations, drawing thousands. Meanwhile, many whites in the community observed Confederate Memorial Day, a month earlier. White Union veterans held their own observances in late May. The tradition of separate Memorial Days for Union veterans from the two races would continue well into the 1930s.[11]

At the 1890 Blue-Gray Reunion at Vicksburg, about four hundred black Union veterans marched proudly in the parade, and white Confederate veterans made a show of the African Americans who had aided their cause. In 1917 there was another reunion, this time led by Frederick A. Roziene, a Chicagoan who had served as a lieutenant in the 49th U.S. Colored Infantry, joining the regiment in 1864, after participating in the siege of Vicksburg with the all-white 72nd Illinois Infantry. Roziene was president of the National Association of Vicksburg Veterans, an organization that lobbied Congress relentlessly to fund a reunion in Vicksburg. When the reunion finally came to pass in 1917, Col. Willard D. Newbill, the event organizer, consciously sought to include black veterans in the ceremonies, although on a segregated basis.[12]

As the veterans of the war passed away, Milliken's Bend faded even further into obscurity. Until the last decade of the twentieth century, the story of Milliken's Bend remained hidden. The Civil War Centennial years produced books about the two other major actions involving black troops in the summer of 1863—Port Hudson and Fort Wagner—but Milliken's Bend, despite having equal significance, remained ignored. In his massive three-volume treatment of the campaign for Vicksburg, published in 1985 and 1986, Ed Bearss devoted less than twenty pages to the fight. This description was about as long as any other work on the subject, and it could be considered generous and thorough, as most other histories of the Vicksburg campaign omitted the Bend entirely. Although there was growing scholarship about African Americans during the war, especially in their role as soldiers, most authors mentioned the fight only in passing. Since the 1990s, however, the fight at Milliken's Bend has begun to receive more attention.[13]

Even today within Madison Parish, the events of 1863 and the fight at Milliken's Bend remain hidden, says Geneva Williams, a longtime resident of the area and local historian. Tina Johnson, director of the Tallulah-Madison Parish Tourism Commission, agrees. Part of her job is to promote the history of the area. Madison Parish is a "gem in the rough when it comes to history," she says, and her mission is to "get the word out" about the many local events of significance. Madison Parish is the birthplace of the first African American female millionaire, Madame C. J. Walker. Delta Airlines got its start there. And President Teddy Roosevelt had a very successful hunting expedition in the parish in 1907, killing three bears.[14]

Most locals, however, know very little about the parish's rich history. Johnson believes part of the problem is that people take their surroundings for granted. They don't think history has anything to do with their lives today. Given the poor economic conditions in the region, most people are concentrating on their daily needs and trying to better themselves and their children. According to Johnson and Williams, the fight at Milliken's Bend and other aspects of local history do not appear to be taught in the public schools. Instead, teachers worry over mandated test scores and teach accordingly. Johnson believes the situation is much the same in neighboring parishes.

Johnson also thinks that in some cases people want to forget the past. An older generation interested in local history has begun to die off, and young people of both races try to distance themselves from the past. This leads to a void in the collective memory of the community. It may be that some of what Johnson has observed is a desire to move away from shameful or racially charged events of history, encompassing slavery, Reconstruction, and the divisiveness of the civil rights movement.

Adam Fairclough, in his book, *Race and Democracy*, finds that the civil rights movement was a contentious time in Madison Parish. Whites who had formerly been friendly toward blacks now gave them a cold shoulder. Others joined White Citizens Councils, formed throughout the state in an effort to shut down NAACP efforts and to block black voting. Blacks saw this increasing racial animosity as an echo of Reconstruction days.[15]

White resident Amy Holmes, daughter of Civil War diarist Kate Stone, also drew comparisons to Reconstruction, though from a different point of view. She had difficulty swallowing the changes that came to Madison Parish in the 1960s. "A negro man defeated white woman candidate for school board in this ward," she wrote John Q. Anderson, who edited Kate's diary for publication. "For some unknown reason a number of whites failed to vote & negroes one and all did vote. We deserve to be ruled by nigs when whites too lazy to vote." Schools were going to be integrated soon, and blacks and whites would no longer be separated in the hospital at Tallulah. She was beside herself. "They will order whites to take them in homes as equals."

She saw blacks' political strides as ominous and insufferable. Blacks still outnumbered whites in the parish, just as they had during the war, and Amy Holmes could see what was next. "They will have a full number to run for Sheriff & other candidate so suppose wil [sic] have a black Sherif [sic] but I may be spared seeing that." "We are back in reconstruction days," she wrote, fearing the worst. "Everything for the black nothing for whites." No doubt she was shaking her head: "Too much for this white."[16]

Zelma C. Wyche was undoubtedly one of the black men who made Amy Holmes so upset. Like black veterans of earlier wars, Wyche thought his military service in World War II would at last earn him the rights and respect that had been so long denied. He was one of the men who successfully sued for the right to vote in Madison Parish, a victory won in 1963, after demanding this right for nearly two decades. Residents in nearby East Carroll and Tensas Parishes had similar hard-fought victories. Many black voters had been subjected to enormously convoluted and "fiendishly difficult" voter registration procedures, which were eventually struck down. In 1969, Wyche became Tallulah's first black police chief, and later, its first black mayor.[17]

About the same time that Wyche won the right to vote, Gary Craven, a white civil rights worker with the Congress of Racial Equality (CORE), who participated in the effort to desegregate restaurants and other public venues, was beaten in Tallulah. The black community responded with massive demonstrations; more than sixty people were arrested at one cafe in a single day and were bailed out in less than twelve hours. Two hundred people gathered to protest segregated school buses. Blacks boycotted the business district, and some shops closed rather than integrate. One grocery store stubbornly endured more than three months of picketing and protest.[18]

Whites fought back, burning homes and businesses and targeting some of the civil rights leaders. Instead of deterring African American activism, such events only made the movement stronger and more determined. As voter registration rolls grew, black candidates began to take offices at all levels of the parish government. It was just a little over one hundred years since black men donned blue uniforms in their fight for personal liberty and freedom on the banks of the Mississippi River at Milliken's Bend. Zelma Wyche and many others, after much courage and action, at last won the rights that had been so long denied.[19]

But even men like Wyche, a prominent local leader and the grandson of a former slave, knew little about Milliken's Bend. He told a newspaper reporter in 1994 that the older generations didn't talk about the Civil War, and shame over slavery ran deep, adding to the silence. That year, the National Park Service dedicated a new informational plaque to honor African American soldiers of the Vicksburg campaign. The plaque specifically refers to events at Milliken's Bend and Goodrich's Landing and is located at the Grant's Canal Unit of the park, near Delta, Louisiana. Some, like Geneva Williams, criticize the location of the Milliken's Bend plaque as being too far from the original site. But, given that the Grant's Canal Unit is the only piece of Vicksburg National Military Park property in Louisiana, the plaque's location does make sense. The National Park Service simply couldn't place it anywhere else in the parish. Robert Walker of Vicksburg and Zelma C. Wyche of Tallulah, both men who were distinguished by being the first black mayors of their respective cities, saw the tribute to Milliken's Bend as long overdue.[20]

Brian Madison Davis, an architecture student at Louisiana Tech University in 1997, recognized both the importance and obscurity of Milliken's Bend when he proposed construction of the Milliken's Bend National Research Center. For his senior thesis, he recommended the preservation and restoration of Dalkeith Plantation, then nearly in shambles. The humble dogtrot house, one of only four Civil War–era structures still standing in the parish at the time, would become a museum, dedicated to the interpretation of the fight at Milliken's Bend. A modern structure would house a research center devoted to the role of blacks in the military during all of America's wars. The center would be unique—no similar place existed elsewhere in the country at that time.

Davis envisioned the center serving a national audience. People would come from all over the country to learn more about blacks in the military and, while there, would be educated about the events at Milliken's Bend. Having such a facility would also provide a place for the battle to be commemorated, since the site of the original battlefield had long ago washed away. Davis saw the center as an important contribution to the local economy and local pride—both battered by poverty. Even more ambitious, he believed it could serve as a place where race relations could be healed through education.

Although undertaken as a school assignment and never carried out, Davis's proposal is quite detailed. More than a decade later, the project still seems substantive enough to consider the possibility of making it a reality. Tallulah's proximity to Vicksburg, its location just off an interstate highway, and the general growing interest in heritage and historical tourism, especially among African Americans, are factors in the project's favor. At the time, Davis predicted that Tallulah and Madison Parish could see about 400,000 visitors annually (40 percent of Vicksburg National Park's visitors), with an economic impact of as much as $35.6 million (in 1996 dollars). Those kinds of figures are hard to ignore. But a young architecture student, just beginning his career, did not have the political and economic capital to make it become a reality.[21]

At the time that plaques were being placed at Grant's Canal and Davis was making his proposal, other efforts were underway in Madison Parish to bring historical awareness to the community. In 1994, the Madison Historical Society was organized when members of the community grew concerned that so much history was being lost and forgotten. In 1997 they established the Hermione House Museum in Tallulah. In better condition than Dalkeith, it was also a surviving Civil War–era building. It is typical of many of the plantation homes that once stood in the area—not a sprawling mansion from Old South myths and movies but rather a modest single-story home, with just three rooms. The Hermione House, originally located two miles south of Milliken's Bend, was moved to the city of Tallulah when it became a museum.

"From the beginning, we've always featured exhibits about both black and white history," Williams says, "and we've always had members from both races." Still, like sites of contested memory relating to the Civil War elsewhere in the South, not everyone wants to remember or commemorate what happened at the Bend. The Civil War still stirs deep feelings on both sides of the racial divide.[22]

During the celebrations of the Civil War Centennial in the 1960s, Milliken's Bend was apparently left to its obscurity. This may have been due in part to tense racial conditions in the parish during the civil rights movement. Or, once again, the Bend may have been overshadowed by events across the river in Vicksburg. Even down to the present day, according to Williams, no reenactments, memorials, or other formal commemorative events have taken place. The only effort to publicly mark the site has come about through numerous plaques that dot the parish. No one seemed to know who put them there, or when, but Terrence J. Winschel, historian at Vicksburg National Military Park, finally solved the mystery when he informed me that the Louisiana Civil War Centennial Commission had erected the markers in the 1960s.[23]

The troops at Milliken's Bend had once had a marker in the Vicksburg park proper, near the site of Grant's Headquarters, but the iron tablet, among many others, was melted down during World War II. The story of Milliken's Bend once again literally became invisible. Then, in the 1980s, the park launched a donation drive to begin to replace the numerous missing markers. Not until the 1990s was the first replacement tablet ordered. That first tablet was the one commemorating the African Brigade, installed at the Grant's Canal Unit in Louisiana. In addition, three other modern interpretive markers at the site tell more about canal operations in 1862 and 1863, and the Colored Troops at Milliken's Bend.[24]

Despite these commemorative efforts led by the National Park Service, both Tina Johnson, who is black, and Geneva Williams, who is white, report the same historical amnesia among local residents. There is strong indifference to the history of the parish among individuals of both races, and these women and the organizations they represent hope to change that. "I'm trying to get people to *know* the history" of the area, Johnson says. Williams's influence in establishing the Hermione House Museum as a tourist destination and a source of local pride serves the same purpose.[25]

Williams believes that an additional reason for the lack of interest in Milliken's Bend is that so many residents live in poverty. About 37 percent of people in the parish were living below the poverty line in 2009. Many people are just doing what they need to survive, and for that reason, historical interest remains low. In such an economic climate, history and commemoration become luxuries, not necessities. Even the museum struggles. "We don't get Federal funding like they do across the river," said Williams. "We are an all-volunteer organization." Even maintaining and staffing the museum is a challenge but one that has been met with success.[26]

Williams is gratified by the attention the Bend has received over the past two decades, making special mention of Terrence J. Winschel's "General's Tour" in *Blue and Gray* magazine in 1996 (which remains the most informative and detailed tour of the region), and Richard Lowe's *Walker's Texas Division C.S.A.*, published in 2004. But Williams wonders why the battle continues to remain so obscure outside of a very few publications.[27]

Despite these many handicaps, both Williams and Johnson find encouraging signs. The Hermione House draws about eight hundred visitors a year. In 2007, the Madison Parish Tourism Commission with Tina Johnson as its director inaugurated the Teddy Bear Festival to celebrate the centennial of Theodore Roosevelt's visit to the parish. It is now an annual event, bringing in important revenue and demonstrating the viability of heritage tourism. The event gives local residents a sense of pride and importance in the role their community played in larger historical events.[28]

Despite these promising beginnings for heritage tourism, both women reported that (as of January 2012) there were still no formal plans to commemorate Milliken's Bend during the upcoming Civil War Sesquicentennial.[29]

Across the river at Vicksburg National Military Park, Milliken's Bend has historically been omitted from the narrative until very recently. In the 1930s, when responsibility for the park passed to the Department of the Interior from the War Department, three men composed the history department of the National Park Service, all of them educated in the North. The scholarship then in vogue was based upon work by Ulrich B. Phillips and William Archibald Dunning. Both scholars had written works considered at the time to be the definitive texts on slavery and the American South. Although their accounts found a ready audience in the South, their books were widely read in graduate schools all throughout the country and were influential for most of the first half of the twentieth century. In Phillips and Dunning's view, slavery had been a "civilizing" influence upon Negroes, whose masters looked after their needs like benevolent fathers. Because this was considered the standard and most authoritative scholarship of the time, it became the foundation for the park's initial interpretive work under the aegis of the National Park Service and remained in place for many years. Given such an interpretation of black history, and its implied irrelevance to the larger narrative of the battle of Vicksburg or the war at large, it is easy to see how and why African Americans—especially the soldiers at Milliken's Bend—were omitted from the story entirely. Prevailing scholarship guided the park's interpretation of the battle then, just as it does, in a radically different direction, today.[30]

The scholarship of the 1930s was not the only reason the fight at the Bend was neglected, however. The battle could be legitimately ignored as being outside of the park's focus. The park was originally established to commemorate and interpret the siege and campaign for Vicksburg proper on the ground where it occurred. A small scrap across the river, which had no impact whatsoever on Grant's operations against the city, really didn't have a place within the overall narrative of actions to take or relieve the river citadel. When viewed within the context of the campaign against Vicksburg, it is a mere "footnote to the battle," says Tim Kavanaugh, an interpreter at Vicksburg National Military Park. If McCulloch's efforts to break Grant's supply lines had succeeded—like the Confederate capture of Holly Springs a year earlier, forcing Grant to backpedal to the north—then Milliken's Bend might have had a significant place in the strategic history of the Vicksburg campaign. But Grant's army and its supply line was already across the river, and Milliken's Bend no longer held the strategic significance it had a few months or even weeks earlier. McCulloch's actions were a strategic failure, essentially pointless, and as such, the fight scarcely bears mentioning. However, viewing Milliken's Bend in the broader overall context of African American participation in the war changes its importance dramatically. Viewed in this way, it becomes "a seminal event," says Kavanaugh, one that requires interpretation, analysis, and attention, both inside and outside of the park boundaries.[31]

In 1990, Congress expanded the park's mission from the limited focus upon interpreting the battle for Vicksburg proper to include the entire Vicksburg campaign, the wartime Union occupation, and the Reconstruction era. By expanding the mission beyond July 4, 1863, this legislation provided a valuable opportunity to interpret all aspects of the U.S. Colored Troops. They were first organized on a grand scale in the Mississippi Valley, during the campaign for Vicksburg, and they were the primary soldiers occupying the city after its surrender until the end of Reconstruction. Two regiments that fought at Milliken's Bend finished their terms of service performing occupation duty in Vicksburg and environs.

The same congressional action in 1990 also authorized the National Park Service to accept a donation of a plot of land in Louisiana containing a fragment of Grant's Canal for incorporation into the park. These two events, enabled by congressional legislation, provided the opportunity to give Milliken's Bend and other events on the western bank of the Mississippi their due. But in typical congressional style, the park's mission was expanded without a simultaneous expansion of funding and staff.[32]

Since 2000, Milliken's Bend and Union African American troops' role in the Vicksburg campaign have gained more attention at the park. Part of this interest is no doubt due to the mandate passed in 2000 calling for a major reinterpretation at all Civil War parks. Prompted by U.S. representative Jesse Jackson Jr.'s resolution to have national battlefields place events in a broader context, including the role of slavery in the war, this action brought about major revisions and reanalysis of interpretations and exhibits at parks throughout the country. Vicksburg was no exception.

A report from the National Park Service to Congress in March 2000 surveyed all Civil War National Parks and evaluated each park's effort to place its battlefield into a broader context, the extent to which the park mentioned the causes of the Civil War, and the extent to which the park specifically addressed slavery as a cause of the war. The report found that Vicksburg addressed the broader themes of the war "moderately" better than some other parks, mostly through temporary exhibits, but found fault with the permanent exhibits in the Visitor Center, which were forty years old. These older exhibits did not address the causes of the war, mentioned slavery "not at all," and did not fulfill the criteria of the expanded mandate for the park.

The study did make it a point to favorably highlight the added exhibits at Grant's Canal—the first new outdoor exhibits in thirty years, made possible through private funding. These exhibits brought attention to the Colored Troops' actions at Milliken's Bend and Goodrich's Landing (Mound Plantation), as well as the use of former slaves as laborers on Grant's and Williams's Canals.

The report also found that other park waysides, the Visitor Center film, and the park's website made no mention of slavery or other causes of the Civil

War. Like the Visitor Center's permanent exhibits, the orientation film was dated and disappointing. Produced not long after the Civil War Centennial, the film was "in dire need of revision and upgrade." A new film would take advantage of the latest technology and learning tools, such as "onscreen maps, charts and diagrams," but in keeping with the new mandate would also address issues like slavery and, presumably, Milliken's Bend.

The study found that "personal services"—interaction with park rangers through interpretive programs, questions, and tours—rarely addressed the issue of slavery as a cause of the Civil War, perhaps because few visitors asked questions on the topic. The report explained: "The staff is trained to respond to questions, but seldom is a request made in regards to slavery. The vast majority of visitor questions focus on the fact that their ancestors fought or died at Vicksburg. The park is hallowed ground to many individuals. It has a deep personal meaning because they can retrace the footsteps of their ancestors and understand the hardships they endured."[33]

In a section of the report titled "Obstacles to Success," which examined issues across all of the Civil War National Battlefield Parks, the greatest obstacle to interpretation of the broader issues of the war, particularly slavery, was that "the immediate emotional public response to the war continues to limit the public discussion of the event." The report implies that it was not the National Park Service that was reluctant to broach the subject of slavery but rather many of its visitors. To that end, the National Park Service would strive to interpret the war "in a manner that interweaves cause, course, consequence for the education and inspiration of the visiting public while fostering an intellectual environment that encourages the broadest discussion of the issues."[34]

A more recent report, a 2008 resource assessment by the National Parks Conservation Association (NPCA), remarks that in honor of the Civil War Sesquicentennial, Vicksburg National Military Park is planning to create the "Vicksburg Campaign Trail." This effort will endeavor to mark sites associated with the Vicksburg campaign and will rely heavily on cooperation between federal, state, and local authorities. The NPCA found that despite Congress's new mandate for the park, increased funding remained lacking, so fulfillment of the mandate was very difficult. The report found that a number of historic resource studies still needed to be completed, including one on African Americans' involvement in the campaign. In 2008, the park had only five full-time interpretive staff on duty, woefully inadequate for the park's 700,000 yearly visitors.[35]

Despite such limited resources, the park has made many significant changes since the 2000 survey by the National Park Service. For instance, the outdated film created in 1969 was finally replaced in 2010. The new film speaks at length about the significance of Milliken's Bend, as well as the influx of former slaves into Union lines, and the U.S. Colored Troops' occupation duty in Vicksburg after the surrender and during Reconstruction. A new fiber-optic map covers the entire Vicksburg campaign and includes Milliken's Bend. An exhibit in the Visitor Center highlights the significance of Milliken's Bend, along with Port Hudson and Fort Wagner, in dramatically changing Northern attitudes about the use and capabilities of black men as soldiers in the Union armies. Tim Kavanaugh reports that Milliken's Bend (as of early 2011) now has more interpretive space at the Visitor Center than Port Gibson, Raymond, Jackson, Champion Hill, and Big Black River combined. It is because of this small action's outsized significance within the larger story of blacks in the military during the Civil War that it has received such treatment.[36]

A park planning document, the Long Range Interpretive Plan, unveiled in 2010, provides extraordinary detail about the future vision for Vicksburg National Military Park. The overarching guide is to employ social history to tell the story of *everyone* affected by the battle—not just the soldiers in the trench lines. Among several proposals or interpretive "themes" are plans to interpret and mark sites related to African American history. These would tell the story of enslaved Vicksburgers laboring on Confederate fortifications, their de facto emancipation on July 4 as the city surrendered, the fight at Milliken's Bend, the use of Colored Troops to occupy the city, the desire of freed men and women to solemnize their marriages, the actions taken by black men to become active citizens and participants in democracy after the war by seeking political office and voting in elections, the eager and rapid learning by African American adults and children as they began to obtain an education, and racial violence and tensions during occupation and Reconstruction. Such a plan represents a revolution in interpretation at the park, compared to just a few decades ago.[37]

Perhaps nothing symbolizes the recent changes at the park more dramatically than the Mississippi African American Monument. Erected in 2004 within park boundaries, the monument honors two African American units that took part in the Vicksburg campaign—the 1st and 3rd Mississippi Infantry, African Descent. The 1st Mississippi was one of the regiments at Milliken's Bend. Often colloquially called the African American Monument, the sculpture was erected by the State of Mississippi and the City of Vicksburg to commemorate Mississippians of African descent, soldiers and civilians.

Like much of the black freedom story, the monument was only achieved after a decades-long struggle. Robert Walker, a descendent of men who fought at Milliken's Bend, began envisioning such a monument in the late 1980s. A native Vicksburger, Walker went to the park often as a child. When he became a historian, he realized that a lot of what he had been taught as a youngster was simply not true. Asked to participate in a program commemorating the 125th anniversary of the siege, Walker did some research on Milliken's Bend and "decided from that point on, I would push until a monument was erected in [the soldiers'] honor." When he became Vicksburg's first African American mayor in 1988, he began a concerted effort to erect on park property a monument to African Americans from Mississippi who had served the Union cause. He felt strongly that "something monumental, significant, needed to be there." It was important that it be on park grounds. By having it in a Federal space instead of, for instance, a city park, the monument would be protected and cared for in perpetuity. Perhaps even more important, with such a monument in place, it would be literally and physically impossible to continue to ignore blacks' actions in a war for their own liberation.[38]

It wasn't until 2002 that Walker's dream began taking physical form when Vicksburg National Military Park approved the construction of a monument on its grounds. In early 2003, Dr. J. Kim Sessums, a white sculptor who had less than ten years' experience working with bronze and who had never executed a large monument, was awarded the commission. Funded with $250,000 from the State of Mississippi and an additional $25,000 from the City of Vicksburg, the monument was formally dedicated on February 14, 2004. The monument features three African American men, two of them soldiers, representing the 1st and 3rd Mississippi Infantry, African Descent. The third figure is a civilian, representing the thousands of teamsters, cooks, and other civilian laborers that provided essential manpower for both armies. The civilian looks behind him—watching slavery recede in the distance. One of the soldiers looks ahead at the bright future of freedom. Together, these two men help the other, a wounded soldier, representing the sacrifices of thousands of black Union soldiers who died during the war. Although the monument was sponsored by the State of Mississippi and is therefore specific to those Mississippi troops who served in the campaign for Vicksburg, it has come to represent the story of all African Americans during the Civil War. It has gained further attention because at its time of construction, it was the largest monument to African American soldiers in any of the Civil War battlefield parks administered by the National Park Service.[39]

When the monument first was announced, press coverage varied wildly. One Associated Press story, running in the *Memphis Commercial Appeal*, claimed that no black troops had been involved in the "battles at Vicksburg, except on the Confederate side," and incredibly questioned their presence at Milliken's Bend, stating that black Union soldiers "were believed to have been involved" there. The paper called the fight at the Bend a "preliminary battle"—though the siege in Mississippi had been well under way since mid-May.[40]

The African American warriors gained more credit two days later when another article from the AP appeared in the same paper. This time, Robert Walker set the record straight, while acknowledging the story's absence in the history books. Referring to enslaved African Americans, Walker said that he and everyone else had been taught that "we were just a part of the controversy that was solved by other people." His own research and the fact that he had forebears who served during the war changed that misconception. "African Americans were involved in this war and in so many crucial battles," he said. Through the monument, more people would learn of the contributions of African American troops and, hopefully, would seek out more information.[41]

Walker was not the first to propose a monument to African Americans in the park. As early as 1907 there was an effort to have a monument to the U.S. Colored Troops, but it was quashed by the secretary of war. (The park and others like it were then under governance of the War Department.) The original focus of the park was the battle for Vicksburg itself; actions elsewhere in the campaign, like Milliken's Bend, would receive limited attention, if any at all. Besides, the secretary responded, the Colored Troops' role in the campaign for Vicksburg already had been commemorated on tablets near Grant's statue. These tablets were some of those melted down during World War II, and they remained absent for nearly fifty years until the 1994 acquisition and interpretation of Grant's Canal.[42]

With the recent dedication of the African American memorial, significant additions at the park interpreting Milliken's Bend, and increasing literature on the fight, the story of this small but historically significant battle finally may be gaining the recognition it deserves. This book, the product of years of research in often obscure sources, is but one contribution. The story is not yet complete. Many questions remain, and yet more research must be undertaken. But if this volume serves no other purpose, perhaps at last the men who fought on the Louisiana levee will get their due—and *be remembered*. Let this final page not be the end of commemoration for Milliken's Bend, but rather let it serve as one part of a multifaceted *beginning* of remembrance for a battle too long forgotten.

APPENDIX A
Unit and Biographical Sketches

UNIT SKETCHES

9th Louisiana Infantry, African Descent (Union)

The 9th Louisiana Infantry, African Descent, was renamed the 1st Mississippi Heavy Artillery, African Descent, in September 1863. This regiment was subsequently renamed the 4th U.S. Colored Heavy Artillery for one month in 1864, and then it became the 5th U.S. Colored Heavy Artillery in April 1864, its final designation. After Milliken's Bend and the fall of Vicksburg, the regiment spent the bulk of the war serving garrison duty on the bluffs at Vicksburg. Col. Hermann Lieb remained in command until the regiment was mustered out in May 1866.[1]

A second but quite distinct black regiment, also named the 9th Louisiana Infantry, organized near Natchez, Mississippi, in the late fall of 1863. John Eaton, the former general superintendent of contrabands, became colonel of the regiment. This unit essentially was a sort of Invalid Corps for black soldiers who could perform garrison or police duty but who were too infirm for service in the field. When all the old state designations were eliminated, it would be renamed the 63rd U.S. Colored Infantry.[2]

11th Louisiana Infantry, African Descent (Union)

In the aftermath of Milliken's Bend, the cowardly Col. Edwin W. Chamberlain was "invited to resign," an offer he gladly accepted. Van E. Young—the same man from the 10th Louisiana Infantry who had caused Col. Isaac F. Shepard so much grief with his recruiting violations on plantations, took Chamberlain's place. It is not clear why Cyrus Sears was not promoted to the position, especially given his strong leadership on the Union right flank during the action at Milliken's Bend. Nor is it clear why Young was selected for the position, given his past history. Lieutenant Colonel Sears remained with the regiment until the close of the war.[3]

Like the 9th Louisiana, the 11th Louisiana spent most of the rest of the war at Vicksburg, performing garrison duty. In March 1864 it was renamed the 49th U.S. Colored Infantry, and it mustered out in March 1866.

13th Louisiana Infantry, African Descent (Union)

Decades after the war, Cyrus Sears claimed that no such regiment as the 13th Louisiana was present at Milliken's Bend. Contemporary records, including Lieb's report and records from Colonel Shepard's African Brigade headquarters, clearly indicate that such a regiment did indeed exist, though it was short-lived. In late June 1863 it was found to have "no legal organization," and the few men present were sent to other regiments.[4]

1st Mississippi Infantry, African Descent (Union)

Col. Isaac F. Shepard returned to command of this regiment once General Hawkins returned from the North to resume command of the African Brigade in August 1863.

At the same time Shepard's regiment was beginning to form in May, there was another 1st Mississippi regiment organizing near Grand Gulf. Shepard believed his regiment had precedent, and it is not known what became of the other 1st Mississippi. Shepard's regiment was an infantry unit; the other Mississippi regiment may have been early fragments of the 1st Mississippi Cavalry (Colored), which was mustered in later in the autumn at Vicksburg.[5]

Shepard's regiment became known as the 51st U.S. Colored Infantry in March 1864. It spent the bulk of its service as garrison forces at Vicksburg, Lake Providence, and Goodrich's Landing, but in 1865 it moved to southern Alabama where it participated in the siege and assault on Fort Blakeley. After a short stint of garrison duty in Mobile, it was sent to Texas where it was mustered out in June 1866.[6]

In the wake of their assault on the Confederate works at Blakeley, as part of an entire division of Colored Troops under the command of Brig. Gen. John P. Hawkins, accusations would arise claiming that the black troops took no prisoners. Lt. Walter Chapman of the 51st said his men "killed all they took to a man." A year earlier, Confederate troops were said to have massacred hundreds at Fort Pillow, Tennessee, galvanizing Union black troops across the entire army to fight without mercy. At Blakeley, the black troops came over the Confederate works with the battle cry, "Remember Fort Pillow." This sent the Rebels scattering, anxious to surrender to white troops nearby.[7]

The men of the 51st also had more personal reasons to hold a grudge. In addition to their experience at Milliken's Bend, a small foraging detachment had been captured by Confederate forces in February 1864. The black enlisted men were killed and mutilated, and the white lieutenant accompanying them was shot and left for dead. The soldiers of the 51st, like their comrades in other black regiments at Blakeley, doubted they would be shown mercy if they were captured, so they may have chosen treat their enemy in the same manner.[8]

Noah Andre Trudeau believes that men from other regiments such as the 68th U.S. Colored Infantry (USCI) and 76th USCI—not the 51st—may have been to blame for any deaths of surrendering Confederates. The facts remain murky. Federal officers from black regiments give contradictory accounts. Some deny that anyone shot down prisoners in cold blood. A few, such as 2nd Lt. Walter Chapman of the 51st USCI, confess that their soldiers did shoot surrendering Confederates, and it was only through the intervention of Yankee officers that a greater massacre was averted. Despite the uncertainty, there seems to be enough evidence to say that at least *some* Confederate prisoners were shown no mercy, and it seems quite likely that the 51st may have been involved.[9]

23rd Iowa Infantry

After Milliken's Bend, the shattered Hawkeyes returned to the other half of their regiment near Vicksburg. After the river citadel surrendered, they advanced against Jackson, Mississippi, then were transferred from the Army of the Tennessee to the Department of the Gulf, where they served in Louisiana, Texas, and Arkansas, seeing no major combat. In April 1865, they were part of the forces that besieged and assaulted Fort Blakeley, and they served occupation duty in Mobile until the regiment was mustered out in July 1865.[10]

16th Texas Infantry
17th Texas Infantry
19th Texas Infantry
16th Texas Cavalry (Dismounted)

All of these regiments have identical histories because they continued to serve together in the same brigade. In the autumn after Milliken's Bend, Brig. Gen. William Read "Dirty Neck Bill" Scurry took command of McCulloch's Brigade, and it remained in the Trans-Mississippi for the duration of the war. The brigade fought in the Red River campaign at Mansfield and Pleasant Hill and, during the Camden Expedition, attacked the Union left at Jenkins' Ferry. It surrendered as part of Edmund Kirby Smith's Army of the Trans-Mississippi on May 26, 1865.[11]

Harrison's 15th Louisiana Cavalry Battalion

Maj. Isaac F. Harrison, the same planter who in 1861 had overheard one of his slaves plotting an uprising on July 4, raised this battalion of seven companies in 1862 from men in northeast and north central Louisiana. It was formally organized in Monroe just five days after Lincoln issued his Preliminary Emancipation Proclamation on September 22, 1862. The battalion spent most of its first year of service defending its home territory in north Louisiana.[12]

About a year later, the unit grew to a full regiment and was redesignated the 3rd Louisiana Cavalry Regiment. Harrison received quick promotions to lieutenant colonel, then colonel. In the spring of 1864, Colonel Harrison led a brigade in the Red River campaign, operating mostly against Yankee gunboats. For the rest of the war, the regiment served mostly in northeastern Louisiana and southern Arkansas. By the time the organization was formally surrendered in late May 1865, most of the men had already gone home.[13]

Parson's Texas Cavalry Brigade

Men of the 12th and 19th Texas Cavalry and two guns of the 10th Texas Field Battery arrived in Louisiana in June 1863. They were only a portion of Parson's Brigade, with the remainder staying in Arkansas under Col. George Washington Carter. Col. William Henry Parsons went in advance of his men, meeting up with them on June 27, right before launching the raid on Goodrich's Landing and Lake Providence, which included the fight at Mound Plantation. As Anne J. Bailey points out, the accusations that some of Parsons's men may have killed black soldiers in cold blood after they were captured at the Mound were not unique. In 1862, near the L'Anguille River in Arkansas, men of the 12th Texas Cavalry were accused by one Wisconsin soldier of murdering numerous black civilians. In 1864, the 30th Texas Cavalry, who would later join Parsons's brigade, took part in what would become known as the Poison Spring Massacre. Edmund Kirby Smith himself admitted to his wife that black Union soldiers at that fight were given no quarter. Wagons drove over the incapacitated wounded soldiers, and some Confederate soldiers calmly shot men in the head if they were unable to flee. Only two black prisoners were taken. Bailey concludes that in all three instances, the cavalrymen were acting in a desperate defensive measure to prevent Yankee incursions into their homeland in north Texas.[14]

In the fall of 1863, Parsons took his men back to Arkansas, where they rejoined the rest of the brigade and a dispute ensued between Parsons and Carter over who should command. In late 1863 the brigade was temporarily split up, with each company returning to its home county to bring in draft dodgers.

In 1864, the brigade came back together. Too late to take an active part in the battles at Mansfield and Pleasant Hill, the cavalrymen attacked Rear Adm. David Dixon Porter's naval forces at Blair's Landing, without success. Brig. Gen. William Steele took command of the brigade shortly thereafter, and it engaged the enemy at Yellow Bayou, suffering significant losses.

The brigade returned to Arkansas, then was sent deep into Texas, driving toward the coast. In the spring of 1865, Parsons returned to command and the brigade was reorganized, but in May it disbanded as the war in the Trans-Mississippi closed.[15]

BIOGRAPHICAL SKETCHES
Confederate

ROBERT T. P. ALLEN

A graduate of West Point in 1834, Robert T. P. Allen served as superintendent of the Kentucky Military Institute in the late 1840s and early 1850s. When he came to Texas in the 1850s, he established Bastrop Military Academy. After commanding the 17th Texas Infantry at Milliken's Bend, in December 1863 he became commander of Camp Ford prison camp near Tyler, Texas, and resigned from the army in July 1864. One of the prisoners at Camp Ford was Lt. John East, a white officer from the 1st Arkansas Infantry, A. D., who had been captured at Mound Plantation. After the war, Allen returned to Kentucky where he again served as superintendent at the military institute. He drowned in Florida in 1888.[16]

GEORGE FLOURNOY

In 1860 George Flournoy was serving as attorney general for the state of Texas. He was a delegate to the Texas Secession Convention and helped author the secession declaration. In the fall of 1861, Gen. Paul Octave Hébert appointed him colonel and authorized him to raise a regiment, which became the 16th Texas Infantry, formally organized in April 1862. After the war, he went to Mexico and served with Maximilian's army. He then returned to Texas, resumed his legal practice, and served as a member of the Constitutional Convention of 1875. In 1876 he moved to California, where he died in 1889.[17]

EDWARD P. GREGG

A lawyer before the war, Lt. Col. Edward Gregg was in charge of the 16th Texas Cavalry (Dismounted) at Milliken's Bend while Col. William Fitzhugh was in Texas on recruiting duty. Gregg was seriously wounded in the thigh but returned to the regiment within a few months. He was captured at Pleasant Hill and was paroled or exchanged within a month. Late in the war, he was promoted to colonel. After the war, he returned to his legal practice and became a judge, living in Marshall and Sherman, Texas. He died in 1894.[18]

ISAAC F. HARRISON

After the war, Isaac Harrison moved to Honduras for a time, then returned to the United States, where he lived in New Orleans, Natchez, and Texas, eventually settling in Fort Worth, where he worked in real estate. He died there in 1890.[19]

PAUL OCTAVE HÉBERT

Paul Octave Hébert remained in command at Monroe for several months. Four months after Milliken's Bend, he proposed arming "able-bodied negro men" for military service for the Confederacy. His proposal was politely denied, citing arms shortages for troops already in the field, as well as an idea "totally at variance with the policy of the Government."[20]

Discipline problems with Parsons and Harrison's troopers and frequent "depredations" by local guerillas in the fall of 1863 led to reprimands from Edmund Kirby Smith. Hébert was removed from his post and sent back to Texas, where the rest of his service was apparently uneventful.

Later biographies would claim Hébert's only Civil War combat experience came at Milliken's Bend, but no evidence has been found in wartime sources to support this statement. Neither Hébert's compiled military service record nor his own personal scrapbook mention his presence at or participation in the fight at the Bend.[21]

In one of those strange twists of fate that was not unusual in later years after the war, two former enemies came together. Hébert was asked by

President U. S. Grant to be a pallbearer at the funeral of Grant's brother-in-law in 1874. The deceased was Lewis Dent, who was once Hébert's prisoner.[22]

Paul Octave Hébert, general, sugar planter, and governor, died in New Orleans in 1880.[23]

HENRY E. MCCULLOCH

The younger brother of Gen. Ben McCulloch, who was killed at Pea Ridge, Arkansas, Henry McCulloch had served with his brother on the Texas frontier as a Ranger and Indian fighter. Probably his greatest military experience prior to the Civil War came in 1840 at the battle of Plum Creek when he fought against the Comanches. He was involved in several other small actions before the Civil War, including serving during the Mexican War as part of a volunteer force to defend the Texas frontier against Indian incursions. In the 1850s he entered politics, served in the state legislature, and became a U.S. Marshal in east Texas. When Texas seceded, he was among the first to receive the surrender of Federal outposts in the state. His request for the surrender of Camp Colorado was refused by its commander, McCulloch's future superior, then-major Edmund Kirby Smith of the U.S. Army.[24]

After the fight at Milliken's Bend, McCulloch was sent in the fall of 1863 back to Texas, where his primary duties were to maintain order and round up draft dodgers and deserters. In his initial announcement of his new position and authority, McCulloch alluded to what he had seen in Louisiana and warned the Texans that their inaction would not do anything to protect them from Yankee offenses. "Your negroes will be taken from you, the men put into the army to fight against you, the able-bodied women and men not too old to labor will be put on *your farms* to work under Yankee overseers," and children and the elderly would be left to starve. Quite clearly, McCulloch was describing what he had seen that previous summer in Louisiana—the black soldiers at Milliken's Bend, the leased government plantations, and the suffering in the contraband camps. McCulloch wanted to make his point very clear to Texans who thought they might be safely away from the front lines. Everything was at stake. "Lincoln's dastard hirelings" were not fighting to restore the Union but "*to free the slave race . . . and enslave the white race,*" he wrote, with as much urgency as he could express in cold type. Even this plea was apparently met with some indifference, for men still did not report when conscripted.[25]

McCulloch took charge of the part of the state that included the area of Gainesville, where the mass hangings had occurred a year earlier. He found so many disloyalists still in the region that he declared he needed a good "fighting, hanging man" who would not hesitate to kill those who resisted authority or the government. He called upon James G. Bourland, who had served as provost marshal during the Great Hanging and demonstrated that he had no difficulty using the most severe tactics. Bourland's actions under McCulloch included such methods as shooting prisoners in cold blood, with the excuse that they were "trying to escape." McCulloch issued orders that anyone killing unarmed prisoners would be court-martialed and tried to rein in Bourland, but he eventually ordered Bourland to go fight Indians because he was too brutal to act within the boundaries McCulloch had established for treatment of deserters and slackers. When the war ended, McCulloch was so reviled by some members of the local populace that he had to have an escort home for his own safety, as he was threatened with death by the deserters and draft-resisters he had pursued.[26]

McCulloch returned to Seguin, where he had settled prior to the war. In 1876 he became superintendent of the State Deaf and Dumb Asylum, but he was forced to resign in 1879 after a state investigation found his administration of the facility to be incompetent. He retired to his farm in Guadalupe County and died on March 12, 1895.[27]

WILLIAM HENRY PARSONS

A veteran of the Mexican War, William Henry Parsons was a farmer and newspaper editor, operating the *Tyler Telegraph* and the *Waco Southwest* before the Civil War. He was a strong advocate of secession but after the war became a Republican "scalawag." He served in the Texas State Senate and as a customs official in Norfolk, Virginia. He "dabbled in health fads and radical politics," and his brother, Albert, a noted Socialist in Chicago, was executed in the wake of the Haymarket Riot. William died in Chicago in 1907.[28]

MILTON WALKER SIMS

Before the war, Milton Walker Sims was an Austin attorney and farmer who owned over one hundred slaves and two farms totaling nearly three thousand acres. Sims joined the Confederate service in April of 1862. His rank and regiment at enlistment is not known, but by the summer of 1863, he had the rank of major and was serving on Gen. Paul Octave Hébert's staff. The story of his capture and imprisonment, the accusations made against him, and his eventual escape and return to Confederate lines is told in Chapter 6. After he made his way back to Hébert's headquarters, he apparently continued in his role as staff officer for most of the rest of the war. Late in the conflict he was made colonel and sent to the Texas frontier to raise a battalion up to regimental strength for action in Arizona and New Mexico, but the war ended before he could complete the task. He settled at Galveston shortly after the war, then later moved to Bryan, Texas. His obituary painted an impressive, heroic picture, calling Sims a "model soldier" who held the memory of the war "sacred." He was "a man of unusual strength of character . . . honor and integrity," and "firm and unswerving in his duty." His family and community would mourn and remember him as "a Southern, Christian gentleman." He died in Bryan on October 4, 1912.[29]

EDMUND KIRBY SMITH

Originally from Florida, Edmund Kirby Smith attended West Point, graduating in 1845. During the Mexican War, he served under Zachary Taylor and was brevetted for gallantry at Cerro Gordo and Churubusco. After the Mexican War he was a math professor at West Point for four years, then became part of a surveying party to establish the border with Mexico. He later served in Texas against the Indians. In charge of the Texas outpost, Camp Colorado, when secession came, and still a U.S. soldier, he refused to surrender the post to Col. Henry E. McCulloch. When Florida seceded, he went with his home state, becoming a lieutenant colonel in the Confederate army. He rapidly was promoted to brigadier general in the summer of 1861. He was wounded at the battle of First Manassas and in the fall of 1861 was promoted to major general. He briefly took command near Knoxville but was then sent to the far west, where he became a lieutenant general and commander of the Trans-Mississippi Department. After the fall of Vicksburg, the Trans-Mississippi was so isolated that it became known as "Kirby-Smithdom," because he had to take on many of the civil responsibilities formerly performed by the Confederate government in Richmond, Virginia, such as preventing cotton speculation, dealing with treasury issues, and seeking support from foreign governments like Mexico. Incredibly, just a little over three months after McCulloch's Brigade attacked regiments composed of former slaves at Milliken's Bend, Smith himself confessed in a letter to his wife on September 21, 1863, that the difficulty of bringing in white men to the army might make it necessary to arm slaves for the Southern cause—if only enough weapons could be found. He stopped the advances up the Red River in Louisiana by Nathaniel Banks in 1864 and thereafter had his capable subordinate Richard Taylor reassigned due to continuous sparring about strategy. Smith was among the last Confederate generals to surrender, not doing so until June 2, 1865.

After the war, he held office in a couple of business enterprises, but he soon returned to the field of education, briefly becoming president of the Western Military Academy in Nashville, Tennessee, then chancellor at the University of Nashville. In 1875, he became a math professor at the University of the South and died in Sewanee, Tennessee, on March 28, 1893.[30]

RICHARD "DICK" TAYLOR

Richard Taylor was the son of president and Mexican War hero Zachary Taylor and brother-in-law to Confederate president Jefferson Davis. Born in 1826, he attended Harvard and Yale and served as his father's clerk during the Mexican War. In the 1850s, Richard Taylor became a Louisiana sugar planter and served in the state senate from 1856 until 1861. He initially served as colonel of the 9th Louisiana Infantry (Confederate) in the Eastern theater of war and advanced rapidly to the rank of major general by 1862. He served during the Seven Days battles around Richmond and during "Stonewall" Jackson's Valley campaign of 1862. He was sent to command the District of West Louisiana in August 1862. After Milliken's Bend, he made a stunning raid on Brashear City and moved to within sixteen miles of New Orleans in the hopes of forcing Union general Nathaniel Banks to abandon his efforts against Port Hudson. Taylor's threat was real, but the surrenders of Port Hudson and Vicksburg meant his efforts were in vain. In the spring of 1864, he fought back Banks's attempt to move up the Red River. Taylor often clashed with his superior, Edmund Kirby Smith, and in the fall of 1864 he was reassigned, although he also received a promotion to lieutenant general. In early 1865 he briefly took command of the shattered remnants of the Army of Tennessee after John Bell Hood had squandered his men in the Nashville campaign. Taylor became the last general to surrender east of the Mississippi in May 1865. He fought against strict Reconstruction and in 1879 penned his memoir, *Destruction and Reconstruction*. He died that same year.[31]

JOHN G. WALKER

A Mexican War veteran, John G. Walker began his Confederate service as colonel of the 2nd Virginia Infantry. He was promoted to brigadier general in January 1862. By the fall of that year he commanded a division. In September he led his troops to capture Loudon Heights at Harpers Ferry, aiding in its surrender. He then led his division into the maelstrom of the West Woods at Sharpsburg. A few months later he was promoted to major general and sent to the Trans-Mississippi Department, where he took charge of a division formerly led by Brig. Gen. Henry McCulloch. This division would soon earn the nickname "Walker's Greyhounds" because of the speed and distance they marched on a regular basis. Taking part in the Red River campaign in 1864, he was wounded at Pleasant Hill. Two months later he briefly took Lt. Gen. Richard Taylor's place as commander of the District of West Louisiana but was then sent west to become commander of the District of Texas, New Mexico, and Arizona. As the Confederacy began to collapse, he had several different commands until the close of the war. Walker fled to Mexico, then England, and engaged in several business enterprises involving the South. He returned to the United States in 1868 and worked predominantly in the railroad and newspaper businesses. He served as a diplomat to Colombia in the 1880s and died in Washington, D.C. in 1893.[32]

RICHARD WATERHOUSE

As part of William R. Scurry's Brigade, Richard Waterhouse and his regiment, the 19th Texas Infantry, fought in the battles of Mansfield and Pleasant Hill. When Scurry was killed at Jenkins' Ferry on April 30, 1864, Waterhouse took command of his brigade. However, the Confederate Senate did not approve his promotion to brigadier general until almost a year later, on March 18, 1865, during the final congressional session. After the war, he resided in San Augustine and Jefferson, Texas, and died on March 2, 1876, as a result of pneumonia after a bad fall.[33]

Civilians
JUDGE LEWIS DENT

A native Missourian, Lewis Dent had gone in the 1840s to California, where he was an attorney and served as a member of the first state constitutional convention. While in California, he married a woman from Mississippi. Two of his uncles were also from Mississippi, so his connections to the region predate the Civil War. Sometime, probably early in 1863, he leased a government plantation in northeast Louisiana not far from Milliken's Bend. It is not known how he became a prisoner of the Confederates, although he may have been taken during one of the cavalry raids by Parsons's or Harrison's troopers. He apparently spent only a month or so in custody. After the war, Dent ran on the National Union Republican Party ticket for the governorship of Mississippi in 1869 but lost. It was hoped he could carry some conservative Southern votes, as he had "extended charity to Confederates held in military confinement," possibly a reference to his efforts to obtain the release of Confederate staff officer M. W. Sims. Dent died in 1874. Present at his funeral, and a pallbearer at the request of President U. S. Grant, was former Confederate general Paul Octave Hébert, who had negotiated Dent's exchange for M. W. Sims.[34]

KATE STONE

Kate returned with her family from their sojourn in Texas in late 1865. Along the way, they stayed briefly in Monroe with the Wadley family, who would soon be moving to Georgia. Upon arriving at their plantation, Brokenburn, the Stones found the place in shambles. The wartime deaths of two of her brothers seemed to make the place even lonelier for Kate. "We must bear our losses as best we can," she wrote. "Nothing is left but to endure."

While on their journey back from Texas in 1865, Kate and her family also stayed over at Bayou DeSaird with the Richardson family. While there, the former Confederate lieutenant Henry Bry Holmes came calling for Miss Kate, having courted her once before in Texas. Kate wrote that although he was quite handsome, he had been "spending a wild summer and fall . . . though he assured me marrying would reform him. I believe not. A dreadful risk for any woman. I fear there is little hope for him." Nevertheless, she married him in 1869, and they initially operated a plantation in Ouachita Parish. Later, they made their home in Tallulah, Madison Parish. Henry became sheriff in 1884, following the term of former Union general Elias Dennis.

Writing in 1900, Kate said that she always "felt the moral guilt of" slavery. She "never regretted the freeing of the Negroes" and explained that, in 1861, the slave owners knew no better. For instance, "Thinking it over by the light of later experience, I know our cook was a hard-worked creature. Then, we never thought about it."

Kate was a well-respected woman in Tallulah and was at the center of the town's social and civic life. She founded the local United Daughters of the Confederacy chapter and led the effort to get a Confederate monument placed at the courthouse. She died in 1907 in Tallulah, survived by her husband and two children, William and Amanda ("Amy").

Upon the publication of her diary by John Q. Anderson, the city of Tallulah declared March 17, 1955, "Kate Stone Day." Ten thousand people gathered for the occasion, and a parade of floats, led by the original Confederate flag from Vicksburg, filled the streets. Next to the Confederate memorial that Kate had helped erect, Anderson presented Miss Amy Holmes, Kate's daughter, with the very first copy of the published diary. Kate's fame soon spread to Amy, and she, too, was feted on numerous occasions. Anderson maintained correspondence and friendship with Miss Amy until her death in 1972.[35]

SARAH WADLEY

Sarah Wadley never married, and she lived with her father and mother until their deaths. After the war, her family moved to Georgia, where her father worked for the Georgia Central Railroad. In 1873 the family moved to a plantation near Bolingbroke, not far from Macon. They named the place Great Hill, after her father's birthplace in New Hampshire. Sarah died on December 7, 1920.[36]

Union

GEORGE L. CONN

Very little is known about George Conn. He was twenty-six when he enlisted as a private in Company D, 48th Indiana Infantry at Rensselaer in August of 1862. Less than a year later, he was serving as a second lieutenant with the 11th Louisiana Infantry, African Descent, at Milliken's Bend. Records from the 48th Indiana show that he was discharged from that regiment sometime in July or August so that he could be mustered in as part of the 11th Louisiana. However, records from the Louisiana regiment show that he was never officially mustered into that unit. Capt. James P. Hall declared that Conn was killed in action at Milliken's Bend, although most other records, including other papers in his compiled service record, listed him as missing and later "murdered by the Rebels" at Monroe. The location of his grave is unknown. His remains may have been reinterred in or near Monroe, or they may have been moved to the national cemetery at Alexandria, Louisiana. No pension was filed on behalf of his heirs or relatives.[37]

DAVID CORNWELL

After the war, David Cornwell lived in Allegan, Michigan, where he farmed, ran a country store, and wrote his memoirs, which totaled nearly 300 pages when they were finally published by his great-grandson John Wearmouth in

1998. They remain one of the most vivid, detailed accounts of not only the fight at Milliken's Bend but one officer's experiences serving with the Colored Troops along the Mississippi River. Cornwell died on May 1, 1911.[38]

ELISHA DEWITT

Elisha DeWitt was just eighteen years old when he enlisted in the 7th Missouri Infantry (U.S.) at Rolla in August 1861. He soon became a sergeant and left that post in the spring of 1863 to serve as a captain in the 9th Louisiana Infantry, African Descent. After his brief time in enemy hands following Milliken's Bend, DeWitt served out his parole at Benton Barracks, St. Louis. He had his appointment to the 9th Louisiana revoked by an order of the secretary of war in late August, and subsequently returned to the 7th Missouri in the fall of 1863. He served until the end of his enlistment in June 1864. Much of his duty with the 7th Missouri before and after Milliken's Bend was as a recruiter. After the war he lived in Texas and Yreka, California. He died in San Francisco on December 15, 1922, and was buried in Evergreen Cemetery in Yreka.[39]

JOHN P. HAWKINS

John P. Hawkins attended West Point, graduating toward the bottom of his class in 1852. Before he took charge of the African Brigade in 1863, most of his Civil War experience came in the commissary department. Early in 1864, he commanded a division of Colored Troops on garrison duty in Vicksburg and then later led a USCT division at Fort Blakeley, Alabama. There, some of his men were accused of shooting down Confederate troops without mercy. Included in his division was the 51st USCI, formerly the 1st Mississippi Infantry, A. D., which fought at Milliken's Bend. Hawkins received a brevet to major general in 1865. After the war he continued in the army, returning to the subsistence department and becoming commissary general of subsistence in 1892. He retired to Indianapolis, where he died on February 7, 1914.[40]

CORYDON HEATH

Divorced before the war, Corydon Heath's ex-wife, Celestia Van der Burgh, later would file for a pension on behalf of their two children, Ada and Jefferson. Claiming that he was serving as a captain at the time of his death, Celestia believed a higher pension should be awarded. Instead, because Heath was still officially on detached service from his original unit, Battery G, 2nd Illinois Light Artillery, where he was a sergeant, Celestia's children received a lower pension. Ada would later name her first son, Corydon Heath Conger, for her father. Corydon continues to be a name passed down to the present day among descendants in Canada and the United States, though at least among the Canadian line, it seems it has been bestowed in honor of more recent generations. Few descendants there are aware of the details of Heath's military service or the circumstances of his death.[41]

Other than the wartime reference to his being buried in a shallow grave near the Ouachita River in Monroe, Heath's final resting place remains unknown. Due to twentieth-century urbanization and river control, it seems likely that at some point his remains may have been discovered and reinterred. It seems equally possible that his body may have been moved to the national cemetery at Alexandria, Louisiana, as part of the great postwar reburials, but if so, his must be one of the more than eight hundred whose identities are unknown.

"BIG JACK" JACKSON

Thus far, it has been impossible to determine the precise identity of the man 1st Lt. David Cornwell called "Big Jack" Jackson. Cornwell and Jack first met near Jackson, Tennessee; one wonders if that is perhaps where Jack took his last name. Jack is typically a nickname for John, but it may have been simply a nickname for the man's last name.[42]

Although a number of men with the surname Jackson served in what ultimately became the 5th U.S. Colored Heavy Artillery, none died on June 7 or as a result of wounds sustained at Milliken's Bend. There were two men named John Jackson, but neither served in Cornwell's Company B, was of great height ("Big Jack" was six-and-a-half feet tall), or died at Milliken's Bend.[43]

One John Jackson was 47 years old, 5' 8", and born in Cleveland County, Mississippi. He enlisted on May 1 at Milliken's Bend, joining Company F. Records are confusing, but he apparently deserted in May "a few hours after his muster into service" or in late June at Vicksburg. In 1886, he applied to have the charge of desertion removed from his record, instead pleading for an honorable discharge, but his effort came to naught. The rest of his story is not known.[44]

A second John Jackson, aged 28, served in Company G, was a little over 5'6", and was born in Jackson, Tennessee. A carpenter, he enlisted at Milliken's Bend on May 1 and was wounded multiple times in the fighting there. After returning to his regiment some months later, he became a cook, but even this proved difficult for him. He received a medical discharge at the end of 1864.[45]

It is entirely possible that Jack Jackson's records are among those missing from the regiment, as a number of records were lost in the action. For instance, in the register of deaths for Company B contained in the regimental descriptive book, no deaths are listed any earlier than August 1863. As a result, we are left with Cornwell's memoirs as virtually the only source for any information about this man.[46]

HERMANN LIEB

Born in Switzerland in 1826, Hermann Lieb came to America in 1852 and lived in Decatur, Illinois, where he began the study of law. Four days after Fort Sumter was fired upon, Lieb enlisted as a private in the three-months 8th Illinois Infantry and remained when the regiment became a three-year unit. His colonel was Richard Oglesby, the future governor of the state. Due to previous military experience in Europe as a young man, Lieb aided Oglesby in providing the rudiments of training for a portion of the new regiment. As a result, Oglesby promoted Lieb to a captaincy. Lieb led a company at Shiloh and, later in the fall of 1862, was promoted to major. He was appointed colonel of the 9th Louisiana Infantry, African Descent, by order of Adjutant General Lorenzo Thomas in April 1863, though, like other officers in the new regiment, he would not be mustered in at that rank until much later. Despite being severely wounded at Milliken's Bend, Lieb continued as the regiment's colonel through its reorganization as the 5th U.S. Colored Heavy Artillery. In March 1865, he was awarded a brevet to brigadier general and continued to lead the regiment until it was mustered out in 1866.

After his service, he returned to Illinois where he became publisher of a German language newspaper, first in Springfield, then in Chicago. In 1906, Lieb was undoubtedly troubled by his wound in his thigh, which still carried the minie ball from forty years earlier. A bill was introduced in Congress to increase his pension to thirty dollars a month. Former assistant secretary of war Charles Dana, former governor Richard Oglesby, and five generals testified on Lieb's behalf. Maj. Gen. Loyd Wheaton, an old comrade from the 8th Illinois, veteran of the Philippine Insurrection, and himself a Medal of Honor winner, declared, "while he had known many brave men, he had known none braver than Herman [sic] Lieb." Lieb died in Chicago on March 5, 1908.[47]

CYRUS SEARS

A lawyer before the war, Cyrus Sears returned to the legal profession briefly afterward. However, he made a poor investment in an attempt to raise cotton near Vicksburg and lost $7,000. He gave up the law, seeking to recoup his earnings by becoming part owner in a machine works back in Ohio known as Stevenson and Sears. In 1876, he became a merchant in Fowler, Ohio, and later moved to Harpster, Ohio. In 1892, he was awarded the Medal of Honor for his actions with the 11th Ohio Battery at Iuka. He died on Nov. 30, 1909. His account of the battle at Milliken's Bend, printed at his own expense as a small booklet in the same year as his death, would remain the only stand-alone publication solely devoted to the battle for more than one hundred years.[48]

ISAAC F. SHEPARD

Harvard-educated, Isaac F. Shepard was an educator, editor, and briefly, a state legislator in Massachusetts. He went to Missouri in 1861 and served on the staff of Gen. Nathaniel Lyon at Wilson's Creek. He became colonel of the 3rd Missouri in 1862 and voluntarily remained at the same rank to take command of a black regiment (the 1st Mississippi Infantry, A. D.) when virtually all other initial officers in the Colored Troops were gaining several grades in rank. He was in charge of the African Brigade through much of the summer of 1863 during the absence of Gen. John P. Hawkins. After Milliken's Bend, Shepard's brigade served garrison duty at Vicksburg. In the fall of 1863, Adjt. Gen. Lorenzo Thomas recommended his promotion to brigadier general. Thomas had recommended his promotion before, but because of Shepard's actions in having a white soldier flogged for punishment by his black enlisted men, the initial request was denied. On Thomas's second attempt, the adjutant general praised Shepard's leadership, pointing out that Shepard had acted on behalf of his men and had been cleared by the court of inquiry, and urged the promotion, to date from the day of Milliken's Bend. The Senate never confirmed Shepard's appointment, and his commission expired in the summer of 1864. After the war he served as state adjutant general of Missouri and became editor of the *Missouri Democrat*. He went to China as a diplomat and in the late 1880s returned to Massachusetts, where he died in 1889.[49]

APPENDIX B

Federal Casualties at Milliken's Bend

Casualty figures on the Federal side at Milliken's Bend vary considerably. First, we must attempt to determine accurate figures for Union losses. Second, when we examine the Federal losses at Milliken's Bend and compare the figures to other regimental losses in the Vicksburg campaign, it becomes clearer that Milliken's Bend was indeed a significant event.

Readers may ask why I am considering only Federal losses. The first reason is that reported Confederate losses are much more consistent, primarily because only a few reports with casualty figures exist. Second, although McCulloch's Brigade certainly suffered at Milliken's Bend—about 12 percent of its force killed, wounded, and missing—its losses were significantly less than those suffered by the Federals.[1] In addition, evaluating the percentage of losses at the regimental level for the Confederates is impossible because no precise figures for the number of men originally engaged are available. For these reasons, I have chosen to concentrate on Union losses and let McCulloch's reports stand on their own.

One further note: because casualties were extremely light in the 13th Louisiana and the 1st Mississippi, these two regiments have been omitted from this study, except when examining the African Brigade as a whole.

PART I. VARIABILITY AND ACCURACY IN UNION REPORTS

A. Initial Reports of Brigade Losses

Col. Hermann Lieb was in temporary command of the African Brigade at Milliken's Bend and was actually present at the time of battle, so his report can be taken as a solid starting point. He claimed that 621 men of the brigade were killed, wounded, or missing. Although Lieb was wounded early in the action, he compiled a report the following day, showing that he was still undertaking his duties as colonel and acting commander of the post.[2]

INITIAL BRIGADE CASUALTY REPORTS

	Killed	Wounded	Missing	Total
Lieb*	101	252	268	621
Dennis	101	285	266	652
Dana**	118	310	not stated	428 (missing omitted)

* Omits losses of the 23rd Iowa
** Includes losses of the 23rd Iowa
Note: All figures contain some inaccuracies.

As reports were made higher up the chain of command, however, more discrepancies crept in. Two additional reports tally the losses at Milliken's Bend—one made by Lieb's superior, Brig. Gen. Elias S. Dennis, and one by Assistant Secretary of War Charles Dana. Neither was present at the battle, and for this reason, their reports are considered unreliable, although some discrepancies can be explained.

Dennis tallied Federal losses at 652. It is not clear if he included figures from the 23rd Iowa, though these numbers could account for the variance between his figures and Lieb's account. Among the casualties reported by Dennis were two officers and 264 enlisted men captured or missing. Most of the missing were black troops, and Dennis expected them to return, claiming "they were badly scattered."[3]

Assistant Secretary of War Charles Dana reported to Stanton that 428 men were dead or wounded, and he omitted the missing. This figure exceeds those killed and wounded reported by Lieb and Dennis, though again, the difference may be the inclusion or exclusion of the losses of the 23rd Iowa. Dana makes it explicit that he includes their losses in his report. Lieb does not include their losses in his report, and in Dennis, it is unclear. It is conceivable that losses for the 23rd Iowa may have been inadvertently counted twice—"invisibly" in Dennis's report and more obviously in Dana's. Dana's figures, however, are considered the least reliable of the reports, and none of the three can be considered entirely accurate.[4]

B. Losses and Numbers of the 11th Louisiana

Just as there were variations in the casualty figures for the brigade, there were inconsistencies with the regimental figures. Differences between Lieb's report and Dana's for the 9th Louisiana, for example, are minimal. By far the most problematic figures in the brigade came from the 11th Louisiana. The problems here are twofold: its number of casualties and its number present at the beginning of the fight.

B.1. Losses of the 11th Louisiana

Lieb gives a total loss for this regiment of 395 men—which is also the number he reported present for duty at the start of the fight. This figure is wrong in both accounts.[5]

Lieb's erroneous numbers for the losses of the 11th Louisiana would be repeated through the years and were not corrected until the publication of the *Supplement to the Official Records* in 1998. Based upon regimental and company records at the National Archives, the *Supplement* is an invaluable resource. In great contrast to the figures given by Lieb, these records reveal the losses for the 11th Louisiana to be considerably less. Total losses for the regiment came in at 201, with only 107 missing, instead of the 243 missing reported by Lieb. Because the figures in the *Supplement* are based upon original regimental reports and returns, it is believed they provide the most accurate figure for the 11th Louisiana's losses.[6]

B.2. Numbers Present in the 11th Louisiana

Determining the 11th Louisiana's original number taken into battle is even more difficult than determining its casualties and borders on the impossible. Lieb, in a report made the day after the battle, said 395 men were present in the 11th Louisiana, but this seems erroneous given much larger numbers reported by others.[7]

Nearly two weeks prior to the battle, Col. Isaac F. Shepard stated that 361 recruits were present in the 11th Louisiana, awaiting medical inspection, but also said, "the entire number in this camp is 683." He may have been referring to the total number of men for the African Brigade, although this seems unlikely given the context of this statement, in the middle of a paragraph about the 11th Louisiana. Forty years later, Capt. Frank Orm would also claim that the 11th brought 680 men to the fight.[8]

About two weeks after Milliken's Bend, Shepard wrote to Adjt. Gen. Lorenzo Thomas and said that the 11th Louisiana brought 458 enlisted men and

CASUALTIES OF THE 11TH LOUISIANA

	Killed	Wounded	Missing	Total
Lieb	33	119	243	395
Supplement	*28*	*66*	*107*	*201*

Note: Italics indicates figures believed to be most reliable.

24 officers to the fight, a total of 482 soldiers. The 458 enlisted men of the 11th Louisiana would allow for a two-week growth of the regiment from the May 24th report of 361 recruits. Still, it is unclear why this number is so much smaller than the 683 that Shepard had reported "in camp" in late May. It may be that many did not pass medical inspection or had to be returned to plantation lessees due to illegal recruiting.[9]

Shepard's postbattle report of 482 soldiers for the regiment gains further credence, however, when one looks at the figures he provides for the *other* regiments of the African Brigade at the fight. They neatly correlate to numbers for all other regiments given by Colonel Lieb the day after the battle, disregarding for the moment Lieb's erroneous report of 395 men for the 11th. Because Shepard's other regimental numbers so closely match those reported by Lieb, I believe that, given the extant resources, the best estimate is that there were 482 officers and enlisted men of the 11th Louisiana present at the start of the battle.[10]

C. Summary

Thus, for the purposes of the next section, I believe that Lieb had the most accurate figures for regimental losses in the African Brigade with exception of the 11th Louisiana. For the losses of the 11th Louisiana, I have chosen to use the *Supplement to the Official Records* as the authoritative source. In addition, I am relying on Shepard's June 23 report for the number of men present in the 11th Louisiana, even though this figure is far from definitive. Finally, for the 23rd Iowa, I use figures recorded in Lt. Aquilla Standifird's diary because his report is from the time of the battle and it seems most accurate when compared to other sources.

STARTING STRENGTH FOR THE 11TH LOUISIANA

Lieb, June 8, 1863	395
Shepard, May 24, 1863	361 "recruits for medical inspection"
	683 "entire number in the camp"
Capt. Frank Orm, 1902	680
Shepard, June 23, 1863	482 (458 enlisted + 24 officers)

Note: Italics indicates figures believed to be most reliable.

CORRECTED CASUALTY NUMBERS AND NUMBERS PRESENT

	Killed	Wounded	Missing	Total Losses	Present
9th Louisiana (Lieb's report)	66	107	22	195	285
13th Louisiana (Lieb's report)	0	5	0	5	108
1st Mississippi (Lieb's report)	2	21	3	26	153
11th Louisiana *(Supplement)*	28	66	107	201	482 (Shepard)
23rd Iowa (Standifird)	23	42	0	65	120
Totals at Milliken's Bend	119	241	132	492	1148

PART II. COMPARATIVE LOSSES DURING
THE VICKSBURG CAMPAIGN

Now that we have a firmer grasp on the actual numbers of men engaged and the losses, we can take a closer look at losses suffered by other regiments during the Vicksburg campaign, as a way of comparing the scale of the casualties at Milliken's Bend.

According to former Vicksburg National Military Park historian Ed Bearss, the 9th Louisiana had the highest numeric loss of any Union regiment in a single day during the entire Vicksburg campaign. Bearss gives its loss as 165. He apparently did not rely upon Lieb's report, which totaled a larger loss of 195 men.[11] Bearss must have ignored the losses of the 11th Louisiana entirely, possibly because of the high and questionable number of missing provided in the majority of published reports. Final numbers for the 11th Louisiana show they lost 201 men from all causes, just slightly more than Lieb's regiment.

Given Bearss' initial assessment that a loss of 165 would denote a regiment with the highest losses in a single day during the Vicksburg campaign, *two* of the regiments that fought at Milliken's Bend, the 11th Louisiana and the 9th Louisiana, would appear to rank in first and second place, respectively, for this distinction.

However, like everything else at Milliken's Bend, it is not that simple. A number of other regiments at other engagements during the Vicksburg campaign lost just as significantly. At Champion Hill, for instance, the 24th Indiana lost 201 men—equal to that of the 11th Louisiana, numerically, but far worse because the Hoosiers had only *eight* men missing—not over a hundred like the Louisiana troops. Other regiments at Champion Hill also had major losses: the 24th Iowa lost 189, and both the 10th Iowa and the 11th Indiana lost 167 from all causes. Four other regiments lost over one hundred men during the same engagement. During the assault on Vicksburg on May 22, 1863, the 22nd Iowa was noteworthy for its loss of 164 men.[12]

Perhaps what Bearss meant to say was that the number of *killed in action* in the 9th Louisiana at Milliken's Bend was the highest loss by any regiment in a single day during the entire campaign. With 66 men dead, no other regiment comes close.[13]

However one does the math, Milliken's Bend earns a place of distinction within the overall Vicksburg campaign.

COMPARISON OF LOSSES DURING VICKSBURG CAMPAIGN

	Killed	Wounded	Missing	Total Losses
24th Indiana (Champion Hill)	27	166	8	201
11th Louisiana (Milliken's Bend)	28	66	107	201
9th Louisiana (Milliken's Bend)	66	107	22	195
24th Iowa (Champion Hill)	35	120	34	189
10th Iowa (Champion Hill)	36	131	—	167
11th Indiana (Champion Hill)	28	126	13	167
22nd Iowa (Assault May 22)	27	118	19	164
93rd Illinois (Champion Hill)	38	113	11	162

Note: Figures for all regiments are based upon Fox, Regimental Losses, 437, except for the 9th and 11th Louisiana, which are based upon the final "corrected" figures in table on p. 204.

APPENDIX C

Report of Col. Isaac F. Shepard to Adjt. Gen. Lorenzo Thomas

Head Quarters U.S. Colored Troops
Milliken's Bend, La. June 23d, 1863

General:

Yours of the 13th, covering several papers, reached me last evening from Louisville, Ky. Your request regarding Gen. Hawkins shall be faithfully observed when I see him, but up to this moment have neither seen, nor heard from him, directly or indirectly, since he left here soon after you did. We have *supposed* he was at Louisville, but from your having forwarded official papers *from there,* we gather that he is not there.

The absence of the General just at the commencement of this great enter-prize was unfortunate. It threw the whole labor upon my shoulders and without staff officers, no Quartermaster, no Commissary,—and with power only to ap-point temporary substitutes, I have had no common work to do. The tri-monthly Report of the result of labors you inaugurated will be sent by this mail, and will show you a grand aggregate of 4464, with 3035 present for duty—the *13th Lou. was* not being authorized by you, as I learn today. All the others are fully armed, equipped, and in growing discipline,—taking more creditable position *in drill* then any troops I ever saw with the same instruction. Thousands of others are recruited before Vicksburg, where Gen. Grant requires them to work in employ-ment of engineers, sappers and miners. Of course the increase of recruits must give way to the urgent work of taking Vicksburg, but Gen. Grant sends assur-ances that very soon he will be done with them, when we must, I think, fill up at once. Until then increase must be slow, from necessity.

The "obstacles" of which I wrote have *all* been overcome, and all our af-fairs run smoothly as could be wished. Gen. Grant has most energetically and promptly met our needs, and reformed all tardiness when he knew of it. But with Gen. Sullivan I am sorry to say I had much inconvenience. His influence was certain [?] against us, and it was felt every way. Subordinates took pattern, if not counsel, and the poor blacks were most inhumanely abused, outraged, pillaged, and even murdered, by white soldiers about us, and redress we could not get. At length I felt impelled to stop the brutality by condign measures. A private of 10th Ill. Cav. kicked a negro soldier tied to a tree, causing dangerous injuries in the abdomen, etc.—went on thence and attempted rape on too [sic] women,—and finally most cruelly kicked a boy to stupidity, cutting a huge gash in his cheek, and neerly [sic] missing his left eye. He was arrested and brought to me, and after heering [sic] the case deemed it right in my indignation to let the black soldiers themselves flagellate him for his crimes, and they did it. This was the 30th of May. The 31st Gen. Sullivan ordered me in arrest. The 1st of June I sent a [illegible] to Gen. Grant asking a Court of Inquiry. It was promptly ordered, and Tuesday the 2d Gen. Sullivan was removed from his command. The 5 the Court were at "the Bend" and for ten days I think, devoted much attention to the developments. They were astounded,—but went away *friend to the blacks.* All were strangers to me, and on the 12th they left for Gen. Grant's H'd Quarters to make their report, followed by my restoration to command on the 14th.

In the mean time had come upon us the attack of Sunday morning the 7th inst., in which, without command, I stood for the encouragement of the blacks, side by side with them in the trenches, as long as to stand was possible. Let me describe in brief the ground, the position, the attack and the results. Two miles above where Gen. Hawkins' quarters were the road, you remember, lead out to Richmond, at nearly right angles to the river. Nearly [parallel?] to the river, 150 yards from it is the levee, which Col. Leib [sic] had ditches *on the inside,* to give the blacks a place to stand protected,—the earth removed being throw[n] on the top of the levee. The camp of the 11th La. = 458 men—of the 9th La. = 285 men—and of the 1st Miss. = 150 men, were all between the ditches Levee and the river = 893 negroes in all. There were about a hundred recruits beside, unorganized. With these the 9th La. had 22 com. officers—the 11th La. = 24 and the 1st Miss. = 3. Total officers = 49. A steamer was at the river bank with the 23d Iowa Inf. not over a hundred fifty men on board, having arrived the evening previous. At three o'clock the camp was alarmed, and the troops readily formed. They were taken to the ditches and posted closely along the levee, the left of the line being nearly opposite the Richmond road. I went at once to the levee, and while standing upon its top, saw defiling from the woods on *the right,* a body of troops. Not knowing the dispositions nor the plans of Col. Leib I supposed in the grey morning they were our pickets coming in. But to my surprize they flanked entirely across the open field, parallel to the Levee, until the right reached the Richmond road, then deliberately halted, came to the front, and [moved?] directly upon us in line of battle, solid, strong and steady. The fire ran along our parapet, the rebels replied within 60 feet of us, and before the *third* volley, a body of cavalry down the Richmond road charged on our right. The 23d Iowa were late off the boats for some cause, and on the double quick through the center of the camp, had only reached this point, not fully in line, when they received this shock,—fell back overpowered, and with them fell back the blacks, like the foot of a compass swinging on its center, while the line of the levee was filled with a mass of the enemy cheering, and waving hats. I *think* they displayed the white flag, with a black crossbones and coffin. I was on the breast works *in line* with it and so saw indistinctly. Others assert it without question. The falling back was not specially disordered, not more so I think than veteran troops must have shown against such odds—at least 2 to one besides cavalry. The larger portion sought cover under the precipitous bank of the river, and making the best use of it for a defence continued a steady fire upon the enemy (now in the camps) with great effect. At the same time a gun boat had come up, and opened with shell, driving back the foe behind the levee, when the black troops once more took position in the trenches and the rebels retired altogether. The fight was short, sharp and desperate on both sides, Muskets were clubbed, and bayonets used freely. Out of the 895 blacks in the engagement, *105 were killed, 233 wounded, 97 missing = total loss 435.* Of these about 60 are known to be prisoners.

Of the 49 white commissioned officers in the affair, 7 *were killed,* 14 *wounded,*—3 prisoners.

There were only 5 *white orderly sergeants* present, of whom 3 *were killed,* and 1 *wounded.*

This is as exact a description of the affair as can be, I think, and demonstrates most surely that we are *not* working useless material. Where before has such fighting been done, under such circumstances? Not one *had ever held a musket* three weeks before—some not 24 hours—untaught—[knowing?] no command, by which they could be moved in masses—and yet standing against disciplined troops till they left *103 dead bodies to be* buried, with a Colonel killed,—a Major in our hands, wounded, and a General's command flying before less than 500 surviving blacks! It is wonderful and suggestive. Perhaps a few officers were not what was expected of them. I think they were not, and when I feel sure shall proceed against such as showed the lack of presence of mind, and personal courage. But the general charge of "cowardice of the officers"—which some northern prints are circulating, is maliciously invented by our domestic foes. 54 white officers in all, *and 28 of them* among the list of casualties! What fight shows so grand a record? What fact so good a defence? I think there will be a future that will make this *first regular battle against the blacks alone* honorably historic. The best of all is our troops are not demoralized by the sad result to them. Not at all disheartened. Indeed they have risen with the event, and proudly walk with a loftier tread than before, of the coming strife that will help wipe out the loss of their comrades. It seems as we say of our father's deeds—"to have cemented devotion to country with the heart's blood."

Since my restoration to command the forces (black) at the Bend, have been steadily at work upon the defences, and we are getting quite a respectable Fort on the site of the battle. I have named it "Fort Thomas" as an appropriate memento of your labors in behalf of these troops, as well as of my personal appreciation of your official position. Gen. Grant has directed a captured battery of artillery to be fited up for use, and during the week we shall see "Fort Thomas" decidedly prepared for a better defence than before.

I trust to see Gen. Hawkins soon, for I am weary with a multitude of labors, and need rest. He will now find it "easy sailing," for the heavy work is all done, and the prejudices are [moving?] overpast—and the departments are all organized and happily working. If I do not break down before he comes, I shall be fortunate, for Mr. Field, Capt. Strickle, Mr. Livermore, and Lt. [Colyer?] of their force are all ill, as well as every *assistant* they have.

I notice by the new order "No. 143" that no person will be allowed to raise but a single regiment. That I suppose cuts off my intended work for promotion. Well, I have never been remarkable *for selfishness*, and as I have worked th[r]ough so much that it was intended Gen. Hawkins should have done—so as long as life continues shall I still labor for a Government I reverence, with all my powers, even if it be in subordinate positions. Most respectfully

Your obedient Servant
Isaac F. Shepard

To
Brig. Gen. L. Thomas

Source: Isaac F. Shepard to General, June 23, 1863 (S-40), Colored Troops Division, Letters Received (entry 360), Records of the Adjutant General's Office (RG94), National Archives, Washington, DC.

APPENDIX D

Reports Investigating the Death of Capt. Corydon Heath

[Note on cover indicates Lieb's report with two enclosures was sent to the Secretary of War "with report on Hon. Mr. Loan's letter" [1] on January 2, 1863.]

Headquarters 1st Miss. Heavy Artillery
Vicksburg Dec. ＿＿＿ 1863.

General

I would respectfully submit for your consideration the following.

Captain Corydon Heath of my Regiment (formerly the 9th La. Vols of A. D.) was taken prisoner at the Battle of Millikens Bend La. June 7th 1863.

I have never except through my Regimental returns made any official report of this case. I waited anxiously hoping that Captain Heath would return or be heard from. But in vain. I have now ample proof to convince me that Capt. Heath with another unfortunate prisoner (a Lieut. of the 11th La. Vols. AD)[2] taken at the same time, were executed at Monroe La. by a military mob. The expedition to that place by Brig. Genl. Stevenson on or about the 28th of August 1863 and the testimony of Brig. Gen. Leggett, Comdg 3d Division 17th A. C. Maj. Davis and Lieut. Wallace of the 1st Arkansas Colored troops (who was a prisoner and sick in Hospital at Monroe La at the time) sufficiently show that the black crime of murder on a prisoner of war has been committed.

Captain Heath was one of my most efficient officers, a nobler patriot and braver soldier his country does not produce. He leaves an interesting family in Illinois to mourn his loss.

Enclosed please find stat[e]ments made by Brig. Genl Leggett and Major Davis.

I am General,
Very Respectfully
Your obt servt
H. Lieb
Col. 1st Miss Heavy Artillery

⁜

Statement of Major John G. Davis Concerning the Murder of Captain Coridon Heath 9th Regiment Louisiana Vols of A. D. a prisoner of War at Monroe State of Louisiana

I being at Monroe, State of Louisiana with the Trans Mississippi expedition on the 28th of August 1863, made it a part of my duty to make inquiry concerning the fate of Captain Coridon Heath of 9th Regiment Louisiana Vols of A. D. who was captured by the Rebels at the Battle of Millikens Bend on the 7th day of June 1863, since which time he had not been heard of.

I first inquired of Citizens who resided at Monroe and they stated that he had been held a prisoner in close confinement at that place, but that a short time before the arrival of the expedition he was taken out of Prison at night and put to Death but could not say in what manner. I next proceeded to the Confederate Hospital and conversed with the Soldiers upon the subject. I found several men who had seen Captain Heath while a Prisoner, and their statements all agreed concerning his Death. Afterwards I conversed with Prisoners who were captured in the vicinity of Monroe, and they informed me positively that said Captain was taken out of Prison by the Rebel authorities at night and hung until Dead.

Jno. G. Davis, Major
1st Miss. Heavy Art. Vols. of A. D.

⁜

Head Quarters 3rd Div. 17th A. C.
Vicksburg Miss. 14th Dec. 1863

Col. H. Lieb
1st Miss. Heavy Art.
Col.

For a few day[s] in the latter part of August last, I was in command of the Post at Monroe on the Washita [sic] River, La. While there, I heard a rumor that two of our officers, who had been taken prisoners were killed in Monroe some weeks before. I immediately sent for some responsible citizens and examined them in reference to the matter, & learned substancially [sic] as follows.

Among the troops taken prisoners at and near Millikens Bend, were Capt. Heath of your Regiment, and a Lieutenant of one of the Colored Regts. These two were hand-cuffed together and confined in the jail at Monroe. The irons with which they were fastened, being too small, caused them great distress, their limbs become badly inflamed and swollen. The citizens complained to the military authorities of the barbarity, and were answered that "they would soon end their misery." The next night they were taken from the jail just after dark, put under charge of a squad of soldiers who took them across the river, that soon after guns were heard, and the squad returned without the prisoners, & reported that they had shot them. One citizen said he went to the place where the firing was heard and found where they were buried.

I intended on the next day to have taken sworn statements of citizens in writing, also to have disinterred the bodies supposed to have been these officers but was ordered back to the Mississippi at dawn of day the next morning.

Further than this I know nothing.

I am Colonel
Your obedient servt
M. D. Leggett
Brig. Genl

Source: H-391, 1864, Letters Received (entry 360), Colored Troops Division, Records of the Adjutant General's Office (RG94), National Archives, Washington, DC.

ABBREVIATIONS

UNIT DESIGNATIONS

A.D. = African Descent
USCHA = U.S. Colored Heavy Artillery
USCI = U.S. Colored Infantry
USCT = U.S. Colored Troops

REPOSITORIES

CAH = Center for American History, University of Texas, Austin, TX

IHS = Manuscript and Visual Collections Department, William Henry Smith Memorial Library, Indiana Historical Society, Indianapolis, IN

LLMVC = Louisiana and Lower Mississippi Valley Collections, LSU Libraries, Baton Rouge, LA

MDAH = Mississippi Department of Archives and History, Jackson, MS

NARA-CP = National Archives and Records Administration, Archives II Building, College Park, MD

NARA-DC = National Archives and Records Administration, Archives I Building, Washington, DC

OPPL = Special Collections Department, Ouachita Parish Public Library, Monroe, LA

SHSI = State Historical Society of Iowa, Des Moines, IA

THM = Historical Research Center, Texas Heritage Museum, Hill College, Hillsboro, TX

TSLAC = Texas State Library and Archives Commission, Austin, TX

TU = Special Collections Department, Tulane University, New Orleans, LA

USAMHI = U.S. Army Military History Institute, Carlisle Barracks, PA

VNMP = Vicksburg National Military Park, Vicksburg, MS

SOURCES

CSR = Compiled Service Record(s)

Mass.-MOLLUS = Massachusetts Commandery Military Order of the Loyal
    Legion

NAMP = National Archives Microfilm (or Microfiche) Publication

NMSUS = *The Negro in the Military Service of the United States 1639–1886,*
    National Archives Microfilm Publications, Microcopy T-823.

ORA = War Department. *The War of the Rebellion: A Compilation of the Official
    Records of the Union and Confederate Armies.* 128 vols. Washington,
    DC: GPO, 1880–1901.

OR Suppl. = Hewett, Janet B. et al., eds., *Supplement to the Official Records of the
    Union and Confederate Armies.* 100 vols. Wilmington, NC: Broadfoot,
    1994–2001.

ORN = Naval War Records Office. *Official Records of the Union and Confederate
    Navies in the War of the Rebellion.* 30 vols. Washington, DC: GPO,
    1894–1922.

RG = Record Group

USACC-pt. 1 = Records of US Army Continental Commands (RG393),
    Part I: Geographical Divisions and Departments and Military
    (Reconstruction) Districts

USACC-pt. 2 = Records of US Army Continental Commands (RG393), Part II:
    Polyonymous Successions of Commands, 1861–1870

NOTES

CHAPTER ONE

1. War Department, *The War of the Rebellion: A Compilation of the Official Records of the Union and Confederate Armies* (Washington, DC: GPO, 1900), series 4, vol. 1, p. 9. Henceforth, *ORA*.

2. Ibid., 8.

3. Ibid., 12.

4. Ibid., 9.

5. Winthrop D. Jordan, *Tumult and Silence at Second Creek: An Inquiry into a Civil War Slave Conspiracy* (Baton Rouge: Louisiana State University Press, 1993).

6. *ORA*, series 4, vol. 1, pp. 8–9.

7. Charles B. Dew, *Apostles of Disunion: Southern Secession Commissioners and the Causes of the Civil War* (Charlottesville: University Press of Virginia, 2001): Georgian Henry L. Benning to Virginia, pp. 64–65; John Smith Preston of South Carolina to Virginia, p. 70; Mississippian Judge Alexander Hamilton Handy to Maryland, p. 33; Isham W. Garrott and Robert Hardy Smith, Alabama, to North Carolina, p. 35.

8. Ernest William Winkler, ed. *Journal of the Secession Convention of Texas* (Austin, TX: Austin Printing, 1912), 120–123. Online as part of Texas Constitutions 1824–1876, Tarlton Law Library / Jamail Legal Research Center at the University of Texas School of Law, The University of Texas at Austin, last modified Sept. 2, 2009, accessed Jan. 14, 2012, http://tarlton.law.utexas.edu/constitutions/pdf/pdf1861/index1861.html, entry for March 9, 1861.

9. The most thorough examination of the "Texas Troubles" appears in Donald E. Reynolds, *Texas Terror: The Slave Insurrection Panic of 1860 and the Secession of the Lower South* (Baton Rouge: Louisiana State University Press, 2007).

10. "Declaration of the Causes which impel the State of Texas to secede from the Federal Union—also the Ordinance of Secession," Printed Ephemera Collection, Portfolio 346, Folder 43, Library of Congress. Online in *An American Time Capsule: Three Centuries of Broadsides and Other Printed Ephemera,* part of *American Memory,* Library of Congress, accessed Jan. 14, 2012, http://hdl.loc.gov/loc.rbc/rbpe.34604300.

11. Ibid.

12. For example, see Armstead L. Robinson, *Bitter Fruits of Bondage: The Demise of Slavery and the Collapse of the Confederacy, 1861–1865* (Charlottesville: University of Virginia Press, 2005), 42–44.

13. *The Negro in the Military Service of the United States 1639–1886,* NAMP Microcopy T-823, roll 5, vol. 7, chap. 8, p. 4448. Henceforth, *NMSUS*.

14. Ibid., 4450.

15. Jordan, *Tumult and Silence at Second Creek*, 4451–4452.

16. Ibid., 4452–4454.

17. Ibid., 4455–4456.

18. Ibid., 4461–4463.

19. Ibid., 4464.

20. Ibid., 4471, 4473–4474.

21. *ORA*, series 1, vol. 14, p. 192.

22. *NMSUS*, roll 5, vol. 7, chap. 8, p. 4475.

23. *Natchez Daily Courier*, Dec. 20, 1862.

24. Ibid., Dec. 24, 1862.

25. Ibid., Jan. 2, 1863.

26. *Report on the Treatment of Prisoners of War by the Rebel Authorities during the War of the Rebellion*, 40th Cong., 3d sess., 1869, H. Rep. 45, serial 1391, 428–430. Henceforth, *Treatment of Prisoners of War.*

27. *Journal of the Congress of the Confederate States of America 1861–1865*, vol. 3, *Journal of the Senate of the First Congress of the Confederate States of America*, 3d sess. (Richmond: Jan. 12, 1863 to May 1, 1863). In U.S. Senate, 58th Cong., 2d sess., 1903–04, S. Doc. 234, vol. 27, serial 4612, pp. 386–387. Henceforth, *Congress of CSA.*

28. "Speech of Hon. William H. Wadsworth of Kentucky, on the Enlistment of Negro Soldiers; delivered in the House of Representatives, January 30, 1863" (Washington: 1863), 8, Alfred H. Stone Collection, v. 58, no. 9, MDAH.

29. "Speech of Hon. Henry May, of Maryland against the war and arming negroes, and for peace and recognition in the House of Representatives, February 2, 1863," Alfred H. Stone Collection, v. 75, no. 19, MDAH; *NMSUS*, roll 2, vol. 3, chap. 5, part 1, pp. 1117, 1081.

30. *ORA*, series 1, vol. 18, pp. 1067–1069; Eugene D. Genovese, *Roll Jordan, Roll: The World the Slaves Made* (New York: Pantheon, 1974), 138.

CHAPTER TWO

1. George M. Frederickson, *The Black Image in the White Mind: The Debate on Afro-American Character and Destiny, 1817–1914* (New York: Harper and Row, 1971), 55.

2. Dunbar Rowland, ed., *Jefferson Davis, Constitutionalist, His Letters, Papers, and Speeches* (Jackson, MS: Mississippi Dept. of Archives and History, 1923), 5:30.

3. Alfred N. Hunt, *Haiti's Influence on Antebellum America: Slumbering Volcano in the Caribbean* (Baton Rouge: Louisiana State University Press, 1988), 46–47. Search of HeritageQuest Online, 1860 census, Louisiana, for birthplace = Santo Domingo and birthplace = Haiti. In the nineteenth century, Haiti was often referred to interchangeably as Santo Domingo (the Spanish colony that changed hands several times in the early nineteenth century, eventually becoming the Dominican Republic in 1844) or Saint Domingue, the French name for the colony, which was overthrown by the Haitian Revolution led by Toussaint Louverture. Joseph C. G. Kennedy, *Population of the United States in 1860 Compiled from the Original Returns of the Eighth Census . . .* (Washington, DC: GPO, 1864), available online from the U.S. Census Bureau at www.census.gov/prod/www/abs/decennial/1860.html/. This compilation does not distinguish between the various

islands, countries, and colonies in the Caribbean. Undoubtedly, persons born in Haiti or Santo Domingo would have been included in the category of "West Indies."

4. Joe Gray Taylor, *Negro Slavery in Louisiana* (Baton Rouge: Louisiana Historical Association, 1963), 212–213.

5. Ibid., 212–213, 218, 220, 222.

6. *Monroe Register,* Jan. 5, 1860.

7. *Daily Mississippian* (Jackson, MS), Jan. 17, 1860.

8. For instance, see Herbert Aptheker, *American Negro Slave Revolts,* 6th ed. (New York: International Publishers, 1993); Dickson D. Bruce Jr., *Violence and Culture in the Antebellum South* (Austin: University of Texas, 1979), 132, 192; Randolph B. Campbell, *An Empire for Slavery: The Peculiar Institution in Texas, 1821–1865* (Baton Rouge: Louisiana State University Press, 1989), 218–219; Kenneth S. Greenberg, *Honor and Slavery: Lies, Duels, Noses, Masks . . .* (Princeton: Princeton University Press, 1996), 102, 144.

9. Armstead L. Robinson, "In the Shadow of Old John Brown: Insurrection Anxiety and Confederate Mobilization, 1861–1863," *Journal of Negro History* 65, no. 4 (Fall 1980): 280.

10. Jordan, *Tumult and Silence at Second Creek,* 308, 14–15, 310.

11. Ibid., 308–310.

12. Ibid.

13. Ibid., 309.

14. John Q. Anderson, ed., *Brokenburn: The Journal of Kate Stone, 1861–1868* (1955; repr. with new intro. by Drew Gilpin Faust, Baton Rouge: Louisiana State University Press, 1995), 37.

15. Ibid., 5–6, 19.

16. Ibid., 248.

17. John F. Walter, Capsule Histories of Texas Units, 16th Texas Infantry and 17th Texas Infantry, THM; William D. Carrigan, *The Making of a Lynching Culture: Violence and Vigilantism in Central Texas, 1836–1916* (Urbana: University of Illinois Press, 2004), 30.

18. Carrigan, *Making of a Lynching Culture,* 40, 41, 36.

19. Ibid., 75; Walter, Capsule Histories of Texas Units, 17th Texas Infantry, THM.

20. Carrigan, *Making of a Lynching Culture,* 77–78; Anne J. Bailey, "A Texas Cavalry Raid: Reaction to Black Soldiers and Contrabands," *Civil War History* 35, no. 2 (1989): 146, 151.

21. Carrigan, *Making of a Lynching Culture,* 79–80.

22. Ibid., 90; E. Russ Williams Jr., *Encyclopedia of Individuals and Founding Families of the Ouachita Valley of Louisiana from 1785 to 1850* (Monroe, LA: Williams Genealogical and Historical Publications, 1996–1997), 2:412. Henceforth, *Founding Families.*

23. Reynolds, *Texas Terror,* 32.

24. Ibid., 42, 151–152.

25. Ibid., 38–39, 120.

26. Typescript of article from *The True Issue,* La Grange, TX, Aug. 23, 1860, in "Slavery" (S2700), AF Files, Austin History Center, Austin, TX.

27. Ibid.

28. Ibid.

29. Ibid.

30. Reynolds, *Texas Terror,* 96.

31. Ibid., 110, 112; entry for Oct. 20, 1860, diary August 8, 1859–May 15, 1865, Sarah Lois Wadley Papers (call number 1258), Manuscripts Department, Southern Historical Collection, University of North Carolina, Chapel Hill, electronic edition, transcript, online as part of *Documenting the American South*, University Library, The University of North Carolina at Chapel Hill, 2000, accessed Jan. 14, 2012, http://docsouth.unc.edu/imls/wadley/wadley.html/. Henceforth, Wadley Diary.

32. Reynolds, *Texas Terror*, 128.

33. Ibid., 112.

34. Ibid., 201–202.

35. Ibid., 149.

36. Ibid., 168.

37. Carrigan, *Making of a Lynching Culture*, 92; Richard B. McCaslin, *Tainted Breeze: The Great Hanging at Gainesville, Texas, 1862* (Baton Rouge: Louisiana State University Press, 1994), 53.

38. McCaslin, *Tainted Breeze*, 2–3.

39. Ibid., 44–46.

40. Ibid., 54.

41. Ibid., 65, 49.

42. Ibid., 65–66.

43. *ORA*, series 1, vol. 9, pp. 735–736.

44. *ORA*, series 1, vol. 53, pp. 828–829.

45. Ibid., 829.

46. McCaslin, *Tainted Breeze*, 113.

47. Lt. Col. Arthur J. L. Fremantle, *Three Months in the Southern States, April–June 1863* (Lincoln: University of Nebraska Press, 1991), 89–90.

48. Ibid., 124, 136, 147, 213.

49. Ibid., 282.

50. Ibid.

CHAPTER THREE

1. *Agriculture of the United States in 1860: compiled from the original returns of the eighth census, under the direction of the Secretary of the Interior by Joseph C. G. Kennedy* (Washington, DC: GPO, 1864). Electronic edition, *Making of America* (Ann Arbor: University of Michigan Library, 2005), pp. 66–69, accessed Jan. 14, 2012, http://name.umdl.umich.edu/AFP3693.0001.001/.

2. Historical Census Browser, Geospatial and Statistical Data Center, University of Virginia, 2004, accessed Jan. 14, 2012, http://fisher.lib.virginia.edu/collections/stats/histcensus/index.html/. Henceforth, Historical Census Browser.

3. Ibid.

4. Abraham Hagaman Memoir, folder 2, bracketed p. 56, MDAH. All subsequent references are to bracketed page numbers.

5. Ibid., 75, 60.

6. *Vicksburg Whig*, June 2, 1858, copy in Milliken's Bend file, Old Court House Museum, Vicksburg, MS.

7. Frances A. Robinson, "Curtains for the Bend," copy in Milliken's Bend file, Old Court House Museum, Vicksburg, MS.

8. Tom Blake, "Carroll Parish, Louisiana: Largest Slaveholders from 1860 Slave Census Schedules and Surname Matches for African Americans on 1870 Census" (Sept. 2001), accessed Jan. 14, 2012, http://freepages.genealogy.rootsweb.com/~ajac/lacarroll.htm/.

9. Taylor, *Negro Slavery in Louisiana*, 102, 100, 68.

10. Narrative of Abbie Lindsay, Arkansas Narratives, vol. 2, part 4, p. 257, digital ID: mesn 024/259255; Narrative of Litt Young, Texas Narratives, vol. 16, part 4, p. 228, digital ID: mesn 164/233227; Narrative of Sarah Wells, Arkansas Narratives, vol. 2, part 7, p. 90, digital ID: mesn 027/094089; Narrative of Ellen Cragin, Arkansas Narratives, vol. 2, part 2, p. 44, digital ID: mesn 022/046042, all in WPA Slave Narrative Project, online as part of *Born in Slavery: Slave Narratives from the Federal Writers' Project, 1936–1938*, part of *American Memory*, Library of Congress, 2001, accessed Jan. 14, 2012, http://memory.loc.gov/ammem/snhtml/snhome.html/. Taylor, *Negro Slavery in Louisiana*, 66.

11. Narrative of Rosa Washington, Texas Narratives, vol. 16, part 4, p. 135, digital ID: mesn 164/140134, online as part of *Born in Slavery*; Narrative of Carlyle Stewart, WPA Collection, Ex-Slave Narrative Project, Mss. 2858, LLMVC; Narrative of William Mathews, Texas Narratives, vol. 16, part 3, pp. 67, 69, digital ID: mesn 163/072067, and Narrative of Mattie Lee, Missouri Narratives, vol. 10, p. 224, digital ID: mesn 100/229224, both online as part of *Born in Slavery*.

12. George P. Rawick, ed., *The American Slave: A Composite Autobiography*, suppl. series 1, vol. 8, *Mississippi Narratives*, part 3 (Westport, CT: Greenwood, 1977), 1329; Ellen Cragin, p. 45, *Born in Slavery*; Narratives of Frances Doby and Carlyle Stewart, WPA Collection, Ex-Slave Narrative Project, Mss. 2858, LLMVC.

13. Ellen Cragin, pp. 42–44, *Born in Slavery*.

14. Claim of George Watt, #11211, Madison Parish, Louisiana; Claim of Martha T. Cleland, #7124, Richland Parish, Louisiana; Claim of Luke Madden, #3171, Madison Parish, Louisiana; Claim of William Hayden, #20964, Madison Parish, Louisiana; all in Settled Case Files for Claims Approved by the Southern Claims Commission, 1871–1880 (entry 732), Records of the Land, Files and Miscellaneous Division, Records of Accounting Officers of the Dept. of Treasury (RG217), NARA-CP. Henceforth, Settled Case Files.

15. Claim of Nancy Short, #5250, Carroll Parish, Louisiana, Settled Case Files.

16. Ted Tunnell, *Crucible of Reconstruction: War, Radicalism and Race in Louisiana 1862–1877* (Baton Rouge: Louisiana State University Press, 1984), 12–13; Williams, *Founding Families*, 2:410.

17. Williams, *Founding Families*, 1:322.

18. Ibid., 2:410–411.

19. Anderson, *Brokenburn*, xxvi; Williams, *Founding Families*, 2:410; Richard N. Current et al., eds., *Encyclopedia of the Confederacy* (New York: Simon and Schuster, 1993), 4:1735.

20. Ouachita Parish, LA Police Jury Minute Book (June 1857–Jan. 1867), 76–77, OPPL.

21. Historical Census Browser; Williams, *Founding Families*, 2:411, 413; Jordan, *Tumult and Silence at Second Creek*, 310.

22. Anderson, *Brokenburn*, 122–124.

23. "Philip Sartorius: Citizen of Vicksburg," *The Rebel Yell* (newsletter of Jackson [MS] Civil War Round Table) 37, no. 5 (Jan. 2001): 3.

24. Anderson, *Brokenburn*, 125, 127.

25. Ibid., 128.

26. Ibid., 145, 148.

27. "Philip Sartorius: Citizen of Vicksburg," 3–5.

28. Ibid., 5.

29. Claim of Margaret Case, #6945, Barred Claims, Barred and Disallowed Case Files of the Southern Claims Commission, 1871–1880, NAMP M1407, fiche 4363, sheet 1, Records of the U.S. House of Representatives (RG233). Henceforth, Barred Claims.

30. Valentine Diary, pp. 211–212, Civil War Diaries, Civil War Papers, Louisiana Historical Association Collection (Coll. #55-B), TU.

31. Anderson, *Brokenburn*, 195–197.

32. Valentine Diary, 212.

33. Valentine Diary, 213–214.

34. Anderson, *Brokenburn*, 212; Valentine Diary, note in front of volume.

35. Claim of Julia H. Morgan and heirs of Keene, #14,601, Carroll Parish, Louisiana, Settled Case Files.

36. Anderson, *Brokenburn*, 208, 177.

37. Claim of Julia H. Morgan and heirs of Keene, #14,601.

38. Anderson, *Brokenburn*, 173, 205.

39. Claim of Mrs. Amanda S. Stone, #16,711, Barred Claims, fiche 4748, sheet 1.

40. Entry for May 16, 1863, Wadley Diary; Anderson, *Brokenburn*, 204.

41. Anderson, *Brokenburn*, 208–210.

42. Entry for May 16, 1863, Wadley Diary; Anderson, *Brokenburn*, 213–214.

43. Entry for May 16, 1863, Wadley Diary; J. P. Blessington, *The Campaigns of Walker's Texas Division* (New York: Lange, Little, 1875), 115.

44. Anderson, *Brokenburn*, 216.

45. Entry for June 19, 1863, Wadley Diary; Anderson, *Brokenburn*, 220.

46. Ingraham's diary was originally published anonymously as "Leaves from the Journal of a Lady Near Port Gibson, Mississippi, Kept During Grant's March Upon Vicksburg, via Grand Gulf and Port Gibson," in Sarah A. Dorsey, *Recollections of Henry Watkins Allen, Brigadier-General Confederate States Army, Ex-Governor of Louisiana* (New York: M. Doolady, 1866), 397–420. Elizabeth Meade Ingraham is identified as the author of the diary in W. Maury Darst, ed., "The Vicksburg Diary of Mrs. Alfred Ingraham (May 2—June 13, 1863)," *Journal of Mississippi History* 44, no. 2 (May 1982): 148–179.

47. "Leaves from the Journal of a Lady," 399–400.

48. Ibid., 400, 401.

49. Ibid., 400, 404.

50. Ibid., 404.

51. Ibid., 405.

52. Ibid., 405, 406.

53. Ibid., 406; Darst, "Vicksburg Diary," 148.

54. "Leaves from the Journal of a Lady," 407.

55. Ibid., 408, 405, 407.

56. Ibid., 409; John Hope Franklin and Loren Schweninger, *Runaway Slaves: Rebels on the Plantation* (New York: Oxford University Press, 1999), 250–251; Greenberg, *Honor and Slavery*, 102; Reynolds, *Texas Terror*, 111–113.

57. "Leaves from the Journal of a Lady," 411, 413.

58. Ibid., 413, 414.

59. Ibid., 414; Ira Berlin et al., eds. *Freedom: A Documentary History of Emancipation, 1861–1867,* series 1, vol. 3, *The Wartime Genesis of Free Labor: The Lower South* (Cambridge: Cambridge University Press, 1990), 701; Bell Irvin Wiley, *The Life of Johnny Reb: The Common Soldier of the Confederacy* (Indianapolis: Bobbs-Merrill, 1943), 136; Bell Irvin Wiley, *The Life of Billy Yank: The Common Soldier of the Union* (Indianapolis: Bobbs-Merrill, 1952), 49.

60. "Leaves from the Journal of a Lady," 414–415.

61. Ibid., 415.

62. Ibid.

63. Ibid., 415, 416.

64. Ibid., 413, 417.

65. Ibid., 418.

66. Elizabeth's diary refers to Frank as being in Company I of the "First Mississippi Regiment." This is incorrect and is probably an error either due to Elizabeth's grief or an oversight by Sarah Dorsey. Frank served in Company I of the 21st Mississippi Infantry. See Janet B. Hewett, ed., *The Roster of Confederate Soldiers, 1861–1865* (Wilmington, NC: Broadfoot, 1996), 8:328.

67. "Leaves from the Journal of a Lady," 420.

CHAPTER FOUR

1. Joseph T. Glatthaar, *Forged in Battle: The Civil War Alliance of Black Soldiers and White Officers* (New York: Free Press, 1990), 4.

2. L. S. Livermore to George B. Fields, [*sic*] Feb. 19, 1863 (L-89), Colored Troops Division, Letters Received (entry 360), Records of the Adjutant General's Office (RG94), NARA-DC.

3. Geo. B. Field to Hon. E. M. Stanton, Mar. 20, 1863 (L-89), ibid.

4. Ibid.

5. Ibid.

6. Anderson, *Brokenburn,* 170–172.

7. Ibid., 173, 175.

8. Field to Stanton, Mar. 20, 1863.

9. Berlin, *Freedom,* series 1, vol. 3, pp. 699–700.

10. Ibid., 3:700–701.

11. Ibid., 3:686–692.

12. Ibid., 3:692.

13. David M. Wray Letter, Mss. 4318, LLMVC. Although his letter is initially dated 1862, a note at the conclusion gives the date of March 18, 1863, and the events he describes correspond with the army's activities in early 1863, such as failed attempts at canal building and a large number of troops camped in the vicinity. Gen. Thomas Williams, the first to attempt a canal in the region, broke ground in June 1862.

14. Samuel Glasgow to My Dear Wife, Apr. 26, 1863, Samuel H. Glasgow Civil War Letters, SHSI; "Siege of Vicksburg," *Cincinnati Daily Commercial,* June 24, 1863; Berlin, *Freedom,* series 1, vol. 3, p. 743.

15. Berlin, *Freedom,* series 1, vol. 3, p. 734–735.

16. Ibid., 3:707–708.

17. Ibid., 3:708–709.

18. Ibid., 3:745.

19. Louis S. Gerteis, *From Contraband to Freedman: Federal Policy Toward Southern Blacks, 1861–1865* (Westport, CT: Greenwood, 1973), 87, 83, 150, 50.

20. Chas. B. Allaire Letter, Mss. 3271, LLMVC; "From the 68th O.V.I.," *Cincinnati Daily Commercial*, Apr. 18, 1863; Manning F. Force, "Personal Recollections of the Vicksburg Campaign," in *Sketches of War History, 1861–1865: Papers Read Before the Ohio Commandery of the Military Order of the Loyal Legion of the United States* (Wilmington, NC: Broadfoot, 1991), 1:293.

21. Wray Letter.

22. "General Thomas in the South-West—His Speech," *Cincinnati Daily Commercial*, Apr. 17, 1863.

23. Ezra J. Warner, *Generals in Blue: Lives of the Union Commanders* (Baton Rouge: Louisiana State University Press, 1964), 502–503; Stewart Sifakis, *Who Was Who in the Civil War* (New York: Facts on File, 1988), 228–229, 650; Orders and Letters Sent, Apr.–Nov. 1863, p. 70, Box 2, and Thomas to Sec. of War Edwin M. Stanton, Dec. 24, 1863, Letters, Enclosures, Telegrams Sent and Special Orders Issued, Nov. 26, 1863 to Feb. 3, 1864, Box 1, both in General Lorenzo Thomas, General's Papers, Subseries I (entry 159), Records of the Adjutant General's Office (RG94), NARA-DC; Dudley Taylor Cornish, *The Sable Arm* (New York: Longmans Green, 1956), 114, 115.

24. "General Thomas in the South-West—His Speech."

25. Ibid.; V. Jacque Voegeli, *Free But Not Equal: The Midwest and the Negro during the Civil War* (Chicago: University Chicago Press, 1967), 2, 17, 18, 92, 170.

26. "General Thomas in the South-West—His Speech."

27. James M. McPherson, *For Cause and Comrades: Why Men Fought in the Civil War* (New York: Oxford University Press, 1997), 123; James M. McPherson, *What They Fought For, 1861–1865* (Baton Rouge: Louisiana State University Press, 1994), 66; Glatthaar, *Forged in Battle*, 31.

28. McPherson, *Cause and Comrades*, 123; Fremantle, *Three Months in the Southern States*, 89.

29. "General Thomas in the South-West—His Speech."

30. David Cornwell Memoir, p. 118, Civil War Miscellaneous Collection, USAMHI.

31. R. L. Howard, *History of the 124th Regiment Illinois Infantry Volunteers: Otherwise Known as the "Hundred and Two Dozen" from August 1862 to August 1865* (Springfield, IL: H. W. Rokker, 1880), 66.

32. "General Thomas in the South-West—His Speech"; "Arming Negroes Along the Mississippi," *Cincinnati Daily Commercial*, Apr. 25, 1863.

33. Cornwell Memoir, 120; Special Order No. 9, Regimental Papers, 5th USCHA, Records of the Adjutant General's Office (RG94), NARA-DC.

34. Ibid.; Jane Martin Johns, *Personal Recollections of Early Decatur, Abraham Lincoln, Richard J. Oglesby and the Civil War* (Decatur, IL: Decatur Chapter Daughters of the American Revolution, 1912), 136–137.

35. Elisha DeWitt CSR, Company K, 7th Missouri Infantry and Company I, 5th USCHA; Frederick H. Dyer, *A Compendium of the War of the Rebellion* (Des Moines, IA: Dyer Publishing, 1908), 1325.

36. Corydon Heath CSR, Battery G, 2nd Illinois Light Artillery; Corydon Heath to Friend Hyde, Aug. 16, 1862, E. B. Gilbert Collection (RC277), Regional History Center, Northern Illinois University, DeKalb, IL; Linda Barnickel, *We Enlisted as Patriots: The Civil War Records of Battery G, 2nd Illinois Light Artillery* (Bowie, MD: Heritage Books, 1998), 91.

37. *ORA*, series 1, vol. 24, part 2, p. 157; Special Order No. 15, Regimental Letters Received and Order Book, 49th USCI, Regimental Books, Records of the Adjutant General's Office (RG94), NARA-DC; George L. Conn CSR, Company D, 48th Indiana Infantry and Company F, 49th USCI; Dyer, *Compendium*, 1137.

38. William F. Fox, *Regimental Losses in the American Civil War* (Albany, NY: Albany Pub., 1889), 462–463; Peter Cozzens, *The Darkest Days of the War: The Battles of Iuka and Corinth* (Chapel Hill: University of North Carolina Press, 1997), 98; *ORA*, series 1, vol. 16, part 1, p. 92; Entry for Cyrus Sears, "Medal of Honor Recipients, Civil War, M–Z" at USAMHI website, accessed Jan. 14, 2012, www.history.army.mil/html/moh/civwarmz.html/; Special Order No. 15.

39. Cornwell Memoir, 122.

40. Ibid.

41. *ORA*, series 1, vol. 24, part 1, p. 78.

42. "The Siege of Vicksburg," *Cincinnati Daily Commercial*, Apr. 22, 1863.

43. "The Contrabands and the War," *Cincinnati Daily Commercial*, Apr. 17, 1863.

44. "The Siege of Vicksburg," Apr. 22, 1863.

45. "General Thomas in the South-West—His Speech."

46. Johns, *Early Decatur*, 136–137.

47. Brig. Gen. John P. Hawkins to Capt. Paddock, Apr. 30, 1863, and Brig. Gen. John P. Hawkins to Brig. Gen. L. Thomas, May 1, 1863, both in African Brigade, District of Northeast Louisiana, Letters Sent (Apr. 1863–Feb. 1864) (entry 2014), USACC-pt. 2, NARA-DC.

48. Brig. Gen. John P. Hawkins to Lt. Col. Van E. Young and Hawkins to Col. H. Scofield, both on May 1, 1863, in ibid.

49. Hawkins to Thomas, May 1, 1863, and Hawkins to Paddock, Apr. 30, 1863.

50. John Wearmouth, ed., *The Cornwell Chronicles: Tales of an American Life . . .* (Bowie, MD: Heritage Books, 1998), 179–180.

51. Wearmouth, *Cornwell Chronicles*, 146–147; Cornwell Memoir, 122. "The non-commissioned staff of the regiments and 1st sergeants of companies of Colored Troops are to be in all cases white men"; so declared an order from Thomas, Orders and Letters Sent, Apr.–Nov. 1863, p. 80, General Lorenzo Thomas, Generals' Papers, Subseries I (entry 159), Records of the Adjutant General's Office (RG94), NARA-DC.

52. Cornwell Memoir, 122–123; Corydon Heath CSR, Battery G, 2nd Illinois Light Artillery.

53. Silas Casey, *Infantry Tactics* (New York: D. Van Nostrand, 1862) 1:12; Cornwell Memoir, 122–124.

54. Cornwell Memoir, 124.

55. Ibid.

56. Ibid., 124–125.

57. Ibid., 127; Special Order No.—(June 2/63), Regimental Letters Received and Order Book, 49th USCI, Regimental Books, Records of the Adjutant General's Office (RG94), NARA-DC.

58. Special Order No. 8, Regimental Letters Received and Order Book, 49th USCI, Regimental Books, Records of the Adjutant General's Office (RG94), NARA-DC.

59. John Y. Simon, ed., *The Papers of Ulysses S. Grant*, vol. 8 (April 1–July 6, 1863) (Carbondale: Southern Illinois Press, 1979), 329–330.

60. Ibid.

61. Report of George B. Field and others, Milliken's Bend, Louisiana, June 9, 1863, file 1315, Letters Received by the Adjutant General (Main Series), 1886 (NAMP M689, roll 437), Correspondence, Records of the Adjutant General's Office (RG94), NARA-DC.

62. Ibid.

63. House, *Report of the Secretary of War*, 38th Cong., 1st sess., 1863, H. Exec. Doc. 1, pt. 5, serial 1184, p. 53; Simon, *Papers of Grant*, 8:329.

64. H. Lieb to General, July 28, 1863, Letter Book, 5th USCHA, Regimental Books, Records of the Adjutant General's Office (RG94), NARA-DC.

65. Col. Isaac F. Shepard to General, May 24, 1863, African Brigade, District of Northeast Louisiana, Letters Sent (Apr. 1863–Feb. 1864) (entry 2014), USACC-pt. 2, NARA-DC.

66. Ibid.

67. Isaac F. Shepard to General, May 24, 1863 (S-13), Colored Troops Division, Letters Received (entry 360), Records of the Adjutant General's Office (RG94), NARA-DC.

68. Ibid.

69. Ibid.

70. *Revised United States Army Regulations of 1861 with an Appendix Containing the Changes and Laws Affecting Army Regulations and Articles of War to June 25, 1863* (Washington, DC: GPO, 1863), 545–546. Henceforth, *Revised U.S. Army Regulations*.

71. Noah Andre Trudeau, *Like Men of War: Black Troops in the Civil War, 1862–1865* (Boston: Little, Brown, 1998), 91–93.

72. Circular, Headquarters, African Brigade, Milliken's Bend, La. May 19, 1863 (S-13), Colored Troops Division, Letters Received (entry 360), Records of the Adjutant General's Office (RG94), NARA-DC.

73. Ibid.

74. Ibid.

75. The precise identity of Griffith is unclear, although it most likely was Eli W. Griffith, a former sergeant in Co. F, 10th Iowa, who became a second lieutenant in the 11th Louisiana Infantry. See Special Order No. 15.

76. Shepard to General, May 24, 1863 (S-13).

77. Hancock's letter specifically mentions a Lt. Col. Young of the 10th Louisiana. Shepard, in his communication, refers to the 11th Louisiana. However, Hancock's information appears to be correct. Cyrus Sears was lieutenant colonel of the 11th Louisiana at this time; the 10th Louisiana's Lt. Col. Van E. Young had already come to Shepard's attention for his recruiting methods on local plantations.

78. Shepard to General, May 24, 1863 (S-13).

79. This and subsequent paragraphs: Court of Inquiry Case File #95, Records of the Office of the Judge Advocate General (Army) (RG153), NARA-DC.

80. Ibid.

81. *ORA*, series 1, vol. 24, part 1, p. 93.

82. Special Order No. 7 (from Isaac Shepard), and Special Order No.—(June 2/63), both

in Regimental Letters Received and Order Book, 49th USCI, Regimental Books, Records of the Adjutant General's Office (RG94), NARA-DC.

83. Cornwell Memoir, 128–129.

84. Cyrus Sears, *Paper of Cyrus Sears [The Battle of Milliken's Bend]* (Columbus, OH: F. J. Heer Printing, 1909), 9; Cornwell Memoir, 137; *ORA*, series 1, vol. 26, part 1, p. 800; Brig. Gen. J. P. Hawkins to Brig. Gen. J. A. Rawlins, Sept. 13, 1863, African Brigade, District of Northeast Louisiana, Letters Sent (Apr. 1863–Feb. 1864) (entry 2014), USACC-pt. 2, NARA-DC.

85. Letter Book, 5th USCHA, Regimental Books, Records of the Adjutant General's Office (RG94), NARA-DC.

86. "The Siege of Vicksburg—Guerillas and the Negro Regiments," *Cincinnati Daily Commercial,* June 10, 1863.

87. Janet B. Hewett et al., eds., *Supplement to the Official Records of the Union and Confederate Armies* (Wilmington, NC: Broadfoot, 1998), part 2, vol. 78, pp. 55, 74. Henceforth, *OR Suppl.*

88. "The Siege of Vicksburg—Guerillas and the Negro Regiments."

CHAPTER FIVE

1. Blessington, *Campaigns of Walker's Texas Division,* 119.

2. "History of the 19th Texas Infantry," in Waterhouse file, in 19th Texas Infantry file, THM.

3. Ibid.; Richard Lowe, *Walker's Texas Division C.S.A.: Greyhounds of the Trans-Mississippi* (Baton Rouge: Louisiana State University Press, 2004), 83–85.

4. "History of 19th Texas Infantry"; E. D. McDaniel to My Dear Lizzie, July 28, 1863, "Letter No. 29," Confederate States of America Records, CAH.

5. "History of 19th Texas Infantry"; Lowe, *Walker's Texas Division C.S.A.,* 83–85.

6. Lowe, *Walker's Texas Division C.S.A.,* 85–86; Norman D. Brown, ed., *Journey to Pleasant Hill: The Civil War Letters of Captain Elijah P. Petty, Walker's Texas Division, C.S.A.* (San Antonio: University of Texas Institute of Texan Cultures, 1982), 232.

7. Blessington, *Campaigns of Walker's Texas Division,* 91.

8. Brown, *Journey to Pleasant Hill,* 233. Often the most reliable source for smaller skirmishes and losses, the entry for the 60th Indiana Infantry in the *Supplement to the Official Records,* part 2, vol. 17, p. 617, provides no additional information about the activities or casualties of this regiment at Perkins' Landing.

9. Blessington, *Campaigns of Walker's Texas Division,* 120.

10. *ORA*, series 1, vol. 24, part 2, p. 458.

11. Blessington, *Campaigns of Walker's Texas Division,* 120.

12. Richard Taylor, *Destruction and Reconstruction: Personal Experiences of the Late War* (New York: D. Appleton, 1879), 138.

13. Blessington, *Campaigns of Walker's Texas Division,* 93–94; Darling Wife from Your husband Ned, June? 1863 Near Delhi, in Edward W. Cade Correspondence, fragment, June 1863, John Q. Anderson Collection, TSLAC.

14. *ORA*, series 1, vol. 24, part 2, p. 458.

15. Ibid., pp. 447, 458; Ira Berlin et al., eds., *Freedom: A Documentary History of Emancipation, 1861–1867,* series 2, *The Black Military Experience* (Cambridge: Cambridge University Press, 1982), 532.

16. *ORA*, series 1, vol. 24, part 2, p. 458.

17. Ibid., pp. 458–459.

18. Ibid.

19. Simon, *Papers of Grant*, 8:328.

20. Cornwell Memoir, 136, 138.

21. Some sources, such as Littell, reported about 130 men present (W. M. Littell to Capt. Wm. T. Rigby, Nov. 17, 1903, 23rd Iowa Infantry, Regimental Files, VNMP). Aquilla Standifird states that 129 men composed the detachment of the 23rd Iowa sent to Milliken's Bend, but only 120 entered the battle, with 9 men remaining on board the boat. Standifird's account seems to be the most accurate when compared with other sources, so I have generally relied upon his figures in my narrative (Aquilla Standifird Civil War diary, Western Historical Manuscript Collection, University of Missouri, Rolla). Cornwell Memoir, 136.

22. *ORA*, series 1, vol. 24, part 2, p. 467. Joseph P. Blessington in his memoir, recalled that this initial action occurred about 4 a.m. (*Campaigns of Walker's Texas Division*, 95).

23. Lowe, *Walker's Texas Division C.S.A.*, 43. Although Lowe's numbers are for Walker's Division as a whole, it is clear that the vast majority of soldiers were armed with smoothbores, and only about nine hundred in the entire division carried Enfields. A fraction of the men carried other types of weaponry.

24. *ORA*, series 1, vol. 24, part 2, pp. 467, 447; Peter W. Gravis, *Twenty-Five Years on the Outside Row of the Northwest Texas Annual Conference: Autobiography of Rev. Peter W. Gravis* (Brownwood, TX: Cross Timbers Press, 1966), 28.

25. Isaac F. Shepard to General, June 23, 1863 (S-40), Colored Troops Division, Letters Received (entry 360), Records of the Adjutant General's Office (RG94), NARA-DC. See Appendix C for a transcript of this document.

26. *ORA*, series 1, vol. 24, part 2, p. 467.

27. Ibid., p. 464.

28. Frank Moore, ed., *Rebellion Record* (New York: Arno Press, 1977), 7:15; Littell to Rigby, Nov. 17, 1903; C. W. C., "How Black Troops Fight," *Daily Cleveland Herald*, June 23, 1863; "The Gunboat Choctaw—Shelling the Rebels after the Battle at Milliken's Bend, La., June 7, 1863," *Frank Leslie's Illustrated Newspaper*, July 4, 1863.

29. *ORA*, series 1, vol. 24, part 2, p. 467; E. D. McDaniel to My Dear Lizzie, July 28, 1863, "Letter No. 29."

30. Isaac F. Shepard to General, June 23, 1863 (S-40). Numbers engaged for the 11th Louisiana vary wildly. See discussion of the 11th Louisiana's numbers in Appendix B.

31. Cyrus Sears in 1909 claimed no such regiment as the 13th Louisiana was present (*Papers of Cyrus Sears*, 11). Lieb filed his report immediately after the battle, and, as acting post commander in charge of the brigade, his report seems more reliable than Sears's memory nearly fifty years later (Cornwell Memoir, 136). Research by William Dobak in post returns for Milliken's Bend in June and July 1863 confirms the existence of the 13th Louisiana, which was determined to have no formal "legal organization." The fledgling regiment was disbanded, and its officers and men reassigned (William Dobak, e-mail to author, Jan. 11, 2007, citing Returns from U.S. Military Posts, NAMP M617, roll 1525, NARA-DC).

32. Cornwell Memoir, 136.

33. Ibid., 136–137; Moore, *Rebellion Record*, 7:12; *ORA*, series 3, vol. 3, p. 453. Miller's letter states that he was in command of Company I, and the introduction to the letter by the editor calls him a captain. However, Elisha DeWitt was captain of this company at the time of the battle. Because DeWitt was captured, it may be that command devolved upon Miller due to the wounding or death of his first lieutenant, forcing him to serve in the capacity of a captain, even though he would have been a second lieutenant. The editor probably simply assumed that because Miller stated he was in command of a company at the fight that he held the rank of captain. See the original order appointing Miller to the position of second lieutenant, Special Orders No. 9. Both Lieb and David Cornwell also refer to Miller as a lieutenant, see Cornwell Memoir, 138.

34. Blessington, *Campaigns of Walker's Texas Division*, 96.

35. "My Dear Pa," June 8, 1863, original letter in private possession, scanned image of original letter provided to author. Quotes are based upon the author's interpretation of the text of the original letter. An earlier edition of a transcript is online, "Battle of Milliken's Bend, Madison Parish, La., June 7, 1863," accessed May 21, 2011, www.rootsweb.ancestry.com/~lamadiso/articles/battle_of_millikens_bend.htm/.

According to family tradition, Henry Dick Lester Sr. was only fifteen years old when he wrote this letter on the back of a piece of wallpaper torn from a house where the soldiers rested shortly after the battle. The letter is now in possession of Lester's granddaughter, who also has a photograph showing him as a young Confederate soldier. The letter itself bears the salutation "My Dear Pa" and is signed, "Your Son," so no names appear on the document itself. The family is confident of its provenance and certain that it was written by Henry Dick Lester Sr.

Regrettably, little information has been found in military records which would formally confirm Lester's presence at Milliken's Bend. Statements made within the body of the letter, although difficult to read, appear to reference the death of Lt. Thomas J. Beaver and the wounding of Capt. Elijah Petty. If correct, it would seem that the writer of the letter was probably a member of Company F, 17th Texas Infantry. However, no Henry Lester has been found as part of this unit.

The lack of official military documentation is frustrating and leaves a number of lingering questions. Nevertheless, the letter remains a rare and important resource as a Confederate eyewitness account of the savage fighting at Milliken's Bend.

36. Cornwell Memoir, 137; Brent Nosworthy, *Roll Call to Destiny: A Soldier's Eye View of Civil War Battles* (New York: Basic Books, 2008), 109–110; Joseph K. Barnes, *The Medical and Surgical History of the War of the Rebellion (1861–1865)* (1870; repr. as *The Medical and Surgical History of the Civil War*, Wilmington, NC: Broadfoot, 1991), 12:685–687.

37. Cornwell Memoir, 132, 135.

38. Ibid., 133.

39. *ORA*, series 1, vol. 24, part 2, p. 467; Blessington, *Campaigns of Walker's Texas Division*, 96; Mamie Yeary, *Reminiscences of the Boys in Gray, 1861–1865* (Dayton, OH: Morningside, 1986), 823. Wright refers to these events as occurring at Perkins' Landing, though it seems more likely to have been at Milliken's Bend. All eyewitnesses universally describe Milliken's Bend as a brutal and bloody battle. This was not the case at Perkins' Landing. No African American troops were present at Perkins' Landing, though the 60th Indiana did receive assistance from black laborers.

Furthermore, only one Confederate casualty was reported at Perkins' Landing; Wright reports the loss of nine men at the "rose fence." This fence sounds like a description of one of the hedges Southern forces had to cross in their advance, where most of the Confederate casualties at Milliken's Bend occurred. Wright reported this information years after the war, and, given the close proximity in time of Perkins' Landing and Milliken's Bend, the similar characteristics in terrain next to the Mississippi River, and the dimming light of memory, such confusion between the two fights is easily explained. Gravis, *Outside Row,* 28.

40. "My Dear Pa," June 8, 1863.

41. *ORA,* series 1, vol. 24, part 2, p. 467.

42. Ibid.

43. Littell to Rigby, Nov. 17, 1903.

44. Samuel H. Glasgow to My Dear Wife, June 11, 1863, Samuel H. Glasgow Civil War Letters, SHSI. Porter consistently but erroneously refers to the Iowa troops as belonging to the 29th Iowa. Naval War Records Office, *Official Records of the Union and Confederate Navies in the War of the Rebellion* (Washington, DC: GPO, 1912), series 1, vol. 25, p. 162. Henceforth, *ORN.*

45. Littell to Rigby, Nov. 17, 1903.

46. Sears, *Paper of Cyrus Sears,* 18–19; Cornwell Memoir, 138; *ORA,* series 3, vol. 3, p. 453.

47. *ORA,* series 3, vol. 3, p. 453, and series 1, vol. 24, part 2, p. 448; T. F. Mays' account, "Fifty Years Ago," *Burleson County Ledger,* June 13, 1913, in Milliken's Bend file, THM; Yeary, *Boys in Gray,* 759.

48. E. D. McDaniel to My Dear Lizzie, July 28, 1863, "Letter No. 29."

49. Moore, *Rebellion Record,* 7:12; *ORA,* series 3, vol. 3, p. 453.

50. Isaac F. Shepard to General, June 23, 1863 (S-40); Cornwell Memoir, 137.

51. Cornwell Memoir, 137.

52. *ORA,* series 1, vol. 24, part 2, p. 459, 464; Moore, *Rebellion Record,* 7:12; Cornwell Memoir, 137.

53. *ORN,* series 1, vol. 25, p. 163.

54. *ORA,* series 1, vol. 24, part 2, p. 468; Col. Isaac F. Shepard to General, May 24, 1863, African Brigade, District of Northeast Louisiana, Letters Sent (Apr. 1863–Feb. 1864) (entry 2014), USACC-pt. 2, NARA-DC.

55. It is unclear who this captain is. Capt. Corydon Heath of the 9th Louisiana was reported as standing in the line on the far Union left when his capture was witnessed by David Cornwell. It was later recorded by Cornwell that Capt. Elisha DeWitt, also of the 9th Louisiana, was still wearing his old sergeant's uniform, so he does not seem a likely candidate either. The third officer captured at Milliken's Bend was 2nd Lt. George F. Conn of the 11th Louisiana. Because of the proximity of the farm to the location of the 11th Louisiana and the large number of missing men from the regiment accounted for in these captures, it is believed that the "captain" may have in fact been Second Lieutenant Conn.

56. *ORA,* series 1, vol. 24, part 2, p. 468–469.

57. Ibid.

58. B. G. Goodrich, "Battle of Millican's Bend," *Confederate Veteran* 8, no. 2 (Feb. 1900): 67.

59. *ORA,* series 1, vol. 24, part 2, p. 447–448.

60. Blessington, *Campaigns of Walker's Texas Division,* 97–99.

61. Cornwell Memoir, 137; *ORA*, series 1, vol. 24, part 2, p. 463, 468–469.

62. *ORA*, series 1, vol. 24, part 2, p. 468, 470, 447–448; Sears, *Paper of Cyrus Sears*, 16.

63. *ORN*, series 1, vol. 25, p. 163.

64. Ibid.; Entry June 7, 1863, USS *Lexington*, Logs of U.S. Naval Ships, Records of the Bureau of Naval Personnel (RG24), NARA-DC.

65. Blessington, *Campaigns of Walker's Texas Division*, 100; Cornwell Memoir, 137; Moore, *Rebellion Record*, 7:12; "My Dear Pa," June 8, 1863.

66. *ORA*, series 1, vol. 24, part 2, p. 459.

67. Ibid.; Blessington, *Campaigns of Walker's Texas Division*, 121; *ORA*, series 1, vol. 24, part 2, p. 464.

68. *ORA*, series 1, vol. 24, part 2, pp. 459–460.

69. Entry June 7, 1863, USS *Choctaw*, Logs of U.S. Naval Ships, Records of the Bureau of Naval Personnel (RG24), NARA-DC.

70. D. E. Young to Dear Wife and Children, June 20, 1863, in 17th Texas Infantry regimental file, THM.

71. Moore, *Rebellion Record*, 7:13; *ORA*, series 3, vol. 3, p. 453.

72. Entry June 7, 1863, USS *Choctaw*, Logs of U.S. Naval Ships, Records of the Bureau of Naval Personnel (RG24), NARA-DC; *ORN*, series 1, vol. 25, p. 163.

73. Register of the Sick and Wounded, pp. 70–71, Van Buren U.S. General Hospital, Milliken's Bend, La., Mar.–June 1863, Field Records of Hospitals—Louisiana, v. 157 (entry 544), Records of the Adjutant General's Office (RG94), NARA-DC.

74. Van Buren Contraband General Hospital, pp. 9–22, 193, Field Records of Hospitals—Louisiana, v. 159 (entry 544), Records of the Adjutant General's Office (RG94), NARA-DC.

75. John Jackson CSR, Company G, 5th USCHA.

76. Herman[n] Lieb and David Cornwell CSR, 5th USCHA.

77. Pension record of William A. Skillen (9th Louisiana Infantry, African Descent, et al.), Civil War Pension Files, Records of the Veterans Administration (RG15), NARA-DC; Cornwell Memoir, 140. Cornwell refers to Skillen as a captain; however, at the time of Milliken's Bend, he was a lieutenant. When he resigned in 1864, due in part from his many wounds sustained at Milliken's Bend, Skillen held the rank of captain.

78. *ORN*, series 1, vol. 25, pp. 164, 162; Brown, *Journey to Pleasant Hill*, 235; John D. Winters, *The Civil War in Louisiana* (Baton Rouge: Louisiana State University Press, 1963), 200–201.

79. Numbers in this and subsequent paragraphs are based upon *corrected* figures, as found in Appendix B, unless otherwise stated.

80. Cornwell Memoir, 137; Elisha DeWitt CSR, 5th USCHA; Fox, *Regimental Losses*, 36, 26. Note that Fox states in one place (p. 36) that the 1st Minnesota had 47 killed—yielding a loss of 18%; in another place (p. 26), he states 50 men were killed, giving a loss of 19%. For a comparison of the 9th Louisiana's losses to other regiments during the Vicksburg campaign, see Appendix B.

81. *Suppl. OR*, part 2, vol. 78, p. 115. Because the figures in the *Supplement* are based upon original regimental reports, I am choosing to rely upon this as the most accurate figure for the 11th Louisiana's losses. See Appendix B for more discussion. Isaac F. Shepard to General, June 23, 1863 (S-40); Morning Reports month of June 1863, Company F, 49th USCI, Regimental Books, Records of the Adjutant General's Office (RG94), NARA-DC.

82. Cornwell Memoir, 137.

83. Standifird Civil War diary; *ORA* series 1, vol. 24, part 1, p. 96; Fox, *Regimental Losses,* 26. For further discussion, see Appendix B.

84. Isaac F. Shepard to General, June 23, 1863 (S-40); Descriptive Book, 49th USCI, Regimental Books, Records of the Adjutant General's Office (RG94), NARA-DC.

85. Isaac F. Shepard to General, June 23, 1863 (S-40).

86. "Report of Killed, wounded and missing of Genl. H. E. McC[ulloch's] Brigade in the engagement of Millikens Bend, June 7th, 18[63]" in 16th Texas Infantry file, THM. Note that this list is predominantly casualties of the 16th Texas Cavalry, although losses for both the 16th Infantry and 16th Cavalry are included on the same page. "19th Texas Casualties at Milliken's Bend," in 19th Texas Infantry file, THM; Register of the Sick and Wounded, Van Buren U.S. General Hospital; Yeary, *Boys in Gray,* 488; Brown, *Journey to Pleasant Hill,* 236.

87. Blessington, *Campaigns of Walker's Texas Division,* 102; *ORA,* series 1, vol. 24, part 2, p. 470.

88. Gravis, *Outside Row,* 28; George T. Boardman Diary, Berta Boardman Maxcy Collection, TSLAC.

89. Blessington, *Campaigns of Walker's Texas Division,* 102.

90. *ORA,* series 1, vol. 24, part 2, pp. 469–470; Harold J. Weiss Jr., "McCulloch, Henry Eustace," *The Handbook of Texas Online* (Texas State Historical Association), accessed Jan. 14, 2012, www.tshaonline.org/handbook/online/articles/fmc35/; Donaly E. Brice, TSLAC, letter to author, May 22, 2008.

91. *ORA,* series 1, vol. 24, part 2, pp. 470, 459; Blessington, *Campaigns of Walker's Texas Division,* 121.

92. *ORA,* series 1, vol. 24, part 2, p. 469; Blessington, *Campaigns of Walker's Texas Division,* 121–122.

93. Cornwell Memoir, 137; Moore, *Rebellion Record,* 7:13.

94. Cornwell Memoir, 137; *ORA,* series 1, vol. 24, part 2, p. 448, and part 1, p. 96.

95. Cornwell Memoir, 137.

96. *ORN,* series 1, vol. 25, p. 164; Moore, *Rebellion Record,* 7:13.

97. *ORA,* series 1, vol. 24, part 2, p. 469.

98. Entry for June 9, 1863, Wadley Diary.

99. Anderson, *Brokenburn,* 218–219.

100. Williams, *Founding Families,* 2:422.

101. *ORA,* series 1, vol. 24, part 2, p. 470.

102. Ibid., p. 469.

103. *ORA,* series 1, vol. 24, part 2, pp. 462–464.

104. Ibid., pp. 459–460; Taylor, *Destruction and Reconstruction,* 138.

105. T. F. Mays' account, "Fifty Years Ago"; Yeary, *Boys in Gray,* 610; Gravis, *Outside Row,* 28; Lowe, *Walker's Texas Division C.S.A.,* 98.

106. *ORA,* series 1, vol. 24, part 1, pp. 95–96.

107. *ORA,* series 1, vol. 24, part 1, p. 102; Sears, *Paper of Cyrus Sears,* 14; Isaac F. Shepard to General, June 23, 1863 (S-40).

108. Ned to My Dear Wife, May 20, 1863, Edward W. Cade Correspondence; Blessington, *Campaigns of Walker's Texas Division,* 115.

109. Cornwell Memoir, 136; *ORA,* series 3, vol. 3, p. 453.

CHAPTER SIX

1. See, for instance, James G. Hollandsworth Jr., "The Execution of White Officers from Black Units by Confederate Forces during the Civil War," *Louisiana History* 35, no. 4 (Fall 1994): 475–489; Richard Lowe, "Battle on the Levee: The Fight at Milliken's Bend," in *Black Soldiers in Blue: African American Troops in the Civil War Era,* ed. John David Smith (Chapel Hill: University of North Carolina Press, 2002), 107–135; George S. Burkhardt, *Confederate Rage, Yankee Wrath: No Quarter in the Civil War* (Carbondale: Southern Illinois University Press, 2007), 56–64; and Bailey, "Texas Cavalry Raid."

2. *Congress of CSA,* 387; *ORA,* series 2, vol. 6, pp. 21–22.

3. *ORA,* series 1, vol. 24, part 1, pp. 95–96.

4. *ORA,* series 1, vol. 24, part 3, p. 425; Brown, *Journey to Pleasant Hill,* 233.

5. Hollandsworth, "Execution of White Officers."

6. Hewett, *Roster of Confederate Soldiers;* Andrew B. Booth, comp., *Records of Louisiana Confederate Soldiers and Louisiana Confederate Commands* (Spartanburg, SC: Reprint Co., 1984); *OR Suppl.,* part 2, vol. 23, p. 528; Entry June 14, 1863, USS *Louisville,* Logs of U.S. Naval Ships, Records of the Bureau of Naval Personnel (RG24), NARA-DC; Thomas B. Carroll CSR, Company K, 3rd (Harrison's) Louisiana Cavalry. Carroll's service records show only his capture at the end of the war and document nothing else, so his wartime experiences remain a mystery. Undoubtedly, Carroll is the same person who filed for a pension from the State of Louisiana after the war, though his middle initial there is given as R. Still, he states in his pension application that he was never taken prisoner (T. R. and Lucy Carroll Confederate Pension Application, Louisiana State Archives).

7. *ORA,* series 2, vol. 6, pp. 21–22.

8. Ibid. For a similar instance of Confederates' linguistic insistence that captured black soldiers were "negroes in arms" and therefore deserving of the death penalty, see Linda Barnickel, "'No Federal Prisoners Among Them': The Execution of Black Union Soldiers at Jackson, Louisiana," *North and South* 12, no. 1 (Feb. 2010): 59–62.

9. *ORA,* series 2, vol. 6, p. 22. A search in the microfilm, Thomas O. Moore Papers, Folder 12 (May–Dec. 1863), Part 2: Louisiana and miscellaneous, Series I: Louisiana State University, reel 19, *Records of Ante-bellum Southern Plantations* (containing portions from Thomas O. Moore Papers, Mss. 305, 893, 1094, LLMVC), found no indication that the attorney general was called upon. Likewise, searches for the latter half of 1863 in Records of the Attorney General, 1860–65 (microfilm roll 7) and Records of the Executive Department, 1860–65 (microfilm roll 14), both part of Records of the Louisiana State Government, 1850–1888, NAMP M359, War Department Collection of Confederate Records (RG109), NARA-DC, found no mention of events at Milliken's Bend or its immediate aftermath.

10. *ORA,* series 1, vol. 24, part 2, p. 461.

11. Moore, *Rebellion Record,* 7:13.

12. *ORA,* series 2, vol. 6, p. 22; No. 37, "An Act Relative to Slaves," and No. 38, "An Act Relative to the Trial of Slaves Accused of Certain Crimes," *Acts of the Extra Session of the 6th Legislature, 1863, vol. 195, held in Shreveport 4 May 1863* (Shreveport: Caddo Gazette, 1863), 27–28, in Records of the Louisiana State Government, 1850–1888, NAMP M359, roll 13, Other Legislative Records, 1860–1864, War Department Collection of Confederate Records (RG109), NARA-DC. Henceforth, "Slavery Acts."

13. *ORA,* series 2, vol. 6, p. 21.

14. Ibid., 6:115.

15. Simon, *Papers of Grant,* 8:401.

16. *ORA,* series 1, vol. 24, part 3, pp. 425–26.

17. Ibid., part 1, p. 110.

18. Ibid., part 3, pp. 443–444.

19. Glatthaar, *Forged in Battle,* 201; "Slavery Acts."

20. *ORA,* series 1, vol. 24, part 3, p. 469.

21. Ibid., p. 590. See also Letters Sent and Orders Issued, p. 129, Provost Marshal, Dept. of Tennessee, "Old Book 36A" (entry 4769), USACC-pt. 1, NARA-DC.

22. *ORA,* series 2, vol. 6, p. 194; M. W. Simms [*sic*] CSR, Confederate Generals and Staff Officers and Nonregimental Enlisted Men; John Y. Simon, ed., *Papers of Ulysses S. Grant,* vol. 9 (July 7–December 31, 1863) (Carbondale: Southern Illinois University Press, 1982), 170.

23. M. W. Simms CSR; Simon, *Papers of Grant,* 9:171.

24. This and subsequent three paragraphs from M. W. Simms CSR.

25. Paul Octave Hébert Scrapbook (Coll. #818), TU.

26. M. W. Simms CSR.

27. Hébert Scrapbook.

28. Entry for M. W. Sims, 6th Precinct, Austin, written p. 55, Travis County, Texas, free population schedules, roll 1306; entry for M. W. Sims, 3rd Precinct, written p. 15, Travis County, Texas, slave population schedules, roll 1312; entry for M. W. Sims, written pp. 11–12, Burleson County, Texas, slave population schedules, roll 1309; all part of NAMP M653, Eighth Census of the United States, 1860, Bureau of the Census (RG29). Henceforth, M. W. Sims 1860 census records.

29. Jesse W. Sparks CSR, Confederate Generals and Staff Officers and Nonregimental Enlisted Men; Simon, *Papers of Grant,* 9:171; Hébert Scrapbook.

30. *ORA,* series 1, vol. 24, part 2, p. 466; Burkhardt, *Confederate Rage, Yankee Wrath,* 64; Trudeau, *Like Men of War,* 101; Gregory J. W. Urwin, "'We Cannot Treat Negroes . . . as Prisoners of War': Racial Atrocities and Reprisals in Civil War Arkansas," in Gregory J. W. Urwin, ed., *Black Flag Over Dixie: Racial Atrocities and Reprisals in the Civil War* (Carbondale: Southern Illinois University Press, 2004), 141.

31. Dr. Anne J. Bailey, on value of captured blacks in letter to author, April 8, 2011.

32. Jon Harrison, ed., "The Confederate Letters of John Simmons," *Chronicles of Smith County, Texas* 14, no. 1 (Summer 1975): 34; Bailey, "Texas Cavalry Raid," 145; Trudeau, *Like Men of War,* 101; Bailey letter to author.

33. Trudeau, *Like Men of War,* 101–102; *ORA,* series 1, vol. 24, part 2, p. 466.

34. *ORA,* series 1, vol. 24, part 2, p. 466; *OR Suppl.,* part 2, vol. 78, pp. 48, 50.

35. Bailey, "Texas Cavalry Raid," 145; Hollandsworth, "Execution of White Officers," 480. The *Official Army Register of the Volunteer Force of the United States Army for the Years 1861, '62, '63, '64, '65 . . .* (Washington, DC: Adjutant General's Office, 1865), part 8, p. 219, and *OR Suppl.,* part 2, vol. 78, p. 48 and 50 both show four officers captured. The *Supplement* is particularly important and generally very reliable, since its source material is original regimental records. This extraordinary resource, exceeded in research value only by the original *Official Records,* had not

been published at the time of Bailey's and Hollandsworth's articles. Pension record of William B. Wallace (1st Arkansas Infantry, African Descent), Civil War and Later Pension Files, Records of the Veterans Administration (RG15), NARA-DC.

36. *ORA*, series 1, vol. 24, part 2, p. 466; Bailey, "Texas Cavalry Raid," 150.

37. *ORN*, series 1, vol. 25, pp. 215–216.

38. Terrence Winschel, e-mail to author, March 14, 2011; [Alfred W. Ellet to wife], "Another deserter . . . ," July 1st, 1863, Ellet Family Papers (M698), Stanford University.

39. Anne J. Bailey, "The Mississippi Marine Brigade: Fighting Rebel Guerillas on Western Waters," *Military History of the Southwest* 22, no. 1 (Spring 1992): 36; Warren Daniel Crandall and Isaac Denison Newell, *History of the Ram Fleet and the Mississippi Marine Brigade* (St. Louis, MO: Buschart Brothers, 1907), 310.

40. *ORA*, series 1, vol. 24, part 2, p. 517.

41. Entry for June 30, 1863, Transcription of Josiah Goodwin's diary by William Wiseley, Josiah Goodwin Diaries and Research Collection, Mss. 4886, LLMVC.

42. *ORA*, series 1, vol. 24, part 3, pp. 589–590. The article would also be copied by other newspapers, such as the *Liberator*, Aug. 21, 1863, and the *Lane* (IL) *Register*, Aug. 8, 1863.

43. Terrence Winschel, e-mail to author, March 14, 2011; Winschel letter to author, Feb. 22, 1995; Terrence J. Winschel, "To Rescue Gibraltar, John Walker's Texas Division and its Expedition to Relieve Fortress Vicksburg," *Civil War Regiments* 3, no. 3 (1993): 53. Winschel stands fast to his position, even after reading this manuscript late in 2011. Charles Dana Gibson and E. Kay Gibson, *Assault and Logistics: Union Army Coastal and River Operations, 1861–1866* (Camden, ME: Ensign, 1995), 310–311. The *Democrat's* account is not mentioned at all in Hollandsworth, "Execution of White Officers"; Bailey, "Texas Cavalry Raid," and "Mississippi Marine Brigade"; or Trudeau, *Like Men of War*, among others.

44. Dyer, *Compendium*, 1303, shows June 30 movement to Tensas Bayou. No activity is shown for the Mississippi Marine Brigade on June 8, the day after Milliken's Bend.

45. *ORN*, series 1, vol. 25, p. 213, 215.

46. William B. Wallace pension record; Hollandsworth, "Execution of White Officers," 480.

47. *ORA*, series 1, vol. 24, part 3, p. 590.

48. Ibid.

49. House, *Exchange of Prisoners*, 38th Cong., 2nd sess., 1865, H. Exec. Doc. 32, serial 1223, p. 53.

50. Ibid., 52.

51. H-391, 1864, Letters Received (entry 360), Colored Troops Division, Records of the Adjutant General's Office (RG94), NARA-DC. Henceforth, H-391. See Appendix D for a transcript of this document.

52. Ibid.

53. Williams, *Founding Families*, 2:183; H-391.

54. Elisha DeWitt CSR, Company I, 5th USCHA and Company K, 7th Missouri Infantry.

55. Cornwell Memoir, 151.

56. However, see Hollandsworth, "Execution of White Officers," concerning deaths of three other white officers elsewhere in Louisiana in 1863 and 1864.

57. Anderson, *Brokenburn*, 239; Hollandsworth, "Execution of White Officers," 480.

58. William B. Wallace CSR, 46th USCI and pension record.

59. H-391.

60. *ORA*, series 1, vol. 24, part 2, p. 466.

61. *ORA*, series 2, vol. 8, p. 659, and vol. 6, p. 115; Lonnie R. Speer, *Portals to Hell: Military Prisons of the Civil War* (Lincoln: University of Nebraska, 1997), 299.

62. Descriptive Book, 49th USCI, Regimental Books, Records of the Adjutant General's Office (RG94), NARA-DC.

63. *OR Suppl.*, part 2, vol. 78, p. 48; Trudeau, *Like Men of War*, 101–102.

64. Boardman Diary.

65. Untitled report, first name entry on page: "One negro boy Amos," concluding statement indicates this report is [Report of Persons and Articles Employed . . . July 1863], Oversize Box 2.325/V3; also Report of Persons and Articles Employed & Hired at Shreveport . . . July 1863 and August 1863, Box 2C489, Trans-Mississippi Quartermaster Dept., Confederate States of America Records, CAH.

66. Nelson Washington and Pleasant Boner, CSR, 49th USCI; pension record of Pleasant Boner alias Barnett (49th USCI), Civil War Pension Files, Records of the Veterans Administration (RG15), NARA-DC.

67. Descriptive Book, Companies A and B, 49th USCI, Regimental Books, Records of the Adjutant General's Office (RG94), NARA-DC.

68. *ORA*, series 1, vol. 24, part 2, p. 457.

69. Ibid., vol. 26, part 2, p. 375; Hébert Scrapbook.

70. Hébert Scrapbook.

71. *ORA*, series 1, vol. 26, part 2, p. 375; Hébert Scrapbook.

72. Anne J. Bailey, *In the Saddle with the Texans: Day-by-Day with Parsons's Texas Cavalry in the Civil War* (Fort Worth: Texas Christian University Press, 1989), 20–21; Bailey, "Texas Cavalry Raid," 151–152; Bailey letter to author. In the latter two sources, Bailey also discusses the involvement of the 30th Texas Cavalry in the Poison Spring Massacre in 1864, but this regiment did not join Parsons's Brigade until later in the war.

73. *ORA*, series 1, vol. 24, part 3, p. 425, and part 2, p. 457; Jordan, *Tumult and Silence at Second Creek*, 14–15.

74. *ORA*, series 1, vol. 26, part 2, p. 472.

75. Brig. Gen. John P. Hawkins to Provost Marshal General, Oct. 5, 1863, African Brigade, District of Northeast Louisiana, Letters Sent (Apr. 1863–Feb. 1864) (entry 2014), USACC-pt. 2, NARA-DC.

CHAPTER SEVEN

1. Isaac F. Shepard to General, June 23, 1863 (S-40).

2. Frank Ross McGregor, *Dearest Susie: A Civil War Infantryman's Letters to His Sweetheart*, ed. Carl E. Hatch (New York: Exposition Press, [1971]), 52, 54–55.

3. Richard N. Ellis, ed., "The Civil War Letters of an Iowa Family," *Annals of Iowa*, 3rd series, 39, no. 8 (Spring 1969): 582.

4. Moore, *Rebellion Record*, 7:13.

5. "The Negro Will Fight," *Chicago Tribune*, June 16, 1863.

6. "The Siege of Vicksburg: The First Engagement for the Negro Soldiers," *Cincinnati Daily Commercial*, June 18, 1863.

7. "Celebration of the Fourth of July," *Pacific Appeal*, July 11, 1863, frame 955, reel 14, *Black Abolitionist Papers, 1830–1865* (Ann Arbor, MI: UMI, 1993); "The Siege of Vicksburg—Guerillas and the Negro Regiments."

8. "Document 44. Editorial by Robert Hamilton," *The Black Abolitionist Papers*, vol. 5, *The United States, 1859–1865*, ed. C. Peter Ripley (Chapel Hill: University of North Carolina Press, 1992), 216, 218.

9. Isaac F. Shepard to General, June 23, 1863 (S-40).

10. "Men of Color, To Arms! Now or Never!" frame 944, reel 14, *Black Abolitionist Papers, 1830–1865*; Glatthaar, *Forged in Battle*, image opposite p. 242.

11. "Colored Regiment of Ohio," *Liberator*, Sept. 4, 1863.

12. "Flag Presentation at Camp William Penn," *Christian Recorder* (Philadelphia, PA), Sept. 5, 1863.

13. "General Thomas in the South-West—His Speech."

14. *Treatment of Prisoners of War*, 429.

15. *ORA*, series 2, vol. 5, pp. 940–941.

16. *ORA*, series 2, vol. 6, pp. 44–45.

17. Philip S. Foner, ed., *The Life and Writings of Frederick Douglass* (New York: International Publishers, 1952), 3:370–371.

18. *ORA*, series 2, vol. 6, p.163.

19. Mark M. Boatner, III, *The Civil War Dictionary*, rev. ed. (New York: Vintage, 1991), 270.

20. *ORA*, series 2, vol. 6, pp. 595–596.

21. Ibid., pp. 616–617.

22. *Congressional Globe*, 38th Cong., 1st sess., 1863, 3, in *A Century of Lawmaking for a New Nation: U.S. Congressional Documents and Debates, 1774–1875*, part of *American Memory*, Library of Congress, accessed Jan. 14, 2012, http://memory.loc.gov/ammem/amlaw/lawhome.html/; Letters Sent by the Office of the Adjutant General, Main Series (1800–1890), vol. 36, Nov. 2, 1863–Mar. 31, 1864, p. 238, NAMP M565, roll 23, Records of the Adjutant General's Office (RG94); Letters Received by the Secretary of War, Main Series (1801–1870), Sept. 1863–Dec. 1863, J–L, file L-802, NAMP M221, roll 237, Records of the Office of the Secretary of War (RG107), both at NARA-DC; Entry for Dec. 16, 1863, Docket Book, Records of the Committee on Military Affairs (38th Cong., 1st Sess.), Records of the U.S. House of Representatives (RG233), as stated by Kate Mollan, Center for Legislative Archives, NARA-DC, in e-mail to author, July 14, 2011.

23. Frank E. Vandiver, ed., "Proceedings of the First Confederate Congress, Fourth Session, 7 Dec. 1863–18 Feb. 1864," *Southern Historical Society Papers*, new series, no. 12, whole no. 50 (Richmond, VA: The Virginia Historical Society, 1953), 366.

24. Confederate States of America, Congress, House, *Joint Resolutions in Reference to the Treatment of Colored Troops*, Feb. 15, 1864, in *Confederate Imprints, 1861–1865* (New Haven, CT: Research Publications, 1974), microfilm reel 7, no. 413.

25. Speer, *Portals to Hell*, 259, 261, caption accompanying bird's-eye view of Andersonville, image between pp. 171 and 173.

26. Speer, *Portals to Hell*, 244, 246.

27. Cornwell Memoir, 151–152.

CHAPTER EIGHT

1. Letter Book, 5th USCHA, Regimental Books, Records of the Adjutant General's Office (RG94), NARA-DC.

2. Ibid.

3. Orders and Letters Sent, Apr.–Nov. 1863, p. 128, Box 2, General Lorenzo Thomas, General's Papers.

4. Order Book, 5th USCHA, Regimental Books, Records of the Adjutant General's Office (RG94), NARA-DC.

5. Letter Book, 5th USCHA; Edward Tick, *War and the Soul: Healing Our Nation's Veterans from Post-traumatic Stress Disorder* (Wheaton, IL: Quest Books, 2005), 99; Eric T. Dean, *Shook Over Hell: Post-traumatic Stress, Vietnam, and the Civil War* (Cambridge, MA: Harvard University Press, 1997), 115–116.

6. Letter Book, 5th USCHA.

7. Ibid.

8. Brig. Gen. John P. Hawkins to Brig. Gen. L. Thomas, Nov. 15, 1863, African Brigade, District of Northeast Louisiana, Letters Sent (Apr. 1863–Feb. 1864) (entry 2014), USACC-pt. 2, NARA-DC.

9. Col. Richard H. Ballinger to Captain, Nov. 13, 1863, District of Northeast Louisiana, Letters Received (Aug. 20, 1863–Dec. 31, 1863) (entry 2016A), USACC-pt. 2, NARA-DC.

10. *OR Suppl.*, part 2, vol. 78, p. 53.

11. John P. Hawkins to Professor C. Mills, Dec. 11, 1863, Letters from General John P. Hawkins, Series I: Caleb Mills Correspondence and Papers, Caleb Mills Family Papers, IHS.

12. Dear Father from B. Marshall Mills, April 19, 1864, Letters from Benjamin Mills, ibid.

13. *Revised U.S. Army Regulations*, 492, 488; August V. Kautz, *The Company Clerk* (Philadelphia: J. B. Lippincott and Co., 1863) 86.

14. Genovese, *Roll Jordan, Roll*, 618.

15. Francis A. Lord, *They Fought for the Union: A Complete Reference Work on the Federal Fighting Man* (New York: Bonanza Books, [1960]), 210–211.

16. Gerteis, *From Contraband to Freedman*, 111, 114; Glatthaar, *Forged in Battle*, 108–116.

17. Case File LL-2492 Giles Simms, Co. F, 49th United States Colored Infantry, Proceedings of U.S. Army Courts-Martial and Military Commissions of Union Soldiers Executed by U.S. Military Authorities, 1861–1866, NAMP M1523, roll 7, Courts-Martial Case Files, 1809–1938, Records of the Office of the Judge Advocate General (Army) (RG153), NARA-DC. Henceforth, Case File LL-2492.

18. Ibid.; Robert Randall CSR, 49th USCI.

19. Van Buren Contraband General Hospital, Field Records of Hospitals—Louisiana, v. 159 (entry 544), Records of the Adjutant General's Office (RG94), shows Warfield was hospitalized after the battle at Milliken's Bend with a contusion on his hip; Rodgers had a gunshot wound in his leg.

20. Case File LL-2492; Register of Deaths, Company F, Descriptive Book, 49th USCI, Regimental Books, Records of the Adjutant General's Office (RG94), NARA-DC.

21. James P. Hall CSR, 49th USCI; Entry for June 7, 1863, Morning Report Book, Company

F, 49th USCI, Regimental Books, Records of the Adjutant General's Office (RG94), NARA-DC; Dear Father and Mother from B. Marshall Mills, May 7, 1864, Letters from Benjamin Mills.

22. Berlin, *Freedom*, series 2, 459–460.

23. Dyer, *Compendium*, 1732.

24. Berlin, *Freedom*, series 2, 459–460; Register of Deaths, Company F, Descriptive Book, 49th USCI.

25. Descriptive Book, 49th USCI, Regimental Books; Special Orders No. 62 (extract), Mar. 17, 1866, Head-quarters, Dept. of Mississippi in 49th USCI, Regimental Papers (entry 57-C), both in Records of the Adjutant General's Office (RG94), NARA-DC. Copy of the latter provided to the author courtesy of William Dobak.

CHAPTER NINE

1. Williams, *Founding Families*, 2:184–186.

2. Ibid., 489, 491.

3. Records Relating to Murders and Outrages, pp. 20–21, 23, Records of the Assistant Commissioner for the State of Louisiana, 1865–1869, NAMP M1027, roll 34, Records of the Bureau of Refugees, Freedmen, and Abandoned Lands (RG105), NARA-DC.

4. Ibid., 20–21, 23, 34–35.

5. Ibid., 20–21.

6. Ibid., 29.

7. Ibid., 20–21.

8. Ibid., 31.

9. Claim of Luke Madden, #3171, Madison Parish, Louisiana, Settled Case Files.

10. Michael J. Pfeifer, "Louisiana Lynchings, 1878–1946," accessed May 20, 2011, http:// academic.evergreen.edu/p/pfeiferm/louisiana.html/. On Nov. 6, 2011, I discovered that this list is no longer available on the Internet. Much of the same information appears in the appendix to Pfeifer's book, *Rough Justice: Lynching and American Society 1874–1947* (Urbana: University Illinois Press, 2004). The information that formerly appeared at Evergreen University's website is available upon request from Dr. Pfeifer at John Jay College of Criminal Justice, Department of History.

11. Includes the parishes of DeSoto, Red River, Webster, Claiborne, Bienville, Winn, Jackson, Lincoln, Union, Morehouse, West Carroll, East Carroll, Richland, Caldwell, Franklin, Madison, and Tensas. It is worth noting that there were significant parish boundary changes and the creation of three new parishes between 1870 and 1880, thus giving Webster, Red River, and Lincoln Parishes lower numbers, since their territory was within Bossier, Claiborne, Bienville, Jackson, and Natchitoches Parishes prior to their formation.

12. Stewart E. Tolnay and E. M. Beck, *A Festival of Violence: An Analysis of Southern Lynchings, 1882–1930* (Urbana: University of Illinois Press, 1995), 19; Pfeifer, "Louisiana Lynchings."

13. Pfeifer, *Rough Justice*, 69–71; W. Fitzhugh Brundage, "The Roar on the Other Side of Silence: Black Resistance and White Violence in the American South, 1880–1940," in W. Fitzhugh Brundage, ed., *Under Sentence of Death: Lynching in the South* (Chapel Hill: University of North Carolina Press, 1997), 271–291.

14. Nell Irvin Painter, *Exodusters: Black Migration to Kansas after Reconstruction* (New York: W. W. Norton, 1986), 29, 82, 97–98, 73; Gilles Vandal, "'Bloody Caddo': White Violence against Blacks in a Louisiana Parish, 1865–1876," *Journal of Social History* 25, no. 2 (Winter 1991): 386, n. 35.

15. Painter, *Exodusters*, 88, 140, 143.

16. William Gillette, *Retreat from Reconstruction 1869–1879* (Baton Rouge: Louisiana State University Press, 1979), 378; David W. Blight, *Race and Reunion: The Civil War in American Memory* (Cambridge, MA: Belknap, 2001), 84, 130–131, former Confederate general Bradley T. Johnson quoted in, 258; F. T. Roche, "Were Negroes in Earlier Wars," *Confederate Veteran* 18 no. 2 (Feb. 1910): 62.

17. Sears, *Paper of Cyrus Sears*, 25, 28.

18. Ibid., 3.

CHAPTER TEN

1. David W. Blight, "'For Something beyond the Battlefield': Frederick Douglass and the Struggle for the Memory of the Civil War," *Journal of American History* 75, no. 4 (Mar. 1989): 1156–1178. These ideas are explored further in Blight's subsequent work, *Race and Reunion*.

2. Andre Fleche, "'Shoulder to Shoulder as Comrades Tried': Black and White Union Veterans and Civil War Memory," *Civil War History* 51 no. 2 (2005): 175–201.

3. Donald R. Shaffer, *After the Glory: The Struggles of Black Civil War Veterans* (Lawrence: University Press of Kansas, 2004), 154–155, 168.

4. Blight, "Something beyond the Battlefield."

5. William Wells Brown, *The Negro in the American Rebellion: His Heroism and His Fidelity* (Boston: Lee and Shepard, 1867), 141.

6. George Washington Williams, *A History of the Negro Troops in the War of the Rebellion, 1861–1865* (New York: Harper and Bros., 1888), 224–226.

7. *National Tribune*, Oct. 10, 1907.

8. Ibid., Feb. 13, 1908; Cornwell Memoir, 139–140.

9. Blessington, *Campaigns of Walker's Texas Division*; Taylor, *Destruction and Reconstruction*, 138.

10. Cornish, *Sable Arm*; Benjamin Quarles, *The Negro in the Civil War* (Boston: Little, Brown, 1953); E. C. Foster, "The Battle at Milliken's Bend," *Crisis* 81, no. 9 (Nov. 1974): 295–300; Martha M. Bigelow, "The Significance of Milliken's Bend in the Civil War," *Journal of Negro History* 45, no. 3 (July 1960): 156–163; Thomas W. Cutrer, ed., "'Bully for Flournoy's Regiment, We Are Some Punkins, You'll Bet': The Civil War Letters of Virgil Sullivan Rabb, Captain, Company 'I' Sixteenth Texas Infantry, C.S.A.," part 1, *Military History of the Southwest* 19, no. 2 (Fall 1989): 161–190; Ed Bearss, ed., "Is This Lt. John Campbell's Letter?" *Annals of Iowa* 39 (Winter 1969): 542–545.

11. Christopher Waldrep, *Vicksburg's Long Shadow: The Civil War Legacy of Race and Remembrance* (Lanham, MD: Rowman and Littlefield, 2005), 82, 279.

12. Ibid., 195, 198–199, 221.

13. Edward Cunningham, *The Port Hudson Campaign 1862–1863* (n.p.: Louisiana State University Press, 1963); Peter Burchard, *One Gallant Rush: Robert Gould Shaw and His Brave Black Regiment* (New York: St. Martin's, 1965); Edwin Cole Bearss, *The Campaign for Vicksburg*, vol. 3, *Unvexed to the Sea* (Dayton, OH: Morningside, 1986), 1175–1189. The first modern work to

examine Milliken's Bend in any significant detail is Glatthaar, *Forged in Battle*. Other works include: Hollandsworth, "Execution of White Officers"; Trudeau, *Like Men of War*; Richard Lowe, "Battle on the Levee: The Fight at Milliken's Bend," in John David Smith, ed., *Black Soldiers in Blue: African American Troops in the Civil War Era* (Chapel Hill: University of North Carolina Press, 2002), 107–135; Lowe, *Walker's Texas Division C.S.A.*; Waldrep, *Vicksburg's Long Shadow*; Burkhardt, *Confederate Rage, Yankee Wrath*; and others. The publication of David Cornwell's memoir, previously available only as a very difficult-to-read typescript in the collections of the U.S. Army Military History Institute, is a very important contribution in making accessible a lengthy and detailed account of a white officer's service with the Colored Troops at Milliken's Bend; see Wearmouth, *Cornwell Chronicles*.

14. Geneva Williams, Madison Historical Society, telephone interview by author, May 20, 2010; Tina Johnson, Director, Tallulah-Madison Parish Tourism Commission, telephone interview by author, June 14, 2010.

15. Adam Fairclough, *Race and Democracy: The Civil Rights Struggle in Louisiana, 1915–1972* (Athens: University of Georgia Press, 1995), 199.

16. Amy [Holmes] to Dear Folks [Mrs. John Q. Anderson], postmarked Aug. 22, 1966, Amy Holmes Correspondence, *Brokenburn* Files, John Q. Anderson Papers, Mss. 2156, 2162, LLMVC.

17. Fairclough, *Race and Democracy*, 105, 306–307, 395.

18. Ibid., 395–396.

19. Ibid., 396–398.

20. "Black Troops Won Liberty as War Prize," *Monroe (LA) News-Star*, Mar. 2, 1994; "Black Union Warriors Recognized," *Clarion-Ledger* (Jackson, MS), Feb. 28, 1994; "Grant's Canal," VNMP website, accessed Jan. 14, 2012, www.nps.gov/vick/historyculture/grants-canal.htm/; Geneva Williams, telephone interview, May 20, 2010.

21. Brian Madison Davis, "Milliken's Bend National Research Center" (B.Arch. thesis, Louisiana Tech University, [1997]), 3. Copy at Hermione House Museum, Tallulah, LA.

22. Geneva Williams, telephone interview, May 20, 2010.

23. Ibid.; Mike Varnedo, Louisiana Division of Historic Preservation, and Tim Kavanaugh, interpreter, VNMP, both in telephone interviews by author, May 21, 2010; Terrence J. Winschel, historian, VNMP, telephone interview by author, Sept. 27, 2010.

24. Terrence J. Winschel, e-mail to author, Feb. 1, 2011.

25. Tina Johnson and Geneva Williams, telephone interviews, June 14 and May 20, 2010, respectively.

26. Madison Parish, Louisiana, State and County Quick Facts, U.S. Census Bureau, last revised Dec. 23, 2011, accessed Jan. 14, 2012, http://quickfacts.census.gov/qfd/states/22/22065 .html/; Geneva Williams, telephone interview, May 20, 2010.

27. Terrence J. Winschel, "The General's Tour—Grant's March through Louisiana: Opening Phase of the Vicksburg Campaign," *Blue and Gray Magazine* 13, no. 5 (June 1996): 51–61; Lowe, *Walker's Texas Division C.S.A*; Geneva Williams, telephone interview, May 20, 2010.

28. Geneva Williams, letter to author, Feb. 16, 2011; Tina Johnson, telephone interview, June 14, 2010.

29. Geneva Williams, telephone interview, Jan. 24, 2012, and Tina Johnson, e-mail to author, Jan. 10, 2012.

30. Waldrep, *Vicksburg's Long Shadow,* 271, 273; Tim Kavanaugh, telephone interview, May 21, 2010.

31. Tim Kavanaugh, telephone interview, May 21, 2010.

32. "Cultural Resource Preservation," VNMP website, accessed Jan. 14, 2012, www.nps.gov/vick/parkmgmt/culresmgt.html/; "Re-enactors Remember U.S. Colored Troops in City," *Vicksburg Post,* undated clipping [probably circa July 5, 2000], Hermione House Museum, Tallulah, LA.

33. National Park Service, *Interpretation at Civil War Sites: A Report to Congress* (Mar. 2000), accessed Jan. 14, 2012, www.cr.nps.gov/history/online_books/icws/index.html/, particularly the section: "Review of Current Conditions," www.cr.nps.gov/history/online_books/icws/icws_review.html/.

34. "Obstacles to Success," *Interpretation at Civil War Sites,* www.cr.nps.gov/history/online_books/icws/icws_obst.html/.

35. National Parks Conservation Association, "State of the Parks: Vicksburg National Military Park, A Resource Assessment" (Oct. 2008), 5–7, 12, accessed Jan. 14, 2012, www.npca.org/about-us/center-for-park-research/stateoftheparks/vicksburg/VICK-web.pdf/.

36. Tim Kavanaugh, telephone interview, Mar. 14, 2011, and letter to author, Mar. 6, 2011.

37. National Park Service et al., *Vicksburg National Military Park: Long Range Interpretive Plan* (n.p.: National Park Service, June 2010), 58–59, 99–100, 102–103, accessed Jan. 14, 2012, www.nps.gov/vick/parkmgmt/loader.cfm?csModule=security/getfile&PageID=296948/.

38. "Monument to Black Troops Close to Reality," *Vicksburg Post,* Feb. 1, 2004; Robert Walker, telephone interview by author, Oct. 4, 2010.

39. J. Kim Sessums, "The Vicksburg Monument: A Personal Journey, Excerpts from the Artist's Journal," accessed Jan. 14, 2012, online at www.jkimsessums.com/cwtribute.html/; "African American Monument" brochure, VNMP, National Park Service, [2006].

40. "Grant Will Go To Creating Monument to Black Federal Troops in Vicksburg," *Commercial Appeal* (Memphis, TN), Mar. 16, 2001, accessed on June 18, 2010, via *Custom Newspapers,* Gale Group database, Gale document number CJ71812254.

41. "Vicksburg Monument to Black Soldiers Will Fill In Missing History," *Commercial Appeal* (Memphis, TN), Mar. 18, 2001, accessed on June 18, 2010, via *Custom Newspapers,* Gale Group database, Gale document number CJ71850198.

42. Timothy B. Smith, *The Golden Age of Battlefield Preservation: The Decade of the 1890s and the Establishment of America's First Five Military Parks* (Knoxville: University of Tennessee Press, 2008), 206; Terrence J. Winschel, telephone interview, Sept. 27, 2010.

APPENDIX A

1. *Official Army Register,* part 8, p. 152; Dyer, *Compendium,* 1721.

2. Sifakis, *Who Was Who,* 199; Gerteis, *From Contraband to Freedman,* 155. Dyer's *Compendium,* 1214, indicates numerous name changes, most of which apply to the "Old" 9th Louisiana. However, only a very sharp reader would catch his distinction in noting the "reorganization" of the regiment, which essentially resulted in reconstituting an entirely new regiment, using the old regiment's name. It is too easy, and too confusing, to erroneously read Dyer's synopsis as describing only a single regiment. The 9th Louisiana (Old), which fought at Milliken's Bend under the command of Col. Hermann Lieb, did *not* became the 63rd U.S. Colored Infantry, as

one might easily conclude from Dyer's summary. Two other sources help clarify the distinctions between the regiments. *OR Suppl.*, part 2, vol. 78, p. 429, and vol. 77, p. 199; and *Official Army Register,* part 8, pp. 152, 236. A definitive source for the changing names of Lieb's regiment can be found in Letter Book, Regimental Books, 5th USCHA.

3. Cyrus Sears to Wm. T. Rigby, March 8, 1902, in 11th Louisiana Infantry, A.D., Regimental Files, VNMP.

4. Sears, *Paper of Cyrus Sears*, 12; Cornwell Memoir, 136; William A. Dobak, e-mail to author, Jan. 11, 2007, citing Post return for Milliken's Bend, June and July, 1863; Isaac F. Shepard to General, June 23, 1863 (S-40).

5. Shepard to General, May 24, 1863, African Brigade, District of Northeast Louisiana, Letters Sent; Dyer, *Compendium*, 1343.

6. Dyer, *Compendium*, 1344, 1732.

7. Chapman quoted in Burkhardt, *Confederate Rage, Yankee Wrath,* 238; Sean Michael O'Brien, *Mobile, 1865: Last Stand of the Confederacy* (Westport, CT: Praeger, 2001), 199.

8. O'Brien, *Mobile,* 99.

9. O'Brien, *Mobile,* 199–200; Trudeau, *Like Men of War,* 406–407; Burkhardt, *Confederate Rage, Yankee Wrath,* 238–239.

10. Dyer, *Compendium,* 1174.

11. Stewart Sifakis, *Compendium of the Confederate Armies: Texas* (New York: Facts on File, 1995), 127–130.

12. Jordan, *Tumult and Silence at Second Creek,* 14; Stewart Sifakis, *Compendium of the Confederate Armies: Louisiana* (New York: Facts on File, 1995), 55.

13. Arthur W. Bergeron, *Guide to Confederate Louisiana Military Units, 1861–1865* (Baton Rouge: Louisiana State University Press, 1996), 43–44.

14. Bailey, "Texas Cavalry Raid," 145–146, 151–152.

15. Anne J. Bailey, "Parsons's Brigade," *Handbook of Texas Online* (Texas State Historical Association), accessed Jan. 14, 2012, www.tshaonline.org/handbook/online/articles/qkp01/.

16. Bruce S. Allardice, *Confederate Colonels: A Biographical Register* (Columbia: University of Missouri Press, 2008), 41; Marcus J. Wright, comp., *Texas in the War, 1861–1865,* ed. Harold B. Simpson (Hillsboro, TX: Hill Junior College Press, 1965), 101.

17. Wright, *Texas in the War,* 107.

18. Edward P. Gregg and William Fitzhugh CSR, 16th Texas Cavalry; Oran Milo Roberts, *Texas,* vol. 11 of *Confederate Military History,* ed. Clement A. Evans (Atlanta, GA: Confederate Publishing Co., 1899), 196; Allardice, *Confederate Colonels,* 174.

19. Allardice, *Confederate Colonels,* 185.

20. *ORA,* series 1, vol. 26, part 2, p. 312.

21. Thomas W. Cutrer, "Hébert, Paul Octave," *Handbook of Texas Online* (Texas State Historical Association), accessed Jan. 14, 2012, www.tshaonline.org/handbook/online/articles/fhe09/; Sifakis, *Who Was Who,* 300; Ezra J. Warner, *Generals in Gray: Lives of the Confederate Commanders* (n.p.: Louisiana State University Press, 1959), 132; Current, *Encyclopedia of Confederacy,* 2:759. The claim that Hébert was at Milliken's Bend probably originates with John Dimitry, *Louisiana,* vol. 10 of *Confederate Military History,* ed. Clement A. Evans (Atlanta, GA: Confederate Publishing Co., 1899), 308.

22. Hébert Scrapbook.

23. Warner, *Generals in Gray*, 132.

24. Weiss, "McCulloch, Henry Eustace," and Thomas W. Cutrer, "Smith, Edmund Kirby," *Handbook of Texas Online* (Texas State Historical Association), accessed Jan. 14, 2012, www.tsha-online.org/handbook/online/articles/fsm09/.

25. *Dallas Herald*, Sept. 30, 1863.

26. McCaslin, *Tainted Breeze*, 143–145; "The Frontier Stands Alone," part of "1864: No Way Out," *Under the Rebel Flag: Life in Texas During the Civil War* (TSLAC), accessed Jan. 14, 2012, www.tsl.state.tx.us/exhibits/civilwar/1864_3.html/; Weiss, "McCulloch, Henry Eustace."

27. Weiss, "McCulloch, Henry Eustace"; Warner, *Generals in Gray*, 201.

28. Allardice, *Confederate Colonels*, 299.

29. M. W. Sims 1860 census records; Adjutant General to Honorable Luther A. Johnson, Dec. 9, 1931 in Mrs. M. W. Sims (#50447), Widow's Application for Pension, TSLAC; "Death of Col. Milton Walker Sims," *Bryan (TX) Weekly News*, Oct. 10, 1912.

30. Cutrer, "Smith, Edmund Kirby," *Handbook of Texas Online*; Warner, *Generals in Gray*, 279–280; Current, *Encyclopedia of Confederacy*, 4:1472–1474; Robert L. Kerby, *Kirby Smith's Confederacy: The Trans-Mississippi South, 1863–1865* (New York: Columbia University Press, 1972), 239; E. B. Long with Barbara Long, *The Civil War Day by Day: An Almanac 1861–1865* (Garden City, NY: Doubleday, 1971), 692; Joseph Howard Parks, *General Edmund Kirby Smith, C.S.A.* (Baton Rouge: Louisiana State University Press, 1954), 478.

31. Current, *Encyclopedia of Confederacy*, 4:1572; John H. Eicher and David J. Eicher, *Civil War High Commands* (Stanford, CA: Stanford University Press, 2001), 885; Lowe, *Walker's Texas Division C.S.A.*, 111–112; Sifakis, *Who Was Who*, 643; Warner, *Generals in Gray*, 299–300.

32. Winschel, "To Rescue Gibraltar," 39; Warner, *Generals in Gray*, 319–320; Sifakis, *Who Was Who*, 684; Thomas W. Cutrer, "Walker, John George," *Handbook of Texas Online* (Texas State Historical Association), accessed Jan. 14, 2012, www.tshaonline.org/handbook/online/articles/fwa20/.

33. Wright, *Texas in the War*, 94; Lowe, *Walker's Texas Division C.S.A.*, 230; Warner, *Generals in Gray*, 327.

34. James Wilford Garner, *Reconstruction in Mississippi* (New York: Macmillan, 1901), 239; William C. Harris, *The Day of the Carpetbagger: Republican Reconstruction in Mississippi* (Baton Rouge: Louisiana State University Press, 1979), 241; Hébert Scrapbook.

35. Anderson, *Brokenburn*, 365, 5–6, xxvii, xi.

36. Sarah Lois Wadley Papers finding aid, Emory University, accessed Jan. 14, 2012, http://marbl.library.emory.edu/findingaids/pdf?id=wadleysarah461_10191/. Surprisingly little biographical information, outside of her own diaries, seems available about Sarah L. Wadley.

37. George L. Conn CSR, 48th Indiana Infantry and 49th USCI.

38. Wearmouth, *Cornwell Chronicles*, 293–294, 291.

39. Letter Book, Regimental Books, 5th USCHA; Elisha DeWitt CSR, 7th Missouri Infantry and pension record.

40. Warner, *Generals in Blue*, 218–219.

41. Corydon Heath minor heirs pension file (2nd Illinois Light Artillery); Charles G. B. Conger, *A Record of the Births, Marriages and Deaths of the Descendants of John Conger of Woodbridge,*

N. J. . . . (Chicago, IL: S. Smith, 1903), 124; Phyllis Conger, telephone interview by author, Nov. 17, 2011.

42. Wearmouth, *Cornwell Chronicles*, 147.

43. Ibid., 146.

44. John Jackson CSR, Company F, 5th USCHA.

45. John Jackson CSR, Company G, 5th USCHA.

46. Descriptive Book, Companies A-E, 5th USCHA, Regimental Books.

47. Wearmouth, *Cornwell Chronicles*, 130; Johns, *Personal Recollections of Early Decatur*, 136–137, 140; Senate, *Report (to Accompany H.R. 7622)*, 59th Cong., 1st Sess., S. Rept. 1561, in Hermann Lieb pension file (5th USCHA).

48. *The History of Wyandot County, Ohio* (Chicago: Leggett, Conaway and Co., 1884), 923–924.

49. Sifakis, *Who Was Who*, 586; Warner, *Generals in Blue*, 435–436; Berlin, *Freedom*, series 2, pp. 414–415.

APPENDIX B

1. McCulloch states he took about 1,500 men into battle. The percentage of his loss is based upon casualty figures provided in his report. *ORA*, series 1, vol. 24, part 2, pp. 469–470.

2. Cornwell Memoir, 137–138.

3. *ORA*, series 1, vol. 24, part 2, p. 448.

4. Ibid., part 1, pp. 95–96.

5. Cornwell Memoir, 136–138.

6. *OR Suppl.*, part 2, vol. 78, p. 115; Cornwell Memoir, 137–138.

7. Cornwell Memoir, 136.

8. Shepard to General, May 24, 1863, African Brigade, District of Northeast Louisiana, Letters Sent; Cornwell Memoir, 139.

9. Shepard to General, May 24, 1863, African Brigade, District of Northeast Louisiana, Letters Sent; Shepard to General, June 23, 1863 (S-40).

10. Shepard to General, June 23, 1863 (S-40); Cornwell Memoir, 137.

11. Bearss, *Campaign for Vicksburg*, 3:1183.

12. Fox, *Regimental Losses*, 437.

13. Based upon battle-by-battle figures provided in Fox, *Regimental Losses*, 437. Note that the much higher numbers that appear in Fox, pp. 18–20, for some of these same regiments are figures for killed *plus* mortally wounded.

APPENDIX D

1. Hon. Benjamin F. Loan, Representative from Missouri (Unconditional Unionist) and member of the House Committee on Military Affairs.

2. 2nd Lt. George L. Conn.

BIBLIOGRAPHY

Although this list includes the vast majority of sources that were most important to my work, it should not be considered a comprehensive listing, particularly for secondary sources. In addition, some works that were cited only once or twice in the notes as supporting information but bear no direct and immediate relationship to the overall story of Milliken's Bend and emancipation have been omitted from this bibliography in the interest of space.

PRIMARY SOURCES
Manuscripts
NATIONAL ARCHIVES—ARCHIVES I BUILDING, WASHINGTON, DC

Records of the Adjutant General's Office (RG94)
Colored Troops Division
   Register of Letters Received (entry 361)
   Letters Received (entry 360)
Field Records of Hospitals—Louisiana (entry 544)
   Van Buren U.S. General Hospital (v. 157)
   Van Buren Contraband General Hospital (v. 159)
General's Papers, Subseries I (entry 159)
   General Lorenzo Thomas
      Letters, Enclosures, Telegrams Sent and Special Orders Issued
      Orders and Letters Sent
Letters Received by the Adjutant General (Main Series), 1886 (NAMP M689, roll 437)
Letters Sent by the Office of the Adjutant General, Main Series (1800–1890), vol. 36, Nov. 2, 1863–Mar. 31, 1864, p. 238, NAMP M565, roll 23
The Negro in the Military Service of the United States 1639–1886. NAMP, Microcopy T-823.
Regimental Books: 5th U.S. Colored Heavy Artillery; 46th U.S. Colored Infantry; 49th U.S. Colored Infantry
Regimental Papers: 5th U.S. Colored Heavy Artillery; 49th U.S. Colored Infantry
Returns from United States Military Posts 1800–1916 (NAMP M617, roll 1525), Milliken's Bend, La.

Records of the Bureau of the Census (RG29)

Eighth Census of the United States, 1860 (NAMP M653), Texas: Burleson County, slave population schedules, roll 1309; Travis County, free and slave population schedules, rolls 1306 and 1312

Records of the Bureau of Refugees, Freedmen, and Abandoned Lands (RG105)

Records of the Assistant Commissioner for the State of Louisiana, 1865–1869 (NAMP M1027, roll 34), Records Relating to Murders and Outrages

Records of the Field Offices for the State of Louisiana, 1863–1872 (NAMP M1905, roll 87), Milliken's Bend and Monroe

Records of the Mississippi Freedmen's Department ("Pre-Bureau Records") (NAMP M1914, roll 1), Letters Sent by John Eaton, General Superintendent of Contrabands

Records of the Bureau of Naval Personnel (RG24)

Logs of U.S. Naval Ships: USS *Black Hawk*, USS *Choctaw*, USS *Lexington*, USS *Louisville*

Records of the Commissary General of Prisoners (RG249)

Commissioner for the Exchange of Prisoners, Letters Received (entry 149)

Papers of General William Hoffman (entry 16)

Records of the Office of the Judge Advocate General (Army) (RG153)

Court of Inquiry Case File #95

Courts-Martial Case Files, 1809–1938, Proceedings of U.S. Army Courts-Martial and Military Commissions of Union Soldiers Executed by U.S. Military Authorities, 1861–1866, Case File LL-2492 Giles Simms (NAMP M1523, roll 7)

Records of the Office of the Secretary of War (RG107)

Letters Received from the Commissary General of Prisoners (entry 32)

Letters Received, Main Series (Sept. 1863–Dec. 1863), file L-802 (NAMP M221, roll 237)

Records of U.S. Army Continental Commands (RG393)

Part I: Geographical Divisions and Departments and Military (Reconstruction) Districts
Dept. of Tennessee, Provost Marshal, Letters Sent and Orders Issued, "Old Book 36A" (entry 4769)

Part II: Polyonymous Successions of Commands, 1861–1870
African Brigade, District of Northeast Louisiana, Letters Sent (entry 2014)
District of Northeast Louisiana, Letters Received (entry 2016A)
Letters and Extracts of Orders Received by Brig. Gen. E. S. Dennis (entry 2017)

Records of the U.S. House of Representatives (RG233)
Barred and Disallowed Case Files of the Southern Claims Commission, 1871–1880, NAMP M1407:
   Margaret Case (Barred Claim #6945, fiche 4363, sheet 1)
   Mrs. Amanda S. Stone (Barred Claim #16,711, fiche 4748, sheet 1)

War Department Collection of Confederate Records (RG109)
Orders and Circulars of the Trans-Mississippi Department (entry 107)
Letters and Telegrams Received and Sent (entry 106)
Letters Sent, Dept. of Trans-Mississippi (Chap. II vol. 70)
Records of the Louisiana State Government, 1850–1888 (NAMP M359)
   Acts of the Extra Session of the 6th Legislature, 1863, Other Legislative
      Records, 1860–1864 (roll 13)
   Records of the Attorney General, 1860–65 (roll 7)
   Records of the Executive Department, 1860–65 (roll 14)

Confederate Compiled Service Records in War Dept. Collection of Confederate Records (RG109)
Generals and Staff Officers: P. O. Hébert, Henry McCulloch, M. W. Sims, E. Kirby Smith, Jesse W. Sparks, Richard Taylor, John G. Walker
3rd (Harrison) Louisiana Cavalry: Thomas B. Carroll
16th Texas Cavalry: William Fitzhugh, Edward P. Gregg

Federal Compiled Service Records
59th Indiana Infantry: Wilfred H. Welman
46th U.S. Colored Infantry: William B. Wallace
49th U.S. Colored Infantry: Pleasant Boner, George L. Conn (also 48th Indiana Infantry), Henry Geesbury, James P. Hall, Robert Randall, Nelson Washington
5th U.S. Colored Heavy Artillery: David Cornwell, Corydon Heath (also Battery G, 2nd Illinois Light Artillery), John G. Davis, Elisha DeWitt (also 7th Missouri Infantry [U.S.]), Herman[n] Lieb

Federal Pension Files
7th Missouri Infantry (U.S.): Elisha DeWitt
46th U.S. Colored Infantry: William B. Wallace
49th U.S. Colored Infantry: George Washington, Pleasant Boner/Barnett, John Gordon
5th U.S. Colored Heavy Artillery: Garrison Connor, Charles Conway (daughters: Louisa Slater and Laura Stanwood), Warren Crump/Jones, Corydon Heath (children: Ada and Jefferson), Lyman Hissong, Daniel Jackson, John Jackson (Company F),

John Jackson (Company G), Hermann Lieb, Lewis Pendleton, William Skillen, Willis Woods, Henry Young (sister: Amanda Young)

NATIONAL ARCHIVES—ARCHIVES II BUILDING, COLLEGE PARK, MD

Records of Accounting Officers of the Dept. of Treasury (RG217)

Settled Case Files for Claims Approved by the Southern Claims Commission, 1871–1880 (entry 732), Records of the Land, Files and Miscellaneous Division. (*Note: Although earlier indexes of these records indicate that files for Ouachita Parish (Monroe, LA) were extant at one time, no such records were identified or located during my visit or through several inquiries with staff. Such records could have proved critical to identifying local Unionists and persons who may have testified (in other records) about their knowledge of the fate of Heath and Conn.*)

Carroll Parish, Louisiana: Julia H. Morgan and heirs of Keene, #14,601; Nancy Short, #5250

Madison Parish, Louisiana: William Hayden, #20964; Luke Madden, #3171; George Watt, #11211

Richland Parish, Louisiana: Martha T. Cleland, #7124

ABRAHAM LINCOLN PRESIDENTIAL LIBRARY, SPRINGFIELD, IL

Lincoln Broadside—LB-621 (Shober, 1865)

AUSTIN HISTORY CENTER, AUSTIN, TX

AF Files

Confederate States of America—Army—16th Texas Infantry

Civil War

Slavery

HERMIONE HOUSE MUSEUM, TALLULAH, LA

Milliken's Bend file

ILLINOIS STATE ARCHIVES, SPRINGFIELD,IL

Civil War Records 2nd Light Artillery Regiment

Muster Rolls of Illinois Regiments. (Microfilm roll #27). Battery G, 2nd Illinois Light Artillery

INDIANA HISTORICAL SOCIETY—MANUSCRIPT AND VISUAL COLLECTIONS DEPARTMENT, WILLIAM HENRY SMITH MEMORIAL LIBRARY, INDIANAPOLIS, IN

Caleb Mills Family Papers

LOUISIANA STATE UNIVERSITY—LOUISIANA AND LOWER MISSISSIPPI VALLEY COLLECTIONS, SPECIAL COLLECTIONS, BATON ROUGE, LA

John Q. Anderson Papers, Mss. 2156, 2162

Chas. B. Allaire Letter, Mss. 3271

John Eaton Letter, Mss. 4106

J. D. Garland Papers, Mss. 153

Josiah Goodwin Diaries and Research Collection, Mss. 4886

Thomas O. Moore Papers, Mss. 305, 893, 1094, portions reproduced in *Records of Ante-bellum Southern Plantations,* Part 2: Louisiana and miscellaneous, Series I: Louisiana State University, reel 19

Honore P. Morancy Family Papers, Mss. 2430

Horace Tibbetts Document, Mss. 1418

WPA Collection. Ex-Slave Narrative Project, Mss. 2858, Narratives of Frances Doby and Carlyle Stewart

David M. Wray Letter, Mss. 4318

LOUISIANA STATE ARCHIVES, BATON ROUGE, LA

Lucy R. Carroll (Thomas B. Carroll) Confederate Pension Application

MISSISSIPPI DEPARTMENT OF ARCHIVES AND HISTORY, JACKSON, MS

Abraham Hagaman Memoir

Alfred H. Stone Collection

NORTHERN ILLINOIS UNIVERSITY—REGIONAL HISTORY CENTER, DEKALB, IL

E. B. Gilbert Collection (RC277)

OLD COURT HOUSE MUSEUM, VICKSBURG, MS

Milliken's Bend file

OUACHITA PARISH COURT HOUSE—CLERK OF COURTS OFFICE, MONROE, LA

Minutes of District Court, 1859–1866

OUACHITA PARISH PUBLIC LIBRARY—SPECIAL COLLECTIONS DEPARTMENT, MONROE, LA

Milliken's Bend file

Ouachita Parish Police Jury Minute Book (June 1857–Jan. 1867)

"The Union March from Milliken's Bend to Hard Times, March 31 to April. 29, 1863." Map. Compiled and drawn by Edwin C. Bearss, Feb. 1963.

SOUTHWEST ARKANSAS REGIONAL ARCHIVES, WASHINGTON, AR

Harvey Alexander Wallace Papers and Diary

STANFORD UNIVERSITY—SPECIAL COLLECTIONS, STANFORD, CA

Ellet Family Papers (M698)

STATE HISTORICAL SOCIETY OF IOWA, DES MOINES, IA

Adjutant General, Military Reports, Civil War, 23rd Iowa Infantry
Samuel H. Glasgow Civil War Letters
David West Collection, Civil War Papers

TALLULAH PUBLIC LIBRARY, TALLULAH, LA

Milliken's Bend file

TEXAS HERITAGE MUSEUM, HISTORICAL
RESEARCH CENTER, HILL COLLEGE, HILLSBORO, TX

Capsule Histories of Federal Units by John Walter
1st Arkansas Colored Infantry, 23rd Iowa Infantry, 9th (Old) Louisiana Colored Infantry, 9th (New) Louisiana Colored Infantry, 11th Louisiana Colored Infantry, 1st Mississippi Colored Infantry, 1st Mississippi Colored Heavy Artillery, 5th U.S. Colored Heavy Artillery, 46th U.S. Colored Infantry, 49th U.S. Colored Infantry, 51st U.S. Colored Infantry
Capsule Histories of Texas Units by John F. Walter
16th Texas Cavalry, 16th Texas Infantry, 17th Texas Infantry, 19th Texas Infantry
Louisiana Capsule Histories by John F. Walter
3rd (Harrison's) Louisiana Cavalry, 15th Louisiana Cavalry Battalion
Vertical Files
16th Texas Cavalry; 16th Texas Infantry; 17th Texas Infantry; 19th Texas Infantry; Camp Ford; Milliken's Bend, Battle of, Louisiana

TEXAS STATE LIBRARY AND ARCHIVES COMMISSION, AUSTIN, TX

George T. Boardman Diary, Berta Boardman Maxcy Collection
Edward W. Cade Correspondence, John Q. Anderson Collection
Francis R. Lubbock, Governor's Papers
Mrs. M. W. Sims Widow's Pension #50447
Lt. Gen. E. Kirby Smith Military Papers
State Adjutant General Records

TULANE UNIVERSITY—SPECIAL COLLECTIONS, NEW ORLEANS, LA

Paul Octave Hébert Scrapbook (Coll. #818)

"Map of the Parish of Madison, La. from United States Surveys" (New Orleans: Mc-Cerren, Landry and Powell, 1860)

Valentine Diary, Civil War Diaries, Civil War Papers, Louisiana Historical Association Collection (Coll. #55-B)

UNIVERSITY OF ARKANSAS—ARCHIVES AND
SPECIAL COLLECTIONS, LITTLE ROCK, AR

Richard Waterhouse Papers

UNIVERSITY OF MISSOURI—WESTERN HISTORICAL
MANUSCRIPT COLLECTION, ROLLA, MO

Aquilla Standifird Civil War Diary (R 458)

UNIVERSITY OF NORTH CAROLINA—SOUTHERN HISTORICAL COLLECTION,
MANUSCRIPTS DEPARTMENT, CHAPEL HILL, NC

Isaac Harrison Memoir, in John Francis Hamtramck Claiborne Papers (#151)

Edmund Kirby-Smith Papers (#404)

John George Walker Papers (#910)

UNIVERSITY OF TEXAS—CENTER FOR AMERICAN HISTORY, AUSTIN, TX

Confederate States of America Records

Ben and Henry Eustace McCulloch Family Papers

E. D. McDaniel Letters

Trans-Mississippi Quartermaster Department Papers

U.S. ARMY MILITARY HISTORY INSTITUTE, CARLISLE BARRACKS, PA

David Cornwell Memoir, Civil War Miscellaneous Collection

"The War of Secession West of the Mississippi River during the Years 1863, 1864 and 1865" by Maj. Gen. John G. Walker, Myron Gwinner Collection

VICKSBURG NATIONAL MILITARY PARK, VICKSBURG, MS

Regimental Files

23rd Iowa; 9th Louisiana Infantry, African Descent; 11th Louisiana Infantry, African Descent

PRIVATE POSSESSION

"My Dear Pa," June 8, 1863, letter, attributed to Henry Dick Lester, unidentified Confederate regiment

"our boys fought bravely," undated fragment, Aaron Trindle letter, 23rd Iowa Infantry

Government Publications and Military Manuals

Casey, Silas. *Infantry Tactics.* Vol. 1. New York: D. Van Nostrand, 1862.

Confederate States of America, Congress, House. *Joint Resolutions in Reference to the Treatment of Colored Troops,* Feb. 15, 1864. In *Confederate Imprints, 1861–1865.* New Haven, CT: Research Publications, 1974. Microfilm reel 7, no. 413.

Davis, Maj. George B., Leslie J. Perry, and Joseph W. Kirkley, eds. *Official Military Atlas of the Civil War.* (Originally published as: *Atlas to Accompany the Official Records of the Union and Confederate Armies,* Washington: GPO, 1891–1895.) New York: Gramercy, 1983.

Hewett, Janet B., et al., eds. *Supplement to the Official Records of the Union and Confederate Armies.* 100 vols. Wilmington, NC: Broadfoot, 1994–2001.

House. *Exchange of Prisoners.* 38th Cong., 2nd sess., 1865. H. Exec. Doc. 32. Serial 1223.

———. *Report of the Secretary of War.* 38th Cong., 1st sess., 1863. H. Exec. Doc. 1, pt. 5. Serial 1184.

———. *Report on the Treatment of Prisoners of War by the Rebel Authorities during the War of the Rebellion.* 40th Cong., 3d sess., 1869. H. Rep. 45. Serial 1391.

Journal of the Congress of the Confederate States of America, 1861–1865. Vol. 3 of *Journal of the Senate of the First Congress of the Confederate States of America,* 3d sess. (Richmond: Jan. 12, 1863 to May 1, 1863). In U.S. Senate, 58th Cong., 2d sess., 1903–04, S. Doc. 234, vol. 27, Serial 4612.

Kautz, August V. *The Company Clerk.* Philadelphia: J. B. Lippincott, 1863.

Official Army Register of the Volunteer Force of the United States Army for the Years 1861, '62, '63, '64, '65 . . . Washington, DC: Adjutant General's Office, 1865.

Naval War Records Office. *Official Records of the Union and Confederate Navies in the War of the Rebellion.* 30 vols. Washington, DC: GPO, 1894–1922.

Revised United States Army Regulations of 1861 with an Appendix Containing the Changes and Laws Affecting Army Regulations and Articles of War to June 25, 1863. Washington, DC: GPO, 1863.

Ross, Joseph B. *Tabular Analysis of the Records of the U.S. Colored Troops and Their Predecessor Units in the National Archives of the United States.* Washington, DC: National Archives and Records Service, 1973.

Senate. *Report of the Freedmen's Inquiry Commission, June 30, 1863.* 38th Cong., 1st sess., 1863. S. Exec. Doc. No. 53. Serial 1176.

Vandiver, Frank E., ed. "Proceedings of the First Confederate Congress, Fourth Session, 7 Dec. 1863–18 Feb. 1864." *Southern Historical Society Papers*, new series, no. 12, whole no. 50. Richmond, VA: Virginia Historical Society, 1953.

War Department. *U.S. Infantry Tactics, For the Instruction, Exercise, and Manoeuvres, of the Soldier, A Company, Line of Skirmishers, and Battalion for the Use of the Colored Troops of the United States Infantry.* New York: D. Van Nostrand, 1863.

———. *The War of the Rebellion: A Compilation of the Official Records of the Union and Confederate Armies.* 128 vols. Washington, DC: GPO, 1880–1901.

Newspapers

(all are Civil War era unless noted)

Bryan (TX) Weekly News—1912
Chicago Tribune
Christian Recorder (Philadelphia, PA)
Cincinnati Daily Commercial
Clarion-Ledger (Jackson, MS)—1994
(Memphis) Commercial Appeal—2001
Daily Cleveland Herald
Daily Mississippian (Jackson, MS)
Daily National Intelligencer (Washington, DC)
(New Orleans) Daily Picayune
Daily Richmond (VA) Examiner
Dallas Herald
Frank Leslie's Illustrated Newspaper
Grant County Witness (Platteville, WI)
Harper's Weekly
Lane (IL) Register
The Liberator
Madison Journal (Tallulah, LA) "Centennial Edition," 14 Aug. 1975
Monroe (LA) News-Star—1994
Monroe (LA) Register
Natchez Daily Courier
National Anti-Slavery Standard
National Tribune—1907
New York Herald
Newark (OH) Advocate
Paulding (OH) Independent
Shreveport Semi-Weekly News
The South-Western (Shreveport, LA)
Tri-Weekly State Gazette (Austin, TX)

True Republican (Sycamore, IL)—1895

Vicksburg Post—2004

Washington (AR) Telegraph

Books

Anderson, John Q., ed. *Brokenburn: The Journal of Kate Stone, 1861–1868*. 1955. Reprinted with new introduction by Drew Gilpin Faust. Baton Rouge: Louisiana State University Press, 1995.

———. *A Texas Surgeon in the C.S.A.* Tuscaloosa, AL: Confederate Publishing Co., 1957.

Appleton's Annual Cyclopedia and Register of Important Events. New York: D. Appleton and Co., 1863.

Bailey, Anne J. *In the Saddle With the Texans: Day-by-Day With Parsons's Cavalry Brigade, 1862–1865*. Abilene, TX: McWhiney Foundation Press, McMurray University, 2004.

Baker, T. Lindsay, and Julie P. Baker, eds. *Till Freedom Cried Out: Memories of Texas Slave Life*. College Station: Texas A&M University Press, 1997.

Barnes, Joseph K. *The Medical and Surgical History of the War of the Rebellion (1861–1865)*. 1870; reprinted as *The Medical and Surgical History of the Civil War*, 12 vols., Wilmington, NC: Broadfoot, 1991.

Barnickel, Linda. *We Enlisted as Patriots: The Civil War Records of Battery G, 2nd Illinois Light Artillery*. Bowie, MD: Heritage Books, 1998.

Berlin, Ira, et al., eds. *Free At Last: A Documentary History of Slavery, Freedom, and the Civil War*. New York: New Press, 1992.

———, et al., eds. *Freedom: A Documentary History of Emancipation, 1861–1867*. Series 2, *The Black Military Experience*. Cambridge: Cambridge University Press, 1982.

———, et al., eds. *Freedom: A Documentary History of Emancipation, 1861–1867*. Series 1, vol. 3, *The Wartime Genesis of Free Labor: The Lower South*. Cambridge: Cambridge University Press, 1990.

———, et al., eds. *Remembering Slavery: African Americans Talk About Their Personal Experiences of Slavery and Emancipation*. New York: New Press, 1998.

Black Abolitionist Papers, 1830–1865. 17 reels of microfilm. Ann Arbor, MI: UMI, 1993.

Blessington, J. P. *The Campaigns of Walker's Texas Division*. New York: Lange, Little and Co., 1875.

Brown, Norman D., ed. *Journey to Pleasant Hill: The Civil War Letters of Captain Elijah P. Petty, Walker's Texas Division, CSA*. San Antonio: University of Texas Institute of Texan Cultures, 1982.

Carleton, Fred. *Roll of Company G, 16th Texas Infantry, Compiled by Memory and From a Partial Copy of the Roster of the Company*. Austin, TX: Bryant P. Dickens, 1899.

Crandall, Warren Daniel, and Isaac Denison Newell. *History of the Ram Fleet and the Mississippi Marine Brigade*. St. Louis, MO: Buschart Brothers, 1907.

Dana, Charles. *Recollections of the Civil War*. New York: D. Appleton, 1902.

Downing, Alexander G. *Downing's Civil War Diary*. Edited by Olynthus B. Clark. Des Moines, IA: Historical Department of Iowa, 1916.

Eaton, John. *Grant, Lincoln and the Freedmen*. New York: Longmans, Green and Co., 1907.

Fleetwood, Christian Abraham. *The Negro As a Soldier*. Washington, DC: Howard University Printing, 1895.

Fleming, Walter L. *Documentary History of Reconstruction, Political, Military, Social, Religious, Educational and Industrial, 1865 to the Present Time*. Cleveland, Ohio: A. H. Clark, 1906.

Foner, Philip S., ed. *The Life and Writings of Frederick Douglass*. Vol. 3. New York: International Publishers, 1952.

Fremantle, Lt. Col. Arthur J. L. *Three Months in the Southern States April–June 1863*. Lincoln: University of Nebraska Press, 1991.

Gautier, George R. *Harder Than Death: The Life of George R. Gautier, an Old Texan, Living at the Confederate Home, Austin, Texas*. N.p., 1902.

Gravis, Peter W. *Twenty-Five Years on the Outside Row of the Northwest Texas Annual Conference: Autobiography of Rev. Peter W. Gravis*. Brownwood, TX: Cross Timbers Press, 1966.

Hallowell, Norwood Penrose. *The Negro As a Soldier in the War of the Rebellion: . . . Read Before the Military Historical Society of Massachusetts, January 5, 1892*. Boston: Little, Brown and Co., 1897.

Hawkins, John Parker. *Memoranda Concerning Some Branches of the Hawkins Family and Connections*. Indianapolis, 1913.

Iowa Adjutant General's Office. *Roster and Record of Iowa Soldiers in the War of the Rebellion*. Vol. 3. Des Moines, IA: E. H. English, 1910.

McGregor, Frank Ross. *Dearest Susie: A Civil War Infantryman's Letters to His Sweetheart*. Edited by Carl E. Hatch. New York: Exposition Press, 1971.

Moat, Louis Shepheard, ed. *Frank Leslie's Illustrated Famous Leaders and Battle Scenes of the Civil War*. New York: Mrs. Frank Leslie, 1896.

Moore, Frank, ed. *Rebellion Record*. Vol. 7. New York: Arno Press, 1977.

Olmsted, Frederick Law. *The Cotton Kingdom*. New York: Modern Library, 1969.

———. *A Journey in the Back Country in the Winter of 1853–4*. New York: G. P. Putnam's Sons, 1907.

Oration by Gen. I. F. Shepard (Adjutant General of Missouri) at Jefferson Barracks, St. Louis, Missouri, Memorial Day May 30, 1870. St. Louis: Missouri Democrat, 1870.

Rainsford, Marcus. *An Historical Account of the Black Empire of Hayti: Comprehending a View of the Principal Transactions in the Revolution of Saint Domingo . . .* [London]: Albion Press, 1805.

Rawick, George P., ed. *The American Slave: A Composite Autobiography*. Suppl. series 1, vol. 8, *Mississippi Narratives*, part 3. Westport, CT: Greenwood Press, 1977.

Report of the Adjutant General of the State of Illinois. Springfield: Baker, Bailhacke, 1867.

Ripley, C. Peter. *The Black Abolitionist Papers.* Vol. 5, *The United States, 1859–1865.* Chapel Hill: University of North Carolina Press, 1992.

Rowland, Dunbar, ed. *Jefferson Davis, Constitutionalist, His Letters, Papers, and Speeches.* Vol. 5. Jackson: Mississippi Dept. of Archives and History, 1923.

Sears, Cyrus. *Paper of Cyrus Sears [The Battle of Milliken's Bend].* Columbus, OH: F. J. Heer Printing, 1909.

Shannon, Fred Albert, ed. *The Civil War Letters of Sergeant Onley Andrus. Illinois Studies in the Social Studies.* Urbana: University of Illinois Press, 1947.

Simon, John Y., ed. *The Papers of Ulysses S. Grant.* Vols. 8 and 9. Carbondale: Southern Illinois University Press, 1979, 1982.

Taylor, Richard. *Destruction and Reconstruction: Personal Experiences of the Late War.* New York: D. Appleton, 1879.

Wearmouth, John, ed. *The Cornwell Chronicles: Tales of an American Life on the Erie Canal, Building Chicago, in the Volunteer Civil War Western Army, on the Farm, in a Country Store.* Bowie, MD: Heritage Books, 1998.

Yeary, Mamie. *Reminiscences of the Boys in Gray, 1861–1865.* Dayton, OH: Morningside, 1986.

Articles and Book Chapters

Bearss, Ed, ed. "The Civil War Diary of Lt. John Q. A. Campbell." *Annals of Iowa* 39 (Winter 1969): 519–541.

———, ed. "Is This Lt. John Campbell's Letter?" *Annals of Iowa* 39 (Winter 1969): 542–545.

Cutrer, Thomas W., ed. "'Bully for Flournoy's Regiment, We Are Some Punkins, You'll Bet': The Civil War Letters of Virgil Sullivan Rabb, Captain, Company 'I' Sixteenth Texas Infantry, C.S.A." Part 1. *Military History of the Southwest* 19, no. 2 (Fall 1989): 161–190.

———, ed. "'An Experience in Soldier's Life': The Civil War Letters of Volney Ellis, Adjutant, Twelfth Texas Infantry Walker's Texas Division, C.S.A." *Military History of the Southwest* 22, no. 2 (Fall 1992): 109–172.

Darst, W. Maury, ed. "The Vicksburg Diary of Mrs. Alfred Ingraham (May 2–June 13, 1863)." *Journal of Mississippi History* 44, no. 2 (May 1982): 148–179.

Ellis, Richard N., ed. "The Civil War Letters of an Iowa Family." *Annals of Iowa* 3rd series, 39, no. 8 (Spring 1969): 561–586.

Force, Manning F. "Personal Recollections of the Vicksburg Campaign." In *Sketches of War History 1861–1865: Papers Read Before the Ohio Commandery of the Military Order of the Loyal Legion of the United States,* vol. 1, 293–309. Cincinnati: Robert Clarke and Co., 1888.

Furness, William Eliot. "The Negro As a Soldier." In *Military Essays and Recollections,*

Papers Read Before the Commandery of the State of Illinois, Military Order of the Loyal Legion of the United States, 457–487. Chicago: McClurg and Co., 1894.

Goodrich, B. G. "Battle of Millican's Bend." *Confederate Veteran* 8, no. 2 (Feb. 1900): 67.

Gray, Andrew, ed. "The Carpetbagger's Letters." *Louisiana History* 20, no. 4 (Fall 1979): 431–451.

Harrison, Jon, ed. "The Confederate Letters of John Simmons." *Chronicles of Smith County, Texas* 14, no. 1 (Summer 1975): 25–57.

"Leaves from the Journal of a Lady Near Port Gibson, Mississippi, Kept During Grant's March Upon Vicksburg, via Grand Gulf and Port Gibson." In Sarah A. Dorsey, *Recollections of Henry Watkins Allen, Brigadier-General Confederate States Army, Ex-Governor of Louisiana,* 397–420. New York: M. Doolady, 1866.

Leggett, Mortimer D. "The Military and the Mob." In *Sketches of War History 1861–1865, Papers Read Before the Ohio Commandery of the Military Order of the Loyal Legion of the United States,* vol. 1, 188–197. Cincinnati: Robert Clarke and Co., 1888.

Roche, F. T. "Were Negroes in Earlier Wars." *Confederate Veteran* 18 no. 2 (Feb. 1910): 62.

Thompson, William Fletcher, Jr. "Pictorial Images of the Negro During the Civil War." *Wisconsin Magazine of History* (Summer 1965): 282–294.

Ullmann, Daniel. *Address by Daniel Ullmann, . . . on the Organization of Colored Troops and the Regeneration of the South . . .* Washington, DC: Great Republic, 1868.

Williams, T. R., Jr. "A Ouachita Family's Texas Sojourn: Excerpts From the Diary of Elizabeth Ann Bartlett Russell." *North Louisiana Historical Association Journal* 15, no. 4 (Fall 1984): 167–172.

Interviews

Conger, Phyllis, related by marriage to Corydon Heath descendent, Nov. 17, 2011
Davis, Brian Madison, historic preservationist, July 19, 2010
Johnson, Tina, Director, Tallulah-Madison Parish Tourism Commission, June 14, 2010
Kavanaugh, Tim, Interpreter, Vicksburg National Military Park May 21, 2010, and Mar. 14, 2011
Slay, David, Park Ranger, Vicksburg National Military Park, May 23, 2010
Varnedo, Mike, Louisiana Division of Historic Preservation, May 21, 2010
Walker, Robert Walker, former mayor of Vicksburg, Oct. 4, 2010
Williams, Geneva, Madison Historical Society, May 20, 2010, and Jan. 24, 2012
Winschel, Terrence, Historian, Vicksburg National Military Park, Sept. 27, 2010

SECONDARY SOURCES
Books

Allardice, Bruce S. *Confederate Colonels: A Biographical Register.* Columbia: University of Missouri Press, 2008.

Ambrose, Stephen E., and Edwin C. Bearss. *Struggle for Vicksburg: The Battles and Siege That Decided the Civil War.* 1967; reissue, n.p.: Eastern Acorn Press, 1982.

Aptheker, Herbert. *American Negro Slave Revolts.* 6th ed. New York: International Publishers, 1993.

Bailey, Anne J. *Between the Enemy and Texas: Parsons's Texas Cavalry in the Civil War.* Fort Worth: Texas Christian University Press, 1989.

Barkley, Mary Starr. *History of Travis County and Austin, 1839–1899.* Waco, TX: Texian Press, 1963.

Bearss, Edwin Cole. *The Campaign for Vicksburg.* Vol. 3, *Unvexed to the Sea.* Dayton, OH: Morningside, 1986.

———. *Texas at Vicksburg.* Austin, TX: Texas State Historical Survey Committee, 1961.

Bergeron, Arthur W. *Guide to Confederate Louisiana Military Units, 1861–1865.* Baton Rouge: Louisiana State University Press, 1996.

Berlin, Ira, et al., eds. *Slaves No More: Three Essays on Emancipation and the Civil War.* New York: Cambridge University Press, 1992.

Blight, David W. *Race and Reunion: The Civil War in American Memory.* Cambridge, MA: Belknap, 2001.

Boatner, Mark M., III. *The Civil War Dictionary.* Rev. ed. New York: Vintage, 1991.

Booth, Andrew B. *Records of Louisiana Confederate Soldiers and Louisiana Confederate Commands.* Spartanburg, SC: Reprint Co., 1984.

Brown, Frank. *Annals of Travis County and of the City of Austin (From the Earliest Times to the Close of 1875).* N.p., [1900].

Brown, William Wells. *The Negro in the American Rebellion: His Heroism and His Fidelity.* Boston: Lee and Shepard, 1867.

Bruce, Dickson D., Jr. *Violence and Culture in the Antebellum South.* Austin: University of Texas Press, 1979.

Brundage, W. Fitzhugh, ed. *Under Sentence of Death: Lynching in the South.* Chapel Hill: University of North Carolina Press, 1997.

Burkhardt, George S. *Confederate Rage, Yankee Wrath: No Quarter in the Civil War.* Carbondale: Southern Illinois University Press, 2007.

Campbell, Randolph B. *An Empire for Slavery: The Peculiar Institution in Texas, 1821–1865.* Baton Rouge: Louisiana State University Press, 1989.

Carrigan, William D. *The Making of a Lynching Culture: Violence and Vigilantism in Central Texas, 1836–1916.* Urbana: University of Illinois Press, 2004.

Carroll, Joseph Cephas. *Slave Insurrections in the United States, 1800–1865.* Boston: Chapman and Grimes, 1938.

Conger, Charles G. B. *A Record of the Births, Marriages and Deaths of the Descendants of John Conger of Woodbridge, N.J.: Through His Grandson, Job Conger, of Woodbridge, N.J. and Albany Co., N.Y.* Chicago: S. Smith, 1903.

Conrad, Glenn R. *A Dictionary of Louisiana Biography.* New Orleans: Louisiana Historical Association, 1988.

Cornish, Dudley Taylor. *The Sable Arm.* New York: Longmans Green and Co., 1956.

Crute, Joseph H., Jr. *Units of the Confederate States Army.* Midlothian, VA: Derwent,
1987.

Cunningham, Edward. *The Port Hudson Campaign, 1862–1863.* N.p.: Louisiana State
University Press, 1963.

Current, Richard N., et al., eds. *Encyclopedia of the Confederacy.* 4 vols. New York:
Simon and Schuster, 1993.

Davis, Edwin Adams, ed. *Heritage of Valor: The Picture Story of Louisiana in the Confederacy.* Baton Rouge: Louisiana State Archives and Records Commission, 1964.

Davis, William C. *Jefferson Davis: The Man and His Hour.* New York: Harper Collins,
1991.

Dew, Charles B. *Apostles of Disunion: Southern Secession Commissioners and the Causes of
the Civil War.* Charlottesville: University Press of Virginia, 2001.

Dimitry, John. *Louisiana.* Vol. 10 of *Confederate Military History,* edited by Clement A.
Evans. Atlanta, GA: Confederate Publishing Co., 1899.

Du Bois, W. E. B. *Black Reconstruction in America.* Introduction by David Levering
Lewis. New York: Free Press, 1998.

Durden, Robert F. *The Gray and the Black: The Confederate Debate on Emancipation.*
Baton Rouge: Louisiana State University Press, 1972.

Dyer, Frederick H. *A Compendium of the War of the Rebellion.* Des Moines, IA: Dyer
Publishing, 1908.

Eicher, John H., and David J. Eicher. *Civil War High Commands.* Stanford, CA: Stanford
University Press, 2001.

Fairclough, Adam. *Race and Democracy: The Civil Rights Struggle in Louisiana, 1915–1972.*
Athens: University of Georgia Press, 1995.

Foner, Eric. *Reconstruction: America's Unfinished Revolution, 1863–1877.* New York:
Harper and Row, 1988.

Fortier, Alcée, ed. *Louisiana: Comprising Sketches of Counties . . .* Atlanta: Southern
Historical Association, 1909.

Fox, William F. *Regimental Losses in the American Civil War, 1861–1865.* Albany, NY:
Albany Publishing Co., 1889.

Frankel, Noralee. *Freedom's Women: Black Women and Families in Civil War Era Mississippi.* Bloomington: University of Indiana Press, 1999.

Franklin, John Hope, and Loren Schweninger. *Runaway Slaves: Rebels on the Plantation.*
New York: Oxford University Press, 1999.

Frederickson, George M. *The Black Image in the White Mind: The Debate on Afro-American Character and Destiny, 1817–1914.* New York: Harper and Row, 1971.

Garner, James Wilford. *Reconstruction in Mississippi*. New York: Macmillan, 1901.

Genovese, Eugene D. *Roll Jordan, Roll: The World the Slaves Made*. New York: Pantheon, 1974.

Gerteis, Louis S. *From Contraband to Freedman: Federal Policy Toward Southern Blacks, 1861–1865*. Westport, CT: Greenwood, 1973.

Gibson, Charles Dana, and E. Kay Gibson. *Assault and Logistics: Union Army Coastal and River Operations, 1861–1866*. Camden, ME: Ensign, 1995.

Gillette, William. *Retreat from Reconstruction, 1869–1879*. Baton Rouge: Louisiana State University Press, 1979.

Ginzburg, Ralph. *100 Years of Lynchings*. Baltimore, MD: Black Classic, 1988.

Glatthaar, Joseph T. *Forged in Battle: The Civil War Alliance of Black Soldiers and White Officers*. New York: Free Press, 1990.

Grabau, Warren E. *Ninety-Eight Days: A Geographer's View of the Vicksburg Campaign*. Knoxville: University of Tennessee Press, 2000.

Grayson County Frontier Village. *The History of Grayson County Texas*. Winston-Salem, NC: Grayson County Frontier Village and Hunter Publishing Co., 1979.

Greenberg, Kenneth S. *Honor and Slavery: Lies, Duels, Noses, Masks, Dressing As a Woman, Gifts, Strangers, Humanitarianism, Death, Slave Rebellions, The Proslavery Argument, Baseball, Hunting, and Gambling in the Old South*. Princeton: Princeton University Press, 1996.

Greenburg, Martin H., and Charles G. Waugh, eds. *The Price of Freedom: Slavery and the Civil War*. 2 vols. Nashville, TN: Cumberland House, 2000.

Hargrove, Hondon B. *Black Union Soldiers in the Civil War*. Jefferson, NC: McFarland, 1988.

Harris, William C. *The Day of the Carpetbagger: Republican Reconstruction in Mississippi*. Baton Rouge: Louisiana State University Press, 1979.

Hearn, Chester G. *Ellet's Brigade: The Strangest Outfit of All*. Baton Rouge: Louisiana State University Press, 2000.

Hewett, Janet B., ed. *The Roster of Confederate Soldiers, 1861–1865*. 16 vols. Wilmington, NC: Broadfoot, 1995–1996.

———, ed. *Texas Confederate Soldiers, 1861–1865*. Wilmington, NC: Broadfoot, 1997.

Hicken, Victor. *Illinois in the Civil War*. Urbana: University of Illinois Press, 1966.

The History of Des Moines County, Iowa Containing a History of the County, Its Cities, Towns, &tc. Chicago: Western Historical Co., 1879.

The History of Wyandot County, Ohio. Chicago: Leggett, Conaway and Co., 1884.

Hollandsworth, James G., Jr. *The Louisiana Native Guards: The Black Military Experience During the Civil War*. Baton Rouge: Louisiana State University Press, 1995.

Howard, R. L. *History of the 124th Regiment Illinois Infantry Volunteers: Otherwise Known as the "Hundred and Two Dozen" from August 1862 to August 1865*. Springfield, IL: H. W. Rokker, 1880.

Hunt, Alfred N. *Haiti's Influence on Antebellum America: Slumbering Volcano in the Caribbean* Baton Rouge: Louisiana State University Press, 1988.

Johns, Jane Martin. *Personal Recollections of Early Decatur, Abraham Lincoln, Richard J. Oglesby and the Civil War.* Decatur, IL: Decatur Chapter Daughters of the American Revolution, 1912.

Jordan, Winthrop D. *Tumult and Silence at Second Creek: An Inquiry into a Civil War Slave Conspiracy.* Baton Rouge: Louisiana State University Press, 1993.

Keen, Sam. *Faces of the Enemy: Reflections of the Hostile Imagination.* San Francisco: Harper, 1991.

Kerby, Robert L. *Kirby Smith's Confederacy: The Trans-Mississippi South, 1863–1865.* New York: Columbia University Press, 1972.

Litwack, Leon F. *Been in the Storm So Long: The Aftermath of Slavery.* New York: Alfred A. Knopf, 1979.

Long, E. B., with Barbara Long. *The Civil War Day by Day: An Almanac, 1861–1865.* Garden City, NY: Doubleday, 1971.

Lowe, Richard. *Walker's Texas Division C.S.A.: Greyhounds of the Trans-Mississippi.* Baton Rouge: Louisiana State University Press, 2004.

Mays, Joe H. *Black Americans and Their Contributions Toward Union Victory in the American Civil War, 1861–1865.* Lanham, MD: University Press of America, 1984.

McCaslin, Richard B. *Tainted Breeze: The Great Hanging at Gainesville, Texas, 1862.* Baton Rouge: Louisiana State University Press, 1994.

McPherson, James M. *For Cause and Comrades: Why Men Fought in the Civil War.* New York: Oxford University Press, 1997.

———. *The Negro's Civil War: How American Negroes Felt and Acted during the War for the Union.* New York: Vintage, 1965.

———. *What They Fought For, 1861–1865.* Baton Rouge: Louisiana State University Press, 1994.

Menn, Joseph Karl. *The Large Slaveholders of Louisiana—1860.* New Orleans: Pelican, 1964.

Moneyhon, Carl, and Bobby Roberts. *Portraits of Conflict: A Photographic History of Texas in the Civil War.* Fayetteville: University of Arkansas Press, 1998.

Mooney, James L. *Dictionary of American Naval Fighting Ships.* Washington: Navy Dept., 1959.

Moore, Claude Hunter. *Thomas Overton Moore, A Confederate Governor.* Clinton, NC: Commercial Printing Co., 1960.

Morris, Thomas D. *Southern Slavery and the Law, 1619–1860.* Chapel Hill: University of North Carolina Press, 1996.

Nosworthy, Brent. *The Bloody Crucible of Courage: Fighting Methods and Combat Experience of the Civil War.* New York: Carroll and Graf, 2003.

Nudelman, Franny. *John Brown's Body: Slavery, Violence, and the Culture of War.* Chapel Hill: University of North Carolina Press, 2004.

O'Brien, Sean Michael. *Mobile, 1865: Last Stand of the Confederacy.* Westport, CT: Praeger, 2001.

Ott, Thomas O. *The Haitian Revolution, 1789–1804.* Knoxville: University of Tennessee Press, 1973.

Painter, Nell Irvin. *Exodusters: Black Migration to Kansas After Reconstruction.* New York: W. W. Norton, 1986.

Parks, Joseph Howard. *General Edmund Kirby Smith, C.S.A.* Baton Rouge: Louisiana State University Press, 1954.

Parrish, T. Michael. *Richard Taylor: Soldier Prince of Dixie.* Chapel Hill: University of North Carolina Press, 1992.

Pfeifer, Michael J. *Rough Justice: Lynching and American Society, 1874–1947.* Urbana: University of Illinois Press, 2004.

Pinkston, Georgia Payne Durham. *A Place to Remember: East Carroll Parish, Louisiana, 1832–1976.* Baton Rouge, LA: Claitor's, 1977.

Powell, Lawrence N. *New Masters: Northern Planters during the Civil War and Reconstruction.* New Haven: Yale University Press, 1980.

Prushankin, Jeffery S. *A Crisis in Confederate Command: Edmund Kirby Smith, Richard Taylor, and the Army of the Trans-Mississippi.* Baton Rouge: Louisiana State University Press, 2005.

Quarles, Benjamin. *The Negro in the Civil War.* Boston: Little, Brown, 1953.

Reynolds, Donald E. *Texas Terror: The Slave Insurrection Panic of 1860 and the Secession of the Lower South.* Baton Rouge: Louisiana State University Press, 2007.

Richard, Allan C., Jr., and Mary Margaret Higginbotham Richard. *The Defense of Vicksburg: A Louisiana Chronicle.* College Station, TX: Texas A&M Press, 2004.

Ringold, May Spencer. *The Role of the State Legislatures in the Confederacy.* Athens: University of Georgia Press, 1966.

Roberts, Oran Milo. *Texas.* Vol. 11 of *Confederate Military History,* edited by Clement A. Evans. Atlanta, GA: Confederate Publishing Co., 1899.

Robinson, Armstead L. *Bitter Fruits of Bondage: The Demise of Slavery and the Collapse of the Confederacy, 1861–1865.* Charlottesville: University of Virginia Press, 2005.

Sanders, Charles W. *While in the Hands of the Enemy: Military Prisons during the Civil War.* Baton Rouge: Louisiana State University Press, 2005.

Schafer, Judith Kelleher. *Slavery, the Civil Law, and the Supreme Court of Louisiana.* Baton Rouge: Louisiana State University Press, 1994.

Schmitz, Sandy L. *Murder, Mayhem and Miscellaneous of Carroll Parish, Louisiana.* Berryville, AR: S&S Press, 2001.

Shaffer, Donald R. *After the Glory: The Struggles of Black Civil War Veterans.* Lawrence: University Press of Kansas, 2004.

Shannon, Fred Albert. *Organization and Administration of the Union Army, 1861–1865.* Gloucester, MA: Peter Smith, 1965.

Sifakis, Stewart. *Compendium of the Confederate Armies: Louisiana.* New York: Facts on File, 1995.

———. *Compendium of the Confederate Armies: Texas.* New York: Facts on File, 1995.

———. *Who Was Who in the Civil War.* New York: Facts on File, 1988.

Silverstone, Paul H. *Warships of the Civil War Navies.* Annapolis, MD: Naval Institute Press, 1989.

Smith, John David, ed. *Black Soldiers in Blue: African American Troops in the Civil War Era.* Chapel Hill: University of North Carolina Press, 2002.

Smith, Timothy B. *The Golden Age of Battlefield Preservation: The Decade of the 1890s and the Establishment of America's First Five Military Parks.* Knoxville: University of Tennessee Press, 2008.

Smith, W. Broadus. *Pioneers of Brazos County, Texas, 1800–1850.* Bryan, TX: The Scribe Shop, 1962.

Sowell, A. J. *Early Settlers and Indian Fighters of Southwest Texas.* Facsimile of 1900 edition. Austin, TX: State House Press, 1986.

Speer, Lonnie R. *Portals to Hell: Military Prisons of the Civil War.* Lincoln: University of Nebraska Press, 1997.

———. *War of Vengeance: Acts of Retaliation Against Civil War POWs.* Mechanicsburg, PA: Stackpole, 2002.

Sutton, Robert K., ed. *Rally on the High Ground: The National Park Service Symposium on the Civil War.* N.p: Eastern National, 2001.

Taylor, Joe Gray. *Negro Slavery in Louisiana.* Baton Rouge: Louisiana Historical Association, 1963.

Tolnay, Stewart E., and E. M. Beck. *A Festival of Violence: An Analysis of Southern Lynchings, 1882–1930.* Urbana: University of Illinois Press, 1995.

Trudeau, Noah Andre. *Like Men of War: Black Troops in the Civil War, 1862–1865.* Boston: Little Brown and Co., 1998.

Tunnell, Ted. *Crucible of Reconstruction: War, Radicalism, and Race in Louisiana, 1862–1877.* Baton Rouge: Louisiana State University Press, 1984.

Urwin, Gregory J. W., ed. *Black Flag Over Dixie: Racial Atrocities and Reprisals in the Civil War.* Carbondale: Southern Illinois University Press, 2004.

Voegeli, V. Jacque. *Free But Not Equal: The Midwest and the Negro during the Civil War.* Chicago: University of Chicago Press, 1967.

Waldrep, Christopher. *Vicksburg's Long Shadow: The Civil War Legacy of Race and Remembrance.* Lanham, MD: Rowman and Littlefield, 2005.

Ward, Andrew. *The Slaves' War.* Boston: Houghton Mifflin, 2008.

Warner, Ezra J. *Generals in Blue: Lives of the Union Commanders.* Baton Rouge: Louisiana State University Press, 1964.

———. *Generals in Gray: Lives of the Confederate Commanders.* N.p.: Louisiana State University Press, 1959.

Westwood, Howard C. *Black Troops, White Commanders and Freedmen during the Civil War.* Carbondale: Southern Illinois University Press, 1992.

Wiley, Bell Irvin. *The Life of Billy Yank: The Common Soldier of the Union.* Indianapolis: Bobbs-Merrill, 1952.

———. *The Life of Johnny Reb: The Common Soldier of the Confederacy.* Indianapolis: Bobbs-Merrill, 1943.

———. *Southern Negroes, 1861–1865.* New Haven, CT: Yale University Press, 1938.

Williams, E. Russ, Jr. *Encyclopedia of Individuals and Founding Families of the Ouachita Valley of Louisiana from 1785 to 1850.* 2 parts. Monroe, LA: Williams Genealogical and Historical Publications, 1996–1997.

Williams, George Washington. *A History of the Negro Troops in the War of the Rebellion, 1861–1865.* New York: Harper and Bros., 1888.

Williamson, Frederick William. *Eastern Louisiana: A History of the Watershed of the Ouachita River and the Florida Parishes.* Louisville, KY: Historical Record Assn., 1939.

Wilson, Joseph T. *The Black Phalanx: A History of the Negro Soldiers of the United States . . .* Springfield, MA: Winter and Co, 1887.

Wilson, Keith P. *Campfires of Freedom: The Camp Life of Black Soldiers During the Civil War.* Kent, OH: Kent State University Press, 2002.

Winschel, Terrence J. *Triumph and Defeat: The Vicksburg Campaign.* 2 vols. New York: Savas Beatie, 2004.

Winters, John D. *The Civil War in Louisiana.* Baton Rouge: Louisiana State University Press, 1963.

Wood, Forrest G. *Black Scare: The Racist Response to Emancipation and Reconstruction.* Berkeley and Los Angeles: University of California Press, 1970.

Wooster, Ralph A. *Texas and Texans in the Civil War.* Austin, TX: Eakin, 1995.

Wright, Marcus J., comp. *Texas in the War 1861–1865.* Edited by Harold B. Simpson. Hillsboro, TX: Hill Junior College Press, 1965.

Wyatt-Brown, Bertram. *Southern Honor: Ethics and Behavior in the Old South.* Oxford: Oxford University Press, 1982.

Yearns, W. Buck, ed. *The Confederate Governors.* Athens: University of Georgia Press, 1985.

Zuczek, Richard, ed. *Encyclopedia of the Reconstruction Era.* Westport, CT: Greenwood, 2006.

Articles and Book Chapters

Aptheker, Herbert. "Negro Casualties in the Civil War." *Journal of Negro History* 32, no. 1 (Jan. 1947): 10–80.

Arnold, George Mike. "Colored Soldiers in the Union Army." *A.M.E. Church Review* (1887): 257–266.

Bailey, Anne J. "The Mississippi Marine Brigade: Fighting Rebel Guerillas on Western Waters." *Military History of the Southwest* 22, no. 1 (Spring 1992): 31–42.

———. "A Texas Cavalry Raid: Reaction to Black Soldiers and Contrabands." *Civil War History* 35, no. 2 (June 1989): 138–152.

Barnickel, Linda. "'No Federal Prisoners Among Them': The Execution of Black Union Soldiers at Jackson, Louisiana." *North and South* 12, no. 1 (Feb. 2010): 59–62.

Bigelow, Martha M. "The Significance of Milliken's Bend in the Civil War." *Journal of Negro History* 45, no. 3 (July 1960): 156–163.

Blassingame, John W. "The Selection of Officers and Non-Commissioned Officers of Negro Troops in the Union Army, 1863–1865." *Negro History Bulletin* 30, no. 1 (Jan. 1967): 8–11.

Blight, David W. "'For Something beyond the Battlefield': Frederick Douglass and the Struggle for the Memory of the Civil War." *Journal of American History* 75, no. 4 (Mar. 1989): 1156–1178.

Brundage, W. Fitzhugh. "The Roar on the Other Side of Silence: Black Resistance and White Violence in the American South, 1880–1940." In *Under Sentence of Death: Lynching in the South,* edited by W. Fitzhugh Brundage, 271–291. Chapel Hill: University of North Carolina Press, 1997.

Burkhardt, George S. "No Quarter! Black Flag Warfare, 1863–1865." *North and South* 10, no. 1 (May 2007): 12–29.

Damico, John Kelly. "Confederate Soldiers Take Matters into Their Own Hands: The End of the Civil War in North Louisiana." *Louisiana History* 39 (Spring 1998): 189–205.

Davies, Wallace E. "The Problem of Race Segregation in the Grand Army of the Republic." *Journal of Southern History* 13, no. 3 (Aug. 1947): 354–372.

Davis, Jackson Beauregard. "The Life of Richard Taylor." *Louisiana Historical Quarterly* 24 (Jan. 1941): 49–126.

De Vries, Freerk. "The Union Ironclad Ram *Choctaw.*" Translated by Erik A. R. Ronnbert Jr. *Nautical Research Journal* 36, no. 3 (Sept. 1991): 116–122.

Dyer, Brainerd. "The Treatment of Colored Union Troops by the Confederates, 1861–1865." *Journal of Negro History* 20 no. 3 (July 1935): 273–286.

Finley, Milton. "The Confederate Capital in the West." *Glimpses of Shreveport.* Edited by Ann M. McLaurin. Natchitoches, LA: Northwestern State University Press, 1985.

Fleche, Andre. "'Shoulder to Shoulder As Comrades Tried': Black and White Union Veterans and Civil War Memory." *Civil War History* 51, no. 2 (2005): 175–201.

Foster, E. C. "The Battle at Milliken's Bend." *Crisis* 81, no. 9 (Nov. 1974): 295–300.

Hollandsworth, James G., Jr. "The Execution of White Officers from Black Units by Confederate Forces during the Civil War." *Louisiana History* 35, no. 4 (Fall 1994): 475–489.

Horton, James Oliver. "Confronting Slavery and Revealing the 'Lost Cause.'" *CRM* 21, no. 4 (1998): 14–20.

Hyde, Samuel C., Jr. "Bushwhacking and Barn Burning: Civil War Operations and the

Florida Parishes' Tradition of Violence." *Louisiana History* 36, no. 2 (Spring 1995): 171–186.

Jones, Terry L. "'The Enemy Cried No Quarter': Courage and Controversy at Milliken's Bend." *Civil War* Issue 68 (June 1998): 38–54.

Lee, Irvin H. "Negro Heroes of the Civil War." *Negro Digest* 15, no. 4 (Feb. 1966): 10–16.

Lowe, Richard. "Battle on the Levee: The Fight at Milliken's Bend." In *Black Soldiers in Blue: African American Troops in the Civil War Era*, edited by John David Smith, 107–135. Chapel Hill: University of North Carolina Press, 2002.

Manning, Chandra. "A 'Vexed Question': White Union Soldiers on Slavery and Race." In *The View from the Ground: Experiences of Civil War Soldiers*, edited by Aaron Sheehan-Dean, 31–66. Lexington: University Press of Kentucky, 2007.

McConnell, Roland C., ed. "Concerning the Procurement of Negro Troops in the South During the Civil War." *Journal of Negro History* 35, no. 3 (July 1950): 315–319.

———. "Louisiana's Black Military History, 1729–1865." In *Louisiana's Black Heritage*, edited by Robert R. Macdonald, John R. Kemp, and Edward F. Haas, 32–62. New Orleans: Louisiana State Museum, 1979.

Metzer, Jacob. "The Records of the U.S. Colored Troops As a Historical Source: An Exploratory Examination." *Historical Methods* 14, no. 3 (Summer 1981): 123–132.

Nichols, James L. "The Operations of Captain N. A. Birge, Confederate Quartermaster at Monroe, Louisiana, 1862–1863." *Louisiana Studies* 1, no. 3 (Fall 1962): 23–29.

Peoples, Morgan D. "'Kansas Fever' in North Louisiana." *Louisiana History* 11, no. 2 (Spring 1970): 121–135.

"Philip Sartorius: Citizen of Vicksburg." *Rebel Yell* (Newsletter of Jackson [MS] Civil War Round Table) 37, no. 5 (Jan. 2001): 2–6.

Phillips, Jason. "A Brothers' War? Exploring Confederate Perceptions of the Enemy." In *The View from the Ground: Experiences of Civil War Soldiers*, edited by Aaron Sheehan-Dean, 67–90. Lexington: University Press of Kentucky, 2007.

Prushankin, Jeffery S. "Milliken's Bend, Battle of (7 June 1863)." *Encyclopedia of the American Civil War: A Political, Social, and Military History*, edited by David S. Heidler and Jeanne T. Heidler, 1330–1331. Santa Barbara, CA: ABC-CLIO, 2000.

Robinson, Armstead L. "In the Shadow of Old John Brown: Insurrection Anxiety and Confederate Mobilization, 1861–1863." *Journal of Negro History* 65, no. 4 (Fall 1980): 279–297.

Sacher, John M. "'A Very Disagreeable Business': Confederate Conscription in Louisiana." *Civil War History* 53, no. 2 (2007): 141–169.

Samito, Christian G. "The Intersection Between Military Justice and Equal Rights: Mutinies, Courts-Martial, and Black Civil War Soldiers." *Civil War History* 53, no. 2 (2007): 170–202.

Stuart, Capt. A. A. "Brevet Brigadier-General S. L. Glasgow." In *Iowa Colonels and Regiments: Being a History of Iowa Regiments in the War of the Rebellion; and Containing a Description of the Battles in Which They Have Fought.* Des Moines, Iowa: Mills and Co., 1865.

Taylor, Ethel. "Discontent in Confederate Louisiana." *Louisiana History* 2 (Fall 1961): 410–428.

Urwin, Gregory J. W. "'We Cannot Treat Negroes . . . as Prisoners of War': Racial Atrocities and Reprisals in Civil War Arkansas." In *Black Flag Over Dixie: Racial Atrocities and Reprisals in the Civil War,* edited by Gregory J. W. Urwin, 132–152. Carbondale: Southern Illinois University Press, 2004.

Vandal, Gilles. "'Bloody Caddo': White Violence against Blacks in a Louisiana Parish, 1865–1876." *Journal of Social History* 25, no. 2 (Winter 1991): 373–388.

Waldrep, Christopher. "Word and Deed: The Language of Lynching, 1820–1953." In *Lethal Imagination: Violence and Brutality in American History,* edited by Michael A. Bellesiles, 229–258. New York: New York University Press, 1999.

Wallenstein, Peter. "Incendiaries All: Southern Politics and the Harpers Ferry Raid." In *His Soul Goes Marching On: Responses to John Brown and the Harpers Ferry Raid,* edited by Paul Finkelman, 149–173. Charlottesville: University Press of Virginia, 1995.

Wesley, Charles H., and Patricia W. Romero. "The Battle of Milliken's Bend." In *Negro Americans in the Civil War: From Slavery to Citizenship,* 86–88. New York: Publishers Co., 1967.

Whittington, G. P. "Thomas O. Moore, Governor of Louisiana, 1860–1864." *Louisiana Historical Quarterly* 13, no. 1 (Jan. 1930): 5–31.

Williams, David. "Waterhouse's 19th Texas Infantry: The Campaigns of a Trans-Mississippi Regiment." *Civil War Historian* 1, no. 6 (Nov./Dec. 2005): 19–21.

Williams, Harry. "Benjamin F. Wade and the Atrocity Propaganda of the Civil War." *Ohio State Archaeological and Historical Quarterly* 48, no. 1 (Jan. 1939): 33–43.

Williams, Walter L. "Again in Chains." *Civil War Times Illustrated* 20, no. 2 (May 1981): 36–43.

Winschel, Terrence J. "The General's Tour: Grant's March Through Louisiana: Opening Phase of the Vicksburg Campaign." *Blue and Gray Magazine* 13, no. 5 (June 1996): 51–61.

———. "Grant's March Through Louisiana: 'The Highest Examples of Military Energy and Perseverance.'" *Blue and Gray Magazine* 13, no. 5 (June 1996): 8–22.

———. "To Rescue Gibraltar: John Walker's Texas Division and Its Expedition to Relieve Fortress Vicksburg." *Civil War Regiments* 3, no. 3 (1993): 33–58.

———. "Walker's Texas Division: Milliken's Bend." *Civil War Regiments* 3, no. 3 (1993): 90–91.

Theses and Dissertations

Davis, Brian Madison. "Milliken's Bend National Research Center." B.Arch. thesis, Louisiana Tech University, [1997].

Foster, Charles Allen. "Reconstruction in Ouachita Parish, Louisiana, 1865–1877." B.A. thesis, History Department, Princeton University, 1963.

Luke, Josephine. "From Slavery to Freedom in Louisiana, 1862–1865." M.A. thesis, Tulane University, 1939.

Messner, William F. "The Federal Army and Blacks in the Gulf Department, 1862–65." Ph.D. dissertation, University of Wisconsin-Madison, 1972.

Owens, Jeffrey Alan. "The Civil War in Tensas Parish, Louisiana: A Community History." M.A. thesis, University of Texas-Tyler, 1990.

Ripley, Charles Peter. "Black, Blue and Gray: Slaves and Freedmen in Civil War Louisiana," Ph.D. dissertation, Florida State University, 1973.

Windham, William Thomas. "General Edmund Kirby Smith and the Confederate Trans-Mississippi Department." M.A. thesis, University of Alabama, 1950.

Online Sources

AMERICAN MEMORY. LIBRARY OF CONGRESS.

An American Time Capsule: Three Centuries of Broadsides and Other Printed Ephemera. "Declaration of the Causes which impel the State of Texas to secede from the Federal Union—also the Ordinance of Secession." Printed Ephemera Collection, Portfolio 346, Folder 43, Library of Congress. Accessed Jan. 14, 2012, http://hdl .loc.gov/loc.rbc/rbpe.34604300/.

Born in Slavery: Slave Narratives from the Federal Writers' Project, 1936–1938. WPA Slave Narrative Project. Accessed Jan. 14, 2012, http://memory.loc.gov/ammem/snhtml/ snhome.html/. Narratives of Ellen Cragin, Mattie Lee, Abbie Lindsay, William Mathews, Rosa Washington, Sarah Wells, Litt Young.

A Century of Lawmaking for a New Nation: U.S. Congressional Documents and Debates, 1774–1875. Congressional Globe, 38th Cong., 1st sess., 1863. Accessed Jan. 14, 2012, http://memory.loc.gov/ammem/amlaw/lawhome.html/.

DOCUMENTING THE AMERICAN SOUTH, UNIVERSITY OF NORTH CAROLINA AT CHAPEL HILL

Diary (August 8, 1859–May 15, 1865), Sarah Lois Wadley Papers (call number 1258), Manuscripts Department, Southern Historical Collection, electronic edition, transcript. Accessed Jan. 14, 2012, http://docsouth.unc.edu/imls/wadley/ wadley.html/.

MAKING OF AMERICA. ANN ARBOR, MI: UNIVERSITY OF MICHIGAN LIBRARY, 2005.

Agriculture of the United States in 1860: compiled from the original returns of the eighth census, under the direction of the Secretary of the Interior by Joseph C.G. Kennedy. Washington, DC: GPO, 1864. Accessed Jan. 14, 2012, http://name.umdl.umich .edu/AFP3693.0001.001/.

TEXAS CONSTITUTIONS 1824–1876, TARLTON LAW LIBRARY / JAMAIL LEGAL
RESEARCH CENTER AT THE UNIVERSITY OF TEXAS SCHOOL OF LAW, THE
UNIVERSITY OF TEXAS AT AUSTIN

Winkler, Ernest William, ed. *Journal of the Secession Convention of Texas*. Austin, TX:
Austin Printing Co., 1912. Last modified September 2, 2009. Accessed Jan. 14,
2012, http://tarlton.law.utexas.edu/constitutions/pdf/pdf1861/index1861.html/.

U.S. ARMY CENTER OF MILITARY HISTORY.

"Medal of Honor Recipients, Civil War, M–Z." Entry for Cyrus Sears. Accessed Jan. 14,
2012, http://www.history.army.mil/html/moh/civwarmz.html/.

U.S. CENSUS BUREAU

Kennedy, Joseph C. G. *Population of the United States in 1860 Compiled from the Original
Returns of the Eighth Census* . . . Washington, DC: GPO, 1864. Accessed Jan. 14,
2012, www.census.gov/prod/www/abs/decennial/1860.html/.
State and County Quick Facts. Madison Parish, Louisiana. Last revised Dec. 23, 2011.
Accessed Jan. 14, 2012, http://quickfacts.census.gov/qfd/states/22/22065.html/.

VICKSBURG NATIONAL MILITARY PARK

"Cultural Resource Preservation." Accessed Jan. 14, 2012, www.nps.gov/vick/park-
mgmt/culresmgt.htm/.
"Grant's Canal." Accessed Jan. 14, 2012, www.nps.gov/vick/historyculture/grants-canal.
htm/.
Vicksburg National Military Park: Long Range Interpretive Plan. June 2010. Accessed
Jan. 14, 2012, www.nps.gov/vick/parkmgmt/loader.cfm?csModule=security/
getfile&PageID=296948/.

Other Online Sources

"Battle of Milliken's Bend, Madison Parish, La., June 7, 1863." Accessed Jan. 14, 2012,
www.rootsweb.ancestry.com/~lamadiso/articles/battle_of_millikens_bend.html/.
Blake, Tom. "Carroll Parish, Louisiana: Largest Slaveholders from 1860 Slave Census
Schedules and Surname Matches for African Americans on 1870 Census." (Sept.
2001). Accessed Jan. 14, 2012, http://freepages.genealogy.rootsweb.com/~ajac/
lacarroll.htm/.
HeritageQuest Online, subscription database, 1860 census, Louisiana. www.heritage-
questonline.com/.
Historical Census Browser, Geospatial and Statistical Data Center, University of Vir-
ginia, 2004. Accessed Jan. 14, 2012, http://fisher.lib.virginia.edu/collections/stats/
histcensus/index.html/.
National Park Service. *Interpretation at Civil War Sites. A Report to Congress*. March 2000.
Accessed Jan. 14, 2012, www.cr.nps.gov/history/online_books/icws/index.htm/.

National Parks Conservation Association. "State of the Parks: Vicksburg National Military Park, A Resource Assessment." Oct. 2008. Accessed Jan. 14, 2012, www.npca.org/about-us/center-for-park-research/stateoftheparks/vicksburg/VICK-web.pdf/.

Pfeifer, Michael J. "Louisiana Lynchings, 1878–1946." Accessed May 20, 2011, http://academic.evergreen.edu/p/pfeiferm/louisiana.html/. As of Nov. 6, 2011, this list was no longer available on the Internet. Much of the same information appears in the appendix to Pfeifer's book, *Rough Justice: Lynching and American Society, 1874–1947* (Urbana: University of Illinois Press, 2004). The information that appeared at Evergreen University's website is available upon request from Dr. Pfeifer at John Jay College of Criminal Justice, Department of History.

Rambow, Paul. *Battery G History.* Accessed Jan. 14, 2012, http://batteryg.org/batteryg/documents/GHistory.doc/.

Sessums, J. Kim. "The Vicksburg Monument: A Personal Journey, Excerpts from the Artist's Journal." Accessed Jan. 14, 2012, www.jkimsessums.com/cwtribute.html/.

Texas State Historical Association. *The Handbook of Texas Online.* Accessed Jan. 2012, www.tshaonline.org/handbook/online/. Articles for Paul Octave Hébert, Henry Eustace McCulloch, Parsons's Brigade, Edmund Kirby Smith, John George Walker.

Texas State Library and Archives Commission. "The Frontier Stands Alone," part of "1864: No Way Out." *Under the Rebel Flag: Life in Texas During the Civil War.* Accessed Jan. 14, 2012, www.tsl.state.tx.us/exhibits/civilwar/1864_3.html/.

INDEX